ANTIRACIST
COUNSELING
in Schools and Communities

edited by
Cheryl Holcomb-McCoy

American Counseling Association
2461 Eisenhower Avenue • Alexandria, VA 22331
www.counseling.org

ANTIRACIST
COUNSELING
in Schools and Communities

American Counseling Association
2461 Eisenhower Avenue • Alexandria, VA 22331

Associate Publisher • Carolyn C. Baker

Digital and Print Development Editor • Nancy Driver

Senior Production Manager • Bonny E. Gaston

Copy Editor • Beth Ciha

Cover and text design by Bonny E. Gaston

Library of Congress Cataloging-in-Publication Data

Names: Holcomb-McCoy, Cheryl, editor. | American Counseling Association.
Title: Antiracist counseling in schools and communities / Cheryl Holcomb-McCoy, editor.
Description: Alexandria, VA : American Counseling Association, 2022. | Includes
   bibliographical references and index.
Identifiers: LCCN 2021033771 | ISBN 9781556204098 (paperback)
Subjects: LCSH: Cross-cultural counseling—United States. | Anti-racism—United States. |
   Social justice—United States. | Racism—United States—Psychological aspects.
Classification: LCC BF636.7.C76 A55 2022 | DDC 158.3—dc23
LC record available at https://lccn.loc.gov/2021033771

DEDICATION

I want to acknowledge and thank my father, Fred Holcomb, and my family, Alvin (husband), Niles (son), and Nia (daughter), for their endless love and support.
I am because of them.

TABLE OF CONTENTS

PREFACE

For there is always light,
if only we're brave enough to see it.
If only we're brave enough to be it.

—**Amanda Gorman,** "The Hill We Climb"

The Inspiration

I watched and cried as 22-year-old Amanda Gorman recited the words above at the inauguration of the 46th president of the United States, Joseph Biden, and the first Black/Asian woman vice president, Kamala Harris. Ms. Gorman's poem, "The Hill We Climb," resonated with me as a middle-aged Black woman and self-proclaimed social justice advocate. After 4 years of an administration that had stoked racial unrest, initiated sweeping anti-immigration policies, and openly devalued women, Amanda Gorman's words summoned both pride and relief. Maybe, just maybe, we are now embarking on an era of harmony in which we can reckon with our country's legacy of racism, sexism, and xenophobia and embrace the greatness of our collective good.

In so many ways, Amanda Gorman's words also reflect our counseling profession's long-standing promise to endear a more inclusive, equitable, and just society. I have always believed professional counselors play an essential role in our nation's quest to be a more perfect union. My decision to become a counselor was based on this belief. For it is counselors who have the skills, awareness, and knowledge to produce social change, solve complex problems, and bring diverse people together; however, as Amanda Gorman implies, counselors have this power only if they are brave enough to act on it.

Although Amanda Gorman's words inspired me, this book was conceptualized long before I knew who she was. The impetus for this book was the series of events that led up to the 2021 presidential inauguration. I could recount hundreds of years of racism and oppression placed on Black and Brown people, but it was the more recent angry white supremacist mob in Charlottesville and the murder of George Floyd, a 46-year-old Black man, that set this book in motion. For those who do not know, Mr. Floyd was murdered by Derek Chauvin, a white Minneapolis police officer, after a convenience store employee called 911 and told the police that Mr. Floyd had bought cigarettes with a counterfeit $20 bill. Seventeen minutes after the first squad car arrived at the scene, Mr. Floyd was unconscious, lifeless, and pinned beneath a police officer. Nine minutes and 29 seconds is the amount of time one officer knelt on the neck of Mr. Floyd, killing him in the street in front of local citizens who recorded the event with their phones. Derek Chauvin was subsequently found guilty of murder. However, on the day of his conviction, just a few miles from the courthouse, another young Black man was killed by a police officer.

Like millions of people around the world, I have watched the senseless murders of unarmed Black people like George Floyd repeatedly on the news. Obsessed with the cruelty of police violence, thousands of protesters marched in the summer of 2020 calling for justice and chanting "Black Lives Matter!" Another inspiration for this book was to call for change in the face of anti-Black racism, anti-Asian racism, anti-Indigenous racism, and the brutality afforded not only George Floyd but also Breonna Taylor, Ahmaud Arbery, Daunte Wright, Rayshard Brooks, Daniel Prude, Atatiana Jefferson, the Atlanta spa workers, the congregants of Charleston's Mother Emanuel Church, and the countless other Black and Brown persons killed by either the police, white supremacists, or hate-filled individuals. I came together with the authors of this book to evoke change, to rise up and speak up for justice. We believe counseling professionals are positioned to *act*! Silence is not an option. This book documents a movement to ensure that counselors, in particular school counselors, take an antiracist stance in their everyday practice. Merely talking about cultural differences and race as a demographic variable is not enough.

Like Amanda Gorman, we argue that counselors can make a difference if they are brave and courageous enough to act.

Reading the Book

Antiracism in counseling requires courage and a high level of understanding of the history of racism in the United States, including the racist structures that have perpetuated white supremacist views. The information presented in this book is intended to facilitate counselors' comprehensive knowledge of antiracism, in particular compared to other constructs such as cultural competence and social justice counseling. As a whole, I firmly believe that antiracism is the foundation of cultural competence and social justice counseling practice. One cannot be a culturally competent counselor or a social justice advocate if antiracism is absent from one's repertoire of understanding. Antiracism is an active stance in which counselors challenge and fight against racist ideas, behaviors, and, most important, policies. Professor Angela Davis, a noted Black activist, has stated, "In a racist society it is not enough to be nonracist, we must be antiracist." More recently, Ibram X. Kendi, an antiracist scholar and 2021 MacArthur Fellow, made the same point to highlight the difference between being not racist and being antiracist. In his book *How to Be an Antiracist*, Kendi lamented that racist ideas have defined our society since its inception, and therefore practices that stem from racist views seem natural. Being antiracist is difficult because it requires us to act differently, think differently, and act in ways that contradict our typical practices and beliefs. Kendi (2019) stated,

"To be an antiracist is a radical choice in the face of our history, requiring a radical reorientation of our consciousness" (p. 23).

Given the shift in mind-set necessary for antiracist counseling practice, this book offers you an opportunity to explore antiracist counseling through the voices of diverse authors who represent expertise across the counseling spectrum as well as intersectional diversity in terms of gender, sexuality, and race. Some are counselor educators, some are practicing school counselors, some are clinical mental health counselors, one is a Postdoctoral Fellow with a background in African American studies, and one is a teacher educator. The authors are diverse, but they all share a unique perspective on antiracism. In addition, many of the authors describe their personal journeys to becoming antiracist counselors. They offer their own self-interrogation of their racial consciousness. Like Kendi, they share their missteps as well as their resilience and willingness to persevere through the journey. Most important, I believe the unwavering and collective sense of urgency among these authors is what makes this book special. Their commitment to social change and lifting up our profession is the thread that binds them together.

Another important aspect of this book is its focus on schools and communities. Why schools? I believe schools are the epicenter of communities and neighborhoods. A strong school contributes to the success of a strong community. So the work of school counselors and clinical mental health counselors is intertwined. Both professionals should work in tandem. Antiracist practice in schools challenges racist practices in communities and vice versa. As more counselors, teachers, and administrators explore the racial histories and legacies of their schools, many are finally asking, "How we can listen to and support Black parents and community members if we aren't emphasizing antiracist practices in schools?" Doing antiracist work means acknowledging that racist beliefs and structures are pervasive in all aspects of our communities—from education to housing to climate change—and then actively doing the work to tear down those beliefs and systems. These beliefs and structures do not exist just in schools *or* communities—they thrive in both interchangeably.

Beware o[...]

Many counselors may reject this boo[...] [be]lieve talking about race and racism is divisive. A wh[...] [a]ll this discussion about racism makes me uncomfor[...] like racism is my fault. I would rather concentrate o[...] d differences. Rehashing our racist past is not needed[...] nd is an excellent example of what Paul Gorski (201[...] My colleague wanted to fall back on comfortable con[...] d culture rather than uncomfortable conversations about the long-standing racialized societal systems that permeate my life as well as hers. In my colleague's perception there was an inherent benefit to maintaining the status quo of these systems, whereas I can clearly see how my family and I are negatively impacted by racism every day. The discomfort associated with these conversations triggers resistance and often anger. Racial equity detours do not represent racial progress. They represent the opposite and sometimes negatively impact the climate of an organization or school. For example, diversity appreciation days are often a comfortable detour for most white people but frustrate Black and Brown individuals who desire a change in racist and oppressive practices. Just think—we love Mexican food but push Mexican students out of our schools. If detours are used continuously in organizations, they exacerbate the frustration and helplessness of Black and Brown people. So this book will *not* ascribe to racial equity detours. Some readers may be uncomfortable with the authors' perspectives. However, discomfort is a part of the journey to an antiracist perspective.

Recently, a discussion of antiracism and critical race theory has been taken up by conservative state legislatures. Republican lawmakers in Texas, for instance, want to ban history lessons that include historical facts about the subjugation of Black and Brown people in the United States (e.g., slavery, colonialism). Many conservative lawmakers and groups confuse antiracism and critical race theory, a theory developed by legal scholars to highlight the experiences and narratives of marginalized people. The two concepts are interrelated, but they are different. The first chapter of this book includes definitions of these concepts so you will be more knowledgeable about the root of these groups' uneasiness and attack on civic education and U.S. history. I argue that the aim of the lawmakers' claims is not only to politicize the history of racism in the United States but also to detour away from correcting racism in this country. The fear of losing the privileges and benefits of whiteness is at the core of this movement to deny historical facts.

Also, it is important to note that many Black and Brown people will criticize this book. Some of my Black colleagues believe that talking about racism and antiracism creates discomfort among their white colleagues and further exacerbates the racial divide. I find this rationale confusing but not surprising because it is a manifestation of internalized racism and oppression. In a study, Robin Nicole Johnson (2012) emphasized that internalized racism involves both conscious and unconscious acceptance of a racial hierarchy in which white people's thoughts, views, and feelings must be protected and valued as most important. Internalized racism also encompasses a wide range of instances in which Black and Brown people accept negative racial stereotypes, adapt to white cultural standards, and embrace any type of thought that denies racism exists. Again, antiracist practice challenges these norms of behavior and cognition and will often create angst among white and Black or Brown colleagues. This book is no exception.

The Use of Racial Labels

Racism and anti-Blackness permeate every aspect of life in the United States and beyond—including the language used to describe people. Throughout history, the use of dehumanizing names and the refusal to manipulate language used to refer to Black adults (e.g., "Mr.," "Mrs.," "Dr.," "Professor") have perpetuated racist ideas about which groups are inferior and superior. For these reasons, it was essential to address the capitalization of "Black" and "Brown" before writing this book. I agonized over whether to capitalize "Black" and "Brown" in the text. Many of the chapter authors shared the same agony. In my chapters, I capitalize "Black" and "Brown" and use these terms to describe the unified and shared oppression and political interests of people of African descent; people who identify as Latinx, Hispanic, or Asian; and people from an Indigenous population. Some of the chapter authors refer to "people of color" rather than "Black" and "Brown" people and some capitalize "white." Some of the authors use *BIPOC* (pronounced "buy-pock"), an inclusive term that stands for "Black, Indigenous, and people of color." It is intended to combat the erasure of these diverse cultures. The inconsistencies in our use of these terms illustrate the diverse viewpoints on which labels are most appropriate. Regardless, the term "minority" is avoided in this book because this label lacks specificity, denotes inferiority, and neglects an overall sense of humanity.

It is noteworthy that many U.S. publishers and authors have adjusted their practices around capitalizing "Black" and "Brown." Many years ago, Kailin (2002) argued that comparing Black and white racial labels is flawed because "white" does not denote a particular ethnicity or nationality. Black, in contrast, represents an ethnicity describing peoples of African descent. She stated,

> One of the reasons people of the African diaspora may call themselves Black rather than a specific ethnicity is because their true ethnicity was robbed from them during slavery when all attempts were made to erase the history and identity of the African peoples. (Kailin, 2002, p. xxi)

Hence, "Black" denotes nationality, whereas "white" denotes skin color. In June 2020, the Associated Press changed its usage rules to capitalize the word "Black" when used in the context of race and culture but will continue its practice of not capitalizing "white." *The New York Times* followed suit and has now changed its policy to capitalize "Black." It is important to note that the term "African American" is not wrong, and some prefer it. However, I believe that capitalizing "Black" and "Brown" is desirable because these descriptors are more inclusive of ethnicities united by shared oppression, race, geography, and culture.

Breathe

As counselors, we have been trained to empathize, to give unconditional positive regard, and to embrace diverse perspectives. These are attributes of an effective counselor. At the same time, it is critical that we acknowledge the difficulty of our work, in particular as we embark on an antiracist journey. Reading this book might trigger intense emotions, including anxiety, fear, frustration, isolation, resentment, and self-blame. For Black and Brown counselors, discussing one's experiences with racism is exhausting and may create feelings of isolation and despair. So I suggest that you breathe before beginning this book and take self-care breaks throughout your reading. Take care of yourself on this antiracist journey. Discuss the concepts with trusted colleagues and others who are on the same journey. Self-preservation and antiracist practice are intertwined and complementary. As Black feminist writer Audre Lorde (1988, p. 129) stated, "Caring for myself is not self-indulgence, it is self-preservation, and that is an act of political warfare."

Breathe. Exhale.

References

Gorski, P. C. (2019). Fighting racism, battling burnout: Causes of activist burnout in US racial justice activists. *Ethnic and Racial Studies*, 42(5), 667–687. https://doi.org/10.1080/01419870.2018.1439981

Johnson, R. N. (2012). The academic opportunity gap: How racism and stereotypes disrupt the education of African American undergraduates. *Race Ethnicity and Education, 15*(5), 633–652.

Kailin, J. (2002). *Antiracist education: From theory to practice*. Rowman & Littlefield.

Kendi, I. X. (2019). *How to be an antiracist*. One World.

Lorde, A. (1988). *A burst of light: Essays*. Firebrand Books.

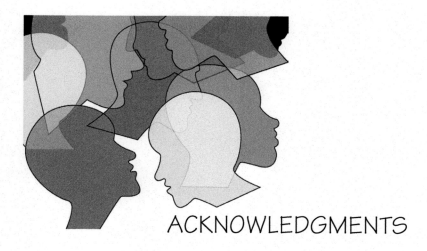

ACKNOWLEDGMENTS

This book is dedicated to the millions of professional school counselors, mental health counselors, and helping professionals who have committed themselves to ensuring justice for their students, their clients, and their clients' communities.

Thanks to everyone on the American Counseling Association's Publications team, including Nancy and the amazing content editors, who helped me so much. Special thanks to Chelsea for her patience and amazing assistance in bringing all the pieces of the book together.

I extend a special acknowledgment to two women who continue to inspire me: Ms. Colethia Holcomb, my late mother, and the late Associate Professor Vivian Lee, an unflappable school counselor educator, human rights activist, and friend.

ABOUT THE EDITOR

Cheryl Holcomb-McCoy, PhD, believes in the revolutionary power of school counseling. A fellow of the American Counseling Association with 30 years of experience as a kindergarten teacher, elementary school counselor, family therapist, and most recently university professor and administrator, she has a wealth of knowledge, expertise, and wisdom. Professor Holcomb-McCoy is currently the dean of the School of Education and a professor at American University (AU). She is also the author of the best selling book *School Counseling to Close the Achievement Gap: A Social Justice Framework for Success*. In her 5 years as dean, Professor Holcomb-McCoy founded AU's Summer Institute on Education, Equity and Justice and the AU Teacher Pipeline Project, a partnership with the (Washington) DC Public Schools and Friendship Charter Schools. She is also actively working to develop an antiracist curriculum for teachers-in-training. Prior to leading the School of Education at AU, she served as vice provost for faculty affairs campus-wide and vice dean of academic affairs in the School of Education at Johns Hopkins University, where she launched the Johns Hopkins School Counseling Fellows Program and the Faculty Diversity Initiative. Professor Holcomb-McCoy has also been an associate professor in the Department of Counseling and Personnel Services at the University of Maryland College Park and director of the School Counseling Program at Brooklyn College of the City University of New York. A decorated scholar, she has written 16 chapters in edited books and more than 40 articles published in peer-reviewed journals. From 2014 to 2016, she served as a consultant to former First Lady Michelle Obama's Reach Higher Initiative, a program dedicated to supporting first-generation students in making it to and through college. She also serves on the board of Martha's Table, a nonprofit that supports health and wellness for children and families in the nation's capital. Professor Holcomb-McCoy's passion for school counseling, mental health, and wellness starts at home. As a proud mother of two, she knows firsthand the importance of systemic change to help students reach their full potential. A proud member of Delta Sigma

Theta Sorority, Inc., Professor Holcomb-McCoy holds bachelor's and master's degrees from the University of Virginia. She earned a doctorate in counseling and counselor education from the University of North Carolina at Greensboro. She lives in Potomac, Maryland, with her husband and two children.

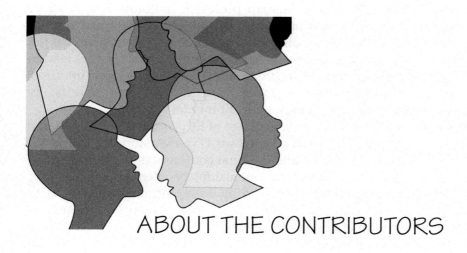

ABOUT THE CONTRIBUTORS

Gretchen Brion-Meisels, EdD, is a lecturer at the Harvard Graduate School of Education whose work draws on critical participatory action research approaches to understand how schools and communities can become more equitable and loving spaces. She completed her EdD at the Harvard Graduate School of Education after spending 10 years as a middle school teacher.

Julia Bryan, PhD, is a professor of counselor education at The Pennsylvania State University. Professor Bryan examines the role of school counselors in school-family-community partnerships and has developed an equity-focused partnership process model to promote care, academic achievement, antiracism, resilience, and equity for marginalized students. She also uses large national secondary data sets to research school counselors' roles in addressing academic achievement, college access, disciplinary referrals, school bonding, and other equity issues in schools that greatly affect students' lives, especially the lives of students of color. Professor Bryan has contributed numerous peer-reviewed empirical publications to the profession, including a special issue of the *Professional School Counseling* journal on collaboration and partnerships with families and communities. Professor Bryan was recently awarded the American Counseling Association's Extended Research Award, the Association for Counselor Education and Supervision's Locke-Paisley Outstanding Mentor Award, and the National Career Development Association's Article of the Year Award.

Janice A. Byrd, PhD, is an assistant professor of counselor education in the Department of Educational Psychology, Counseling, and Special Education at The Pennsylvania State University. She earned her PhD in counselor education and supervision from the University of Iowa and has previous experience as a school counselor and career counselor. She has also counseled, taught, and mentored youth. Professor Byrd's scholarship seeks to situate the lived experiences of Black students within the broader ecological context to systematically examine how their personal, social, academic, and career success is interrupted and/or enhanced by school, family, community, and policies throughout all stages of the educational pipeline (i.e., K–12, postsecondary, and graduate studies).

Aubrey D. Daniels, PhD, LPC, is an assistant professor of counseling at Rider University. Her research is focused on complex trauma and the impacts it has on individuals and family systems both long term and short term. Much of her research focuses on the construct of resilience. She studies what factors lead to resilience despite the experience of trauma. Similar to her research interests, Professor Daniels's clinical practice is focused on trauma, more specifically childhood and complex trauma, crisis, and adult mental health.

Beth O. Day-Hairston, PhD, is dean of the College of Education and Professional Studies at Fort Valley State University. Professor Day-Hairston has presented extensively at numerous local, state, and national conferences on differentiated instruction, service learning, coteaching, inclusion, problem-based learning, experiential teaching, best practices for working with culturally and linguistically diverse families, best practices for teaching at-risk students, and teaching strategies for working with children with behavioral and emotional disorders. Professor Day-Hairston is the recipient the 2010 Wachovia Excellence in Teaching Award for Winston-Salem State University and the recipient of the 2000 Alumni Achiever of the Year Award for the School of Education and Performance at Winston-Salem State University.

Norma L. Day-Vines, PhD, serves as associate dean for faculty development in the School of Education at Johns Hopkins University and maintains a faculty appointment as professor of counseling and human development. Prior to joining the faculty at Johns Hopkins University, she held tenured faculty positions at Virginia Tech and William & Mary. Professor Day-Vines's research agenda examines the importance of multiculturalism as an indispensable tool in the delivery of culturally competent counseling and educational services for clients and students from marginalized groups. More specifically, she specializes in the measurement of attitudes toward discussing the contextual dimensions of race, ethnicity, and culture with ethnic minority clients or students and the identification of strategies that reduce barriers to well-being. She has consulted with school districts across the country to address issues related to diversity, equity, and inclusion. Her scholarship has appeared in leading counseling journals, such as the *Journal of Counseling & Development*, the *Journal of Multicultural Counseling and Development*, the *Journal of Measurement and Evaluation in Counseling and Development*, and *Professional School Counseling*. Professor Day-Vines was recognized with an Exemplary Diversity Leadership Award in 2013 by the Association for Multicultural Counseling and Development. In 2018 she received an Excellence in Teaching Award at Johns Hopkins University, and in 2019 she was awarded a Presidential Citation from the American Counseling Association in recognition of her scholarship on multiculturalism.

Traci Dennis, EdD, is a professorial lecturer in American University's School of Education. In her current role, she teaches undergraduate and graduate students in various education courses. Professor Dennis has a strong record of teaching in underfunded prekindergarten–Grade 12 schools. Her scholarly work focuses on examining how Black students experience school and schooling and the intersection of anti-Black racism and antiracist teaching. Through her teaching and scholarship, she aims to address the impact of inequities in education on students of color; support the development of antiracist knowledges, literacies, and capacities among teacher candidates; and assist teacher candidates in translating antiracist theories and research into practice in pre-kindergarten–Grade 12 schools, classrooms, and curricula. Her goal is to use research to counter harmful dominant narratives, improve educational outcomes for students experiencing marginalization and oppression, amplify the voices of racially minoritized students, and create opportunities for adaptive and sustainable change.

Mary Edwin, PhD, LPC, NCC, is an assistant professor of counselor education at the University of Missouri–St. Louis. She received her doctoral degree from Pennsylvania State University, where she also served as a career counselor. Prior to earning her doctoral degree, Professor Edwin served as an elementary and middle school counselor. Her research interests include career development across the life span and fostering career development in K–12 schools.

Derek Francis, MA, is the manager of counseling services for Minneapolis Public Schools and a professional development consultant for Hatching Results. Derek, who specializes in helping students and staff build trusting cross-cultural relationships, has presented at state and national conferences around the country. In the summer of 2020, Derek led a webinar for more than 25,000 counselors and educators on proactive school counseling after a major racial incident. Some of Derek's published work includes contributions to *Contemporary Case Studies in School Counseling*, the published blog "This Is Not a Fire Drill—Supporting Students After George Floyd," and articles published for the American School Counselors Association and in the *American School Board Journal*. Derek was quoted in the November 2020 *Time* magazine article titled "'You Can't Be Silent.' Schools Brace for the Presidential Election Aftermath." Derek believes that school counselors are key to bridging our country's racial divide. Spending time with his daughter, eating, and traveling are Derek's favorite hobbies.

Dana Griffin, PhD, is an associate professor at the University of North Carolina at Chapel Hill, where she teaches in the School of Counseling, Human Development and Family Studies, and Applied Developmental Sciences and Special Education programs in the School of Education. Professor Griffin also serves as a consultant for the university's World View program, where she travels to school districts across North Carolina conducting workshops with schools on how to have courageous conversations around diversity, equity, and inclusion. Professor Griffin teaches a variety of courses related to her research and interests in social justice and advocacy, cultural diversity, parent involvement, adolescent development, and school-family-community partnerships. Across these courses, Professor Griffin emphasizes the need for counselors, teachers, administrators, and other school stakeholders to address their biases and fight against institutional racism and other isms that exist in schools to meet the academic, social, and emotional needs of students, in particular Black, Indigenous, and other students of color and low-income students.

Dominiqua M. Griffin, PhD, NCC, is an assistant professor of school counseling at California State University, Fresno, and the program coordinator for the Master's in School Counseling and Pupil Personnel Services program. She focuses on school counseling and international education to advance school counseling domestically and internationally. She centers Barbadian school counseling roles. Professor Griffin's research extends to school-family-community partnerships and compassion fatigue in K–12 educators.

Paul C. Harris, PhD, is an associate professor in the Counselor Education program at Pennsylvania State University. He earned his BSEd in health and physical education with a concentration in sports medicine and his MEd in school counseling from the University of Virginia. He worked as a high school counselor for several years prior to completing his PhD in counselor education from the University of Maryland, whose program emphasized promoting systemic equity, access, and justice in schools through counseling. He also holds an MDiv from Virginia Union University. Professor Harris's research focuses on achieving three goals: (a) improving the college and career readiness of underserved students, (b) promoting the identity development of Black male student athletes, and (c) facilitating the empowerment of antiracist school counselors. He is the creator of Men Passionately Pursuing Purpose, a program that exists to see Black male athletes thrive in and outside of sport. He is also the former president of the Virginia School Counselor Association and a former member of the board of directors of the American School Counselor Association.

Malik S. Henfield, PhD, is the founding dean of and a professor in the Institute for Racial Justice at Loyola University Chicago. He received a BA in biology from Francis Marion University, an MEd and EdS in school counseling from the University of South Carolina, and a PhD in counselor education from The Ohio State University. Professor Henfield's scholarship situates Black students' lived experiences in a broader ecological milieu to critically explore how their personal, social, academic, and career success is impeded and enhanced by school, family, and community contexts. His research has resulted in external funding, including most recently a grant from the National Science Foundation focused on increasing the number of students of color entering computer science professions and a grant from the Institute of Education Sciences aimed at determining the extent to which school districts provide equity and excellence in their gifted education programming.

Lynette M. Henry, PhD, is the manager of college success programs in the Office of Counseling and College and Career Readiness in Fairfax County Public Schools. She uses a systems approach to close opportunity gaps for college for students who are historically underserved in college. She manages programs designed to promote high-quality college access, readiness, and success among many underrepresented students. Many of the students served by these programs are the first in their families to attend college. Professor Henry has served in the field of education for the past 26 years, from prekindergarten through college, as a professor, school counselor, college and career counselor, and teacher in the United States and Barbados. Her passion for giving children access to opportunities through innovative school-family-community partnerships has led to her receiving the Superintendent We Deliver Miracles Award from the School District of Hillsborough County and Hillsborough Education Foundation for going above and beyond for schoolchildren and the community, the Ida S. Baker Diversity Educator of the Year from Just Elementary School (School District of Hillsborough County), and the Outstanding School Counseling Professional of the Year from Hayfield Secondary School (Fairfax County Public Schools).

Erik M. Hines, PhD, is an associate professor in the Department of Educational Psychology and Learning Systems at Florida State University as well as the coordinator of the Counselor Education Program and School Counseling Track. Professor Hines prepares graduate students to be professional school counselors. Professor Hines's research agenda centers around (a) the college and career readiness of African American males; (b) parental involvement and its impact on academic achievement among students of color; and (c) improving and increasing post-secondary opportunities for first-generation students, low-income students, and students of color (in particular African American males). In 2020 Professor Hines was selected as a fellow of the American Counseling Association.

Kara Ieva, PhD, is an associate professor in the Counseling in Educational Settings program at Rowan University. Her educational career, which spans more than 20 years, includes work as a Spanish teacher, as a professional school counselor, and in school counselor education. She received her BA in Spanish secondary education and an MEd in secondary education curriculum and administration from Towson University. In addition, she earned an MEd in school counseling from Loyola College in Maryland and her PhD in counselor education from the University of Central Florida. Kara's areas of research interest include promoting equity and wellness in education for children and adolescents from marginalized populations in the areas of college and career access, social-emotional development, and group counseling. She consults with regional school districts and provides professional development to prekindergarten–Grade 12 school counselors, teachers, and administrators on how to embed culturally affirming social-emotional development into curricula and strategies for cultivating safe and welcoming mental health and a neurodiverse culture in schools.

Kaprea Johnson, PhD, is an associate professor in counselor education at Virginia Commonwealth University. Her interests are broadly situated in interrogating education and health care systems as it relates to addressing social determinants of health needs, equity, access, and justice. In education, she is interested in school counseling practice, training needs, and outcomes in underresourced schools that serve predominantly minorities. She is an experienced scholar with more than $4.5 million in grant-funded projects as either a principal investigator or a co–principal investigator, 51 peer-reviewed journal publications, two books, more than 80 presentations, and several practitioner-oriented publications. She is passionate about supporting the mental health and wellness needs of youth through assisting in the development of caring, knowledgeable, anti-racist, equity-driven school counselors.

Erin Mason, PhD, LPC, CPCS, is an assistant professor at Georgia State University in Atlanta and was previously a faculty member at DePaul University in Chicago. She spent 13 years as a middle school counselor. Her greatest joys as a counselor educator come from teaching, and she values most the fact that students provide her with ongoing opportunities to learn. Professor Mason's primary area of interest is the relationship between professional identity and professional practice in school counseling. Her scholarship has covered antiracism, antibias, and a justice philosophy for school counseling and school counselor preparation.

Renae D. Mayes, PhD, is an associate professor in the Department of Disability and Psychoeducational Studies at the University of Arizona, where she prepares master's- and doctoral-level students to be counselors and counselor educators. Professor Mayes's research agenda centers around the academic success and college readiness of gifted Black students with dis/abilities and Black girls. Her research details the experiences of students and families navigating schools while also providing recommendations for dismantling systems of oppression through policy and practice. Furthermore, Professor Mayes has extended this research to include implications for leadership, advocacy, and collaboration for school counselors and school administrators.

Laura Owen, PhD, is the executive director of the Center for Equity and Post-secondary Attainment at San Diego State University. Formerly an urban school counselor and district counseling supervisor, she is a passionate advocate for closing college opportunity gaps. Her research focuses on evaluating the impact of interventions and programs designed to address the systems, structures, and policies that drive inequitable access to high-quality postsecondary advising support. Laura has researched interventions targeting financial aid and completion of the Free Application for Federal Student Aid, the transition from high school to college, text messaging and virtual advising, the impact of technology on college-going decisions, and how students prefer to receive college and career information. Her research includes interventions and partnerships with nonprofit college access organizations, technology companies, cross-institutional researchers, and school districts from Baltimore, Maryland, to San Diego, California.

Whitney Polk, PhD, is a licensed professional counselor in Pennsylvania and previously provided therapy to K–12 students in Philadelphia public schools. She is currently a National Science Foundation Postdoctoral Fellow at the University of Pennsylvania researching discrimination, school discipline, and youth mental health.

Mandy Savitz-Romer, PhD, is the Nancy Pforzheimer Aronson Senior Lecturer in Human Development and Education at the Harvard Graduate School of Education. Her research examines how schools structure counseling support systems and specifically what conditions are critical to effective practice. Professor Savitz-Romer is the author of *Fulfilling the Promise: Reimagining School Counseling to Advance Student Success* and coauthor of *Ready, Willing, and Able: A Developmental Approach to College Access and Success*.

Joshua Schuschke, PhD, is an assistant professor at Johns Hopkins University. Professor Schuschke is a scholar of Black academic identity development across multiple media contexts. He earned his PhD in 2019 from the University of Southern California's Rossier School of Education's Urban Education Policy program. His concentration was in educational psychology with a special focus on intersectional educational experiences. Before his doctoral studies, Professor Schuschke earned his BS and MA degrees in Pan-African Studies from his hometown school, the University of Louisville. In his master's thesis he developed a theoretical framework of online Black academic identity development for Black students through the use of social media platform affordances. Professor Schuschke's dissertation, *#RepresentationMatters: Constructing Black Academic Identities Through Popular & Social Media*, received the University of Southern California Rossier School of Education PhD Dissertation of the Year Award.

M. Ann Shillingford, PhD, is an associate professor of counselor education at the University of Central Florida in Orlando. Professor Shillingford has written several articles and book chapters on multicultural issues focused in particular on disparities among people of color. Professor Shillingford has a keen interest in exploring measures to deconstruct educational, social, and health disparities among marginalized communities. Professor Shillingford's coedited book *The Journey Unraveled: College and Career Readiness of African American Students* was published in the fall of 2015. Her coedited book *Demystifying the DSM for School Counselors* was published in September 2020.

Sam Steen, PhD, is an associate professor in the College of Education at George Mason University. He is also co–academic coordinator of the school counseling program. He specializes in group work and cultivating Black students' academic identity development. Professor Steen was a school counselor for 10 years, and his practitioner experiences shape his research agenda, approach to teaching, and service. He is a fellow of the Association for Specialists in Group Work, a division of the American Counseling Association. Recently, Professor Steen received the Professional Advancement Award from the Association for Specialists in Group Work recognizing his outstanding efforts in advancing the field of group work though research and the development of a new and innovative strategies for schools, families, and marginalized communities.

Jaelyn O. Vines is an undergraduate student at North Carolina A&T State University. She graduated from the Oldfields School in Maryland.

Ahmad R. Washington, PhD, is an assistant professor in the Department of Counseling and Human Development at the University of Louisville. He teaches in the School Counseling program, where he works with preservice school counseling students as they prepare to transition into the profession. Professor Washington received his BS in psychology from Francis Marion University, his MA in clinical counseling from Webster University, and his PhD in counselor education and supervision from the University of Iowa in 2013.

Joseph M. Williams, PhD, is an associate professor of counselor education at the University of Virginia. He is a faculty affiliate with Youth-Nex: The Center to Promote Effective Youth Development and with the Center for Race and Public Education in the South. His primary research focuses on resilience-based interventions and policies at the micro and macro levels that neutralize or offset the detrimental effect of racism and poverty on the academic, personal/social, and career development of K–12 students. Besides publishing scholarly articles and book chapters in these areas, he also consults with school districts, communities, associations, and corporations to improve diversity, inclusion, and equity efforts and engage people in productive dialogue and action. Professor Williams earned his PhD in counselor education and supervision from the University of Iowa and his MS in clinical mental health counseling from Minnesota State University. He has more than 10 years of practical experience counseling children and adolescents in both school and mental health settings.

Valaida (Val) L. Wise, EdD, is the principal consultant at her firm Dr. Valaida Wise Consulting, LLC. The firm supports schools and other organizations in the areas of diversity, equity and inclusion, governance, and leadership. She is also a faculty member in the Graduate School of Education at Johns Hopkins University in Baltimore, Maryland, where she teaches diversity, equity, inclusion, and issues of social justice. An educator for more than 25 years, Professor Wise has served as the head of several independent schools in the Washington, DC, region. Professor Wise is the chair of the board at Creative Minds International Public Charter School; is chair of the board at McLean School in Potomac, Maryland; and also serves on the boards of several other professional organizations and independent schools.

CHAPTER 1

The Pathway to Antiracism: Defining Moments in Counseling History

Cheryl Holcomb-McCoy

Racism and white supremacy have a long-standing and tumultuous history in the United States. Ever since 1619, when 20 to 30 enslaved Africans landed in the English colony of Virginia, racism has shaped Americans' lives and brutally shaped the lives of Black Americans. According to historian Carol Anderson (2016), James Madison called chattel slavery America's "original sin." This inhumane sin was documented in Article I, Section 2, of the Constitution, which declared each enslaved African to be three fifths of a person. It was again documented in Article IV, Section 2, the Fugitive Slave Clause. This clause stated that the owner of a slave had the right to seize and repossess that slave in another state, further underscoring the fact that Black Africans were property, not humans with rights. All in all, these facts are evidence that U.S. history is grounded in significant systems of oppression, fueled by the belief that the white race is inherently superior to other races. Slavery as well as the colonization of Indigenous American societies upheld this belief, and the results live within us today.

After the Civil War, there was an attempt to redeem the country's original sin with three Reconstruction-era amendments to the Constitution (i.e., the 13th, 14th, and 15th Amendments) and the Freedmen's Bureau. The amendments were designed to ensure equality for emancipated enslaved persons.

- The 13th Amendment bans slavery and all involuntary servitude, except in the case of punishment for a crime.
- The 14th Amendment defines a citizen as any person born or naturalized in the United States, overturning the 1857 *Dred Scott v. Sandford* Supreme Court ruling, which stated that Black people were not eligible for citizenship.

- The 15th Amendment prohibits governments from denying U.S. citizens the right to vote based on race, color, or past servitude.

In addition, Congress established the Freedmen's Bureau to provide land, medical facilities, and education to newly freed Black persons transitioning from slavery to freedom. Despite these efforts, the civil rights of Black persons were not sustained, and the courts failed to ensure that Black persons received due process based on the amendments. More important, a refusal to redistribute land to Blacks led to long-standing economic constraints and future racialized practices such as redlining, housing discrimination, and segregation in schools. The Freedmen's Bureau, which was responsible for founding many historically Black colleges, was terminated in 1872, which led to the mistreatment of Black Americans through state and local statutes that legalized segregation by race and other discriminatory laws and practices. These practices, popularly known as Jim Crow laws, existed for about 100 years, until 1968. Jim Crow laws resulted in Black Americans being denied the right to vote, the right to hold jobs, the right to an education, and the right to a fair criminal justice system. Those who challenged Jim Crow laws faced arrest, fines, violence, and death (e.g., lynching). Sadly, 4,075 Black Americans were lynched in Alabama, Arkansas, Florida, Georgia, Kentucky, Louisiana, Mississippi, North Carolina, South Carolina, Tennessee, Texas, and Virginia between 1877 and 1950 (Equal Justice Initiative, 2021). Moreover, the overrepresentation of Black and Brown persons in the prison system has resulted in a new racial caste system (Alexander, 2010).

In addition to mass incarceration, inequality and segregation in schools has led to a long legacy of educational oppression. Black and Brown students continue to be overrepresented in special education (Elder et al., 2019), underrepresented in gifted classes (Ford et al., 2011), tracked to low-level classes (Mickelson, 2001), and criminalized and removed from schools (Morris, 2016). They are also the students who are least likely to attend 4-year colleges and universities (The Education Trust, 2020). According to Horace Mann (1848), education is "the great equalizer of the conditions of men—the balance-wheel of the social machinery" (Massachusetts Board of Education, 1849, p. 59). But Mann went on to state that education doesn't change the "moral nature" of people (p. 60). Thus, for Black and Brown students, racism within education systems has created the opposite. Education injustice, stoked by racist views and policies, has perpetuated and sustained unshakeable disparities in education.

Given these hundreds of years of oppressive practices, there is no way that any American escapes the impact of racism. Although some might argue that racism is a Black problem, history refutes that notion. The effects of racism touch white persons as much as they touch those who identify as Black or Brown. In a recent report, McKinsey and Company (2019) estimated that if the wealth gap caused by systemic racism were addressed, the U.S. gross national product could be 4% to 6% higher. A higher gross domestic product ultimately means more jobs and higher salaries for all Americans.

Racism also affects the interpersonal relationships of white people. Many may have lost relationships with friends, family members, and coworkers to disagreements, fights, and tension over racism. Racism also distorts white people's perceptions of what to fear. Many are taught to fear Black and Brown people without considering other human and environmental factors that influence behavior and life outcomes. For instance, Black and Brown people—not the economic opportunity system—are often scapegoated as the problem. So the costs of racism are devastating to white people, especially those without the resources to buffer the effects. They are not the same costs of day-to-day violence, discrimination, and harassment that plague Black people. Nevertheless, they are high costs that most people are trained to ignore, deny, or rationalize away.

A History of Racism in Counseling

Helping professionals, in particular counselors, have also been touched by racism. Over the past 4 decades, social scientists, including counselors, have moved away from defining race in biological terms and toward defining it as a social and political construct that in turn impacts the counseling process as well as counselors' and clients' conceptualization of problems. The foundational theories and frameworks of professional counseling emerged from a predominantly white, middle-class context (Gerig, 2014; Ratts & Pedersen, 2014). Therefore, racism within the profession has not necessarily been a focal point. Over the past 30 years, much has been written about clients who do not originate from the dominant society (Butler & Shilling-ford-Butler, 2014; Wade, 2006). However, less has been written about racism within the profession. D'Andrea (1992) challenged the profession to take on racism and even warned of silence denoting professionals' complicity in racism in communities where they worked. In a more recent opinion piece in *Counseling Today*, Arredondo et al. (2020) suggested that there are still unintentional and covert forms of racism and racial injustice within counselor training, research, and practice.

Several iterations of counseling movements have emerged out of the experiences of Black and Brown counselors and clients (e.g., the Black psychology movement). Each movement has addressed racism but without specific attention to antiracism. The remainder of this chapter provides descriptions of these counseling movements: Black/African-centered psychology (e.g., Jones, 1972), cross-cultural counseling and psychology (e.g., Atkinson et al., 1989), multicultural counseling (e.g., Lee, 1991), and social justice counseling and advocacy (Holcomb-McCoy, 2007). Having a common language makes it easier to communicate a commitment to racial equity and creates a platform for coordinated work toward antiracist outcomes. Also, this chapter includes definitions of antiracism and antiracist counseling and introduces an antiracist framework of school counseling.

Black/African-Centered Psychology

More than 40 years ago, White (1972) argued that the lived experiences of persons of African ancestry in the United States demanded a shift in conceptualizing psychology. With the assassination of Martin Luther King Jr. came an intense need to lift up the Black community and an affirmation of Blackness. This era heralded the beginning of the Black psychology movement, which solidified when the Association of Black Psychologists (ABPsi) was established in 1968 at the annual convention of the American Psychological Association. ABPsi emerged out of the American Psychological Association's lack of responsiveness to the needs of Black psychologists and the communities they served. In the press release announcing its establishment, the need for a community-centered organization committed to ethnocentrism and the needs of Black people and Black psychologists was stated as the impetus for the new organization (Williams, 1974, pp. 11–12). See Box 1 for Black/African-centered psychology scholars in the field. ABPsi (2021) defined Black/African-centered psychology as follows:

It is the intention of the Committee to Advance African Psychology (CAAP) to establish a framework for content provided during the African Psychology Institute (API) that adheres to the values and principles expressed therein. In recognition of the diverse historical experiences and cultural expressions within and between peoples of African ancestry, the following is the accepted definition:

> "Black/African Centered psychology is a dynamic manifestation of unifying African principles, values and traditions. It is the self-conscious "centering" of psychological analyses and applications in African realities, cultures, and epistemologies. Black/African centered psychology, as a system of thought and action, examines the processes that allow for the illumination and liberation of the Spirit. Relying on the principles of harmony within the universe as a natural order of existence, Black/African centered psychology recognizes: the Spirit that permeates everything that is; the notion that everything in the universe is interconnected; the value that the collective is the most salient element of existence; and the idea that communal self knowledge is the key to mental health. Black/African Centered psychology is ultimately concerned with understanding the systems of meaning of human beingness, the features of human functioning, and the restoration of normal/natural order to human development. As such, it is used to resolve personal and social problems and to promote optimal functioning." (paras. 1–2)

Overall, the Black psychology movement was a period of academic progression in combining and applying Black studies with traditional psychological frameworks, encapsulating new approaches, terms, and structures for understanding Black people. Akbar (2004) described Black/African-centered psychology as follows:

> [It] is not a thing, but a place—a view, a perspective, a way of observing. African Psychology does not claim to be an exclusive body of knowledge, though a body of knowledge will continue to be generated from the place. It is a perspective that is lodged in the historical importance of the human view from the land known as Africa. (p. ix)

In a special issue of the journal *Cultural Diversity and Ethnic Minority Psychology*, Holliday (2009) outlined the history of African Americans and Blacks in psychology in the United States. It is interesting that Holliday noted that in 1934, the *Journal of Negro Education* (published by Howard University) developed a special issue of 14 papers that challenged the functions and findings of research on racial differences.

Cross-Cultural and Multicultural Counseling and Psychology

In 1982, Derald Wing Sue and six of his colleagues ignited the cross-cultural and multicultural counseling movement when they published the article "Position Paper: Cross-Cultural Counseling Competencies." Sue et

BOX 1

Scholars: Black/African-Centered Psychology

Na'im Akbar, PhD
Faye Belgrave, PhD
Kevin Cokley, PhD
Cheryl Grills, PhD
Asa Hilliard, PhD
Kobi Kambon, PhD
Linda James Myers, PhD
Wade Nobles, PhD
Joseph White, PhD
Robert Lee Williams, PhD

al. (1982) argued that traditional mental health practices (including counseling) and research were irrelevant to ethnic minorities. They proposed a push for new approaches to counseling that would be more appropriate for the culturally different. Sue et al.'s framework for cross-cultural counseling led to the triad of components of cultural competence: cultural knowledge, cultural awareness, and cross-cultural skills. A plethora of literature emerged from Sue et al.'s article. Pedersen (1990) even described the cross-cultural and multicultural counseling movement as the fourth force in counseling because of its rapid growth and visibility in the field.

In addition to components of cultural competence, the cross-cultural counseling movement focuses on studying similarities and differences in individual psychological functioning based on cultural and/or ethnic background. Scholars and researchers of cross-cultural counseling and multicultural counseling regard culture as essential to psychological functioning, an integral context for psychological development and behavior. Multicultural counseling specifically addresses factors within the counseling process when the client and counselor represent different cultures. This strengths-based approach considers the sociocultural factors that impact the client and counselor. The client's and the counselor's race and racism are considered, but the framework for multicultural and cross-cultural counseling is culture, not race. See Box 2 for cross-cultural scholars.

In 1972, another group formed specifically to address the issues of Black and Brown counselors and clients. The new group, the Association for Non-White Concerns in Personnel and Guidance, became a separate division of the American Personnel and Guidance Association, which is now the American Counseling Association (ACA). Before the group was formed, its members had limited representation and no voting rights on the board of directors of the American Personnel and Guidance Association. The individual most often identified as the father of the Association for Non-White Concerns in Personnel and Guidance is Samuel H. Johnson. The name of the group was changed to the Association for Multicultural Counseling and Development (AMCD) in 1985 to more accurately reflect its efforts. The mission of the association is

BOX 2 — Scholars: Cross-Cultural/ Multicultural Counseling

Patricia Arredondo, PhD
Donald Atkinson, PhD
Robert Carter, PhD
Madonna Constantine, PhD
Michael D'Andrea, PhD
Donald Pope Davis, PhD
Janet Helms, PhD
Allen Ivey, PhD
Courtland Lee, PhD
Don C. Locke, PhD
Paul Pedersen, PhD
Joseph Ponterotto, PhD
Gargi Roysicar, PhD
Derald Wing Sue, PhD
Clemmont E. Vontress, PhD

- [To] recognize the human diversity and multicultural nature of our society;
- To enhance the development, human rights, and the psychological health of ethnic/racial populations and all people as critical to the social, educational, political, professional, and personal reform in the United States and globally;
- To identify and work to eliminate conditions that create barriers to the individual development of marginalized populations;
- To develop, implement, and/or foster interest in charitable, scientific, and educational programs designed to further the interests of marginalized populations;

- To secure equality and access of treatment, advancement, qualifications, and status [for] individuals and families in counseling, wellness, and mental health work;
- To publish a journal and other scientific-educational and professional materials with the purpose of raising the standards of all who work in providing counseling, wellness, and mental health. (AMCD, n.d., "Our Mission")

> **BOX 3**   Scholars:
> Social Justice
> Counseling and Advocacy
>
> Mary Smith Arnold, PhD
> Fred Bemak, PhD
> Stuart Chen-Hayes, PhD
> Rita Chung, PhD
> Reese House, PhD
> Michael Hutchins, PhD
> Mark Kiselica, PhD
> Judith Lewis, PhD
> Manivong Ratts, PhD
> Anneliese Singh, PhD
> Rebecca Toporek, PhD
> Edil Torres-Rivera, PhD

In April 1991, AMCD approved Sue et al.'s (1982) rationale for a multicultural and/or cross-cultural perspective in counseling. AMCD proposed 31 multicultural counseling competencies and strongly encouraged ACA (then known as the American Association of Counseling and Development) to adopt the competencies in accreditation criteria. The competencies were approved and became a standard for counseling training and practice (Sue, Arredondo, and McDavis, 1982).

Social Justice Counseling and Advocacy

In 1994, a group of counseling professionals convened to better commit to multiculturalism and broader social justice issues. The group members represented many organizations within ACA, such as AMCD, the Association for Specialists in Group Work, and the National Career Development Association. After numerous meetings with ACA leadership, the group became an organizational affiliate in 1999 and was called Counselors for Social Justice (CSJ; J. Anderson et al., 2015). In 2000, the ACA Governing Council accepted CSJ as an official division of ACA, making it an additional division devoted to the concerns of Black and Brown populations, but with a broader focus than just racism. With social justice as a focal point, CSJ advocates for health care, for access for the disabled, against discrimination of sexual and gender minorities, for immigration, and against economic disparities.

In 2003, CSJ promoted the endorsement of the ACA Advocacy Competencies (Toporek et al., 2009). These competencies laid the groundwork for counselors intervening for systems change. Since 2007, CSJ has partnered with Psychologists for Social Responsibility to publish the *Journal for Social Action in Counseling and Psychology*, a leading journal in the field.

In 2015, the ACA Governing Council approved a new set of competencies that blended the Multicultural Counseling Competencies (Sue et al., 1982, 1992) with the Social Justice Counseling Competencies put forth by CSJ. The new competencies, called the Multicultural and Social Justice Counseling Competencies, specifically highlight the intersection of identities and the dynamics of power, privilege, and oppression that influence the counseling relationship. The domains reflect the different factors that lead to multicultural and social justice competence: awareness, client worldview, counseling relationship, counseling, and advocacy interventions (Ratts et al., 2015). See Box 3 for social justice scholars.

Defining Antiracism

The beauty of antiracism is that you don't have to pretend to be free of racism to be an antiracist. Antiracism is the commitment to fight racism wherever you find it, includ-ing in yourself. And it's the only way forward.

—**Ijeoma Oluo**

Recently, literature about racism and antiracism—like Ijeoma Oluo's *So You Want to Talk About Race*, Ibram Kendi's *How to Be an Antiracist*, and Robin DiAngelo's *White Fragility*—has risen to the top of the *New York Times* best sellers list. But what is antira-cism? Simply put, being *antiracist* refers to taking an active approach to dismantling racist practices, racial hatred, systemic racism, and the oppression of historically op-pressed racial groups. In Britain, antiracism evolved as a critique of the multicultural education movement, which some believed accepted deficit perspectives of Black and Brown students and ignored the systems and policies that resulted in uneven student outcomes (Gillborn, 2006). Thus, antiracism in education focuses on the dominant systems that uphold racist views and ideas, like standardized testing, curriculum, educator preparation, discipline, and other schooling policies that disproportionately impact Black and Brown communities.

Although there is a plethora of literature on the history of slavery in the United States and on movements against slavery (e.g., abolition), there is a lack of litera-ture describing the history of antiracist thought. William Lloyd Garrison emerged as a prominent abolitionist and early antiracist. Garrison founded the newspaper *The Liberator* and the American Anti-Slavery Society. Initially fearful of integrating former slaves into white society, Garrison later talked about his flawed thinking, openly discussed the horrors of slavery, and advocated for abolition.

Herbert Aptheker (1992), a historian and controversial political activist, wrote one of the few U.S. books to use antiracism as a construct before the 2000s. The book, titled *Anti-Racism in U.S. History: The First Two Hundred Years*, challenged the view that whites universally accepted racism. Aptheker attempted to debunk the myth that white people never cared about the plight of African Americans until just before the outbreak of the Civil War.

Angela Davis, a feminist and political activist, has written extensively about antiracism and more specifically the idea that antiracism must disrupt the social constructions of both race and gender (Davis, 1981, 1985). For many years, Davis has argued that racism, sexism, capitalism, and heterosexism work together to compound oppression. Her famous quote "In a racist society it is not enough to be nonracist, we must be antiracist" has become popular and is a defining aspect of today's conceptualization of antiracism.

Other Forms of Racism

Anti-Black racism is typically characterized as prejudice and bias that is directed at people of African descent. At the core of anti-Blackness is a devaluation and marginalization of Black people through policies and practices, such as continued overpolicing in Black communities, the criminalization of Black children, and bru-tality against Black people in general. Colorism, a type of discrimination in which lighter skin is privileged over darker skin, is aligned with the concept of anti-Black racism. Non-Black people with dark skin, such as Native Americans or darker Cuban Americans, are often faced with anti-Black racism.

The Black Lives Matter (BLM) movement has highlighted the global history of anti-Black racism and simultaneously propelled a national focus on antiracism. BLM, founded in 2013 in response to the killings of unarmed Black people, has become a global movement to eradicate white supremacy and combat anti-Black racism. The popularity of BLM has grown dramatically since 2013. Public opinion on BLM was net negative in 2018 and grew increasingly popular throughout 2019 and 2020. A June 2020 poll found that 67% of adult Americans expressed some support for the BLM movement. This shift in support indicates increased societal understanding of systemic injustices based on race and targeted violence toward Black people. It is essential to recognize that acknowledging that Black lives matter does not negate anyone else's life or imply that others do not matter. In a society in which the experiences and input of Black and Brown populations are not honored and racist policies are common, counseling professionals must speak out against unjust and racist systems.

The increased incidence of anti-Asian and anti-immigrant racism—fueled in part by former President Donald Trump's xenophobic response to novel coronavirus and immigration policies—has prompted an outcry among Asian American and immigrant communities, sparking nationwide protests led by the rallying cries "Stop Asian Hate" and "Defund Hate!" Some people still have trouble grasping the idea that Asian Americans can be victims of racism at all, in part because of the myth of the model minority—the narrative that Asians have managed to succeed economically and educationally in the United States, especially in comparison with other racial groups.

Antiracism Is Not Critical Race Theory

In recent years, the concept of antiracism has been used synonymously with critical race theory (CRT), a theory originated by Derrick Bell, a legal scholar who argued that traditional approaches to legal studies lacked the voice and narratives of marginalized persons (Delgado, 1995; Delgado & Stefancic, 2000). Bell described CRT as a form of law that speaks to the social and cultural contexts in which individuals live. Critical race theorists view racism as a normal part of American society that is woven into the fabric of all U.S. systems in such a way that people of all races see it as normal. The dominant strategy of CRT is to unmask and expose racism and racist practices and policies. As a matter of fact, CRT led to the study of microaggressions, subtle insults (verbal, nonverbal, and/or visual) directed toward people of color, often automatically or unconsciously. Antiracism, in contrast, denotes actions to dismantle racist practices, policies, and structures. Following is an excerpt from one of Derrick Bell's (1995) law review papers explaining how antiracism intersects with CRT:

> Critical race theory writing and lecturing is characterized by frequent use of the first person, storytelling, narrative, allegory, interdisciplinary treatment of law, and the unapologetic use of creativity. The work is often disruptive because its commitment to antiracism goes well beyond civil rights, integration, affirmative action, and other liberal measures. This is not to say that critical race theory adherents automatically or uniformly "trash" liberal ideology and method (as many adherents of critical legal studies do). Rather, they are highly suspicious of the liberal agenda, distrust its method, and want to retain what they see as a valuable strain of egalitarianism which may exist despite, and not because of, liberalism. (p. 899)

Antiracism and School/Community Counseling

With the murder of George Floyd coupled with the rise of white supremacist groups (e.g., the Proud Boys, the Aryan Brotherhood), counseling professionals are paying increased attention to issues of racism and are articulating a desire to be antiracist, in particular in school settings (American School Counselor Association [ASCA], 2021). Shifting to antiracist counseling requires more than focusing on multiculturalism, diversity, and inclusion. It involves more than collecting data, reading books by Black authors, and empathizing with Black and Brown clients. Being an antiracist counselor requires interrogating one's racial consciousness and the impact of one's behaviors in counseling relationships with Black and Brown students or clients. Counselors must name the importance of the links among race, racism, and counseling. Counseling, in particular school counseling, is a racialized process, given the racist practices and policies that are embedded in schools and communities. Thus, if counselors do not address embedded racist and biased practices and policies in schools, then they are likely to reproduce racial structures and hierarchies in their practice.

Lori Gottlieb (2020) wrote a revealing, poignant opinion piece in *The Washington Post* titled "I Thought I Was an Antiracist Therapist. Then I Looked More Closely." Gottlieb admitted that her graduate training in cultural competence did not prepare her to delve deeply into the racism of her patients as well as her own racist beliefs and ideas. She gave the following example:

> I'm seeing a black patient, a woman who looks a lot like me on paper—we're both professionals, we went to the same college, we're moms of kids about the same ages. And because of our similarities—and also my unstated reluctance to go there—we tacitly collude in pretending that she isn't black and I'm not white. Until one day she tells me about an incident at her company, where she is one of the few black executives: Her white boss chose a white woman for a promotion that she had fully expected to earn, and my patient would have been the first black executive to be promoted to this level. The white woman was not nearly as experienced or qualified, my patient tells me. And she says this is the story of her life—a story she hadn't told me about until that day.
>
> We may have a lot in common, but unlike her, I had never walked into a classroom at our college and wondered if I had to prove myself worthy of being there; I hadn't sat in the dining hall and overheard someone talking about "affirmative-action" students who got into the school more easily; I never stepped foot in a job interview and watched someone try to cover her surprise because, based on my résumé, she had expected my skin to be lighter. (Gottlieb, 2020, paras. 6–7)

An antiracist perspective in counseling is long overdue. Even professional associations are joining the call. ACA (2020) issued the following statement on antiracism:

> Racism, police brutality, systemic violence, and the dehumanizing forces of oppression, powerlessness, and White supremacy have eroded the very fabric of humanity which ideally binds our society together. Macrolevel systemic racism extends to disparities in institutional policies and procedures in physical and mental healthcare, education, the judicial system, employment, sports and entertainment, and the brutal violence of law enforcement. These larger societal oppressions lead to inaccessibility to resources and social marginalization,

which descend finally to individual racist attitudes, implicit biases, stereotypes, microaggressions, and even death. The ongoing and historical injustices are not acknowledged by those who want to be in power or protect their entitlements. Some who do acknowledge, do so reactively, temporarily, or superficially and thus, no meaningful change occurs. Anti-Black racism is often reframed as accidental, an unfortunate incident, or as the criminality of the victim.

Words cannot truly capture our feelings. We are angry, exhausted, grieving, suffering, furious, and in despair. The American Counseling Association is pained by the murders of George Floyd, Rayshard Brooks, Ahmaud Arbery, Breonna Taylor, Tamir Rice, Eric Garner, Sandra Bland, Michael Brown, and countless other Black/African Americans who unfortunately remain nameless. We stand in solidarity with our Black siblings in denouncing the historical legacy and destruction caused by institutionalized racism and violence against Black people, perpetuated at the hands of law enforcement, the hatred bred of White supremacy, the deafening silence of dehumanizing and complicit inaction to address these systemic ills within our society. As counselors, we listen, we empathize, and agree with protesters that when absolute justice is established, peace will follow. Enough is enough, we cannot continue to watch fellow Black Americans being murdered, as the very life force is suffocated out of them.

The American Counseling Association is built on enduring values and a mission that promotes: human dignity and diversity, respect, the attainment of a quality of life for all, empowerment, integrity, social justice advocacy, equity, and inclusion. If we remain silent, and do not promote racial justice, these words become harmful and meaningless for our members and the counseling community. Given the rapidly evolving double pandemic of COVID-19 and the continued exposure of Black people to institutionalized racism, ACA wants to be clear about where we stand and the ongoing actions we will take. As proactive leaders, counselors, mentors, supervisors, scholars, and trainers we will break away from this structure of racism trauma, and the violence born on the necks of Black people.

Our stance is: Black Lives Matter. We have a moral and professional obligation to deconstruct institutions which have historically been designed to benefit White America. These systems must be dismantled in order to level the playing field for Black communities. Allyship is not enough. We strive to create liberated spaces in the fight against white supremacy and the dehumanization of Black people. The burden of transgenerational trauma should not be shouldered by Black Americans even though they have remained resilient.

ASCA (2020), similarly, issued a statement:

> The American School Counselor Association condemns violence and the systemic and institutional racism that marginalizes African Americans. ASCA calls on all Americans to end the cycle of racism and on leaders to enact and enforce laws protecting members of the Black community and give them the same opportunities to lead successful and productive lives that other Americans enjoy. The recent deaths of Ahmaud Arbery, Breonna Taylor and George Floyd did not occur in schools or involve students; however, these and other violent acts can indirectly cause long-term harm to students. Witnessing brutality or experiencing the death of a family member or friend constitutes an adverse childhood experience, which can affect students well into adulthood. More broadly, systemic racism perpetuates discrimination, bigotry and prejudice that has relegated African Americans to generations of poverty, underemployment, substandard housing, poor health care and second-class citizenship.

These statements by ACA and ASCA, although timely and needed, declare a not-racist stance. The words do not clearly articulate an antiracist position because action steps, including policy and practice changes, are not delineated. Because racism is perpetuated every day, an antiracist approach requires a systemic approach to change that includes daily practice. Therefore, the work of advancing antiracist counseling requires changing everyday racist practices and policies. ASCA, through its standards in practice, offers school counselors some guidance on addressing racism as it relates to the ASCA National Model (ASCA, 2021). A more concise explanation of intentional action steps for dismantling racist school counselor practices and programs in schools is warranted, however. See, https://www.schoolcounselor.org/getmedia/542b085a-7eda-48ba-906e-24cd3f08a03f/SIP-Racism-Bias.pdf.

An Antiracist Framework of School Counseling

In 2007, I introduced a framework for social justice school counseling that included six key components: (a) counseling and intervention planning; (b) consultation; (c) connecting schools, families, and communities; (d) collecting and using data; (e) challenging bias; and (f) coordinating student services and support (Holcomb-McCoy, 2007). The framework was introduced as a means of integrating more systemic and structural analysis into the practice of school counseling. Lee (2005), Bemak and Chung (2005), and Green and Keys (2001) called for school counseling that acknowledges broad, systematic societal inequities and oppression as well as the need for more intentionality on the part of school counselors. Much like its predecessors—multicultural and cross-cultural counseling—social justice counseling addresses cultural differences between the client and counselor, but it also emphasizes human rights, justice, and the most vulnerable populations. Addressing oppression in all forms is the focus of social justice counseling.

Similar to a social justice framework, an antiracist framework of school counseling is needed now more than ever to focus precisely on dismantling racist practices and policies in schools. Thus, I have revised the social justice framework to include antiracist principles, which means that issues of racism are intentionally addressed and not implied. The revised framework is based on the following assumptions about counseling:

- The status quo in counseling practices and programs is characterized by an inequitable distribution of power and resources based on race, socioeconomic status, ethnicity, ability, language, and so on.
- Racism is embedded in the fabric of our schools and communities.
- Racism influences our behavior and attitudes.
- We as counselors (and our clients and students) have internalized racist attitudes, ideas, understandings, and patterns of thought that allow us to function in racist and oppressive systems.

Table 1.1 presents key elements of an antiracist framework of school counseling.

A note regarding the shift to a more antiracist approach in counseling: Some counseling professionals might view "antiracist" as a code word for "anti-white."

TABLE 1.1 • Key Elements of Antiracist School Counseling	
Key Element	Description
Human growth and development	Use of theories of human development and behavior that are grounded in understanding Black and Brown people; use of Black psychology, African-centered psychology, Latinx psychology, and/ or any theory, approach, or intervention developed by and for Black and Brown people
Antiracist counseling and consultation	Use of strengths-based counseling and consultation techniques and strategies to lift up and validate the lived experiences of Black and Brown students, clients, and/or families
Policy change	Emphasis on changing school policies and practices that impact the schooling and counseling experiences of Black and Brown students (e.g., discipline policies, standardized testing)
Dismantling of racism and promotion of racial equity	Being a bystander to racism is harmful; challenge unequal systems of power that harm Black and Brown people; the goal of school counseling is to ensure racial and education justice
Data	Use of data to uncover racial disparities and inequities at the classroom, school, and district or community levels

This thinking became popular among many white supremacists in 2006 when Bob Whitaker's (2021) essay "Mantra" was released. Whitaker, a segregationist, falsely accused antiracist scholars of trying to destroy the white race. This is not true. The goal of antiracism is to eliminate racial injustices so all people can have the opportunity to live productively. More important, antiracist counselors recognize that antiracism is a way of life in which one acknowledges that racism negatively shapes society; thus, combatting it in our lives and our students' or clients' lives shapes a better and more harmonious society.

Conclusion

The history of racism in the United States has been long and painful. Amid escalating tensions across racial groups due to long-standing racial injustices, antiracism is an essential concept in determining meaningful societal change and building effective counseling practices. Racialized school policies and practices (e.g., discipline policies, testing policies, tracking, the identification of gifted students) have blocked the access of millions of children and parents across the country to positive opportunities for a productive life. Likewise, decades of school and community counseling without a focus on dismantling racist policies and practices have hindered racial justice and ensuring access to equal opportunities for all. Although it may be time to shift and examine racism in our profession, it is not time to give up. We as counselors must move forward with an antiracist focus and perspective if we want change!

References

Akbar, N. (Ed.). (2004). *Akbar papers in African psychology*. Mind Productions.

Alexander, M. (2010). *The new Jim Crow: Mass incarceration in the age of colorblindness*. The New Press.

American Counseling Association. (2020, June 22). *ACA anti-racism statement*. https://www.counseling.org/news/updates/news-detail/2020/06/22/aca-anti-racism-statement

American School Counselor Association. (2020, May). *ASCA condemns violence and institutional racism.* https://www.schoolcounselor.org/getmedia/3695e7a7-5cac-4adb-a31b-35641287807f/Statement-Systemic-Racism-5-2020.pdf

American School Counselor Association. (2021). *ASCA research report: State of the profession 2020.* https://www.schoolcounselor.org/getmedia/bb23299b-678d-4bce-8863-cfcb55f7df87/2020-State-of-the-Profession.pdf

Anderson, C. (2016). *White rage: The unspoken truth of our racial divide.* Bloomsbury.

Anderson, J., Hilert, A., Lara, M., Martinez, R., & Mavaneh, S. S. (2015, December). *The history of Counselors for Social Justice (CSJ).* https://www.counseling-csj.org/uploads/1/2/3/6/123630265/history_csj-history-final-version-january-3-2016.pdf

Aptheker, H. (1992). *Anti-racism in U.S. history: The first two hundred years.* Greenwood Press.

Arredondo, P., D'Andrea, M., & Lee, C. (2020, September 10). Unmasking white supremacy and racism in the counseling profession. *Counseling Today.* https://ct.counseling.org/2020/09/unmasking-white-supremacy-and-racism-in-the-counseling-profession/

Association for Multicultural Counseling and Development. (n.d.). *About us.* https://www.multiculturalcounselingdevelopment.org/about

Association of Black Psychologists. (2021). *Black/African-centered psychology.* https://www.abpsi.org/pdf/AfricanCenteredPsychologydefinition.pdf

Atkinson, D., Morten, G., & Sue, D. W. (1989). *Counseling American minorities: A cross-cultural perspective.* McGraw-Hill.

Bell, D. A. (1995). Who's afraid of critical race theory? *University of Illinois Law Review, 1995,* 893–910.

Bemak, F., & Chung, R. (2005). Advocacy as a critical role for urban school counselors: Working toward equity and social justice. *Professional School Counseling, 8*(3), 196.

Butler, S. K., & Shillingford-Butler, M. A. (2014). Counseling Black clients. In M. J. Ratts & P. D. Pedersen (Eds.), *Counseling for multiculturalism and social justice* (4th ed., pp. 143–157). American Counseling Association.

D'Andrea, M. (1992, October). The violence of our silence: Some thoughts about racism, counseling, and development. *The Guidepost,* 14.

Davis, A. Y. (1981). *Women, race and class.* Vintage Books.

Davis, A. Y. (1985). *Violence against women and the ongoing challenge to racism.* Kitchen Table.

Delgado, R. (Ed.). (1995). *Critical race theory: The cutting edge.* Temple University Press.

Delgado, R., & Stefancic, J. (2000). *Critical race theory: The cutting edge.* Temple University Press.

Dred Scott v. Sandford, 60 U.S. (19 How.) 393 (1857) (enslaved party), superseded by constitutional amendment, U.S. CONST. amend. XIII.

Elder, T. E., Figlio, D. N., Imberman, S. A., & Persico, C. L. (2019). *School segregation and racial gaps in special education identification.* National Bureau of Economic Research. https://www.nber.org/system/files/working_papers/w25829/w25829.pdf

Equal Justice Initiative. (2021). *Lynching in America: Confronting the legacy of racial terror* (3rd ed.). https://lynchinginamerica.eji.org/report/

Ford, D., Moore, J. L., & Scott, M. T. (2011). Key theories and frameworks for improving the recruitment and retention of African American students in gifted education. *Journal of Negro Education, 80*(3), 239–253.

Gerig, M. S. (2014). *Foundations for clinical mental health counseling: An introduction to the profession*. Pearson.

Gillborn, D. (2006). Critical race theory and education: Racism and anti-racism in educational theory and praxis. *Discourse: Studies in the Cultural Politics of Education, 27*(1), 11–32.

Gottlieb, L. (2020, June 18). I thought I was an antiracist therapist. Then I looked more closely. *The Washington Post*. https://www.washingtonpost.com/opinions/2020/06/18/i-thought-i-was-an-antiracist-therapist-then-i-looked-more-closely/

Green, A., & Keys, S. G. (2001). Expanding the developmental school counseling paradigm: Meeting the needs of the 21st century student. *Professional School Counseling, 5*(2), 84–95.

Holcomb-McCoy, C. (2007). *School counseling to close the achievement gap: A social justice framework for success*. Corwin Press.

Holliday, B. G. (2009). The history and visions of African American psychology: Multiple pathways to place, space, and authority. *Cultural Diversity and Ethnic Minority Psychology, 15*(4), 317–337. https://doi.org/10.1037/a0016971

Jones, R. L. (1972). *Black psychology*. Harper & Row.

Lee, C. C. (1991). Cultural dynamics: Their importance in multicultural counseling. In C. C. Lee & B. L. Richardson (Eds.), *Multicultural issues in counseling: New approaches to diversity* (pp. 11–17). American Counseling Association.

Lee, C. C. (2005). Urban school counseling: Context, characteristics, and competencies. *Professional School Counseling, 8*(3), 184–188.

Massachusetts Board of Education. (1849). *Twelfth annual report of the Board of Education together with the twelfth annual report of the secretary of the board*. https://archives.lib.state.ma.us/handle/2452/204731.

McKinsey and Company. (2019, August). *The economic impact of closing the racial wealth gap*. https://www.mckinsey.com/~/media/mckinsey/industries/public%20and%20social%20sector/our%20insights/the%20economic%20impact%20of%20closing%20the%20racial%20wealth%20gap/the-economic-impact-of-closing-the-racial-wealth-gap-final.pdf

Mickelson, R. A. (2001). Subverting Swann: First- and second-generation segregation in the Charlotte-Mecklenburg schools. *American Educational Research Journal, 38*(2), 215–252.

Morris, M. W. (2016). *Pushout: The criminalization of Black girls in schools*. The New Press.

Pedersen, P. (1990). The multicultural perspective as a fourth force in counseling. *Journal of Mental Health Counseling, 12*(1), 93–95.

Ratts, M. J., & Pedersen, P. B. (2014). *Counseling for multiculturalism and social justice: Integration, theory, and application* (4th ed.). American Counseling Association.

Ratts, M. J., Singh, A. A., Nassar-McMillan, S., Butler, S. K., & McCullough, J. R. (2015). *Multicultural and social justice counseling competencies*. Association for Multicultural Counseling and Development. https://www.counseling.org/docs/default-source/competencies/multicultural-and-social-justice-counseling-competencies.pdf?sfvrsn=20

Sue, D. W., Arredondo, P., & McDavis, R. J. (1992). Multicultural counseling competencies and standards: A call to the profession. *Journal of Counseling & Development, 70*(4), 477–486. https://doi.org/10.1002/j.1556-6676.1992.tb01642.x

Sue, D. W., Bernier, J. E., Durran A., Feinberg, L., Pedersen, P., Smith, E. J., & Vasquez-Nuttall, E. (1982). Position paper: Cross-cultural counseling competencies. *The Counseling Psychologist*, *10*(2), 45–52. https://doi.org/10.1177/0011000082102008

The Education Trust. (2020). *"Segregation forever"? The continued underrepresentation of Black and Latino undergraduates at the nation's 101 most selective public colleges and universities*. https://edtrust.org/wp-content/uploads/2014/09/Segregation-Forever-The-Continued-Underrepresentation-of-Black-and-Latino-Undergraduates-at-the-Nations-101-Most-Selective-Public-Colleges-and-Universities-July-21-2020.pdf

Toporek, R. L., Lewis, J. A., & Crethar, H. C. (2009). Promoting systemic change through the ACA Advocacy Competencies. *Journal of Counseling & Development*, *87*(3), 260–268.

Wade, J. C. (2006). The case of the angry Black man. In M. Englar-Carlson & M. A. Stevens (Eds.), *In the room with men: A casebook of therapeutic change* (pp. 177–196). American Psychological Association.

Whitaker, B. (2021). *The mantra*. https://www.robertwwhitaker.com/mantra/

White, J. L. (1972). Toward a Black psychology. In R. Jones (Ed.), *Black psychology* (pp. 43–50). Harper & Row.

Williams, R. (1974). A history of the Association of Black Psychologists: Early formation and development. *Journal of Black Psychology*, *1*(1), 9–24. https://doi.org/10.1177/009579847400100102

CHAPTER 2

Decolonizing the Counseling Canon

Ahmad R. Washington, Janice A. Byrd, and Joseph M. Williams

In the wake of the unrepentant dehumanization and gratuitous murders of Ahmaud Arbery, Breonna Taylor, Sandra Bland, Tamir Rice, and others by members of law enforcement and rogue white vigilantes, the American Counseling Association (ACA) disseminated a position statement denouncing racism and professing its commitment to fighting white supremacy and anti-Black racism (ACA, 2020). Specifically, ACA reiterated its expectation that all counselors representing all subspecialties (e.g., school counseling, addictions, clinical mental health) embrace the ideal of social justice and engage in antiracist advocacy and reform efforts. In part, the statement read, "Racism, police brutality, systemic violence, and the dehumanizing forces of oppression, powerlessness, and White supremacy have eroded the very fabric of humanity which ideally binds our society together" (ACA, 2020, para. 2). Although ACA's statement represents a promising step in the right direction, what cannot be overlooked is the counseling profession's historical obliviousness and lack of meaningful and sustained attention to anti-Black racism (Washington & Henfield, 2019).

ACA's effectiveness in achieving its ultimate mission depends, first and foremost, on how it theorizes the problem of anti-Blackness. The extant counseling literature reveals that the current discourse regarding social justice counseling evolved out of a clear need to name the ethnocentrism and cultural encapsulation throughout the profession writ large (Smith, 2015). Lance C. Smith and others (e.g., Holcomb-McCoy, 2004; Sue & Sue, 2019; Suite et al., 2007) have succinctly charted this evolution and emphasized the inherent limitations, blind spots, and shortcomings of previous iterations of cross-cultural considerations in counseling. As instrumental as these writings on the subject have been, we believe that virtually all dominant counseling ideologies and praxes (e.g., cognitive and behavioral therapies) and even theories of human/group subordination often considered radical (e.g., traditional feminist theory) do not adequately describe the essential and constitutive elements of anti-Blackness in our society. In this chapter, we submit our thesis, which is unlike intrapsychic theories of helping (e.g., cognitive behavioral approaches) or theories of cultural difference (e.g., multiculturalism) or pragmatic reform to foster assimilation (e.g., social justice). We propose a decolonial analytical framework that more effectively brings into relief the Manichean dialectic (meaning dichotomous and routinely and ritualistically antagonistic) that produces social death that includes gratuitous violence (Patterson, 1982; Vargas, 2010).

For Orlando Patterson, slavery, as a form of social death, consists of three constitutive elements. By accentuating the psychological and sociological facets of slavery and social death rather than the idea that slavery is primarily about economic exploitation, Patterson helps us understand how Black people continue to be subjected to a form of antagonism that exceeds economic exploitation and disenfranchisement. S[ ] itutive components:

(handwritten note: Modernity. Violence against Black thru clue to European expansion + imperialism)

1. *Gratuitous* [ ]ulnerable to wanton physical violence, viole[ ]n the commission of a crime or an unwillingn[ ]rm or acquiesce to the dictates of a particular [ ]: (e.g., going on a run, shopping at the grocer[ ]
2. *Natal aliena*[ ] arrangements are habitually disregarded, an[ ]ways subject to overbearing surveillance and [ ]croachments of the state (e.g., murderous no-[ ] [ ]dustrial complex).
3. *General dishonor*—Black people are routinely subjected to blatant and egregious disregard and disrespect without the slightest consideration or hesitation, evidenced in, for instance, a general refusal to accept and respect Black people's traditions (e.g., names, color, forms of Black cultural production).

Our utilization and reliance on Patterson's (1982) work, invoked here and throughout this chapter, represents an intentional desire to bring a foundational antagonism—social death—into sharper relief. In other words, Patterson's conception provides an unfiltered analytic lens through which we better understand the forms of violence (e.g., gratuitous violence, natal alienation, general dishonor) that saturate the Black body as a consequence of European expansion and imperialism, a project called *modernity*. Furthermore, we submit that modernity and the legacies of modernity are inextricably tethered to a humanistic logic of white supremacy that proliferated during a time commonly referred to as the period of European enlightenment.

Although counselor educators have emphasized the criticality of understanding how the period of European enlightenment informs contemporary counseling epistemologies and dominant orientations toward the therapeutic encounter (e.g., the client-counselor dyad) and revered research practices (e.g., researcher objectivity), this emphasis often ignores or evades an engagement, whatsoever, with the myriad forms of violence enacted on the Black body in this process. For instance, although Hansen (2006) went to great lengths to illuminate the epistemologies that characterized modernity and European enlightenment before contrasting these epistemologies with those associated with later scientific paradigms, like postmodernity, Hansen ignored how dominant theorists and knowledge claims associated with modernity and European enlightenment were transfixed on the Black subject. Unfortunately, Hansen's characterization almost completely occludes any theorization of the utility and fungibility of the Black body in the formation of a world-altering system of knowledge claims that made the modern colonial world we occupy come into formation (Ani, 1994; Castro-Gómez & Martin, 2002; Horne, 2020; Morrison, 2017).

Our engagement with discourses on colonization and decolonization is grounded in a body of interdisciplinary Black critical thinking, from within the humanities and social sciences in particular, that examines how the gratuitous and mundane nature of colonial violence impinges on the psychic and social-emotional well-being of the Black subject. Specifically, Fanon's (1963, 2008) revolutionary and incisive ideas on the sociogenetic etiology of Black suffering and Black self-alienation, a phenomenon often distilled into more palatable phraseology (e.g., internalized racism), are integral to the tapestry of decolonial counseling epistemologies and practices we employ vis-à-vis the Black body as it is understood within the context of enduring forms of coloniality (McKittrick, 2015; Wynter, 2003). Rather than merely highlighting and celebrating differences and cultural identities or championing more equitable access to marginalized groups, as is often the case in multicultural counseling and social justice counseling discourses, our amalgam of decolonial counseling epistemologies and practices resembles Joseph's (2015) orientation to clinical work. Our ideas on a decolonial theory of counseling can best be understood as a conscious effort to highlight a reoccurring and ubiquitous trend in counseling discourses, specifically the

> inattention to the complicit influences of colonial and imperial projects on the practices and technologies of dehumanization, taxonomization, and the establishment of human hierarchies to rationalize violence through the implementation of racial and eugenic rationale … but also the historical, political, and social practices that were developed to achieve oppression and exploitation. (Joseph, 2015, p. 1021)

In other words, we intend to make a clear distinction between theoretical and pragmatic frameworks of helping (e.g., multicultural counseling, social justice counseling) that suggest Black suffering can be ameliorated or even decelerated through discourses of respect for cultural differences or progressive ideologies of social inclusion. With this as our point of departure, we propose a decolonial theory of counseling that refuses to shy away from the structural nature of social death. Our candor and forthright engagement with social death and decolonial theory represents our desire to abandon Eurocentric scientific paradigms and psychological theories that suggest that adjustment and assimilation to an inherently unjust society, a society that habitually denies people of color access, constitutes psychological health and wellness (King, 1968). By intentionally naming historical events (e.g., the rise of European enlightenment, the formation of the new world) and emphasizing how these events reverberate through and restructure our contemporary colonial context (e.g., the hypersegregation and overpolicing of Black communities), we take up a position, as counselor educators, grounded in an undying and unapologetic love for Black people. This position requires and necessitates radical love and honesty and the eschewing of analytical and theoretical perspectives that obscure and mythicize the terror Black people live through (Washington & Henfield, 2019). We assert that a decolonial theory of counseling (Bulhan, 1990; Fanon, 1963, 2008) must engage concepts like social death, meaning a cancerous colonial context in which Black people are treated as nonbeings and perpetually subjected to gratuitous violence (Patterson, 2018).

We begin by exploring how the gratuitous and whimsical fashion on non-beingness imposed on the Black sentient being has continually helped consolidate the psychological and integrity of other social groups since 642 AD (Judy, 1993). We hope to illuminate disciplines (e.g., Black studies, Indigenous studies) and discourses/frameworks (e.g., decolonization, the master/slave dialectic; Bulhan, 1990; Fanon, 1963) not typically broached in the counseling literature to deepen our understanding of social oppression that manifests as the murders of Ahmaud Arbery, Breonna Taylor, George Floyd, Rayshard Brooks, Tony McDade, and others. We then demonstrate how anthropology, psychology, counseling, and other helping professions provide the ideological sinew that holds colonial and postcolonial social societies intact.

Whiteness in the Counseling Profession

In the 1960s, the proliferation of decolonial, postcolonial, and critical cultural theories across academic discourses and within the general public coincided with prolonged revolutionary struggles for human rights, human dignity, and racial justice (Stanfield, 1985). These struggles for human dignity and racial justice were inspired by streams of radical consciousness that critiqued European colonialism and imperialism, in particular the profound impact European colonialism, neocolonialism, and neo-imperialism have on the material conditions of people of color throughout the world (Fanon, 1963; Morrison, 2017). As part of their work, many decolonial, postcolonial, and critical cultural theories have "fought against the traditional concept of difference" (Guthrie, 2004, p. xiii) by examining the role European enlightenment—a seismic shift in the arc of epistemological and methodological paradigms—played in justifying the physical demarcation (e.g., Manifest Destiny as land seizure) between the old and new worlds/territories (Horne, 2018).

What is pernicious is that the physical boundaries erected between the two territories—the old and new worlds/territories—were supposedly derived from irrefutable scientific evidence—namely, natural anthropological observation and the manipulation of variables through laboratory experiments that demonstrated stark group differences. In his theorization of the psychology of oppression, Bulhan (1990) provided a list of prominent philosophers and psychologists (e.g., David Hume, Thomas Malthus, Francis Galton, Lewis Terman) who, at one point or another, subscribed to and publicly endorsed biological/genetic or cultural discourses/explanations of difference. By compiling the list, Bulhan illustrated how enthralled and deeply invested early theorists and psychologists were in calcifying beliefs that these differences in technological development, for instance, were attributable to biological racial determinism, such as skull shape and size as proxies for intelligence or social deviance, or antiquated and naive sociocultural practices (e.g., correspondence/complementarity/harmony with nature).

Bulhan (1990) pushed the reader to comprehend how these figures and the monumental significance ascribed to their ideas (e.g., Charles Darwin's doctrine of survival of the fittest, Galton's politics of sterilization of the unfit, the Malthusian principle of famine and drought as solutions to global oversaturation/overpopulation of inferior people) helped substantiate a Manichean framework that structured the project of modernity (Castro-Gómez & Martin, 2002). The Old World (e.g., Africa as the Dark Continent) was considered a wild, savage, and unbridled space occupied by inadequate/adolescent and inferior beings; conversely, the New World represented refinement, sophistication, and immeasurable opportunities for expansion, prosperity, and wealth accumulation for those deemed acceptable based on Eurocentric standards of decorum, civility, and social life (Castro-Gómez & Martin, 2002; Stanfield, 1985). Promoting this Manichean dichotomy/doctrine—the irreconcilable differences between the social and cultural practices of the Indigenous, the African, and other peoples of color (e.g., old, primitive, inferior world) and the sociocultural mores of European imperial powers—was of the utmost importance in the formation of the social sciences, psychology notwithstanding (Guthrie, 2004).

In addition, decolonial and postcolonial theories of the 1960s drew parallels between colonial domination that characterized the project of modernity, initiated with Christopher Columbus's nautical exploit in 1492 (Clarke, 1998), and newer forms of surveillance, subordination, and oppression that were implemented as economic innovation and urbanization bourgeoned in this country (e.g., housing segregation and the confinement of Black people to urban ghettos during early American urban industrialization). For historians of this ilk, it is vital to fully comprehend how European enlightenment—in particular, the emphasis placed on reason and rational thinking as quintessential characteristics of human beings, and in particular, white men (e.g., autonomous and self-governed, individuated, competitive, ruggedly individual, and having a strong work ethic)—helped codify categories and taxonomies of individual and social group difference and social policies that remain salient to this day (e.g., residential and housing segregation).

Quintessential characteristics of European American culture and behavior have been so systematically integrated into psychological nomenclature (e.g., normalcy, abnormality, deviant behavior, approved therapeutic practices) that it is rare when we consider the adverse implications this hegemonic imposition of European American culture has had on the cultural other. As Stanfield (1985) wrote, "Economics, psychology, and sociology were dominated by middle-class white Anglo-Saxon Protestant males who sought to define and explain the human problems produced by the changing socio-economic and political order of their ethnic-based cognition" (pp. 404–405). Grier (2004) corroborated the assertion that psychological nomenclature has been an important and indispensable handmaiden in maintaining the status quo by recreating racial stratification, in particular during critical and socially contentious historical periods in this country (e.g., World War I, European immigration, Black northern migration), when he stated the following:

> Psychological tests were devised and interpreted to demonstrate that not only were Blacks intellectually inferior to Europeans but that they were particularly suited to perform manual labor, as if this pseudoscience had as its purpose providing a scientific basis for slavery and peonage. (p. xii)

A fundamental starting point in reimagining the helping profession, then, requires appreciating how European standards and whiteness are veiled and universalized throughout the counseling profession (Cushman, 1996; Katz, 1985; Marsella, 2015). This reimagining is a process that requires a critical awareness not only of the innocuous and systemic presence of white supremacy within the field of counseling but also of how the white imagination, invested in maintaining the Manichean dialect, is impervious to rhetoric and pedagogical interventions (e.g., antiracist training, unconscious bias training; Wilderson, 2010).

Part of this interrogation means revealing how the hegemony of Western thought was operationalized in counseling and psychology's fundamental ideological bedrock to naturalize and then codify common sense about the non-beingness of Blackness and how the Black stands outside of humanity (Guthrie, 2004). As countless literary critics and social scientists have pointed out, many of the espoused values of the United States (e.g., meritocracy) came by drawing a definitive line of demarcation between the formerly enslaved Black subject and the disenfranchised white settler. This understanding is indispensable to our departure from the colonial and imperialistic origins of oppression and the helping professions.

Articulating Departures From the Colonial Counseling Canon

Many analyses of European enlightenment often begin by critiquing the veracity of objective claims to knowledge construction about categories and discourses of social difference derived from Western episteme. This critique is important because Western episteme was crucial in justifying the violence that constructed the New World. This is important because these social categories (Black/non-Black) are the consequence of colonialism and power dynamics in this country rather than objective truths obtained through the institutionalized methods of Western empirical science. As Smith (2015) astutely pointed out, frameworks of multiculturalism (e.g., respect for difference and diversity that do not undertake analyses of structural position seriously) and liberal ideas of social justice, which claim to ameliorate forms of cultural and social exclusion Black people encounter, are often rooted in deficit-based social reform programs predicated on the notion of preexisting forms of Black cultural pathology (e.g., mentoring programs, social-emotional learning, standards of mind-sets and behavior).

When contemplating a departure from the counseling canon, we would be remiss not to ponder the words of James Baldwin (1962): "Not everything that is faced can be changed; but nothing can be changed until it is faced" (p. T11). The school counseling profession, a microcosm of America and broadly the Western world, perpetually avoids reckoning with its role in maintaining systemic racism. This avoidance creates incongruence between avowed values and tangible actions across the profession that is observed systemically and individually. For Black counselor educators who embody a critical standpoint, navigating incongruent landscapes in various spaces creates an internal twoness that illuminates the inconsistencies within oneself and throughout the profession (Du Bois, 1903/2015). Sometimes, in an attempt to reconcile these feelings while in this struggle, the desire to influence change within inherently racist spaces (i.e., counseling, higher education, K–12 schools; Arredondo et al., 2020; Watkins, 2001; Wilder, 2013) becomes paramount. This existential meaningless is compounded by the unspoken expectation that we rely on the very scientific discourses that problematized Blackness to achieve self-affirmation, professional acceptance, or professional recognition.

This conundrum is typified in Audre Lorde's (1984) insightful articulation "the master's tools will never dismantle the master's house" (p. 110). Although Lorde's aspiration to deconstruct the master's house resonates, feeling disempowerment to intervene in interrupting the structural nature of anti-Blackness is disheartening. Holding this awareness while attempting to create a community where future school counselors can authentically grapple with how they perceive themselves and the history of the profession represents a daunting challenge (Singh et al., 2010). To dismantle racism in the world, our profession, and our schools, individuals must first have critical awareness and then commit to a journey of internal transformation. More important, having a critical awareness of the systemic presence of racism within the field of school counseling builds a space to (a) understand how racism and white supremacy are reproduced and what interrupting this reproduction requires and (b) anticipate and navigate roadblocks that derail progress.

Counselor educators, school counselors, and school counselors-in-training are encouraged to adopt a lifelong critical self-awareness whereby they continuously reflect on their own bias, worldview, and positionality (Ratts et al., 2016). Holcomb-McCoy's (2004) checklist provides a useful tool for engaging in this reflective practice. Aimed at the white school counselors who dominate the field (American School Counselor Association, 2020; Mitcham-Smith, 2007), Holcomb-McCoy's tool offers a comprehensive set of prompts that allows one to critically self-reflect their whiteness and other layers of their social status (e.g., class), their awareness of racism, and their potential to counsel Black and Brown students. Exploration of oneself is a foundational practice in producing systemic change. When speaking of the threat of whiteness, Bettina Love (2019) stated the following:

> Whiteness cannot enter spaces focused on abolitionist teaching. Whiteness is addicted to centering itself, addicted to attention, and making everyone feel guilty for working toward its elimination. Whiteness will never allow true solidarity to take place. Those who cling to their Whiteness cannot participate in abolitionist teaching because they are a distraction, are unproductive, and will undermine freedom at every step, sometimes in the name of social justice. Being an abolitionist means you are ready to lose something, you are ready to let go of your privilege, you are ready to be in solidarity with dark people by recognizing your Whiteness in dark spaces, recognizing how it can take up space if unchecked, using your Whiteness in White spaces to advocate for and with dark people. And you understand that your White privilege allows you to take risks that dark people cannot take in the fight for educational justice. (p. 159)

Although Love speaks of abolitionist teaching, her observations are applicable for all who engage with Black students in educational settings. Whiteness permeates the psyche and influences thoughts and behaviors and should be interrogated and challenged (Malott & Paone, 2011). School counselors of color should also engage in ongoing reflection. Like the teachers represented in Kohli's (2014) research examining how teachers of color actively work to develop racially just classrooms, school counselors of color would benefit from engaging in critical self-awareness work to combat internalized racism that may cause them to support white supremacy ideologies, policies, and practices.

SEL as upholding white supremacy

Some of the ideas and practices upheld by the school counseling profession perpetuate white supremacy and systematically harm Black students. Such ideas include theories like social-emotional learning (Griffin et al., 2020; King-White & Kurt, 2019) and grit (Duckworth et al., 2007). Social-emotional learning is influenced by Eurocentric norms and justifies the draconian disciplining of Black and Brown students (Kaler-Jones, 2020; Love, 2019). These tools are not different from the American School Counselor Association's (2014) *Mindsets and Behaviors for Student Success*. This tool provides "35 mindset and behavior standards to identify and prioritize the specific attitudes, knowledge, and skills students should be able to demonstrate as a result of a school counseling program" (p. 1). Although the mind-set and behavior standards are informed by college and career readiness scholarship and other empirical studies exploring how students learn, there is little acknowledgment that this literature centers whiteness and provides student self-management and social skills dispositions where success can theoretically be achieved through respectability (Love, 2019; Morris, 2016). Success, conceptualized this way, ignores how oppression constrains one's capacity to be successful and further romanticizes the Western myth of meritocracy (Bell, 2002). For example, the self-management skill "demonstrate the ability to overcome barriers to learning" places the responsibility on the Black or Brown student to overcome racist structures and practices like standardized tests (Au, 2016), disproportionately funded schools (Vaught, 2009), and overpolicing (Morris, 2016; Washington & Henfield, 2018). In addition, social skills like "use effective oral and written communication skills and listening skills" can be used subjectively to elevate students who speak standard English but subjugate students who do not speak English as their first language or who use culturally specific vernacular that is stereotyped as ignorant or less intelligent by the dominant culture (general dishonor). These skills do not hold racist school leaders, policies, and structures responsible for creating and maintaining toxic spaces for Black students to navigate.

In addition, these skills, like the previously mentioned theories, render the experiences of students of color obtuse, not normal, and in need of correcting. If these theories or tools are used by individuals who do not hold a critical standpoint, they can be physically and psychologically dangerous. Most important, students who hold a critical awareness of the system and attempt to advocate for themselves are criminalized, viewed as noncompliant, and labeled "troublemakers." Viewing Black people as noncompliant aligns with a history deeply rooted in psychology. Black people who dared to seek freedom from bondage or refused to remain quiet were violently punished for questioning their oppression and subordination (Guthrie, 2004).

When facing oneself and others in dismantling systems of oppression, there are many strategies in which one may actively engage to facilitate an ongoing reflective practice to name racism and white supremacy. In addition to using Holcomb-McCoy's (2004) checklist, these strategies include, but are not limited to, (a) actively engaging in critical dialogues about race (Kohli, 2014; Singh et al., 2010); (b) engaging in self-exploration activities that enhance one's awareness of one's worldview and positionality (Singh, 2019); (c) examining what it means to be white (Malott & Paone, 2011); (d) increasing one's knowledge of the history of oppression; and (e) building genuine working relationships with students, families, and communities (Singh et al., 2010; Washington & Henfield, 2019).

A Political Critical Standpoint

In this section we argue that decolonizing the Western hegemony in the counseling canon requires that counseling professionals acquire a political critical standpoint. Prilleltensky (1994) used the term "political critical standpoint" to refer to a critical awareness (i.e., active, persistent, and careful consideration) of the social, political, and moral assumptions implicit in psychological and counseling theories and practices. A political critical standpoint acknowledges that the counseling canon is not value neutral or immune to the influence of Western ideologies used to justify the existing racial hierarchy. Despite pretensions of being morally, politically, and ethically neutral, counseling, which is heavily influenced by psychology, is fundamentally Eurocentric, both in theory and in practice (Katz, 1985; Sue, 2006; Sue & Sue, 1999; White, 1984). So it should come as no surprise that the counseling canon (i.e., the body of books, narratives, theories, and other texts considered to be the most important and influential in counseling) inherently reflects whiteness and that this reflection acts as the profession's unnamed norms. Whiteness refers to how white people, their customs, their culture, and their beliefs operate as the standard by which all other racial groups are compared. Thus, any behaviors, values, beliefs, and lifestyles that differ from white American norms are seen as deficient, inferior, and even deviant (Prilleltensky, 1994; Rivera & Torres, 2015; White & Parham, 1990).

The Western hegemony in the counseling canon has served to perpetuate a view that cultural difference is inherently pathological and has also undergirded racist research and counseling practices (Sue et al., 1992). Several writers (Bulhan, 1990; Guthrie, 1970; Katz, 1985; Naidoo, 1996; Prilleltensky, 1994; Sue et al., 1992) have highlighted how psychology and counseling theories and practices tend to support the racist status quo by (a) attributing excessive weight to individual factors in explaining clients'/students' problems and social behavior while largely ignoring social determinants of mental health, such as racial discrimination and social inequalities; (b) endorsing microlevel counseling interventions for social, political, and economic problems impacting clients/students of color, thereby diverting attention away from macrolevel skills (e.g., advocacy, policy analysis, community organizing) to address large-scale social issues such as anti-Black racism; (c) rejecting the notion that biases and dominant (i.e., white) values are inherent in theories of counseling, career development, and human development and their translation into common practice; and (d) portraying values that benefit the dominant (i.e., white) segments of society as benefiting society as a whole.

Consequently the profession is adversely impacted because (a) knowledge and understanding of people from a range of racial and ethnic backgrounds is tightly restricted; (b) our ability to work effectively in cross-cultural situations is severely hindered; (c) the value and usefulness of the healing practices of Indigenous people is deprecated; (d) clients/students are less informed of how racism precipitates their presenting concerns, which makes them less likely to engage in social action that promotes macrosystemic social change; and (e) counselors are less likely to draw connections between clients'/students' presenting concerns and the larger context in which they live or to engage in social justice advocacy with and on behalf of clients/students (Bulhan, 1990; Guthrie, 1970; Katz, 1985; Naidoo, 1996; Prilleltensky, 1994; Sue et al., 1992; Williams et al., 2013).

A Political Critical Standpoint Lens to the Counseling Canon:
In Practice and Research

Here we detail how developing this critical standpoint represents a critical first step toward the ambitious goal of achieving a decolonized and antiracist approach to counselor pedagogy and praxis (Prilleltensky, 1994). We believe that teaching is a political act (Freire, 1972). Teaching counseling students how to see, name, and challenge racial injustice and sharing knowledge and ideas is inherently political.

Over the arcs of our respective careers, we the authors have all lamented the following: How effective are my interventions in cultivating students' critical consciousness (i.e., the ability to recognize and analyze systems of anti-Blackness and the commitment to take action against these systems) if those interventions still conform to the dictates inherent to the traditional European counseling canon (Henfield et al., 2017)? For example, to teach theories is to engage in an exercise of promoting and endorsing theories that are supposedly universal when they are in fact a set of language, stories, and theories reflecting the traditions of economically secure, traditionally educated, socially privileged white men and white women. Symbolically, this advances the idea that within the profession there is a body of scholarship that warrants our attention and respect that is juxtaposed against emergent theories from marginalized thinkers that can be engaged only obliquely. The exclusion of Black scholars (and other nondominant perspectives and forms of texts) within the counseling canon communicates to counseling students, in subtle and profound ways, that a decolonial or antiracist perspective is not central to the counseling profession or one's professional identity (Goodman et al., 2015). The literary counseling canon permeates our profession on many levels and undoubtedly shapes counseling's professional values. Disrupting the counseling canon and moving toward antiracist teaching requires a willingness to examine the underlying cultural (i.e., white) values and social, political, and moral assumptions that serve as the foundation for counseling (Wrenn, 1962).

Case Study

Naomi is a Black American assistant professor in a counselor education program in a Mid-Atlantic university. Her counseling students are primarily white, middle-class, heterosexual, and often cisgender women. Naomi desires to equip her students with the critical knowledge and skills necessary to interrogate and transform their beliefs and attitudes about race and develop an antiracist identity as counselors. However, when determining what to assign students to read, she experiences a double consciousness that threatens her efforts to remain congruent with an antiracist positionality. The feeling of twoness often comes when she must choose between teaching (Council for Accreditation of Counseling and Related Educational Programs and state-level) content that will likely appear on standard certification and licensing exams or scholarship that infuses a critical lens. In taking a political critical standpoint, Naomi uses critical race theory as an interpretive lens to help students analyze the underlying cultural (i.e., white) values and social, political, and moral assumptions that serve as the foundation for the counseling canon—including the content knowledge required for certification and licensure. Naomi also integrates Black perspectives into her counseling courses to help students develop a framework that informs antiracist practice. By integrating Black perspectives throughout her courses, Naomi helps students recognize the history and cultures of Black people, value differences and strengths in Black communities, reject white norms in counseling, and adopt a political ideology from which to fight racism.

Naomi understands that developing a political critical standpoint represents ongoing professional development and does not end with incorporating racial content and frameworks into her courses. It requires that she apply the critical standpoint into her various spheres of influence (e.g., her counseling program; colleagues; and service to her department, college, university, and the counseling profession) and needs to be valued as much as publication and scholarship. Naomi struggles with holding her counselor education program accountable for inadequately preparing their counseling graduates to work with racially/ethnically diverse students/clients while at the same time being collegial and not appearing confrontational. Unfortunately, taking a political critical standpoint has subjected Naomi to hypervisibility (e.g., being overly criticized, policed, targeted for retaliation) by colleagues and students who feel threatened by a challenge to the status quo. Naomi's political critical standpoint is often perceived as aggressive, anachronistic, or too political or described condescendingly by her colleagues with adjectives like "interesting," a word not typically associated with objective or rigorous perspectives or methodological approaches. Navigating her counseling program and university as a consciously critical Black woman comes with uncertainties that manifest as Naomi's constant internal and external struggles. These struggles become an additional burden she must traverse when doing the ongoing self-work necessary to honor what it means to be antiracist.

Conclusion

Counselor educators must challenge the traditional counseling canon to create the more inclusive, representative, and equitable curriculum that students deserve—one that stimulates students to doubt, challenge, and reject preconceived notions of objective knowledge claims derived from Western episteme. The following strategies can be used to help counselors develop a political critical standpoint:

1. Acknowledge that the counseling profession is neither sociopolitically neutral nor immune to the influence of Western racial ideologies that support a racist status quo.
2. Acknowledge that your own knowledge is (to a certain degree) situated in dominant perspectives and social and political experiences that shape how you see and understand the world and determine which behaviors, values, worldviews, paradigms, sets of beliefs, and practices of others are considered healthy, credible, and relevant.
3. Familiarize yourself with components of counseling theories that (a) consider the social determinants of mental health and need to modify environmental conditions conducive to pathology; (b) question the capacity of the present social system to enhance the well-being of Blacks, Indigenous people, and people of color; and (c) critique socially structured inequalities and their psychological effects (Prilleltensky, 1994).

4. Use critical race theory as an interpretive lens to analyze and critique the Western hegemony embedded within the counseling canon, such as (a) whiteness as normative and nonracial; (b) the silence of marginalized narratives; (c) liberal principles of neutrality, fairness, and meritocracy; (d) color blindness; and (e) the inextricability of race, power, and privilege (e.g., Crenshaw et al., 1995).
5. Seek insights from Black feminism and Black feminist epistemologies/counseling practices to (a) develop a critical lens and language with which to scrutinize the ideological repercussions of psychology, (b) examine previously ignored issues, (c) formulate and test new (and old) hypotheses, and (d) develop alternative theoretical paradigms that are sensitive to the realities and contextualized lives of oppressed groups (e.g., Thomas, 2004).
6. Plan for and engage in racial justice action that goes beyond merely developing a political critical standpoint.

References

American Counseling Association. (2020, June 22). *ACA anti-racism statement.* https://www.counseling.org/news/updates/news-detail/2020/06/22/aca-anti-racism-statement

American School Counselor Association. (2014). *Mindsets and behaviors for student success: K-12 college- and career-readiness standards for every student.*

American School Counselor Association. (2020, November 10). *Member demographics.* https://www.schoolcounselor.org/getmedia/9c1d81ab-2484-4615-9dd7-d788a241beaf/member-demographics.pdf

Ani, M. (1994). *Yurugu: An African-centered critique of European cultural thought and behavior.* Africa World Press.

Arredondo, P., D'Andrea, M., & Lee, C. (2020, September 10). Unmasking white supremacy and racism in the counseling profession. *Counseling Today.* https://ct.counseling.org/2020/09/unmasking-white-supremacy-and-racism-in-the-counseling-profession/

Au, W. (2016). Meritocracy 2.0: High-stakes, standardized testing as a racial project of neoliberal multiculturalism. *Educational Policy, 30*(1), 39–62.

Baldwin, J. (1962, January 14). As much truth as one can bear. *The New York Times,* T11.

Bell, D. (2002). *Ethical ambition: Living a life of meaning and worth.* Bloomsbury.

Bulhan, H. A. (1990, November). *Afro-centric psychology: Perspectives and practice* [Opening address]. UWC conference Psychology and Apartheid.

Castro-Gómez, S., & Martin, D. A. (2002). The social sciences, epistemic violence, and the problem of the "invention of the other." *Nepantla, 3*(2), 269–285.

Clarke, J. H. (1998). *Christopher Columbus and the Afrikan holocaust: Slavery and the rise of European capitalism.* A&B.

Crenshaw, K., Gotanda, N., Peller, G., & Thomas, K. (Eds.). (1995). *Critical race theory: The key writings that formed the movement.* The New Press.

Cushman, P. (1996). *Constructing the self, constructing America: A cultural history of psychotherapy.* Da Capo Press.

Du Bois, W. E. B. (2015). *The souls of Black folk.* Yale University Press. (Original work published 1903).

Duckworth, A. L., Peterson, C., Matthews, M. D., & Kelly, D. R. (2007). Grit: Perseverance and passion for long-term goals. *Journal of Personality and Social Psychology, 92*(6), 1087–1101. https://doi.org/10.1037/0022-3514.92.6.1087

Fanon, F. (1963). *The wretched of the earth*. Grove Press.

Fanon, F. (2008). *Black skin, white masks*. Grove Press.

Freire, P. (1972). *Pedagogy of the oppressed*. Penguin Books.

Goodman, R. D., Williams, J. M., Chung, R. C. Y., Talleyrand, R. M., Douglass, A. M., McMahon, H. G., & Bemak, F. (2015). Decolonizing traditional pedagogies and practices in counseling and psychology education: A move towards social justice and action. In R. D. Goodman & P. C. Gorski (Eds.), *Decolonizing "multicultural" counseling through social justice* (pp. 147–164). Springer.

Grier, W. H. (2004). Foreword. In R. V. Guthrie, *Even the rat was white: A historical view of psychology* (pp. xi–xii). Pearson Education.

Griffin, C. B., Gray, D., Hope, E., Metzger, I. W., & Henderson, D. X. (2020). Do coping responses and racial identity promote school adjustment among Black youth? Applying an equity-elaborated social–emotional learning lens. *Urban Education*. Advance online publication. https://doi.org/10.1177/0042085920933346

Guthrie, R. (1970). *Even the rat was white*. Harper & Row.

Guthrie, R. V. (2004). *Even the rat was white: A historical view of psychology*. Pearson Education.

Hansen, J. T. (2006). Counseling theories within a postmodernist epistemology: New roles for theories in counseling practice. *Journal of Counseling & Development, 84*(3), 291–297. https://doi.org/10.1002/j.1556-6678.2006.tb00408.x

Henfield, M. S., Washington, A. R., Rue, L. D. L., & Byrd, J. A. (2017). Black male school counselor educator contextual explorations in leadership. *Professional School Counseling, 21*(1b), 1–10. https://doi.org/10.1177/2156759X18773591

Holcomb-McCoy, C. (2004). Assessing the multicultural competence of school counselors: A checklist. *Professional School Counseling, 7*(3), 178–186.

Horne, G. (2018). *The apocalypse of settler colonialism: The roots of slavery, white supremacy, and capitalism in 17th century North America and the Caribbean*. New York University Press.

Horne, G. (2020). *The dawning of the apocalypse: The roots of slavery, white supremacy, settler colonialism, and capitalism in the long sixteenth century*. Monthly Review Press.

Joseph, A. J. (2015). The necessity of an attention to Eurocentrism and colonial technologies: An addition to critical mental health literature. *Disability & Society, 30*(7), 1021–1041.

Judy, R. A. T. (1993). *(Dis)forming the American canon: African-Arabic slave narratives and the vernacular*. University of Minnesota Press.

Kaler-Jones, C. (2020, May 7). *When SEL is used as another form of policing*. Medium. https://medium.com/@justschools/when-sel-is-used-as-another-form-of-policing-fa53cf85dce4

Katz, J. (1985). The sociopolitical nature of counseling. *Counselling Psychologist, 13*(4), 615–624.

King, M. L., Jr. (1968). The role of the behavioral scientist in the civil rights movement. *American Psychologist, 23*(3), 180–186.

King-White, D., & Kurt, L. (2019). The role of school counselors in the RTI process at the secondary level. In P. L. Epler (Ed.), *Advanced strategies and models for integrating RTI in secondary schools* (pp. 78–88). IGI Global.

Kohli, R. (2014). Unpacking internalized racism: Teachers of color striving for racially just classrooms. *Race Ethnicity and Education, 17*(3), 367–387. https://doi.org/10.1080/13613324.2013.832935

Lorde, A. (1984). The master's tools will never dismantle the master's house. In *Sister outsider: Essays and speeches by Audre Lorde* (pp. 110–113). The Crossing Press.

Love, B. L. (2019). *We want to do more than survive: Abolitionist teaching and the pursuit of educational freedom*. Beacon Press.

Malott, K. M., & Paone, T. R. (2011). The meaning of whiteness: Addressing the taboo in counselor education. In *VISTAS 2011*. https://www.counseling.org/Resources/Library/VISTAS/2011-V-Online/Article_28.pdf

Marsella, A. J. (2015). Decolonization of mind and behavior: A responsibility of professional counselors. In R. D. Goodman & P. C. Gorski (Eds.), *Decolonizing "multicultural" counseling through social justice* (pp. vii–x). Springer.

McKittrick, K. (Ed.). (2015). *Sylvia Wynter: On being human as praxis*. Duke University Press.

Mitcham-Smith, M. (2007). Advocacy—Professional school counselors closing the achievement gap through empowerment: A response to Hipolito-Delgado and Lee. *Professional School Counseling, 10*(4), 341–343. https://doi.org/10.1177/2156759X0701000405

Morris, M. (2016). *Pushout: The criminalization of Black girls in schools*. The New Press.

Morrison, T. (2017). *The origin of others*. Harvard University Press.

Naidoo, A. V. (1996). Challenging the hegemony of Eurocentric psychology. *Journal of Community and Health Sciences, 2*(2), 9–16.

Patterson, O. (1982). *Slavery and social death: A comparative study, with a new preface*. Harvard University Press.

Patterson, O. (2018). *Slavery and social death: A comparative study*. Harvard University Press.

Prilleltensky, I. (1994). *The morals and politics of psychology: Psychological discourse and the status quo*. State University of New York Press.

Ratts, M. J., Singh, A. A., Nassar-McMillan, S., Butler, S. K., & McCullough, J. R. (2016). Multicultural and social justice counseling competencies: Guidelines for the counseling profession. *Journal of Multicultural Counseling and Development, 44*(1), 28–48.

Rivera, E. T., & Torres, I. (2015). Tools of oppression and control in counseling: Making the invisible, visible. *Griot, 8*(1), 119–127.

Singh, A. A. (2019). *The racial healing handbook: Practical activities to help you challenge privilege, confront systemic racism, and engage in collective healing*. New Harbinger.

Singh, A. A., Urbano, A., Haston, M., & McMahan, E. (2010). School counselors' strategies for social justice change: A grounded theory of what works in the real world. *Professional School Counseling, 13*(3), 135–145. https://doi.org/10.1177/2156759X1001300301

Smith, L. C. (2015). Alterity models in counseling: When we talk about diversity, what are we actually talking about? *International Journal for the Advancement of Counselling, 37*(3), 248–261. https://doi.org/10.1007/s10447-015-9241-8

Stanfield, J. H. (1985). The ethnocentric basis of social science knowledge production. *Review of Research in Education, 12*, 387–415.

Sue, D. W. (2006). The invisible whiteness of being: Whiteness, white supremacy, white privilege, and racism. In M. G. Constantine & D. W. Sue (Eds.), *Addressing racism: Facilitating cultural competence in mental health and educational settings* (pp. 15–30). Wiley.

Sue, D. W., Arredondo, P., & McDavis, R. J. (1992). Multicultural counseling competencies and standards: A call to the profession. *Journal of Multicultural Counseling and Development, 20*(2), 64–88.

Sue, D. W., & Sue, D. (1999). *Counseling the culturally different: Theory and practice.* Wiley.

Sue, D. W., & Sue, D. (2019). *Counseling the culturally different: Theory and practice* (8th ed.). Wiley.

Suite, D. H., La Bril, R., Primm, A., & Harrison-Ross, P. (2007). Beyond misdiagnosis, misunderstanding and mistrust: Relevance of the historical perspective in the medical and mental health treatment of people of color. *Journal of the National Medical Association, 99*(8), 879–885.

Thomas, V. G. (2004). The psychology of Black women: Studying women's lives in context. *Journal of Black Psychology, 30*(3), 286–306.

Vargas, J. H. C. (2010). *Never meant to survive: Genocide and utopias in Black diaspora communities.* Rowman & Littlefield.

Vaught, S. E. (2009). The color of money: School funding and the commodification of Black children. *Urban Education, 44*(5), 545–570.

Washington, A., & Henfield, M. (2018). Introduction: School-to-prison pipeline special issue. *Taboo, 17*(4). https://doi.org/10.31390/taboo.17.4.01

Washington, A. R., & Henfield, M. S. (2019). What do the AMCD Multicultural and Social Justice Counseling Competencies mean in the context of Black Lives Matter? *Journal of Multicultural Counseling and Development, 47*(3), 148–160. https://doi.org/10.1002/jmcd.12138

Watkins, W. H. (2001). *The white architects of Black education: Ideology and power in America, 1865-1954.* Teachers College Press.

White, J. L. (1984). Toward a Black psychology. In R. L. Jones (Ed.), *Black psychology* (pp. 5–16). Harper & Row.

White, J. L., & Parham, T. A. (1990). *The psychology of Blacks.* Prentice Hall.

Wilder, C. S. (2013). *Ebony and ivy: Race, slavery, and the troubled history of America's universities.* Bloomsbury Press.

Wilderson, F. B., III. (2010). *Red, white and Black.* Duke University Press.

Williams, J. M., Greenleaf, A. T., & Duys, D. K. (2013). Who's to blame? Client problems and the causal attributions made by counselors-in-training. *Journal of Counselor Preparation and Supervision, 5*(2), Article 1. https://digitalcommons.sacredheart.edu/jcpc/vol5/iss2/1/

Wrenn, C. G. (1962). The culturally encapsulated counselor. *Harvard Educational Review, 32*(4), 444–449.

Wynter, S. (2003). Unsettling the coloniality of being/power/truth/freedom: Towards the human, after man, its overrepresentation—An argument. *CR: The New Centennial Review, 3*(3), 257–337.

CHAPTER 3

Addressing Anti-Black Racism in a School Counseling Context

Norma L. Day-Vines, Beth O. Day-Hairston, Valaida L. Wise, and Jaelyn O. Vines

On Memorial Day 2020, the nation and the world watched in utter horror as an unarmed African American civilian, George Floyd, pleaded for his life while lying prostrate with his hands cuffed tightly behind his back on a Minneapolis street corner. Police officer Derek Chauvin ignored Floyd's supplications for air while nonchalantly repositioning his knee on Floyd's lifeless neck, even as Floyd gasped for his final breath of oxygen. Were it not for a teenager with the temerity to capture the footage digitally, George Floyd would have died in obscurity, with the taken-for-granted assumption that he had provoked the police by resisting arrest. Instead, the visual of his murder looped in constant rotation on Facebook, Instagram, and Twitter feeds, not to mention every major television network around the world, and each successive loop retraumatized countless African American men, women, children, and adolescents who knew intuitively "but for the grace of God, goeth I." That is church speak for "it could have been me."

At the time of Floyd's death, a global pandemic immobilized all but essential employees and most Americans were sheltering in place at home; otherwise, he might have died in vain, much like the nearly 1,000 others who are murdered annually at the hands of police. *The Washington Post* has tracked fatal police shootings since 2014 after discovering that the FBI undercounts such shootings because local police departments are not required to report these data (Berman et al., 2020). For months, George Floyd's murder galvanized a multiracial coalition of outraged protestors who marched in the midst of a global pandemic in more than 140 cities throughout the United States, as well as the United Kingdom, New Zealand, Canada, and Brazil, to express solidarity with African Americans who have decried state-sanctioned violence since the antebellum period (Al Jazeera, 2020).

Discussing why it took the nation several hundred years to come to terms with the endemic nature of racism in general and anti-Black racism in particular lies beyond the scope of this chapter, despite the fact that this issue warrants serious consideration. In any case, this chapter addresses anti-Blackness as it is manifested in our professional counseling associations, defines anti-Blackness, and addresses the consequences of anti-Blackness. We present a conceptual framework, the continuum of broaching behavior, that school counselors can enlist as they work to discuss the contextual dimensions of race, ethnicity, and culture with students in prekindergarten–16 settings and with adult clients. Afterward, we argue that the continuum of broaching behavior is a necessary albeit insufficient criterion for fostering openness to discussions of anti-Blackness. Although school counselors can talk individually with students about anti-Black racism, a more compelling approach involves school-based interventions. Thus, we recast the continuum of broaching behavior as an organizational development framework that describes the role schools play in fostering a sense of safety and openness for African American students.

In the section that follows we describe how corporations and professional associations responded to the George Floyd murder. We note that compared with other organizations, the American School Counselor Association (ASCA) in particular provided an underwhelming response that did not position students and their families to feel supported in the organization's attempt to condemn state-sanctioned violence.

Organizational Responses to George Floyd's Murder

In response to the widespread national and international outcry following George Floyd's murder, many corporations, universities, and professional associations issued declarations and position statements affirming their solidarity with the African American community. The ice cream company Ben & Jerry's issued perhaps one of the more compelling statements, titled "Silence Is NOT an Option," which contested the notion that Floyd's death was the result of some bad cops on the police force and instead attributed his death to "white supremacy" and "the predictable consequence of a racist and prejudiced system and culture that has treated Black bodies as the enemy from the beginning" (Ben & Jerry's, n.d., para. 3). Not only did the ice cream company name the elephant in the room (i.e., white supremacy), it also identified a set of actionable items, insisting that (a) President Donald Trump commit to a formal process of healing and reconciliation in lieu of attacking protestors, (b) Congress create a commission to study the impact of slavery from 1619 to the present and generate remedies, (c) a national task force draft legislation aimed at ending racial violence and increasing police accountability, and (d) the U.S. Department of Justice "[defend] the rights of Black and Brown people" (Ben & Jerry's, n.d., para. 9).

Ben & Jerry's statement lies in marked contrast to pronouncements issued by other corporations, universities, and professional associations, as we demonstrate later in this chapter. In fact, England and Purcell (2020) eschewed their university for its lackluster response to George Floyd's murder and argued that institutions of higher education were far more preoccupied with managing risk, minimizing legal liability, and appeasing trustee board members than expressing condolences to hurting African American faculty, students, and staff or pledging an earnest commitment to the eradication of racism and white supremacy. England and Pur-cell asserted that their institution's written statement did not denounce the police officers responsible for Floyd's death, condemn the system of policing in which racism flourished, or demand justice; as a consequence, it rang hollow. Moreover, when universities neglect to take a decisive stance on anti-Blackness, they label those who dare to speak up as "agitators" espousing values and viewpoints that are antithetical to the organization's mission, which in some cases jeopardizes their prospects for tenure and other forms of mobility. In addition, issuing statements that are devoid of substance is more offensive than saying nothing at all, because such statements normalize racism by intimating there is not an investment in all constituent groups. Similarly, when school-based professional associations neglect to develop comprehensive statements on anti-Black racism and white supremacy, it constrains the profession's ability to advance in ways that eliminate systemic barriers for the students it purports to support.

Robert Starratt (1994) asserted that educators should develop ethical schools by engaging in ethics of critique, justice, and care. An ethic of critique involves an assessment of structures and practices that impede the development of ethical schools. An ethic of justice involves our responsibility to correct structural inequal-ities by ensuring that arrangements are just and equitable relative to individual and collective needs. Starratt noted that as we critique and rectify problems in education, we must do so with an ethic of care and compassion. It is in this spirit that we discuss ASCA's response to the heinous murder of George Floyd.

In the section that follows, we argue that ASCA's statement did little to advance the social justice aims it claims to value following George Floyd's death. After-ward, we establish a rationale for the use of the term "anti-Blackness" by docu-menting parallels between historical forms of anti-Blackness and contemporary manifestations. The first author was trained as a school counselor and counselor educator and devoted her entire career to school counseling and related matters. Thus, she holds dear the profession that cultivated her skills as a professor and scholar yet recognizes that ASCA can reach even higher heights by developing a deep structural understanding of anti-Black racism and its impact on far too many African American students.

ASCA's Performative Response to George Floyd's Murder

In the aftermath of George Floyd's murder, ASCA (2020) released a statement ti-tled "ASCA Condemns Violence and Institutional Racism." For many readers, the title of the document called into question which specific group constituted the target audience, because it was not entirely clear whether the condemnation of violence was a reaction to violence perpetrated against George Floyd, an effort to caution Black Lives Matter protestors about taking an aggressive stance against state-sanctioned violence, or both. Thus, the statement acted as a dog whistle sig-naling that there were problematic behaviors on both sides. Yet the mostly peace-ful marches of Black Lives Matter protests and sympathizers paled in comparison to the deadly insurrection that ensued at the U.S. Capitol on January 6, 2021. Certainly, more clarity is warranted.

In any case, many readers categorized ASCA's (2020) statement as what C. Mor-ris (2020) referred to as "performative allyship," because the statement provided a rhetorical commitment to antiracism that lacked both depth and substance. Performative allyship and antiracism often result from fear of reprisal by certain constituent groups. It is regrettable that this lack of substance and authentic commitment contribute to the reproduction of inequality within educational systems at both structural (e.g., policies, practices) and individual (individual acts of meanness, microaggressions) levels. Allyship and antiracism are intended to be transformative, not performative. Be that as it may, ASCA's statement called for an end to racism, more opportunity structures for African Americans, and an acknowledgment that witnessing violence is an adverse experience. More than being an adverse experience, watching George Floyd's murder repeatedly has the potential to trigger vicarious traumatization or the internalization of trauma that results from witnessing acts of violence rather than being the target of violence (M. A. Seitz, 2020).

Next ASCA (2020) discussed issues related to discipline and disproportionality; the mental health concerns of African Americans, including suicide; and the impact of the novel coronavirus COVID-19 on the African American community. Although these are veritable realities within the African American community that have resulted from the virtually uninterrupted forms of systemic racism that have persisted since the antebellum period, discussion of these challenges functioned as a distraction that deflected attention from George Floyd's murder.

ASCA (2020) advocated for tolerance and social justice and the need to recognize the intrinsic value of every student irrespective of their race, ethnicity, or culture. The word "tolerance" has a negative connotation that implies enduring something or someone you would prefer not to encounter rather than accepting and appreciating it. The statement closed with a recommendation to treat African Americans with respect. According to the research of Bonilla-Silva (2010), racism is not always flagrant. In fact, racism has evolved from blatant to more subtle and nuanced forms of contempt and dehumanization over the years. In addition, racism is often cloaked in semantic tactics that at first glance appear neutral to camouflage racially charged values and viewpoints. Similarly, bell hooks (1992) asserted that "goodwill can co-exist with racist thinking and white supremacist attitudes" (p. 16). As Bonilla-Silva maintained, racism and white supremacy are structural issues and should not be misconstrued as accusations directed toward individuals.

In all fairness, ASCA (2020) did acknowledge systemic racism as problematic and posted a set of resources several months after its initial statement was posted; however, unlike Ben & Jerry's, ASCA stopped short of attributing Floyd's death to white supremacy. Nor did ASCA outline specific actions school counselors could take.

As C. Morris (2020) contended,

> Performative allyship does not engage on a complex level. It consists of low level, often ill-informed rhetorical statements that are usually obvious to Black and Brown employees and real allies, of the anti racist, racially inclusive agenda. It lacks genuine concern and does little to acknowledge the very behaviours that support structural and process driven racism. ("Moving Forward With Real Allyship," para. 1)

In the section that follows, we compare ASCA's initial response to George Floyd's murder to responses from other professional associations. In particular, we note that ASCA's response left many socially conscious school counselors reeling because it lacked a depth of analysis, an earnest commitment to antiracist school counseling, and a delineation of action steps. We make this claim not in an effort to cast aspersions on the profession but because we prize the academic, career, and personal-social development of African American students over professional solidarity. To privilege silence on the issue of anti-Black racism means that we cannot stand in the vanguard of social justice, advocacy, and systemic change.

Statements From Other Professional Associations

Compared to ASCA, the American Counseling Association (ACA, 2020) provided a much more compelling and thoughtful response that described the impact of systemic racism on multiple institutions (e.g., physical and mental health care, education, the judicial system, employment, law enforcement) and the role of structural inequality in perpetuating inequitable institutional policies and practices that have impacted African Americans historically and in contemporary times at both the macrolevel (e.g., societally) and microlevel (e.g., in terms of individual racist attitudes and behaviors). To its credit, ACA acknowledged anti-Black racism by addressing the emotional weight and psychic wounds far too many African Americans bear and the complicit inaction that results from silence. ACA took a bold stance by stating that the Black Lives Matter movement was a moral imperative. In addition, ACA pledged its commitment to fighting white supremacy and the dehumanization of Black people by dismantling formidable systems of oppression.

The National Association of School Psychologists (NASP) issued a call to action and engaged in what Patricia Hill Collins (2009) referred to as "antiracist resistance." NASP (2020) called for an end to racism and identified concrete steps that school psychologists can take, such as examining their own implicit and explicit biases, speaking up, recognizing how stress imposes acute stress and trauma on students and staff who experience racism, and naming racism as racism. On a related note, Metzl and Hansen (2014) noted that multicultural competence is a necessary albeit insufficient condition for demonstrating the ability to work effectively with people from marginalized groups. They argued that beyond demonstrating multicultural counseling competence, helping professionals must be able to name and label the specific structural forces that contribute to racial inequalities such as white supremacy. NASP admonished psychologists to talk candidly about race, make meaningful connections with students and families, ensure that school resource officers are carefully selected and trained, and work to eliminate systemic inequities. Although the NASP statement did not mention African American students specifically, it did appear inclusive and action oriented.

The School Social Work Association of America (SSWAA, 2020) issued a solidarity statement with Black Lives Matter urging school social workers to break the legacy of white supremacy and model antiracism. They referenced an incident in Central Park when Amy Cooper, a white woman, called 911 on an African American man when he asked her to leash her dog. Indignant, Cooper called 911 and erroneously reported that she was being threatened by an African American man who was birdwatching in the park. SSWAA asserted that Cooper weaponized her whiteness by endangering the African American man's life. More important, SSWAA drew parallels between the Central Park incident and the murder of George Floyd, noting that Cooper's effort to invoke the police could have resulted in deleterious consequences. Consistent with contestations made by Kendi (2019),

SSWAA argued that it is not enough for school social workers to not be racist—they must be antiracist and address situational and structural racism.

As school counselors work to support African American students and combat anti-Blackness, they must be able to broach the contextual dimensions of race, ethnicity, and culture with students both individually and systemically. In the section that follows, we distinguish between antiracism and anti-Blackness with a detailed set of examples. Afterward, we review the continuum of broaching behavior as a framework that school counselors can use to discuss students' concerns about anti-Blackness. For some students, this may involve working to reconcile the confusing barrage of events that have taken place since the murder of George Floyd. For other students, it may involve discussing the exhausting impact of personal encounters with anti-Blackness within schools, such as issues related to discipline and disproportionality, low expectations, or microaggressive behaviors. And although helping students manage personal concerns is important, it is woefully inadequate. Later in the chapter we adapt the continuum of broaching behavior from an individual counseling model to an organizational development framework to document school-based responses to anti-Blackness, but first we distinguish between the terms "racism" and "anti-Black racism."

Racism Versus Anti-Black Racism

Scholars have long since rejected the premise that race is a biological construct that consigns people to specific groups based on their phenotypic characteristics. They argue instead that racial categories reflect arbitrary classification systems that rank people hierarchically by consigning them to dominant or subordinate statuses (Smedley & Smedley, 2005). Dominant group members ordinarily use ranking systems to mete out differential resources, treatment, opportunity structures, policies, and practices in ways that advance their own interests and disadvantage the interests of subordinate group members (Feagin, 2004). Racism is continually produced and reproduced as it both exposes and conceals the exploitation, propagation of false ideologies, maintenance of inequalities and unjustly gained resources, power, and sociopolitical realities of people of African origin (Bonilla-Silva, 2010; Feagin, 2004). See Wilkerson (2020) for a more elaborated discussion of hierarchical ranking systems (e.g., caste) that stratify groups of people according to their presumed worth and humanity.

Racism is a catchall term that does not adequately capture the specific and unique manner in which African Americans experience oppression. *Anti-Blackness* is a more precise term that refers to society's inability to recognize the humanity of African Americans and reflects hatred that targets African Americans in an effort to valorize whiteness (Ross, 2020). It is disturbing that anti-Blackness manifests itself in schools, as evidenced by, among other things, the disproportionate number of African American students who experience school referral, suspension, expulsion, special education placements, the school-to-prison pipeline, or dropout relative to their white peers; the lower graduation rates, low expectations, deficit paradigms, and school funding patterns that affect African American students; the exposure of far too many African American students to lead poisoning that impacts cognitive functioning; and the limited availability of school counselors in urban school districts (Alexander, 2012; Benjamin, 2019; Collins, 2009; Garcia & Guerra, 2004; Rothstein, 2017; H. A. Washington, 2019).

Jones (2000) identified three forms of racism: (a) institutional, (b) personally mediated, and (c) internalized. Anti-Blackness, a very specific variant of racism directed expressly toward people of African descent, cannot be understood absent the unique historical context of enslavement and colonization in which it is rooted (A. R. Washington & Henfield, 2019). In this chapter, we specify anti-Blackness so as not to confuse the term with more generic forms of racism that do not center the African American experience. Anti-Blackness acknowledges the fact that racism impacts different groups differently. As a consequence, we enlist Jones's definition of racism as a framework for contextualizing anti-Black racism. Using Jones's definition of racism with an anti-Black racial lens, then, we argue that anti-Blackness at the institutional level accounts for the historical underpinnings and concomitant structural forms of disadvantage that are codified in policies, laws, and practices that have impeded African American students' access to resources such as adequate schooling, housing, employment, and health care both historically and contemporaneously. As we demonstrate in the section that follows, the manifestation of anti-Blackness is not static but is constantly evolving, such that blatant forms of racism exhibited during the antebellum slave period and beyond took on more subtle and nuanced forms during the latter part of the 20th century and the first 2 decades of the 21st century in an effort to disguise racist behavior and intent; however, the social, psychological, and material consequences remain similar.

Institutionalized Anti-Black Racism

The disproportionate referral, suspension, expulsion, and subsequent criminalization of far too many African American students has given rise to the school-to-prison pipeline (Skiba et al., 2014). The dizzying number of punitive disciplinary approaches must be situated within an analytic framework that demonstrates the symbiotic relationship between certain dehumanizing practices for policing Black bodies historically, such as slave patrols, slave codes, Jim Crow laws, convict leasing programs, and lynching, and more recent forms of anti-Black racism that perpetuate reliance on hypersurveillance tactics as a response to student misbehavior, including zero-tolerance policies, resource officers, metal detectors, racial profiling, the 1994 crime bill, vigilante violence, police brutality, and mass incarceration (M. W. Morris, 2016; Parker, 2017; Rosenfeld, 2019; A. R. Washington & Henfield, 2019). More precisely, norms, ideologies, laws, and policies that were codified historically continue today in more nuanced forms that rationalize the suspension and expulsion of African American students as acceptable, normative, and even warranted. A spate of previous research has demonstrated connections between school suspension and later incarceration (M. W. Morris, 2016; Mowen et al., 2020; Skiba et al., 2014). It is disturbing that whether African American youngsters spend 30 minutes or 30 years in prison, the consequences are essentially the same: Upon their release from prison, African American youngsters effectively lose their civil rights and are ushered into what Alexander (2012) referred to as an "underworld of legal discrimination and permanent social exclusion" (p. 13), wherein they surrender the right to the vote, public housing, meaningful employment, and education, all of which are related to the social determinants of well-being, without which the cycle of poverty continues unabated.

The blatant disregard for and dehumanization of Black bodies during the antebellum period was reconstituted as lynching during the 20th century and later vigilante violence (e.g., Emmett Till, the teenager who was lynched in Mississippi in 1955 after being falsely accused of whistling at a white woman) that has continued into the 21st century, snuffing out far too many young African Americans in the prime of their lives, like Trayvon Martin and Ahmaud Arbery, not to mention the state-sanctioned violence that killed Freddie Gray, Tamir Rice, Sandra Bland, George Floyd, and a litany of other African Americans. These atrocities are indicative of a racial caste system that is alive and well (Alexander, 2012; Onwuachi-Willig, 2017; Parker, 2017; Wilkerson, 2020). It is disturbing that in the vast majority of police-involved murders, officers are neither charged nor convicted (Berman et al., 2020). Although it may be difficult to acknowledge, it is not difficult to recognize the parallels between the presumed criminality of African Americans in particular and the 1994 crime bill wherein legislators and the media labeled young African Americans as the face of "superpredators" (Retro Report, 2014).

Institutionalized forms of anti-Blackness are not relegated merely to hypersurveillance and policing of African Americans. As Welsing (1991) suggested, anti-Blackness pervades every area of people's activity. Charity Hudley et al. (2020) asserted that "whether acknowledged or not, race is central, not peripheral or irrelevant, to every aspect of academic knowledge production" (p. e211). It is regrettable that much of African American history is obscured given the romanticized manner in which many schools portray America's past. Sanitized versions of history unabashedly perpetuate myths about Christopher Columbus discovering America, the Pilgrims inviting Indigenous People to dinner, and slavery being a benign yet unfortunate part of the country's past, with little to no connection to settler colonialism and its impact on the social, psychological, and economic well-being of those who were duly affected by the necropolitical effort to determine what groups were worthy of living or dying (Mbembe, 2003). Textbook companies seldom make connections between westward expansion (e.g., Manifest Destiny) and the annihilation of Indigenous Peoples. Publishers devote even less attention to the manner in which the slave economy helped the United States become a world superpower, leaving schoolchildren to imbibe a colossal set of dehumanizing myths about African Americans (Wilder, 2013). Partial truths fuel gross misunderstandings of U.S. history and by extension perpetuate negative attributions that pathologize African Americans, characterizing them in the racial imagination as lazy, inferior, and bellicose, justifying dehumanizing treatment while falsely extolling the virtues of whiteness and thereby reifying white supremacy. Efforts at dismantling romanticized notions of U.S. history are regarded as un-American propaganda when in actuality they serve as a manifestation of anti-Black racism (Bryan & Gerald, 2020).

Other forms of anti-Blackness abound. A growing cadre of scholarship unmasks medical abuses throughout the annals of time that have resulted in experimentation on African American bodies (Hogarth, 2017; Skloot, 2011; Wilkerson, 2020). For instance, James Marion Sims, considered the father of gynecology, conducted gynecological experiments on slave women without their permission or the benefit of anesthesia. Thomas Jefferson perfected the smallpox vaccine on his slaves before using it on his family. This level of disregard was unconscionable and reflects contempt for the humanity of African Americans (H. A. Washington, 2006). As if that were not enough, reports of medical abuses creep well into the mid-20th century and beyond. Doctors engaged in unethical medical experimentation by administering fenfluramine, a drug with known side effects, to test the relationship between serotonin levels and aggression in an effort to identify a "mean gene" in African American boys (H. A. Washington, 2006, p. 275). In 1951, Henrietta Lacks was diagnosed with cervical cancer. Because her cells replicated continuously, doctors used them to conduct medical research, but without Lacks's permission. Unbeknownst to her family until years after she died, the oncology community had launched a multi-billion-dollar industry around her cancer cells, which were used to achieve a number of medical breakthroughs (Skloot, 2011). As late as the 1970s, doctors used coercive tactics to examine boys with an extra Y chromosome to study the possibility of male hypercriminality (H. A. Washington, 2006).

More recently, published reports indicate that African Americans in particular contract and die from the COVID-19 virus at disproportionately higher rates than whites; however, African Americans are less likely to have access to quality health care and more likely to have comorbidities and work as essential employees—circumstances that advocates refer to as health justice issues (Artiga et al., 2020; Benfer & Wiley, 2020). Rana Zoe Mungin was an early casualty of the systemic failures that visit far too many African Americans. Mungin, a social studies teacher in New York, presented three times for medical treatment at a local hospital, and each time she was denied hospital admission. During her second visit, the ambulance attendant stated that she was having a panic attack. By the time she was finally admitted to the hospital, it was too late; Paula A. Johnson (2020), epidemiologist and 14th president of Wellesley College, speculated whether the same fate would have befallen a white man.

Housing is yet another institution that negatively impacts African Americans. For years, common lore presupposed that segregated communities were the result of de facto (i.e., happenstance) rather than de jure (i.e., legalized) segregation (Rothstein, 2017). However, a spate of recent research shows that federal and local policies prohibited many African Americans from accessing opportunities that would have contributed to the transfer of wealth from one generation to the next (Rothstein, 2017; Sarra & Wade, 2020). Exclusionary zoning ordinances, redlining, blockbusting, racially restrictive covenants, the withholding of government construction funds to corporations that sold homes to African Americans, and prohibitions against accessing low-interest mortgages were historically used to warehouse African Americans in the least desirable sections of town. The decades between the inception of government-backed programs designed to stimulate American prosperity but denied to African Americans and African Americans' eventual accessing of these programs can be measured in the unrealized appreciation in home values. Racism is not static, and more recent manifestations of anti-Black policies and practices abound in the form of the predatory lending crisis of 2008, which exacerbated the wealth gap between African Americans and their white counterparts and negatively affected African Americans' economic well-being. White borrowers obtained conventional home loans while mortgage companies directed many African Americans to subprime loans even when they qualified for better terms (Patillo, 2013; Sarra & Wade, 2020). Home values contribute to the intergenerational wealth that has been elusive for so many African Americans. Economist Dana Peterson estimated the cost of racial bias at $16 trillion, just since 2000 (Kishan, 2020). Property values are inextricably bound to property taxes, which in turn shape school funding, student achievement, and school quality.

Voter suppression is yet another domain of anti-Black racism that has a negative impact on African American students, especially because citizens vote for the politicians they believe will support their interests. These politicians in turn make important decisions about how resources are dispersed and which laws are enacted around police accountability, education, health care, unemployment, housing, and so on. Despite the fact that the 15th Amendment granted African American men the right to vote in 1868, historical barriers have persisted. For instance, grandfather clauses, which stipulated that citizens could vote only if their grandfather had voted, effectively excluded African Americans from enfranchisement, and literacy tests and poll taxes imposed impediments to voting during the 1940s (American Civil Liberties Union, n.d.; Kendi, 2016). In 1959, many sharecroppers in Fayette and Haywood Counties, Tennessee, who registered to vote lost their homes, jobs, and credit. White merchants would not sell them goods and services, and white doctors would not provide medical care. So much for the Hippocratic Oath. Evicted with nowhere to go, propertied African Americans allowed them to build tent cities on their land (Momodu, 2020). In 1964, the 24th Amendment to the Constitution prohibited poll taxes and literacy tests, but that did not stop Bloody Sunday on the Edmund Pettus Bridge in 1965 when Martin Luther King Jr., John Lewis, and a host of other protestors were beaten mercilessly as they marched for voting rights in Alabama. This atrocity prompted the passage of the Voting Rights Act of 1965, which was designed to eliminate discrimination and illegal barriers to voting (American Civil Liberties Union, n.d.).

Since the election of former President Barack Obama, concerns about a growing Black and Brown electorate have prompted numerous efforts to curtail African Americans' access to the ballot. These voter suppression measures include gerrymandering (i.e., partisan redistricting that undermines the strength of Black and Brown voters); voter restriction laws that invoke bureaucracies such as voter identification laws; the elimination of preclearance measures from the U.S. Department of Justice that required Southern states to obtain approval before changing voting provisions (*Shelby County v. Holder*); and a reduction in the number of early voting days, preregistration for 16- and 17-year-olds, and same-day registration (Kasino, 2019). These tactics are especially egregious because they compromise democracy.

In addition to anti-Black racism in education, the carceral state, health, housing, and voting rights, other forms of anti-Black racism abound. For instance, the proliferation of technology is not a neutral enterprise. In fact, Benjamin (2019) provided compelling evidence that seemingly unbiased approaches to technology such as coding and the use of algorithms appear neutral on the surface but in reality use data to reinscribe and perpetuate the discrimination, stigmatization, and exploitation of many African Americans. Incidentally, Benjamin referred to this practice as the New Jim Code, a play on Michelle Alexander's (2012) seminal text *The New Jim Crow*.

Environmental racism (H. A. Washington, 2019) jeopardizes the health and often neuropsychological performance of African American students. Compared with their white counterparts, African American students and families are more likely to reside in communities that have pollution levels that violate the standards of the U.S. Environmental Protection Agency. Residence near oil and gas facilities, landfills, and chemical plants predisposes people to childhood diseases such as asthma and leukemia. Prolonged exposure to pesticides, lead, waterborne poisons, microbes, and pathogens diminishes intellectual functioning. It is interesting that the American Academy of Pediatrics defined *racism* as a social determinant of health that is exacerbated by economic, political, and social conditions, much like the ones described above (Trent et al., 2019). Chronic exposure to racialized stress increases cortisol levels, which in turn contributes to effects on the autonomic nervous system, immune suppression, and heart disease, all of which put children on a trajectory to have poor health outcomes.

Personally Mediated Anti-Black Racism

Personally mediated racism, a type of racism identified by Jones (2000), refers to varying forms of prejudice and discrimination, such as lack of respect, suspicion, devaluation, scapegoating, and dehumanization. It also includes assumptions that are made about African American children that devalue their worth and well-being.

Scholars have argued vociferously about the manner in which educators enact varying forms of domination, control, and white supremacy to undermine the ability of African American children to flourish socially and academically. For instance, McKenzie and Scheurich (2004) coined the term "equity traps" to describe the pejorative assumptions educators make about students of color that interfere with their ability to create equitable learning environments. They identified four specific equity traps that we see as forms of anti-Black racism: (a) deficit viewpoints, (b) racial erasure, (c) avoidance and employment of the gaze, and (d) paralogical beliefs and behaviors. The first equity trap, deficit viewpoints, refers to negative attitudes that undermine one's ability to see African American students as capable and competent, such that one's emphasis focuses on failure versus success (Delpit, 1995; Garcia & Guerra, 2004). This kind of negativity stifles productivity, engagement, connection, a sense of belonging, and trust. A large corpus of scholarship documents negative attitudes governing African American students' behavior, academic abilities, potentiality, and so on, without attention to students' strengths and sources of resilience (Day-Vines & Terriquez, 2008; Garcia & Guerra, 2004). Moreover, African American students encounter enormous amounts of unfair treatment, which has a detrimental impact on school performance (Chavous et al., 2008; Le & Stockdale, 2011). Linguists have documented the negative attitudes educators have toward African American students who speak African American English in lieu of more standardized varieties of English (Charity Hudley & Mallinson, 2010). More specifically, students in Lewis's (2005) study who spoke African American English were deemed as having limited communicative competence.

The second equity trap, racial erasure, refers to a form of color-blind racism wherein perpetrators deny racist tendencies by asserting that they do not see race to minimize their own racism. An emerging body of scholarship corroborates the findings of McKenzie and Scheurich (2004)—namely, that color blindness reflects an attempt to shield hidden biases. The groundbreaking research of Bonilla-Silva (2010) documented the semantic tactics that many whites in his study used in conversation, such as prefacing racially charged viewpoints with statements such as "I'm not racist, but ...." Additional behaviors included expressing ambivalence about controversial subjects, voicing clear preferences for conservative viewpoints, attributing racialized issues to anything but race, blaming African Americans for problems, and exhibiting rhetorical incoherence when discussing race.

Lewis (2005) conducted an ethnographic study in the United States to examine how race, ethnicity, and culture shape social interactions in school settings. Although adults in the study asserted that race was inconsequential, in actuality the community claimed obliviousness to the effects of color and tended to ignore racial factors associated with student conflict. For instance, half of the children Lewis interviewed admitted to not playing with a student of color because they were different. It is regrettable that school staff attributed interpersonal conflicts to the student of color and perceived conflicts to be exaggerated claims of mistreatment. An emerging body of educational research suggests that when concerns are raised about controversial topics related to racial bias, school districts enlist bureaucratic practices such as ignoring, minimizing, and denying accusations in ways that perpetuate racial marginalization (Akom, 2008; Khalifa & Briscoe, 2015).

The third equity trap, avoidance and employment of the gaze, refers to the use of surveillance efforts to control behavior. For example, white teachers in McKenzie and Scheurich's (2004) study sought employment in predominantly Black/Brown schools to avoid the gaze or the demands for accountability insisted on by parents in more affluent school districts. By working in diverse schools, teachers were able to escape censure for rude, disrespectful behavior directed toward students. In predominantly Black/Brown schools, white teachers used the gaze to rebuke other teachers whose values, beliefs, and statements did not comport with more conservative anti-Black viewpoints.

The final equity trap, paralogical beliefs and behaviors, refers to the tendency to draw conclusions from a false premise by projecting onto Black or Brown students. For instance, teachers in the McKenzie and Scheurich (2004) study reported that they would lose control and scream at children yet asserted the children were to blame for their loss of self-control. These equity traps reflect a form of personally mediated behavior that results in the perpetuation of anti-Blackness.

Internalized Anti-Black Racism

Jones's (2000) final component of racism is internalized racism. Anti-Black internalized racism refers to the premise that over time encounters with racism and discrimination result in people from marginalized groups believing and enacting the negative stereotypes perpetuated against them. Prolonged exposure to internalized racism can lead to self-doubt and self-deprecation (Davis & Ernst, 2019). Many African American students are susceptible to stereotype threat, a specific form of internalized oppression that results when individuals' performance declines because they begin to believe negative stereotypes that have been perpetrated against them (Perry et al., 2004; Steele, 1997). Some African American students experience traumatization from the barrage of societal messages that work to convince them they are inadequate. As stated above, chronic exposure to racism, discrimination, and implicit bias is associated with diminished social-emotional functioning, worse mental health, certain physical diseases (e.g., autoimmune diseases), and diminished academic achievement (Pascoe & Richman, 2009).

The foregoing discussion suggests that the past serves as prologue for the present and future. School counselors must understand the sociopolitical realities of African American children and their impact on their education. By extension, professional associations and universities must stand valiantly at the forefront of providing clarity and taking a stance that recognizes the deep structural historical issues that shape, perpetuate, and reinforce contemporary issues. Weak position statements do little in the way of creating structures that shift a history of exploitation and white supremacy. Not understanding the interconnections among racism, discrimination, and educational experience means not being positioned to help students.

In the remainder of this chapter, we present an empirically supported continuum and conceptual framework that school counselors can use as they address the contextual dimensions of race, ethnicity, and culture with students. We argue that the counselor's broaching behavior could have more utility if it is adapted as an organizational development framework that considers the integral role that schools play in shaping a school culture that eschews anti-Black racism.

The Continuum of Broaching Behavior

Broaching refers to the counselor's ability to explore the contextual dimensions of race, ethnicity, and culture with clients during treatment (Day-Vines et al., 2007). Essentially, broaching behavior results when the counselor pays selective attention to cultural factors that may impact the client's sociopolitical experience. That is, the counselor does not define the client's race or culture as the primary source of concern but considers the client in a cultural context.

An emerging body of literature has demonstrated the utility of discussing racialized concerns with adolescents. Van Ausdale and Feagin (2001) found that as early as preschool, children subjected one another to racial mistreatment. Similarly, Seele's (2012) qualitative research demonstrated that young children between the ages of 4 and 6 created social hierarchies within their peer groups based on their linguistic and racial differences. Talking about these distressing events with students can alleviate psychological distress. For instance, Scott and House (2005) studied a sample of African American high school students and concluded that high levels of discrimination distress were associated with avoidant coping styles, whereas feelings of mastery and control were associated with coping strategies such as seeking social support and problem-solving. Powell and Jacob Arriola (2003) reached similar conclusions.

Other research has demonstrated that counselors who possess race-neutral attitudes have lower levels of self-reported multicultural counseling competence (Burkard & Knox, 2004; Neville et al., 2006). Given the power dynamics that govern the counseling relationship, a counselor's disavowal of the client's cultural context may prevent the client from addressing pertinent counseling concerns related to race, ethnicity, and culture (Pope-Davis et al., 2002; Thompson et al., 1994). The foregoing discussion implies that counselors have a compelling rationale for discussing the extent to which issues related to race and representation may influence the client's sociocultural and sociopolitical reality.

The continuum of broaching behavior describes four empirically supported styles that school counselors may rely on to either initiate or respond to issues related to race, ethnicity, and culture during treatment: (a) avoidant, (b) continuing/incongruent, (c) integrated/congruent, and (d) infusing (Day-Vines et al., 2007, 2013). Avoidant school counselors ignore or minimize students' racial, ethnic, and cultural concerns because they contend that broaching is unnecessary. Continuing/incongruent school counselors are open to broaching the contextual dimensions of race, ethnicity, and culture with students but lack the accompanying skill set. Integrated/congruent school counselors explore students' racial, ethnic, and cultural concerns in ways that help them feel heard or understood. Infusing school counselors broach as part of their professional identity and enlist social justice frameworks.

An emerging body of research supports the need for school counselors to develop their broaching capability. Day-Vines et al. (in press) compared the broaching efforts of school counselors, clinical mental health counselors, and counselor trainees. Their findings indicated that school counselors and white counselors had higher avoidant scores than clinical mental health counselors and counselor trainees. School counselors scored higher than counselor trainees on the Infusing subscale. In a related study examining the relationship between school counselors' racial identity and their broaching behavior, findings indicated that school counselor trainees operating at lower levels of racial identity functioning were more likely to have avoidant broaching attitudes (Day-Vines, Brodar, et al., 2021). Similarly, school counselor trainees operating at higher levels of racial identity functioning endorsed more infusing attitudes and behaviors. In the paragraphs that follow, we present a hypothetical situation and describe how counselors along the continuum of broaching behavior may respond. See Table 3.1 for more information on the continuum.

For example, Eboni, a seventh-grade African American female student, approaches her school counselor to discuss the hurt she feels when one of her peers calls her the N-word. Eboni is crushed because she is convinced that her teacher heard this racial slur but ignored it, despite the fact that a number of students laughed, which was even more humiliating. An avoidant school counselor would likely redirect Eboni's attention to more generic topics, such as her academic performance. More disturbing, the school counselor may suggest that Eboni misheard her classmate, especially if the teacher did not address the matter. A continuing/incongruent school counselor would explore Eboni's concerns but do so awkwardly and mechanically. The counselor may talk using what Bonilla-Silva (2010) referred to as rhetorical incoherence, having difficulty acknowledging Eboni's concerns because they might fear being seen as biased. An integrated/congruent school counselor would broach effectively and would normalize Eboni's concerns by providing a sense of safety and trust that would allow Eboni to talk openly about how she has been impacted by her peer's comments. They would help Eboni construe this unfortunate event as an act of anti-Blackness. An infusing school counselor would recognize that Eboni's concerns are part of a larger constellation of social justice issues that plague many African American students in the school. The school counselor who recognizes that a significant number of students are similarly situated might work with the administration, faculty, staff, and student government leaders to generate a plan of action to support African American students who are reeling under the weight of intense and unrelenting forms of anti-Blackness. The school counselor may work with various constituents in the school to schedule listening tours with students and parents and so on. Elsewhere Day-Vines and colleagues have provided more detailed guidelines for specific broaching strategies (Day-Vines et al., 2018, 2020; Day-Vines, Cluxton-Keller, et al., 2021).

An Organizational Continuum of Broaching Behavior

Although the continuum of broaching behavior identifies how individual school counselors facilitate discussions of anti-Blackness, these conversations are limited

TABLE 3.1 • The Continuum of Broaching Behavior in School Contexts

Mode of Response	Avoidant	Continuing/ Incongruent	Integrated/ Congruent	Infusing
Symbol	*Avoiders*	*Bumblers*	*Heroes*	*Champions*
School stance	• Refusal to address controversial issues (reprimand quietly, no school-wide communique) • Issue is not considered a teachable moment	• Bumblers address controversial issues but awkwardly, mechanically, superficially, inappropriately	• Heroes address controversial issues • Thoughtful, well-intentioned statements and actions (individual teachers and/or administrators have mastered the art and science of addressing controversial topics, are comfortable talking about race)	• Social justice interventions/activities • School-wide professional development • All stakeholders
What is said/ done	• Nothing	• Statements are made but are not thought through systematically	• Thoughtful and heartfelt statements by individual members of the school staff or leadership	• Champions engage racial and cultural issues directly and effectively school-wide • Diversity, equity, and inclusion (DEI) are part of the school-wide culture
Rationale	• Fear of being seen as racist • Fear of reprisal by powerful parent groups • Fear of losing funders • Desire for problem to disappear • Lack of a skillset to address concerns • No consensus about how the organization feels	• Lack of tools to manage controversial issues that arise	• Socially conscious school personnel champion issues of DEI because it is the right thing to do	• Champions address issues related to DEI functions as part of the school culture, vision, and mission
Individual teachers	• Fearful of talking about race • Avoiders believe that students are color-blind	• Bumblers recognize that racialized issues warrant discussion but do not have the tools to facilitate dialogue effectively	• Heroes have a heightened sense of critical consciousness • Heroes have a deep structural understanding of racial issues • Heroes have made individual efforts	• All personnel have been trained as part of a school-wide initiative that imparts knowledge and skills to address racialized issues

(Continued)

Mode of Response	Avoidant	Continuing/ Incongruent	Integrated/ Congruent	Infusing
Symbol	*Avoiders*	*Bumblers*	*Heroes*	*Champions*
Administrative response	• Top-down mandate by the administration to ignore the issue • Discipline is handled quietly • No training on handling issues	• Top-down mandate to discuss race, ethnicity, and culture without guidance	• Training occurs but is not infused throughout the school	• Equity audit • School-wide training • Faculty, staff, and students are social justice minded
Presence of systematic approach to DEI	• Little collection, analysis, and application of data points • Race and equity are not reflected in hiring, onboarding, and evaluation processes • No apparent commitment to diversity in hiring	• Data are collected, disaggregated, and reported • Bumblers accept or do not critique disparities • Administration does not know what to do with data to guide changes • Rhetorical commitment to diversity	• Collection, analysis, and disaggregation of data are done by individual teachers • Highly diverse faculty/ staff • Aspirational commitment to diversity	• Collection, analysis, and application of data points • Data are disaggregated appropriately with an eye toward racial equity • Race and equity are reflected in hiring, onboarding, and evaluation processes
Themes	• Silence	• Limited engagement	• Some of us	• All of us

TABLE 3.1 • The Continuum of Broaching Behavior in School Contexts (*Continued*)

unless they are part of a systematic, coordinated plan of action that operates on an organizational level designed to root out anti-Blackness in schools. Wise and Day-Vines (2020) adapted the continuum of broaching behavior to reflect school-based responses. Essentially, they argued that if meaningful change is to take place, schools (and not just school counselors) must respond systemically (see Table 3.1). Schools operating within the avoidant category discount racialized issues for fear that addressing such topics will spark volatile debate, expose biases, polarize the school community, and lead to accusations of racism. Administrators may address issues quietly in ways that do not provide for a transformation of school culture. For instance, school officials may opt not to respond because they believe it will divert attention from the learning process and upset a number of families. A consequence of suppressing racialized concerns may be that issues spiral out of control unnecessarily because they were not dealt with when they were still manageable. Furthermore, not holding students and teachers accountable reinforces and perpetuates anti-Blackness. Table 3.1 delineates an avoidant school's response. The emblem for avoidant schools is an ostrich whose head is in the sand ignoring pertinent issues. Ironically, an ostrich has wings but cannot fly. The predominant theme for avoidant schools is "silence."

As schools advance along the continuum, they engage in continuing/incongruent responses. School administrators may recognize that such issues warrant attention yet lack the tools to respond appropriately to anti-Blackness. They may react to racialized incidents awkwardly or inappropriately. Much like ASCA in responding to George Floyd's murder, the school may issue a statement that seems equivocal at best. An equivocal statement dismisses the continued dehumanization that far too many Black and Brown children experience repeatedly. The graphic representation for continuing/incongruent schools is a caution sign, which reflects the fallout that can occur from mismanaging an instance of anti-Blackness. The theme for continuing/incongruent schools is "limited engagement."

Schools responding from an integrated/congruent stance demonstrate openness to addressing issues related to race, ethnicity, and culture. Such schools may respond by engaging in thoughtful reflection before issuing a public statement and consider their institutional commitment to social justice as well as the consequences of rendering responses that may be nonfacilitative. Ultimately, they generate a response that recognizes the historical legacy of racism and discrimination in the United States, the need to stand in solidarity with Black and Brown students, and the school's commitment to antiracist practice. On the surface, integrated/congruent school officials seem to manage incidents appropriately; however, in reality, a handful of socially conscious teachers and school counselors shoulder the responsibility for managing crisis situations. A thumbs-up sign characterizes integrated/congruent schools, and the predominant theme is "some of us."

Schools operating in the infusing category possess the tools and resources to address anti-Blackness directly and effectively. In addition to reiterating their commitment to anti-Blackness, infusing schools examine their policies and practices to make sure they do not deliberately or inadvertently penalize African American students. For instance, they may have systematic ongoing training and support for faculty to engage in antiracist dialogue and education, begin the process of unlearning racism and by extension anti-Black racism, look at structures within the school that disadvantage students, review data (e.g., school-level data that track advanced course-taking patterns or discipline practices by race and class), enlist constituent groups such as parents and students to share their perceptions of the school climate, examine the curriculum to make sure it is bias free, and review policies to make sure they do not penalize students from marginalized groups unfairly. The graphic representation for infusing schools is a recycling symbol, which reflects the fact that schools work consistently to root out anti-Blackness systematically. The theme for infusing schools is "all of us," which reflects the fact that the entire school community is committed to the eradication of anti-Blackness.

We believe this work cannot be accomplished through single-session professional development workshops, feel-good book readings, or the hiring of diversity officers who have limited support or authority. The implementation of ongoing, systematic training (e.g., in cultural competence, antibias, antiracism, anti-Blackness) in which members of the school community develop the ability to broach difficult conversations and set up more equitable school practices rests heavily on doing self-awareness/self-interrogation work that brings into focus one's attitudes, biases, and assumptions; engaging in introspective reflection on both an individual and organizational level; and most important having the will to transform schools.

Conclusion

The egregious murder of George Floyd sent shockwaves throughout the nation and the world, especially as it was paired with a global pandemic and an unanticipated financial maelstrom. Multiple organizations stepped forward to offer condolences, express solidarity with African Americans who felt most vulnerable to state-sanctioned violence, and pledge a commitment to the eradication of anti-Blackness. Some organizations articulated their stances better than others. For instance, Ben & Jerry's took a courageous stance by making a set of demands. In addition, school-based professional associations jumped into the fray. ASCA made an effort to address systemic racism but stopped short of identifying the antiracist resistance strategies that school counselors can enlist. NASP and SSWAA went further by identifying specific actions that its members could take, recommending that school-based support personnel name systemic racism and white supremacy to make the implicit explicit and as a consequence refrain from normalizing racism. None of the organizations reviewed in this chapter used the term "anti-Black racism."

It is clear that school-based professional associations exhibited certain strengths in demonstrating solidarity with African Americans in particular who were impacted by George Floyd's murder. Stronger statements were associated with an ability to (a) make connections between historical encounters with racism and white supremacy and more contemporary manifestations, (b) declare a commitment to eradicating oppression, (c) focus exclusively on the concern as it related to state-sanctioned and vigilante violence, (d) delineate action-oriented steps, (e) acknowledge the depth of the pain that African Americans endure, and (f) name systemic forms of oppression. None of the organizations reviewed used the term "anti-Blackness" to articulate the specific and unique historical encounters of oppression that originated during the antebellum period and evolved from more blatant forms of dehumanization to more invisible forms of dehumanization, despite the fact that George Floyd's murder provided a clear example of anti-Black racism. This suggests that there may be opportunities for school-based professional associations such as ASCA to better understand how history informs students' sociopolitical realities, codify this in position statements, and press for training so school counselors can better support the students they serve.

The fact that our school counseling association struggles to articulate the manner in which African American students experience intense and unrelenting exposure to and consequences of anti-Blackness suggests that individual schools and school counselors may not have the tools to broach anti-Blackness on an individual counseling level or on a macro, school-based level. Future research should assess the extent to which schools are able to infuse broaching elements into the school culture.

At some point, the noise surrounding the heinous killing of George Floyd will subside, we will have a medical response to COVID-19, and the unrest will cease. Everyone will go back home and life will resume. But will there be real, substantive change? Will schools have the necessary tools to manage the change required? That will depend on you.

References

Akom, A. A. (2008). Black metropolis and mental life: Beyond the "burden of 'acting white'" toward a third wave of critical racial studies. *Anthropology & Education Quarterly, 39*(3), 247–265.

Al Jazeera. (2020, June 11). *A timeline of the George Floyd and anti-police brutality protests.* https://www.aljazeera.com/news/2020/06/timeline-george-floyd-protests-200610194807385.html

Alexander, M. (2012). *The new Jim Crow: Mass incarceration in the age of colorblindness* (Rev. ed.). The New Press.

American Civil Liberties Union. (n.d.). *Voting Rights Act: Major dates in history.* https://www.aclu.org/issues/voting-rights/voting-rights-act/history-voting-rights-act

American Counseling Association. (2020, June 22). *ACA anti-racism statement.* https://ct.counseling.org/2020/06/aca-anti-racism-statement/

American School Counselor Association. (2020, May). *ASCA condemns violence and institutional racism.* https://www.schoolcounselor.org/getmedia/3695e7a7-5cac-4adb-a31b-35641287807f/Statement-Systemic-Racism-5-2020.pdf

Artiga, S., Corallo, B., & Pham, O. (2020, August 17). *Racial disparities in COVID-19: Key findings from available data and analysis.* Kaiser Family Foundation. https://www.kff.org/report-section/racial-disparities-in-covid-19-key-findings-from-available-data-and-analysis-issue-brief/

Ben & Jerry's. (n.d.). *Silence is not an option.* https://www.benjerry.com/about-us/media-center/dismantle-white-supremacy

Benfer, E. A., & Wiley, L. F. (2020, March 19). *Health justice strategies to combat CO-VID-19: Protecting vulnerable communities during a pandemic.* Project HOPE. https://www.healthaffairs.org/do/10.1377/hblog20200319.757883/full/

Benjamin, R. (2019). *Race after technology: Abolitionist tools for the new Jim code.* Polity.

Berman, M., Sullivan, J., Tate, J., & Jenkins, J. (2020, June 8). Protests spread over police shootings. Police promised reforms. Every year, they still shoot and kill nearly 1,000 people. *The Washington Post.* https://www.washingtonpost.com/investigations/protests-spread-over-police-shootings-police-promised-reforms-every-year-they-still-shoot-nearly-1000-people/2020/06/08/5c204f0c-a67c-11ea-b473-04905b1af82b_story.html

Bonilla-Silva, E. (2010). *Racism without racists: Color-blind racism and racial inequality in contemporary America* (3rd ed.). Rowman & Littlefield.

Bryan, K. C., & Gerald, J. P. B. (2020, August 17). The weaponization of English. *Language Magazine: Improving Literacy and Communication.* https://www.languagemagazine.com/2020/08/17/the-weaponization-of-english/

Burkard, A. W., & Knox, S. (2004). Effect of therapist color-blindness on empathy and attributions in cross-cultural counseling. *Journal of Counseling Psychology, 51*(4), 387–397.

Charity Hudley, A., & Mallinson, C. (2010). *Understanding English language variation in U.S. schools.* Teachers College Press.

Charity Hudley, A. H., Mallinson, C., & Bucholtz, M. (2020). Toward racial justice in linguistics: Interdisciplinary insights into theorizing race in the discipline and diversifying the profession. *Proceedings of the Linguistic Society of America, 96*(4), e200–e235. https://www.linguisticsociety.org/sites/default/files/e01_96.4CharityHudley.pdf

Chavous, T. M., Rivas-Drak, D., Smalls, C., Griffin, T., & Cogburn, C. (2008). Gender matters, too: The influences of school racial discrimination and racial identity on academic engagement outcomes among African American adolescents. *Developmental Psychology, 44*(3), 637–654.

Collins, P. H. (2009). *Another kind of public education: Race, schools, the media, and democratic possibilities.* Beacon Press.

Davis, A. M., & Ernst, R. (2019). Racial gaslighting. *Politics, Groups, and Identities, 7*(4), 761–774.

Day-Vines, N. L., Booker Ammah, B., Steen, S., & Arnold, K. M. (2018). Getting comfortable with discomfort: Preparing counselor trainees to broach racial, ethnic, and cultural factors with clients during counseling. *Journal for the Advancement of Counselling, 40*(2), 89–104. https://doi.org/10.1007/s10447-017-9308-9

Day-Vines, N. L., Brodar, J., Hicks, D., Fernandez, E., Garcia, K., & Jones, K. (2021). *An investigation of the relationship between school counselor trainees' broaching behavior and racial identity attitudes*. Unpublished manuscript.

Day-Vines, N. L., Bryan, J., & Griffin, D. (2013). The Broaching Attitudes and Behavior Survey (BABS): An exploratory assessment of its dimensionality. *Journal of Multicultural Counseling and Development, 41*(4), 210–223.

Day-Vines, N. L., Bryan, J., Griffin, D., & Brodar, J. (in press). Grappling with race: A national study of the broaching behaviors of school counselors, clinical mental health counselors, and counselor trainees. *Journal of Multicultural Counseling and Development*.

Day-Vines, N. L., Cluxton-Keller, F., Agorsor, C., & Gubara, S. (2021). Strategies for broaching the subjects of race, ethnicity, and culture. *Journal of Counseling & Development, 99*(3), 348–357. https://doi.org/10.1002/jcad.12380

Day-Vines, N. L., Cluxton-Keller, F., Agorsor, C., Gubara, S., & Otabil, N. (2020). The multidimensional model of broaching behavior. *Journal of Counseling & Development, 98*(1), 107–118. https://doi.org/10.1002/jcad.12304

Day-Vines, N. L., & Terriquez, V. (2008). A strengths-based approach to promoting prosocial behavior among African American and Latino students. *Professional School Counseling, 12*(2), 170–175.

Day-Vines, N. L., Wood, S., Grothaus, T., Craigen, L., Holman, A., Dotson-Blake, K., & Douglass, M. (2007). Broaching the subjects of race, ethnicity, and culture during the counseling process. *Journal of Counseling & Development, 85*(4), 401–409.

Delpit, L. (1995). *Other people's children: Cultural conflict in the classroom*. The New Press.

England, J., & Purcell, R. (2020). Higher ed's toothless response to the killing of George Floyd. *The Chronicle of Higher Education*. https://www.chronicle.com/article/higher-eds-toothless-response-to-the-killing-of-george-floyd

Feagin, J. (2004). Toward an integrated theory of systemic racism. In M. Krysan & A. E. Lewis (Eds.), *The changing terrain of race and ethnicity* (pp. 203–223). Russell Sage Foundation.

Garcia, S. B., & Guerra, P. L. (2004). Deconstructing deficit thinking: Working with educators to create more equitable learning environments. *Education and Urban Society, 36*(2), 150–168.

Hogarth, R. (2017). *Medicalizing Blackness: Making racial difference in the Atlantic world, 1780-1840*. University of North Carolina Press.

hooks, b. (1992). *Black looks: Race and representation*. South End Press.

Johnson, P. A. (2020, May 31). *A 30-year-old teacher's Covid-19 death tells us volumes*. CNN. https://www.cnn.com/2020/05/31/opinions/higher-education-coronavirus-opportunity-for-a-more-just-world-johnson/index.html

Jones, C. P. (2000). Levels of racism: A theoretic framework and a gardener's tale. *American Journal of Public Health, 90*(8), 1212–1215.

Kasino, M. (Director). (2019). *Rigged: The voter suppression playbook* [Documentary]. The American Issues Initiative.

Kendi, I. X. (2016). *Stamped from the beginning: The definitive history of racist ideas in America*. Nation Books.

Kendi, I. X. (2019). *How to be an antiracist*. One World.

Khalifa, M. A., & Briscoe, F. (2015). A counternarrative autoethnography exploring school districts' role in reproducing racism: Willful blindness to racial inequities. *Teachers College Record, 117*(8), 1–34.

Kishan, S. (2020, October 20). Economist found $16 trillion when she tallied cost of racial bias. *Bloomberg Businessweek*. https://www.bloomberg.com/news/articles/2020-10-20/racism-and-inequity-have-cost-the-u-s-16-trillion-wall-street-economist-says

Le, T. N., & Stockdale, G. (2011). The influence of school demographic factors and perceived student discrimination on delinquency trajectory in adolescence. *Journal of Adolescent Health*, *49*(4), 407–413.

Lewis, A. E. (2005). *Race in the schoolyard: Negotiating the color line in classrooms and communities*. Rutgers University Press.

Mbembe, A. (2003). Necropolitics. *Public Culture*, *15*(1), 11–40.

McKenzie, K. B., & Scheurich, J. J. (2004). Equity traps: A useful construct for preparing principals to lead schools that are successful with racially diverse students. *Educational Administration Quarterly*, *40*(5), 601–632.

Metzl, J. M., & Hansen, H. (2014, February). Structural competency: Theorizing a new medical engagement with stigma and inequality. *Social Science & Medicine*, *103*, 126–133. https://doi.org/10.1016/j.socscimed.2013.06.032

Momodu, S. (2020, May 13). *Tent cities of Fayette and Haywood Counties (1960-1962)*. https://www.blackpast.org/african-american-history/tent-cities-of-fayette-and-haywood-counties-1960-1962/

Morris, C. (2020, November 26). Performative allyship: What are the signs and why leaders get exposed. *Forbes*. https://www.forbes.com/sites/carmenmorris/2020/11/26/performative-allyship-what-are-the-signs-and-why-leaders-get-exposed/?sh=4d773c1822ec

Morris, M. W. (2016). *Pushout: The criminalization of Black girls in schools*. The New Press.

Mowen, T. J., Brent, J. J., & Boman, J. H. (2020). The effect of school discipline on offending across time. *Justice Quarterly*, *37*(4), 739–760. https://doi.org/10.1080/07418825.2019.1625428

National Association of School Psychologists. (2020, May 29). *NASP calls for action to end racism and violence against people of color*. https://www.nasponline.org/about-school-psychology/media-room/press-releases/nasp-calls-for-action-to-end-racism-and-violence-against-people-of-color

Neville, H., Spanierman, L., & Doan, B. (2006). Exploring the association between color-blind racial ideology and multicultural counseling competence. *Cultural Diversity and Ethnic Minority Psychology*, *12*(2), 275–290.

Onwuachi-Willig, A. (2017). Policing the boundaries of whiteness: The tragedy of being "out of place" from Emmett Till to Trayvon Martin. *Iowa Law Review*, *102*(3), 1113–1185.

Parker, L. (2017). Schools and the no-prison phenomenon: Anti-Blackness and secondary policing in the Black Lives Matter era. *Journal of Educational Controversy*, *12*(1), Article 11. https://cedar.wwu.edu/jec/vol12/iss1/11

Pascoe, E. A., & Richman, L. S. (2009). Perceived discrimination and health: A meta-analytic review. *Psychological Bulletin*, *135*(4), 531–554. https://doi.org/10.1037/a0016059

Patillo, M. (2013). *Black picket fences: Privilege and peril among the Black middle class* (2nd ed.). University of Chicago Press.

Perry, T., Steele, C. M., & Hilliard, A. (2004). *Young, gifted and Black: Promoting high achievement among African-American students*. Beacon Press.

Pope-Davis, D. B., Toporek, R. L., Ortega-Villalobos, L., Ligiéro, D. P., Brittan-Powell, C. S., Liu, W. M., Bashshur, M. R., Codrington, J. N., & Liang, C. T. H. (2002). Client perspectives of multicultural counseling competence: A qualitative examination. *The Counseling Psychologist*, *30*(3), 355–393.

Powell, C. L., & Jacob Arriola, K. R. (2003). Relationship between psychosocial factors and academic achievement among African American students. *Journal of Educational Research, 96*(3), 175–181.

Retro Report (2014). The superpredator scare. *New York Times.* https://www.nytimes.com/video/us/100000002807771/the-superpredator-scare.html/

Rosenfeld, R. (2019). *The 1994 crime bill: Legacy and lessons—Overview and reflections.* Council on Criminal Justice.

Ross, K. M. (2020, June 4). Call it what it is: Anti-Blackness. *The New York Times.* https://www.nytimes.com/2020/06/04/opinion/george-floyd-anti-blackness.html

Rothstein, R. (2017). *The color of law: A forgotten history of how our government segregated America.* Liveright.

Sarra, J., & Wade, C. (2020). *Predatory lending and the destruction of the African-American dream.* Cambridge University Press.

School Social Work Association of America. (2020, May 31). *Solidarity statement with Black Lives Matter.* https://aab82939-3e7b-497d-8f30-a85373757e29.filesusr.com/ugd/486e55_0be666d8efd241aba23af719e33856fc.pdf

Scott, L. D., & House, L. (2005). Relationship of distress and perceived control to coping with perceived racial discrimination among Black youth. *Journal of Black Psychology, 31*(3), 254–272.

Seele, C. (2012). Ethnicity and early childhood. *International Journal of Early Childhood, 44*(3), 307–325.

Seitz, M. A. (2020, June 9). *The quiet trauma of watching police brutality on our screens.* Vulture. https://www.vulture.com/2020/06/police-brutality-footage-vicarious-trauma.html

Skiba, R. J., Arredondo, M. I., & Williams, N. T. (2014). More than a metaphor: The contribution of exclusionary discipline to a school-to-prison pipeline. *Equity & Excellence in Education 47*(4), 546–564.

Skloot, R. (2011). *The immortal life of Henrietta Lacks.* Broadway Books.

Smedley, A., & Smedley, B. D. (2005). Race as biology is fiction, racism as a social problem is real: Anthropological and historical perspectives on the social construction of race. *American Psychologist, 60*(1), 16–26.

Starratt, R. J. (1994). *Building an ethical school: A practical response to the moral crisis in schools.* The Falmer Press.

Steele, C. (1997). A threat in the air: How stereotypes shape intellectual identity and performance. *American Psychologist, 52*(6), 613–629.

Thompson, C. E., Worthington, R., & Atkinson, D. R. (1994). Counselor content orientation, counselor race, and Black women's cultural mistrust and self-disclosures. *Journal of Counseling Psychology, 41*(2), 155–161.

Trent, M., Dooley, D. G., & Dougé, J. (2019). The impact of racism on child and adolescent health. *Pediatrics, 144*(2), e20191765. https://doi.org/10.1542/peds.2019-1765

Van Ausdale, D., & Feagin, J. R. (2001). *The first R: How children learn race and racism.* Rowman & Littlefield.

Washington, A. R., & Henfield, M. S. (2019). What do the AMCD multicultural and social justice counseling competencies mean in the context of Black Lives Matter? *Journal of Multicultural Counseling and Development, 47*(3), 148–160. https://doi.org/10.1002/jmcd.12138

Washington, H. A. (2006). *Medical apartheid: The dark history of medical experimentation on Black Americans from colonial times to the present.* Anchor.

Washington, H. A. (2019). *A terrible thing to waste: Environmental racism and its assault on the American mind*. Little, Brown Spark.

Welsing, F. C. (1991). *The Isis papers: The keys to the colors*. Third World Press.

Wilder, C. S. (2013). *Ebony and ivy: Race, slavery, and the troubled history of America's universities*. Bloomsbury Press.

Wilkerson, I. (2020). *Caste: The origins of our discontents*. Random House.

Wise, V., & Day-Vines, N. L. (2020, June 22). What do we do now about racism? *Independent Ideas Blog, National Association of Independent Schools*. https://www.nais.org/learn/independent-ideas/june-2020/what-do-we-do-now-about-racism/

CHAPTER 4

Proactively Addressing Racial Incidents in Schools: Two Perspectives

Derek Francis and Erin Mason

A 2019 report by the Southern Poverty Law Center, *Hate at School*, summarizes findings from 821 media stories in 2018 and a survey of 2,776 K–12 U.S. educators related to school-based hate incidents. The educators who participated reported 3,265 hate incidents in their schools for the fall of 2018. Racism accounted for 63% of media-reported events and 33% of educator-reported events—more than any other category of hate incidents. This statistic might seem surprising when we consider that in 2008 the United States elected its first African American president. Some felt that Barack Obama's inauguration was a sign that our country welcomed and celebrated diversity. We may even have dared to think that Martin Luther King Jr.'s dream was coming to fruition. However, the ensuing years have proved that hatred, bigotry, and racism are still a part of the fabric of our country, and work still lies ahead as hate crimes, prejudice, discrimination, and violence have escalated in our schools.

Responding to racial incidents in schools begins with considering how race is conceptualized and treated as a topic in general. If schools aid in cognitive and social development, they can also promote racial and ethnic identity development. The school years hold prime opportunities for all children to develop a critical awareness of identity and social consciousness. Multiple scholars (Corenblum & Armstrong, 2012; Gonzalez et al., 2020; Pica-Smith & Poynton, 2015; Rivas-Drake et al., 2017) have demonstrated that this is especially important for children from traditionally marginalized groups. The practice of providing space for youth to explore their racial and ethnic identities with thoughtful educators can lead to more positive interactions between and across various racial and ethnic groups (Rivas-Drake & Umaña-Taylor, 2019a).

School counselors must be at the forefront of this practice of providing such spaces for students. School counselors are charged to create school environments in which racially diverse students have their identities validated, learn about the history of racism in the United States, and gain skills to navigate the world and their future based on their identities. We believe school counselors must be committed and proactive to create antiracist school environments that ensure that racially diverse students feel welcomed, included, and—most important—that they matter!

In this chapter, we share our perspectives and insights on creating antiracist learning environments and, more important, how to respond to racial incidents in schools. Representing diverse lived experiences, we reflect on our own internal dialogues because we believe school counselors must explore their thoughts and biases. Counselors must be able to communicate with students as compassionate, culturally competent, and antiracist adults. We also provide recommendations for every level of programming.

Throughout we highlight many scholars and writers, many of whom represent racial diversity. We do this purposefully and intentionally (a) to immerse ourselves in the work of authors of color to ground ourselves during the writing process, (b) to ensure you are aware of their work and its practical applications, and (c) to model the importance of shifting away from the dominant white voices that often permeate our literature.

Our Positionality

As coauthors, we present our varied perspectives. Most notable is that some school counselors of color may resonate with Derek's messaging and experiences as an African American, whereas some white school counselors may connect with Erin's views. We provide male and female counterpoints as well. On both race and gender, where school counseling as a profession is concerned, Derek's points are essential to elevate, but many readers may represent more like Erin. The school counseling profession is still primarily populated by white (76%) women (85%), according to demographics from the American School Counselor Association (ASCA, 2020). Below are each of our views on 2020, in particular the racial events involving the killing of unarmed Black men and women.

Derek's Message

Events of 2020, including the murders of Breonna Taylor, Ahmaud Arbery, and, in my hometown of Minneapolis, Minnesota, George Perry Floyd, revealed a horrifying truth about the state of race relations in our country. Here this was in my city, on my streets, and I thought to myself, "That could have so easily been me or someone in my family or one of my students." I could feel and hear the pain of the people marching beside me. The title of an article by Carvelle Wallace (2017), a *New York Times* best selling author, rang true: "If you are Black in America, riots are a spiritual impulse, not a political strategy." George Floyd's murder caused me to feel completely depleted and enraged that this was still occurring in our society, in plain sight, and conviction in my heart began to hit me. With advancements in technology, racism now gets exposed live. America did not begin to reckon with its racism until black-and-white videos showing white police officers beating Black people to a pulp while at diners and voting stations were released. And in May 2020, a brave Minneapolis teenager brought us back to those same images of brutality.

According to 2020 U.S. Census data, Minneapolis's population is 63.6% white followed by 19.2% Black, the second-highest percentage of the population (U.S. Census Bureau, n.d.). Minnesota is 83% white, followed by 7% Black. I hope this puts into perspective why it is alarming that in the Twin Cities metro area, three out of the four most recent police shootings have involved unarmed Black men. I tend to be the only Black person among my professional colleagues, in family settings, and in my community; thus, navigating the discomfort of talking about race is something I have learned to endure. During the novel coronavirus COVID-19 pandemic, George Floyd's murder left no escape from having difficult conversations and brought the pain of our country's racism to the forefront of my day-to-day interactions.

Whether it was slavery, Jim Crow, health, or housing disparities, Black lives have historically not mattered as much as the lives of whites. The 2016 and 2020 presidential elections shed light on the pervasiveness of racism. Schools across the country saw an increase in hate speech and chants of "Build the Wall" and "White Power." If I felt the effects of racism in my personal life and relationships, I could not imagine the toll current events were taking on my students, in particular Black, Brown, and Indigenous students. Racism continues to happen in our communities and schools and impacts children's ability to learn. Racism affects how students achieve because it impacts them socially and emotionally. I believe that as school counselors we have a duty to our students to make them feel safe and seen and celebrated so they can focus on achieving their most significant and most ambitious dreams.

Erin's Perspective

I am grateful to Derek for the opportunity to contribute to this work and to learn from him. When he asked me to collaborate on this chapter I sought to understand his experiences as an African American man in Minneapolis at the time of Floyd's killing and as a school counseling director who had to consider the impact of such an event on local schools and the community. Ahmaud Arbery was killed several months before Floyd near a town in South Georgia with which I am familiar. Rayshard Brooks was killed a few weeks after Floyd about 10 miles southeast of where I live in Atlanta. Breonna Taylor could easily have been one of my graduate students. I was sad, angry, and activated, but my experience could in no way compare to Derek's or that of others who are Black. So I sought out more conversations about race, racism, and antiracism in school counseling with new and familiar colleagues and renewed my belief that our profession as a whole can be an agent of change.

I bear in mind the personal racial privilege I have had during my lifetime as well as the history of racial privilege that exists through my American and Eurocentric lineage. I also have economic, linguistic, sexual orientation, and gender identity privileges. My status as a professor, my college education, and my 26 years in school counseling are privileges that allow me to influence the profession. Any transparency about my own experiences, I hope, will be helpful, especially to those who may relate and seek a path to raising their consciousness and that in their schools.

As a white woman, I must do more to prepare antiracist school counselors by continuing to challenge my own biases and taking action. Beloved friends and colleagues of all races point out blind spots in my words, actions, and writing. When posting or wearing images related to human rights, like a Black Lives Matter shirt, I am sometimes cited for virtue signaling and performative behavior. When this happens, I reflect, consult with others, process in counseling, make corrections, and then get back to work. At this point in my career, I can say I have been a good school counselor and counselor educator, and I would have been better had I known much of what is in this chapter. Fortunately, it is never too late for each of us to grow, learn, and be a part of the change.

Rethinking the School Counselor's Role

To think of ourselves as proactive and antiracist, we must rethink our role as school counselors. We must fight the narrative of the passive, reactive guidance counselor who perpetuates white supremacist norms of education that advantage some students over others. We must take on an active and visible leadership role amid sometimes tense and even toxic racialized cultures within our schools.

During the summer of 2020, ASCA (n.d.) issued a Standards in Practice document, *Eliminating Racism and Bias in Schools: The School Counselor's Role*. The document states, "Through implementation of a school counseling program, school counselors promote equity and access for all students and make a significant impact on creating a school culture free from racism and bias" (p. 1). ASCA, and our profession as a whole, have historically taken a passive stance on issues like racism. Where Derek lives this is called, "Minnesota Nice" and we need to confront it in ourselves, in our schools, and especially with each other. In order to create spaces free from racism in school, school counselors must actively condemn the pattern of hate and bias that disrupt schools and communities.

Activist Angela Davis gives the charge "in a racist society it is not enough to be nonracist, we must be antiracist." The modern day school counselor must shift *now* from being just a peacekeeper to being a justice-seeker. The ASCA Standards in Practice on *Critical Race Theory* (September 2021) state "school counselors work toward cultural competence and engage in anti-racist actions by advocating to change racist policies, procedures, practices, guidelines and laws contributing to inequities in students' academic, career and social/emotional development (p. 2). Regardless of who tells us this work must be done, it is not easy work, but it must be at the very core of who we are as school counselors for the sake of all our students.

We have to consider ourselves healers during this time; our students need us to lead in the restoration of their spirits so they too can emerge into the world as agents of change. We cannot shy away from uncomfortable conversations about race. These conversations are too important. Race impacts how we navigate the world socially and emotionally, and to avoid this topic is negligent. New documents and updates to existing documents are progress in ASCA's attempts to be proactive, but they are not enough. Our national association must clearly articulate that school counselors work from an antiracist stance to actively dismantle the systemic racism in schools. School counselors must take ownership in healing our country's racial divide.

Derek's Perspective

Just because George Floyd was not killed by police officers in your city does not mean the emotional impact will not hit your students, in particular Black and Brown students. At the time of George Floyd's death, the world had changed drastically because of the COVID-19 pandemic. Movie theaters and restaurants were closed, LeBron James and Anthony Davis were not on TV dominating, March Madness and the Olympics had been canceled. TV viewership had increased dramatically across the country, so there was no escaping the news of George Floyd's murder. Colleagues from around Minnesota reached out to me, letting me know how sorry they were this had happened in Minneapolis. When I asked how they planned to discuss the event with their students, none had a plan to provide support or knew how. I received just as many calls from colleagues asking me to help them with how to respond to their students. This response left me feeling angry and opened my eyes to a lack of preparation and education in my school counseling field and possibly a lack of understanding of the impact that watching a Black man being murdered by the police has on students, in particular Black and Brown students. School counselors need to have difficult and emotionally gutting conversations about racism, oppression, privilege, and action, and they need to acknowledge the feelings and experiences of Black and Brown students.

If you choose to accept your role as a change agent, please buckle up and read on because this chapter is for those who are ready to begin now.

The remainder of this chapter focuses on the following:

- The nature of racial incidents in schools
- The emotional impact of racial incidents on students and school staff
- Proactive strategies for school counselors
- Students and schools: tiered options and more
- Staff: calling in, calling out, and more
- Self: cultural humility

The Nature of Racial Incidents in Schools

A brief review of historical racism in schools is essential because it helps us understand the magnitude of the job ahead. Dismantling systemic racism is daunting but imperative as we work to build a future in which equity and opportunity exist as a norm rather than an anomaly. Throughout our history, racism has been an oppressive force impacting the educational system and the educational outcomes of students of different racial backgrounds. Our country's history of slavery and systemic racism affects how schools and communities interact with each other socially today. The Southern Poverty Law Center reported in 2018 that 10% of high school seniors did not know that slavery was the reason for the Civil War. This statistic reveals that many of our schools omit crucial history, which has shaped our country and our schools' race relations.

Racism has undergone mutations within our society. Slavery mutated into separate but equal, which mutated again into housing restrictions, which mutated into the school-to-prison pipeline, which mutated again into police brutality, which mutated again into "Make America Great Again." To bring awareness to how racism has mutated and continued to thrive, we must teach our history with truth and compassion. Furthermore, teaching slavery must include drawing the long, full arc of the oppression of people of color for centuries into the current times so students understand how its vestiges still manifest in contemporary society. These manifestations include the school-to-prison pipeline and the mass incarceration of Black men (Alexander, 2010).

We also cannot assume that conversations about race and racism happen in students' homes and communities. When was the first time you were aware of or had a conversation about your racial/ethnic identity? Were you explicitly taught what racism is, how it plays out in our day-to-day lives, and how to speak up against it? If a family member says something racist or discriminatory at dinner, does anyone say anything, or is there just awkward silence? Have you built authentic cross-cultural relationships with people of color to understand racism experienced daily, sometimes even by you? We recommend that school counselors, our primary audience, make sure they are well educated about the history of racism and act as change agents to encourage accurate teaching of the history of racism in their schools. See the "Additional Resources" section at the end of this chapter for teaching resources.

Derek's Perspective

My parents talked about race and ethnicity as far back as I can remember. My mom was born and grew up in Liberia and immersed me in the culture and tradition from birth. My dad was born in the small town of Exmore, Virginia, then moved to Long Island, New York. Most early conversations about race happened while I was watching my parents blend American culture and Liberian culture. We would talk about the differences between Liberian family functions and American cultural events. Even though my parents grew up in different parts of the world, they were unified in their openness to addressing race and culture. Their strong faith in God guided their hearts for teaching me how we should treat people. Growing up, my brothers and I were told, "Treat everyone equal. If people are racist to you tell us, don't get upset. You will face racism as Black children, but know that there's nothing wrong with who you are." When we experienced racism in school my parents would talk to us about what had happened. My mom continues to help me learn about my ethnic and racial identity by visiting spaces in Liberia where her family lived and in South Carolina where our family members were slaves.

As a parent, I am intentional about raising my biracial daughter in an environment that is diverse and respectful of people from all backgrounds. My daughter's mother and her family had a much different pattern around the topic of race. I was the first and only person of color within their extended family, and I picked up through dinner table conversations racist comments that would be said and not addressed. I recall the discomfort of watching a basketball game with my then in-laws. One of the basketball players had a traditional Nigerian name, and I would sit silently and endure hearing extended family members making fun of the name and saying it was "made up."

Having difficult conversations in the family is a part of my values. As I think about my daughter's race and ethnic development, I know the messaging she hears about people of different backgrounds will have a huge impact on her. Commitment to addressing racism cannot just be a professional thing; it is personal for me. As a person of color I believe these hard conversations are interconnected in all aspects of our lives. There is no off switch. Reflecting on my personal history as an African American allows me to understand what has contributed to my identity and helped me to succeed despite inequities in our society. Having cross-cultural friendships changed my life. Neither of my parents had any close friends of different races, but they always encouraged us to be open to befriending kids of other races. My parents were aware of the transition to our new, less diverse suburban environment and would sometimes say, "You will have to work twice as hard and keep out of trouble." Like most Black kids, I got The Talk quite often.

I have enjoyed sharing my whole racial and cultural self with those in my life. I find joy in understanding others' cultures and hardships and having more humility and empathy. Research supports the benefits of cross-cultural friendships (Rivas-Drake et al., 2017). It is not enough to just be together in diverse schools; we must get to know one another as well. Getting to know one another allows for the formation of authentic relationships. Often children leave our educational system with the same or even more bias than they had when they entered our schools.

In second grade, my family moved from a two-bedroom apartment in South Minneapolis—which at the time was very diverse, with Hmong, Somali, and Latinx families making up a large percentage of the student body—to Brooklyn Park, a suburb with schools that were 80% white. I had some fears and insecurities that I still battle today, such as, Will anyone want to be my friend? Will they be afraid of me? Will I be the only Black boy? Will the teachers be nice to me? Some of those fears come from stereotypes I had about predominantly white suburban areas. My dad worked in nursing with a colleague who lived on the same block as our new house. She had a son named Brandon who was in my grade and was white. When I met him, he helped me feel comfortable, like I was not alone. He seemed to see my humanity, himself in me. Brandon became the first person of another race I could have authentic conversations with about race. I remember leaving a Boy Scout meeting at one of the den leaders' homes, and Brandon and I both noticed that the den leader had been treating me differently from the other children. On our walk home I shared with Brandon how uncomfortable I felt, and he listened, affirmed that he had noticed too, and supported me by saying it was not right. We would go on to be friends throughout high school, through college, and now as fathers.

School counselors are positioned to teach youth antiracism skills of speaking up, empathy, reporting, and changed behavior. Youth see racism happening daily and need these essential interpersonal skills. As school counselors, we foster these relationships by helping students find a sense of pride in who they are racially and culturally. We also need to help shift the negative perception of talking about race, ethnicity, and culture. We must help students unlearn the negative stereotypes they may have learned from home, news, or social media. Not just students, but families and community members need to have real conversations about the racism in their community. How many other children did that den leader impact? How can the Boy Scouts and other organizations address racism in adults and make changes? How can we normalize, or even create excitement around, students learning more about people from different backgrounds? Our country's racial climate hinges on this. Racial unity among all people is central to our calling as school counselors.

The Emotional Impact of Racial Incidents in Schools

Students of color experience "spirit murdering" (Love, 2016, p. 22), a form of racial violence that kills their humanity and steals their sense of self-worth. In the wake of George Floyd's murder and the resulting protests, we saw the role schools play in spirit murdering and its widespread effect. Black students turned to social media to share their pain and the racism they endured in schools. Early Instagram accounts included Black@Chapin and Black@Brearley. Many "Black at" accounts continue to document student and alumni experiences of racist treatment by other students, staff, or parents as well as the lack of accountability on the part of schools in addressing such incidents in both K–12 and higher education settings across the country. These accounts describe some schools' decades of cultures of normalizing racism and white supremacy (O'Kane & Wilson, 2020). Private schools are highlighted in these accounts, including Benilde-St. Margaret's in Minneapolis. Current and former students criticized the Benilde-St. Margaret administration for not taking an urgent stance on Floyd's killing or supporting its Black students and, during the summer of 2020, for promising listening sessions that never transpired (thepinkreportnews, 2020). Through systemic change and early antiracist efforts, our country has the hope to heal its ongoing transgressions with racism.

The emotional impact of racial incidents in schools is lasting. Students of color frequently experience race-related trauma and stress in their daily lives, which leads to lifetime battles with anger, anxiety, and depression, among other mental health concerns (Anderson et al., 2019). Schools then perpetuate and exacerbate this trauma by replicating racism in society at large. Some examples of this include instances when schools disproportionately discipline students of color over other students, when hate speech and symbols are allowed to be displayed, or when racial slurs in literature are read aloud in the classroom (Essien, 2020; Gaffney, 2019; Jernigan & Daniel, 2011).

Derek's Perspective

I spent my first 4 years as a school counselor at North High in Minneapolis. Because of declining enrollment and a myriad of other factors beyond the scope of this book, North High had a 44% graduation rate and was on the brink of closing. We had amazing teachers from around the district and a strong African American principal who pushed us. After 4 years, we were able to increase the graduation rate to around 89%. Because of the rich Black history in the community, Black students felt comfortable being themselves. Passing time and eating lunch felt like being at a family get-together. Students at North and later Champlin Park made me aware that racial incidents occurred in the school and that more needed to be done. This was not just a school issue but a statewide one. "Minnesota nice" was a term used to describe the social climate, and this niceness often left no room for topics like race. Conversations about race were often avoided, especially in mixed-race spaces, to retain a polite, friendly, peaceful, and extremely conflict-avoidant and change-resistant social environment.

Students of color are aware of the often traumatic racial climate in Minnesota schools. Amid the social unrest in the summer of 2020, hundreds of stories emerged from current and former students detailing "acts of racism and discrimination, exposing a culture in the Minnesota education system that students say often disregards or gaslights concerns from students of color" (Most, 2020, para. 4). A Google search for racial incidents in Minnesota displays a long list of xenophobic, racist, homophobic, and anti-immigration acts within K–12 schools. Chaska High School had five racial incidents, including multiple blackface postings in the yearbook, on social media, and at a football game.

Transitioning from an urban, predominantly Black school to a suburban school like Champlin Park in Anoka-Hennepin was significant for my counseling career and racial identity. I had graduated from Champlin Park and had spent some time there as an intern. Many of the building staff when I was a student were still there and became my coworkers. I was even working with the counselor I had had as a student. This dualism was unique, in particular because I had changed since high school. As a student, I followed the rules, did well in school (3.8 grade point average), participated in varsity basketball, and socialized with many students and staff. Very rarely in high school did I have conversations about race with the staff. In the years leading up to my time as a counselor at Champlin Park, acts of racism and discrimination had increased throughout the district. In March 2012, the Office for Civil Rights and U.S. Department of Justice investigated Anoka-Hennepin's school district, which resulted in a consent decree in which the district agreed to take action around sex-based harassment and other forms of harassment and to meet with an equity consultant (Office for Civil Rights, 2020). In my time as a student, intern, and school counselor at Champlin Park, I did experience moments of intentional, authentic conversation about race with students and staff. Still, there were many times when racism played out systemically or interpersonally, and many staff went silent.

Going from Minneapolis to Anoka-Hennepin looks different when you are a person of color in school counseling. Minneapolis is the third largest district in Minnesota, and about one third of the department is made up of counselors of color. In Anoka-Hennepin, the state's largest school district, I was the only full-time school counselor of color. I cannot stress enough that systemic racism in hiring practices must be addressed. Within my first year back in Minneapolis Public Schools, we hired five counselors of color while Anoka-Hennepin did not hire any. Candidates of color whom we would have loved to hire in Minneapolis had positions been available were not invited to interviews.

When I arrived at Champlin Park as a school counselor, students and staff made me very aware of my presence in the building. I was one of two African American educators out of a staff of 150. I stand at 6 feet 4 inches, most days I have earrings in, on Fridays I am in Nike Air Forces or Air Maxes, and my arms are tatted. Not a week went by the first year when a student did not ask whether I was security, a custodian, a para, or a coach. Building relationships with students and helping them see themselves and their potential is my passion in life. In every school in which I have worked, I have made it a point to know the students I serve. Food, music, sports, race, and culture are topics I engage with students on the most. I have dunked on students, showed students how to fry chicken, and engaged in conversations about what their parents taught them about Black people. As my students would say, "Mr. Francis is a whole vibe."

Within my first couple days as a school counselor at Champlin Park, I could feel the racial tension in the atmosphere. I had navigated spaces as one of few people of color, but this was different because I had many students of all races in the building who were mature enough to understand and vocalize the racism they witnessed or experienced. I remember seeing the faces of Black students when they found out I was their counselor. There was an unspoken sense of comfort, trust, an affinity that came naturally. The boys of color in particular gave me a natural respect that I relished and honored. Students, staff, and families listened when I spoke up. I imagine many had never had an African American man in a position of authority in education. I never turned away students who wanted to connect with me but were assigned to a different counselor.

Sports was a massive part of the school culture at Champlin Park. With a student body of 3,000, varsity sporting events felt like college game day. Basketball, football, and volleyball were competitive and ranked statewide annually. The volleyball team wrapped up a regular season with a 10–2 record and qualified for the state tournament, and on the bus ride home from the win spirits were high and the team was singing along to hip-hop music. What took place on this bus ride would change the tone of the entire school year. One white girl said the N-word within a song's lyrics repeatedly while her white friend recorded her. The video was uploaded to social media, and the news spread like wildfire. One student of color posted online immediately, saying, "Wow, this is so messed up!" Another posted, "Take this down, look at this!?!" Local news outlets began to hear about the incident, and the coverage began. In a previous book, *Contemporary Case Studies in School Counseling*, I shared details of students' emotions in the days after the post: "Adding to the tension in the building, racial slurs stating, 'I hate Black people,' appeared in three bathroom stalls, and on social media, offensive remarks popped up: 'We brought you here. Without us, you wouldn't be anything.'" (Ohrtman & Heltner, 2019, p.35)

Students of color shared their rage, heartbreak, fear, and betrayal with me, and I felt these same emotions alongside them. I remember several students stopping by that following Monday to ask whether I had heard about what happened. Many students, especially students of color, were not surprised that the consequences were minimal. They shared that microaggressions had been frequent up until this point with no consequences. I began to hear more and more expressions of anger from students of color. One of my students of color who sat right next to a student who had made racist comments on social media shared how challenging it was for her to focus in class knowing that students felt that way about people who looked like her. Several students opened up about fighting the urge to retaliate against the students because they were so hurt. Our school community was hurting.

The game had been on a Tuesday, and by Thursday the climate in the high school was toxic and the student body had become divided. The privilege of the volleyball student athlete became apparent as things unfolded. There was an unspoken sense of protection by school leaders of these student athletes. These incidents were not new to the school; this one was just so direct and public that you could not ignore it. Some students had built-up resentment and anger toward the girls' volleyball team. On one side of the issue were students and staff who empathized with the two white students; these folks questioned the consequences assigned to the girls, arguing that the intent was not to offend—rather, the girls were just having fun. On the other side, many people felt the incident required a response that included mediation, restorative justice, and education surrounding race relations. More than 200 students of all races at the high school organized a peaceful protest and walkout. Students wanted to raise awareness of racism and discrimination at the school; they wanted their feelings and emotions to be heard and proposed more education and open dialogue about race relations at the high school and in the community.

My own emotions were a rollercoaster that week. This ended up being one of the toughest moments of my career. I struggled to feel supported by my white coworkers who could not understand, relate to, or validate the pains of racism in the building. There were moments when parents who did not know I was African American called to discuss their anger at how African American students were disrupting the school and because of "their behavior" parents were considering transferring their students to another district where "this type of behavior isn't tolerated." I did not realize how hard the racism from this experience had hit me until months later. I struggled with self-confidence and considered leaving the school counseling profession.

Being a school counselor or educator of color is rewarding but a burden. When I graduated from the University of Minnesota in 2012, I was one of two Black students in the school counseling track and knew of two Black male school counselors in the state. The amount of direct racism I experienced from past-presidents and board members as perhaps the first Black man on the board of the Minnesota School Counselors Association still hurts today. For several years the Minnesota School Counselors Association had a lobbyist who also had an interest in supporting a local county in creating private prisons. Several board and association members attempted to educate the government relations team and sitting president about the harmful impact of private prisons and argued that we should avoid partnering with him. I shared with association leaders how I had been pulled over more than 20 times in the past 5 years and noted that policing in Minneapolis was problematic. We shared students' stories of being racially profiled. Our voices were ignored, and hundreds of counselors left the association. Hearing the voices of counselors of color is crucial for the development of our field. The isolation, the feeling of being a token, and the feeling of not being fully respected as an equal contributor in that space get emotionally tiring.

I knew I could not tread lightly around racism in schools if I remained a school counselor. Educators must develop empathy and compassion for marginalized students in their buildings. No longer can you just enjoy being in proximity to students of color without knowing the full context of what they have experienced. If you are going to celebrate students of color on the football field, in the choir, or at homecoming, then you need to be attentive to the emotional stressors of racism in your building. The racial incident on the bus led to opportunities to talk about race with students and families on a deeper level. I became more vulnerable about what I had experienced personally, and students opened up as well. I needed the students to know that I was human, African American, and a real person who could relate to their feelings.

The best mentor and colleague I have had the opportunity to work with is Jim Bierma. Several times I considered a career change, and Jim helped me rediscover my passion for school counseling. In 2019, I decided to take my talents back to Minneapolis Public Schools as district lead counselor and 6 months later transitioned into being manager of counseling. As manager of counseling services, I lead monthly professional developments addressing staff bias, privilege, and microaggressions. Preparing for and responding to racial incidents has helped our counselors be proactive rather than reactive when incidents occur. When the emotional response to the murder of George Floyd erupted, school counselors led virtual and small-group meetings for students to process what they were seeing, hearing, and feeling as the events unfolded. The counselors in Minneapolis Public Schools feel like family, and I am so happy to be a part of this team.

Strategies for Students and Schools: Tiered Options and More

"Where do we start?" This is a question we both often hear from school counselors who want to be instrumental in addressing racial incidents in their schools. The starting point is not the same for every school because the racial climate of each setting is unique. It is ideal to start from a proactive position before an incident occurs. Often, however, this is not the way things happen, and an incident becomes the opportunity for change, as was the case for Derek at Champlin Park. Here we tackle what we think are the two most challenging starting points for many school counselors.

Responding at the Point of Incident

School counselors may feel ill equipped to know how to handle one of the most critical points in a racial incident, the point of crisis, as the incident is happening and just afterward. Incidents often happen in public spaces (e.g., buses, busy hallways, full classrooms) and may involve multiple parties. Plan how you will respond and discuss your plans with your supervisor and your coworkers. Learning for Justice (2017) has a full curriculum titled Responding to Hate and Bias at School that Derek has worked from and that we suggest you explore. For the crisis phase these nine recommendations are made:

1. Put safety first
2. Denounce the act
3. Investigate
4. Involve others
5. Work with the media
6. Provide accurate information—and dispel misinformation
7. Seek justice, avoid blame
8. Support targeted students
9. Promote healing (Learning for Justice, 2017, p. 16)

Although school counselors may be apprehensive, they have relevant skills in counseling, collaboration, and leadership to respond in this phase. Calming and de-escalation techniques as well as validation and active listening are very useful. It will be necessary to leave some tasks, such as investigating and working with the media, to the administration and district staff in disciplinary roles but provide consultation. Most important, school counselors must take an antiracist stance, not a neutral one, so the message is clear that racism is never acceptable.

Advocating for Policy Change

On the other end of the spectrum of responding at the point of incident is the need to advocate for policy change so there are more equitable outcomes in the long run. This is another area in which school counselors may feel less prepared and in which ethically they cannot take a neutral stance. Despite heightened national attention on racial injustice, a recent survey from ASCA (2021) showed that only 22% of respondents indicated they were taking action to address racially discriminatory policies or using data to challenge course enrollment patterns (p. 12). On the whole, the report demonstrated that school counselors are doing more to address racism among students (e.g., monitoring of behavior, classroom lessons, individual counseling) than they are to address institutional racism (e.g., policies, staff). We have not evolved our practice to create safe school climates for students of color. For there to be any progress school counselors have to retool.

Recommendations

1. Allocate more program time to reviewing and revising policies that may be racist, inequitable, or noninclusive.
2. Seek out in-school antiracist allies and community members to join your advocacy efforts.
3. Conduct focus groups with students to better understand issues beyond quantitative data.
4. Propose policy changes backed by data, starting with your administration.

School-Wide and Classroom Strategies

One way to reduce racism in schools is to normalize conversations about race throughout the school. This practice begins with your counseling office and district-level team agreeing to hold space for race-related issues. When going through the student handbook at the beginning of the school year, be specific about what racism looks and sounds like in school. Schools tend to have a racial climate in which students know the specific spaces (e.g., unmonitored stairwells, unsupervised passing times) and people (e.g., disengaged faculty, staff with a color-blind mentality) that allow for racist comments. Social media and other technology now double as platforms for students to carry out racism. Counteract these negative spaces by providing regular opportunities for students to discuss race with caring, justice-oriented adults in the school.

Erin's Perspective

The middle of my career coincided with 9/11. This historic time in our country shook the general sense of security many Americans had and challenged our Western privilege. The time was novel and extreme, and I recall many ethnic, racial, and xenophobic incidents at my school. I leaned into my multicultural training, did what I knew how to do to support the few Muslim and Middle Eastern students we had who were targeted, and researched and shared anything I could find with staff. The most intense work I did was in the classroom addressing students' unfounded fears and suspicions based on multiple factors, including race. I borrowed from a packaged Facing History and Ourselves curriculum at the time, but now there is a fully expanded website with an abundance of resources (see "Additional Resources").

Using Classroom Lessons to Explore Racial Identity

In Minneapolis Public Schools, counselors lead lessons in sixth through 12th grades, helping students share their social identity, hear about others' social identity, and look for similarities and differences. Racial and ethnic groups that have historically been portrayed from a deficit standpoint must be represented from a nonbiased perspective. Do not just talk about slavery or the struggle to end segregation. Educate students on the inventors, doctors, teachers, politicians, and other strong leaders who went before them. Provide context for students on the strength of the people who share their racial and ethnic lineage. Counselors should deliver antiracist lessons throughout the year, providing strategies for speaking up when they see discrimination.

Matthew R. Kay, an educator and public speaker, developed a framework for having conversations about race in schools that he outlined in his book *Not Light, but Fire* (Kay, 2018). Kay's (2018) framework encourages educators to create space for students to learn how to have healthy dialogue: "Dialogic pedagogy disrupts the traditional classroom power dynamic, positioning school as a place where students have an equal share in their education" (p. 5). Children need spaces to learn about the emotional impact of hurtful words and build empathy for classmates of all backgrounds. If your school has an advisory program, have at least monthly lessons that provide proactive skills for creating a healthy cross-cultural climate.

As another example, Rivas-Drake and Umaña-Taylor (2019b) implemented the Identity Project, a 12-week classroom-based project during which high school students explored their own ethnic and racial identities with the facilitation of a teacher. There were no differences between the experimental and control groups on surveys related to ethnic and racial identity at the beginning of the study. However, 6 weeks after the study, students in the experimental group scored significantly higher than students in the control group on understanding their ethnic and racial backgrounds—this was the case for students of color and white students. Most impressive is that surveys conducted a full year after the study showed statistically significant increases in identity development for students who participated in the project and significant increases in grades and self-esteem and decreases in depression.

Minneapolis Public Schools is proactive in social-emotional development by requiring an Ethnic Studies class for graduation. Part of the course curriculum focuses on ethnic/racial identity development because children's perception of their racial identity impacts their academic and career outlook. This work does not have to wait until kids get to school. Parents are the initial influencers of their children's racial/ethnic lens, and school counselors at *every* level have a role to play. According to Umaña-Taylor et al. (2014), children follow an ethnic and racial identity development trajectory with cognitive milestones shaped by their social and environmental contexts. Early childhood is when children pick up on ethnic and racial labeling, whereas middle childhood is the phase when an awareness of bias is most likely to emerge. The nature of adolescent development is that more negotiating of identity and self with the world can present itself at school and in society (Umaña-Taylor et al., 2014). Therefore, elementary counselors need to take a preventive approach and begin correcting social behaviors that reenact early racist and biased beliefs and creating school cultures that value diversity. However, data from the Southern Poverty Law Center (2018) indicate that high schools and middle schools account for the majority of hate-based incidents in schools, 37% and 27%, respectively. So middle and high school counselors must be able to intervene directly in racial incidents in addition to doing prevention and postvention work.

Prepping Students for Responses to Racial Incidents

At the beginning of the year, highlight the fact that if there is a racial incident at school a planned process will occur, and racism will not be tolerated. When racist incidents happen at school it is essential to have a plan for responding. These are opportunities to show the importance of our role as school counselors. Dialogue with students on race needs to be ongoing in schools, and being able to discuss race and racism should be a *minimum* requirement for school counselors. We urge district leaders to prepare for racial incidents like they would for a fire drill. Be proactive and hopefully nothing will happen. The point of incident was covered earlier, but we encourage you to see the other sections of Learning for Justice's (2017) Responding to Hate and Bias at School curriculum for how to assess a school's culture ahead of potential incidents and how to respond after an incident has occurred.

Recommendations

1. Normalize and encourage discussions of race and racial and ethnic identity school-wide.
2. Involve students in planning activities designed for discussions of race, identity development, and consciousness-raising.
3. Thoughtfully integrate discussions of race into learning experiences across a range of subjects through interdisciplinary exercises.

Small-Group Strategies

Derek's Perspective

Small groups can be very effective for building multicultural relationships in schools and reducing racism. For some students, a smaller setting is needed to learn and be vulnerable talking about race. Create small groups that provide an opportunity for students to be in spaces with kids from different backgrounds. When I coached basketball and led food clubs after school, there were natural moments when we had conversations about what it meant to be inclusive. Often small groups are used to help students find racial or ethnic affinity. For instance, high schools and colleges have Black student unions or Asian student associations. When led by staff with a common racial or ethnic identity, these spaces are sometimes the only safe places students of color can open up and receive acknowledgment of the microaggressions and bias they experience daily. Small-group spaces help students realize they are not alone in their feelings, not the only ones. Someone else in their building understands. That is powerful. Students must be able to express their full range of emotions after racial incidents occur. When schools do not help students process racism, it leaves them to process some strong emotions independently. The racial incident that just occurred in your school might mark your first time addressing racism head on, but for some of your students it might be their third incident in school this year. I have been in small groups in which students get loud or even swear in authentic anger about the racism they have just experienced. Allow them to feel—do not stifle their emotions because you are uncomfortable. Those feelings let the unaddressed compound and carry on into adulthood.

In the days after the racist incident at Champlin Park, I began leading impromptu lunch groups in which students would come by and talk about what they were hearing on social media and in class. Students would crowd into my office and share what they thought should happen. One of the best small-group experiences I led was with three white female students after their friend posted a racist comment toward a Black student at school. The girls had many questions about why certain words could be said by some people and not others. They were curious about how hearing the N-word made me feel. I was curious about what messaging they had received from their parents about race. The most powerful part of the small-group space involved brainstorming strategies for how to correct errors. The girls encouraged their friend who had made the racist comment to push through her shame and make an apology.

Recommendations

1. Use small groups for affinity grouping by race to support affirmation, awareness, and growth.
2. Use a leader or coleader who matches the racial representation of the group members for emotional safety.
3. Remember that providing opportunities for students to openly discuss experiences with identity and race may be more useful than strictly following a curriculum.

Individual Counseling Strategies

Derek's Perspective

Talking about race one-on-one with students is a beautiful journey. I was intentional in looking for opportunities to talk with students about race, culture, and identity. I realized that I could leverage my presence so all students felt comfortable being vulnerable about race and racism. There was an unspoken understanding among my students of color that I could relate to their school experience. As you grow in your self-awareness, be mindful and become more comfortable connecting with students about their racial identity. How are you actively building relationships with students in your building who have been marginalized racially? How has racism impacted students and their families on a personal level? What traumas do they have from having previously been called the N-word at school? And when students of color transfer in, who helps them navigate the social isolation they may feel being in a space where their cultural and racial backgrounds are not reflected?

My approach to talking about race with students varied depending on the student's racial and cultural background. For most of my white students, I was the first person of color with whom they had ever had a conversation about race. When students made errors around race, I would offer grace when correcting them. Giving students skills to build empathy and humility is crucial. I would ask white students to consider what it would be like at a school where most teachers did not look like them. When racism happened to Black peers, I would provide strategies for white students to be allies and speak up.

My passion for addressing racism in schools really grew when I would meet with students of color in the days after major racist events. My presence to them represented safety, understanding, an advocate, someone who listened. Many times students came to me because other staff had dismissed their attempts get support. The students would usually share about previous times they had experienced racism or talks they had had at home. White educators can support students of color after they experience racism. Be honest with students about your own racial identity. Acknowledge that you may not fully understand how racism feels for them but that you want to support them. I want to encourage school counselors to stop and listen to students hurt from racism. Let them know that racism is wrong and that you see and value them. This will help students feel more connected and supported. Even just one staff person doing this check-in can make a difference.

Broaching Race With Students: Derek's Perspective

Broaching a challenging conversation about race with a student individually is committing to racial equity (Day-Vines et al., 2020). Early in my career, I found myself reserving conversations about race for students of color. The students of color, in most cases, had had more race conversations at home or in social spaces than school staff. Talking with white students about race meant I had to address my own internal biases. I avoided conversations with white students because I assumed they would say something messed up or turn it into an "ask a Black guy" session. But it is all about perspective. I would rather help a student work through a racist error than not engage in a conversation and miss a learning opportunity.

If communities are more racially diverse, this does not mean they are integrated. Communities need to be taught how to learn about people of different backgrounds. Researcher Deborah Plummer et al. found in a 2016 study that Asian, Hispanic, and multiracial participants were more likely to have cross-racial friendships than Black and white participants. They also found that social and historical context shaped the depth and breadth of cross-cultural friendships. Plummer (2019) published a book on her research and her personal experiences in which she offered recommendations for how to engage intentionally in cross-racial friendships. Educators must be intentional in creating cross-cultural learning opportunities for students and their families. I remember at Monroe Elementary School we did a cultural parade in which, with the help of your family, you decorated a wagon with your family's cultural or ethnic heritage. I remember how much my mom loved putting the decorations on the wagon!

Recommendations
1. Engage students in discussions of their race and ethnicity and learn what they value about their many identities.
2. Share any of your own identities and discuss how differences between you and your students can sometimes help (i.e., provide a different perspective) or get in the way (i.e., highlight power or privilege).

Strategies for Staff: Calling Out, Calling In, and More

School counselors also need to support the racial identity development and consciousness-raising of staff. The systemic racism baked into schools is not the fault of students; it is the outcome of decades of adult influence via state and federal legislation, school and district administration, local parent-teacher associations, community partners, families, and school staff. Racial identity development requires specific and curious attention (Singh, 2019). Those who appreciate an ecological systems perspective may understand racial incidents, which may be interpreted as problematic in schools, as feedback to the system that something needs to be addressed. The health and sustainability of a system are determined by how it makes meaning of the feedback it receives (McMahon et al., 2014). When it comes to making meaning, individual educators must consider how they make meaning of the feedback they receive just as much as schools do.

Calling Out and Calling In: Erin's Perspective

As a white woman from the South, I was raised in a culture that often valued courtesy and politeness, even if it might be mistaken for agreement. As a new school counselor, I found learning to advocate a bit counterintuitive. I taught myself that if I wanted to speak up, I had to start with raising my hand. Raising my hand in a meeting or classroom would hold me accountable for calling someone out and saying something like "Wait a minute. What are you saying here?" or "I need you to explain what you mean by that." Asserting myself, rather than staying in the background, is not always easy, but it is critical to ensuring an antiracist stance instead of a neutral one.

Calling others out is one strategy, but another is calling in. *The New York Times* did a feature on civil rights activist and professor Loretta Ross and her calling-in campaign (Bennett, 2020). Ross delineates calling in from calling out based largely on power differentials. Those in power need to be called out because they are responsible for oppressive decision-making and policies. However, calling in is for times when deeper, more intimate conversations need to be had to understand those with less power or cases when people may have equal power. Ross also published a 2019 article for *Teaching Tolerance* on the importance of using the calling-in strategy with students that can be used for training educators (see "Additional Resources").

Providing Training and Development

Authors such as Atkins and Oglesby (2019), in their book *Interrupting Racism: Equity and Social Justice in School Counseling*, propose that change must occur at the self, student, and staff level for systems-level shifts to begin to take place. The authors provided excellent case examples for discussion. Every school is its own microcosm, its own unique context, and each will be at a different starting point when it comes to exploring topics of race. Training on implicit bias is one place to start. Indeed, school counselors can provide professional development, but *only* if they have done their own work to identify and address their own biases. However, much of the research on training on diversity and implicit bias does not show it to be impactful over time. Instead, the focus of school staff should be on empathy training and strategies (e.g., slowing down, deep breathing) that help adults mitigate stress reactions when working with students (Sparks, 2020). Understanding racial bias intellectually does not do much good if school staff members do not know how to recognize it or what to do when it is creating relational damage.

One of the books we recommend for use with school staff is Anneliese Singh's (2019) *The Racial Healing Handbook: Practical Activities to Help You Challenge Privilege, Confront Systemic Racism and Engage in Collective Healing*. Singh's deep expertise is brilliantly accessible in this text, as is her genuine invitation to bring the reader into doing the work necessary to generate insight. She covers history, models, and provides graphics, reflection exercises, and suggested activities for both people of color and white people. The book is flexible enough to read from beginning to end or to start where your school staff is most ready.

Recommendations

1. Remember that school staff may be just as lacking in their racial identity development as students, so they can also benefit from activities that promote open discussions of racism as well as celebrations of diversity.
2. Plan ongoing and intentional professional development on antiracism designed to change school policies and staff behavior rather than one-off trainings.

Strategies for Self: Cultural Humility

In the process of writing this chapter, both of us frequently referred back to the significance of cultural humility as an integral part of our work in dealing with racial incidents as school counselors and of our work in our current roles. We believe cultural humility is at the heart of the internal ongoing work school counselors must do to main an antiracist stance.

Ongoing Self-Reflection: Derek's Perspective

One of the practices I have found to be useful in learning about others' racial and ethnic backgrounds is using cultural humility. The term first appeared in the medical field to help physicians learn more about patients and clients of different backgrounds. School counselors must foster an environment in which marginalized students can share the racism they experience in school.

Ongoing self-reflection is vital for practicing cultural humility. How do you see that person? You will need to examine the messaging you received about people of different backgrounds. We will never be experts in someone else's experience. Many people come in new to antiracism and social justice work with the passion and conviction to do something. To take a stand, you first need to take a seat and listen. A key component of growing in humility means_understanding your own identity, privileges, and biases and what identities hold power. Self-reflection involves being aware that you have been in spaces where someone, maybe even someone close to you, has said or done racist things and you have either been silent or turned the other way. You cannot wear a Black Lives Matter shirt to school on Friday and on Saturday be at a bonfire calmly eating s'mores while spewing racist comments.

I know sometimes we think of privilege only in terms of racial privilege, but as a straight, tall, handsome (my mom says so at least), cisgender, middle-aged man, my presence carries *tons* of privilege. There are things I never have to worry about that students and other colleagues think about daily. That privilege carries so much power in our broken world and can marginalize those without privilege. Male privilege hit me in my 20s while I was talking to female friends or work colleagues who would share stories of guys in college who did some horrible things to them and never owned up or apologized.

During my sixth year as a school counselor, I worked with a student for only 3 months but we bonded quickly. The student shared that he had come out to his friends as gay, and he planned to take a date to the upcoming school dance. The student initially was excited about the dance, but then in the week leading up to it his mood changed. The extraverted social butterfly that I am, I kept pointing out how exciting the dance would be and providing strategies for things they could do before the dance. I realized I was missing the mark in supporting this student from his body language. He was not as excited or engaged as when we talked about other things. I knew something was up, and it was something real. Finally, I asked with humility, "I want to understand better the stressors and struggles you experience socially and emotionally." I stumbled to get these words out, and the student asked me something I remember to this day: "Do you remember ever having to come out to your parents as straight? How long did it take you? Were you worried about introducing your prom date to your parents? How about holding hands or dancing with your date or taking pictures?" That student served me humble pie with whipped cream on top. All the moments I had shared that were exciting for me in my context were painful and took mental energy for the student. If this one student felt this way, others before him may have as well. Instead of always going to training sessions on race or college and career readiness, I opted for going to those on sexual and gender minority topics, reading more books, and playing bingo at local gay bars to grow in authentic relationships with sexual and gender minorities in my community.

Humility is that heart-centered commitment to submitting to understanding what another person needs from their viewpoint. Humility is seeing the situation through that person's context. Context leads to compassion and compassion to humility. As educators, we have to fight that urge to be right and the nervousness of how people will view us if we get it wrong. You will get it wrong at times. You will fall a thousand times. The beautiful thing about education is that it is reciprocal. Sometimes you are the teacher, and other times you are the student. To be an effective educator for all students, you have to continually be in the pattern of doing racial equity reflection and growth. This work is hard and draining, but the reward is seeing someone else's full humanity, pain, struggles, and potential and using your gifts to help them grow.

"Having Lunch With My Bias": Erin's Perspective

Cultural humility was not a concept that was around when I was in grad school in the mid-1990s, but it has been beneficial to know about it when it comes to understanding my response to racial incidents. Hook et al. (2013) described cultural humility both as intrapersonal components like reflection about biases and also as "an interpersonal stance that is other-oriented rather than self-focused, characterized by respect and lack of superiority toward an individual's cultural background and experience" (p. 353). Counseling skills and cultural humility pair well together. According to Mosher et al. (2017), therapists who are culturally humble

> (a) intentionally self-reflect and make a consistent effort to reduce their limitations and biases; (b) focus on learning from their clients' cultural backgrounds and experiences; (c) search for opportunities to build respectful, mutual partnerships with their clients; and (d) are motivated throughout their lives to learn more about various cultural beliefs. (p. 224)

In my ongoing pursuit of how to respond to racial incidents in the diverse schools in which I worked, I could not ignore my privilege. I *believed* I connected with students individually, in small groups, and in classrooms on topics of race, discrimination, and injustice and was empathic about their experiences of marginalization. I *believed* I advocated on behalf of my students. I *believed* I did my job well and was impactful—and surely was to some extent. I felt emotionally invested and spent at the end of the day, but still there was a safe distance to retreat to. As Derek and I have discussed, white privilege gives me an emotional off switch that he does not have.

Derek told me this phrase about "having lunch with your bias," which resonated with me as I recalled some of the moments I had had as a school counselor when I had failed to see my bias. For example, when I was in the first year of my career, I met with the father of a Black female student. She had strong standardized test scores, but she was failing most of her classes because she was missing assignments. When her father came in to meet with me, I showed him the report of her missing assignments and contrasted it against her high test scores. He asked whether she might be considered for the gifted program and suggested that she might not be challenged enough in her current classes. As an alternative, I asked whether she was just slacking and not doing her work at home. The father then said, "You're a racist!" At that moment I was stunned and apologized profusely, but the damage was done, and he stormed out. Initially, as I replayed the event in my head, I knew I had apologized because he was upset with me and I was protecting myself—which was my white fragility. In the days that followed, and after consultation with some colleagues, I had lunch with my bias and reflected on the fact that my racist belief had rejected her capacity for intellectual rigor and instead labeled her as "lazy" and "irresponsible." Yes, it was painful to think I had this racist belief, *and* it gave me a vital awareness that I needed to carry into the future. When I am stuck in my privilege, cultural humility is central to helping me get unstuck. I am highly motivated to be part of collaborative solutions, and I cannot do that if I am mired down by fragility or defensiveness.

Recommendations

1. Always remember that race is a social construct that began as a way to justify slavery.
2. If you are the dominant culture in a space, commit to doing additional work. This may mean doing research ahead of time to understand the culture of those lesser represented groups and being extra aware of and sensitive to the fact that your presence may create hesitation or necessitate caution.
3. Approach with care and curiosity. This applies to understanding labels, terms, concepts, names, symbols, phrases, or other cultural conventions with which you are unfamiliar.

Conclusion: A Vaccine for Racism

The 2020 COVID-19 pandemic changed the lives of people around the world. News of a vaccine came as a relief. There is a renewed joy that life will one day return to normal, when we will be able to go to restaurants and attend in-person classes and enjoy life together with those we love. As we move into our post-COVID society, we wonder whether there is a vaccine for combatting racism. We believe it comes down to how we see one another. Do we look at one another equally, or are we continuing to hold negative biases toward certain races? How can we address the bias and filters that get in the way of seeing people who do not look like us as less than equal? How can we use meals, music, and cultural traditions to tell stories that unite cross-culturally?

With the current political and racial divide in our country, we will continue to see public reactions that will impact the classroom. We are finishing writing this chapter just days after the U.S. Capitol was breached by angry insurgent supporters of Donald Trump. We hope you felt something in your stomach tell you "I have to address the situation with students. I can't be silent." As the late Congressman John Lewis said, "When you see something that is not right, not just, not fair, you have a moral obligation to say something, to do something. Our children and their children will ask us, 'What did you do? What did you say?'" (C-SPAN, 2019, 1:10). We hope that in 100 years, history will show how school counselors in the United States helped bring an end to racist incidents in schools and communities in America.

References

Alexander, M. (2010). *The new Jim Crow: Mass incarceration in the age of colorblindness*. The New Press.

American School Counselor Association. (n.d.). *School counseling standards and practice: Eliminating racism and bias in schools: The school counselor's role*. https://www.schoolcounselor.org/getmedia/542b085a-7eda-48ba-906e-24cd3f08a03f/SIP-Racism-Bias.pdf

American School Counselor Association. (2020, July). *Member demographics*. https://www.schoolcounselor.org/getmedia/9c1d81ab-2484-4615-9dd7-d788a241beaf/member-demographics.pdf

American School Counselor Association. (2021). *ASCA research report: State of the profession 2020*. https://www.schoolcounselor.org/getmedia/bb23299b-678d-4bce-8863-cfcb55f7df87/2020-State-of-the-Profession.pdf

Anderson, R. E., Saleem, F. T., & Huguley, J. P. (2019). Choosing to see the racial stress that afflicts our Black students. *Phi Delta Kappan, 101*(3), 20–25. https://doi.org/10.1177/0031721719885911

Atkins, R., & Oglesby, A. (2019). *Interrupting racism: Equity and social justice in school counseling*. Routledge.

Bennett, J. (2020, November 19). What if instead of calling people out, we called them in? *The New York Times*. https://www.nytimes.com/2020/11/19/style/loretta-ross-smith-college-cancel-culture.html

Corenblum, B., & Armstrong, H. D. (2012). Racial-ethnic identity development in children in a racial-ethnic minority group. *Canadian Journal of Behavioural Science/Revue Canadienne Des Sciences Du Comportement, 44*(2), 124–137.

C-SPAN. (2019, December 18). *Representative John Lewis speaks in favor of articles of impeachment against President Trump* [Video]. https://www.c-span.org/video/?c4842224/representative-john-lewis-speaks-favor-articles-impeachment-president-trump

Day-Vines, N. L., Cluxton-Keller, F., Agorsor, C., Gubara, S., & Otabil, N. A. A. (2020). The multidimensional model of broaching behavior. *Journal of Counseling & Development, 98*(1), 107–118. https://doi.org/10.1002/jcad.12304

Essien, E. (2020, January 27). The N-word: Confronting racial slurs in literature. *Book Riot*. https://bookriot.com/racial-slurs-in-literature/

Gaffney, C. (2019, Summer). When schools cause trauma. *Teaching Tolerance, 62*. https://www.learningforjustice.org/magazine/summer-2019/when-schools-cause-trauma

Gonzalez, M., Kokozos, M., Byrd, C. M., & McKee, K. E. (2020). Critical positive youth development: A framework for centering critical consciousness. *Journal of Youth Development, 15*(6), 24–43. https://doi.org/10.5195/jyd.2020.859

Hook, J. N., Davis, D. E., Owen, J., Worthington, E. L., & Utsey, S. O. (2013). Cultural humility: Measuring openness to culturally diverse clients. *Journal of Counseling Psychology, 60*(3), 353–366. https://doi.org/10.1037/a0032595

Jernigan, M. M., & Daniel, J. H. (2011). Racial trauma in the lives of Black children and adolescents: Challenges and clinical implications. *Journal of Child & Adolescent Trauma, 4*(2), 123–141. https://doi.org/10.1080/19361521.2011.574678

Kay, M. R. (2018). *Not light, but fire: How to lead meaningful race conversations in the classroom.* Stenhouse.

Learning for Justice. (2017). *Responding to hate and bias at school.* https://www.learningforjustice.org/magazine/publications/responding-to-hate-and-bias-at-school

Love, B. L. (2016). Anti-Black state violence, classroom edition: The spirit murdering of Black children. *Journal of Curriculum and Pedagogy, 13*(1), 22–25. https://doi.org/10.1080/15505170.2016.1138258

McMahon, H. G., Mason, E. C. M., Daluga-Guenther, N., & Ruiz, A. (2014). An ecological model of professional school counseling. *Journal of Counseling & Development, 92*(4), 459–471. https://doi.org/10.1002/j.1556-6676.2014.00172.x

Mosher, D. K., Hook, J. N., Captari, L. E., Davis, D. E., DeBlaere, C., & Owen, J. (2017). Cultural humility: A therapeutic framework for engaging diverse clients. *Practice Innovations, 2*(4), 221–233. https://doi.org/10.1037/pri0000055

Most, B. (2020, August 1). UMN students lead callouts against racism in Minnesota public schools. *The Minnesota Daily.* https://mndaily.com/261890/news/achighschoolcallout/

Office for Civil Rights. (2020, January 15). *Title IX: Sex-based harassment: Anoka-Hennepin School District (MN) (#05115901).* https://www2.ed.gov/about/offices/list/ocr/docs/investigations/05115901.html

Ohrtman, M., & Heltner, E. (Eds). (2019). *Contemporary case studies in school counseling.* Rowman & Littlefield.

O'Kane, C., & Wilson, O. (2020, September 14). *"A long time coming": Black students turn to social media to expose racism at private schools.* CBS News. https://www.cbsnews.com/news/Black-at-instagram-students-private-school-racism-social-media/

Pica-Smith, C., & Poynton, T. A. (2015). Supporting interethnic and interracial friendships among youth to reduce prejudice and racism in schools: The role of the school counselor. *Professional School Counseling, 18*(1), 82–89.

Plummer, D. L. (2019). *Some of my friends are …: The daunting challenges and untapped benefits of cross-racial friendships.* Beacon Press.

Plummer, D. L., Stone, R. T., Powell, L., & Allison, J. (2016). Patterns of adult cross-racial friendships: A context for understanding contemporary race relations. *Cultural Diversity and Ethnic Minority Psychology, 22*(4), 479–494. https://doi.org/10.1037/cdp0000079

Rivas-Drake, D., & Umaña-Taylor, A. (2019a). *Below the surface: Talking with teens about race, ethnicity, and identity.* Princeton University Press. https://doi.org/10.2307/j.ctvc77kmw

Rivas-Drake, D., & Umaña-Taylor, A. J. (2019b). Engaging in meaningful conversations: The need to foster ethnic-racial identity in school. *American Educator, 43*(3), 18–22.

Rivas-Drake, D., Umaña-Taylor, A. J., Schaefer, D. R., & Medina, M. (2017). Ethnic-racial identity and friendships in early adolescence. *Child Development, 88*(3), 710–724. https://doi.org/10.1111/cdev.12790

Ross, L. (2019, Spring). Speaking up without tearing down. *Teaching Tolerance, 61.* https://www.tolerance.org/magazine/spring-2019/speaking-up-without-tearing-down

Singh, A. A. (2019). *The racial healing handbook: Practical activities to help you challenge privilege, confront systemic racism and engage in collective healing.* New Harbinger.

Southern Poverty Law Center. (2018, January 31). *SPLC report: U.S. education on American slavery sorely lacking.* https://www.splcenter.org/news/2018/01/31/splc-report-us-education-american-slavery-sorely-lacking

Southern Poverty Law Center. (2019). *Hate at school.* https://www.splcenter.org/sites/default/files/tt_2019_hate_at_school_report_final_0.pdf

Sparks, S. D. (2020, November 17). *Training bias out of teachers: Research shows little promise so far.* Education Week. https://www.edweek.org/leadership/training-bias-out-of-teachers-research-shows-little-promise-so-far/2020/11

thepinkreportnews. (2020, August 20). Black at Benilde: Black students at elite Minnesota private school recommend enrolling elsewhere. *The Pink Report News.* https://thepinkreportnews.com/2020/08/20/black-at-benilde-black-students-at-elite-minnesota-private-school-recommend-enrolling-elsewhere/

Umaña-Taylor, A. J., Quintana, S. M., Lee, R. M., Cross, W. E., Rivas-Drake, D., Schwartz, S. J., Syed, M., Yipp, T., & Seaton, E. (2014). Ethnic and racial identity during adolescence and into young adulthood: An integrated conceptualization. *Child Development, 85*(1), 21–39. https://doi.org/10.1111/cdev.12196

U.S. Census Bureau. (n.d.). *QuickFacts: Minneapolis city, Minnesota.* https://www.census.gov/quickfacts/fact/table/minneapoliscityminnesota/RHI125219

Wallace, C. (2017, June 5). If you're black in America, riots are a spiritual impulse not a political strategy. *Timeline.* https://timeline.com/long-hot-summer-riots-8db9fff6c9c1

Additional Resources

Facing History and Ourselves
    https://www.facinghistory.org
Learning for Justice, Teaching Hard History: American Slavery
    https://www.tolerance.org/frameworks/teaching-hard-history/american-slavery
PBS, *Race: The Power of an Illusion*
    https://www.racepowerofanillusion.org/
Seed the Way, Resources
    www.seedtheway.com/resources.html

CHAPTER 5

College and Career Readiness for Students of Color: Using an Antiracist Ecological Framework

Erik M. Hines, Paul C. Harris, Renae D. Mayes, and Laura Owen

Now more than ever, education or training beyond a high school diploma is necessary. Many high-paying jobs and careers require some training or skill to execute. Furthermore, over a lifetime, a person with a college degree can earn over $1 million more than someone with just a high school diploma (Carnevale et al., 2015). Yet despite increased opportunities to pursue postsecondary education and training, not all individuals have access to it, and barriers prevent them from improving their career and life outcomes. For example, African American and Latinx students may be overlooked or persuaded not to pursue education or training beyond high school because of assumptions made about their cognitive ability (e.g., Are they smart enough to attend college?), socioeconomic status (e.g., Can they afford college?), or linguistics (e.g., they can be mistakenly considered not college ready based on their communication skills). Therefore, more research is needed to address the aforementioned issues. Furthermore, school counselors must take an antiracist approach to college and career readiness (CCR), as many students, specifically those from vulnerable populations, are being left behind from engaging in postsecondary opportunities because of racism, lack of access to rigorous coursework, limited information on financial aid and college options, bias, and stereotypes. The purpose of this chapter is to provide an antiracist ecological approach to CCR, as school counselors need to play an active role in speaking out against racism and ending racial inequity in the postsecondary preparation process.

The report *High School Benchmarks 2020* noted that high school graduation rates remained steady for the class of 2019–2020, but direct enrollment from high school to college fell sharply, with an overall decline of 21.7% (National Student Clearinghouse Research Center, 2020). However, when we examine the results by socioeconomic status they are even more alarming, with college enrollment dropping 29.2% for low-income students compared to 16.9% for higher income students. Enrollment for students transitioning from high-poverty schools fell by 32.6% versus 16.4% for students from low-poverty schools, and the college enrollment of high–Black, Indigenous, and people of color (BIPOC) schools declined by 26.4% while that of low-BIPOC schools decreased by 18.0% (National Student Clearinghouse Research Center, 2020). Early indications suggest that 2021 enrollment rates may reveal even more dramatic decreases. The high school class of 2020–2021 submitted 8% fewer fall college applications and applications from students who requested fee waivers from the Common App (https://www.commonapp.org), and the percentage of applicants who were first in their family to attend college fell by 16% (Goldman & Korn, 2020). In addition, the Federal Student Aid Office in the U.S. Department of Education reported that Free Application for Federal Student Aid (FAFSA) completion rates were down 16.6% in 2020 compared to previous years (Watson & Pananjady, 2020).

Students who delay enrollment are less likely to gain a postsecondary credential compared to their peers who enroll on time (Horn et al., 2006). Although attempts have been made for several decades to close college opportunity gaps, they continue to fall short and leave too many students behind, in particular Black, Brown, and Indigenous students. In light of alarming declines in enrollment that disproportionately affect students attending low-poverty and high-BIPOC schools, as well as those who are first in their family to attend college, immediate action is necessary to stem the tide and ensure that policies ensure equitable outcomes and more opportunities for low-income, first-generation Black, Hispanic, and Native American youth.

Given the importance of CCR, it is critical to examine the roles that school staff, in particular school counselors, play in perpetuating racism in the CCR process. School counselors are often key personnel charged with engaging students in their career development, which includes building career aspirations, engaging in career exploration, and facilitating postsecondary planning (American School Counselor Association [ASCA], 2019). As they engage in this work with every student, it is important for school counselors to understand that their own racist ideas along with structural racism may perpetuate disparities in CCR. For example, student athletes, in particular Black boy student athletes, may have limited exposure to school counselors for their CCR because they are perceived as being athletes only rather than carrying multiple identities and roles (student, athlete, Black boy, etc.; Harris et al., in press). Or Black girls may not receive any support for CCR, as they are often subjected to adultification, which means they are perceived as not needing help or as already knowing (R. Epstein et al., 2017; Mayes & Vega, in press). Adultification aligns with racism in that it is a form of dehumanization, assuming less innocence and more culpability in Black girls and boys and robbing them of the innocence that makes childhood distinct from all other developmental periods (Goff et al., 2014). At its worst, adultification can be fatal in that it perpetuates a false narrative of malicious intent in Black children versus immature decision-making. This was made abundantly clear in the case of Tamir Rice, the 12-year-old Black child who was killed by a police officer in 2014 when he was seen with a toy gun. These examples call for a deeper understanding of intersectionality in anti-racist CCR work. Intersectionality (Crenshaw, 1989, 1991, 2015) refers to the ways in which individuals may experience overlapping marginalization and oppressive systems based on the intersections of their identities. Intersectionality as a part of antiracist works holds individuals as being multidimensional and possessing multiple minoritized identities that each have sociopolitical and developmental implications (Crenshaw, 1989, 1991).

In addition to racist ideas, structural racism, including policies in prekindergarten–Grade 12 schools, impede CCR. State school funding policies and structures often ensure that wealthy communities receive the most funding and resources; schools in Black, Brown, and Indigenous communities have for decades received fewer resources and had fewer jobs to ensure families' economic mobility (Darling-Hammond, 2004, 2007; Love, 2019). Limited funding means that schools that serve historically oppressed racial groups often have dilapidated physical structures, high staff turnover, and limited student supports and educational opportunities. Across all school settings, policies and practices related to school discipline disproportionately target Black and Brown students, thrusting them into the school-to-prison pipeline and denying them the chance to learn (Love, 2019). Furthermore, policies and practices related to enrollment in rigorous courses (advanced placement courses, gifted education, honors courses, etc.) often screen out and overlook Black and Brown students, which leads to their underrepresentation in said courses (Wright et al., 2017). Taken together, these policies and related practices overlook and police Black and Brown students' brilliance in a way that limits opportunities in prekindergarten–Grade 12 school and subsequent postsecondary opportunities.

With these structural challenges stemming from racist ideas and practices, school counselors must embrace an antiracist approach to their CCR work. An antiracist approach allows school counselors to identify, challenge, and change their racist beliefs and practices. An antiracist lens also helps school counselors challenge the policies that make up their comprehensive CCR activities, with a particular focus on how such activities and policies center the wholeness and humanness of each of their students, especially their historically minoritized students. This chapter includes a review of the literature pertaining to CCR, a detailed description of the role of school counselors in this CCR, and discussion of an antiracist ecological framework that can guide school counselors' CCR practices in the future.

Literature Review

Indicators of CCR and Enrollment Patterns

CCR involves the attainment of various skills that facilitate students' successful matriculation to postsecondary education or entry into the workforce. It has been a topic of national conversation for decades but was given more emphasis in 2010 by the U.S. Department of Education through the revision and reauthorization of the Elementary and Secondary Education Act of 1965, now known as the Every Student Succeeds Act (ESSA, 2015). ESSA noted that postsecondary education was increasingly becoming a necessity for social, economic, and political mobility (Hines, Harris, et al., 2020).

It is important to note that CCR is not built on the assumption that all students should go to college. Rather, it is built on the moral imperative that all students should have that choice. Historically this choice was made early and often for Black and Brown students by the systems that served them. This practice, known as tracking, dates back to the 1920s and generally refers to the grouping of students based on perceived ability. Such grouping has often been determined from incomplete and biased means such as standardized test performance. Over time, Black and Brown students and students from low-income backgrounds have been disproportionately placed in lower tracks (LaPrade, 2011; "Teaching Inequality," 1989).

Antiracist CCR practice, then, calls for purposefully preparing all students to choose to attend college if they want to do so. Cultivating the requisite skills in Black students and students of color as well as removing the barriers to their acquiring such skills is imperative. Specifically, it requires naming and actively resisting racist policies and practices that lead to unmet indicators of CCR for Black students. Critical indicators of CCR include mastery of key content knowledge, cognitive strategies, academic behaviors (study skills and habits), and contextual skills (understanding of the college lifestyle; Conley, 2010; Malin et al., 2017). Black students have historically been underserved toward these ends.

Although each of these indicators is relevant for Black students, course enrollment patterns reveal particularly significant disparities from their white counterparts. School counselors can have a significant influence on these patterns, which can translate into a higher percentage of Black students being ready for and successful in college. When enrolled in honors and advanced placement courses, Black students are often very successful; however, they are underrepresented in both (Patrick et al., 2020). Subsequently, the stratification in college enrollment based on race has been stark for decades, with Black students continuing to lag.

Historical Context

When considering current indicators of CCR along with enrollment trends, it is important to understand that we did not arrive here by happenstance. These enrollment statistics and indicators are a by-product of anti-Blackness that exists across every facet of U.S. institutions and structures. With the enslavement and subjugation of Africans, the United States began its structural commitments to anti-Blackness (Booth, 2019). These beginnings led to the codification of laws and codes that promoted white lives through the limitation of Black bodies (Anderson, 2016). Not only did this stratify opportunity, and thus income, to privilege white bodies, but it also policed Black bodies, often brutally and fatally, as a response to political and economic gains (Anderson, 2016; Booth, 2019; Love, 2019). Essentially,

> the trigger of White rage, inevitably, is Black advancement. It is not the mere presence of Black people that is the problem; rather it is Blackness with ambition, with drive, with purpose, with aspirations, and with demands for full and equal citizenship. (Anderson, 2016, p. 2)

White rage has built the U.S. capitalist system where, to thrive, Black bodies need to remain poor and indebted to whites (Love, 2019). Although it might seem as though our current economic structure has repaired this troubled history, it builds on it. Capitalism's inherent relationship with anti-Blackness allows for Black bodies to earn less than their counterparts despite similar education (Gould, 2020). It allows for the state to benefit from the labor of Black bodies through mass incarceration (Alexander, 2010). It allows for the state-sanctioned murder of Black bodies (Anderson, 2016; Love, 2019). It allows for underfunded and underresourced schools that primarily serve Black bodies (Darling-Hammond, 2004, 2007; Love,

2019). It allows for Black bodies to be excluded from schools by being pushed into the school-to-prison pipeline as early as prekindergarten (Love, 2019; Powell, 2014). It allows for Black bodies to be overlooked when it comes to referrals for gifted education (Wright et al., 2017).

The Role of the School Counselor

School counselors have a critical role in disrupting these anti-Black and antiracist patterns within education. The role of a school counselor is to contribute to the removal of individual and systemic barriers to the social-emotional, academic, and career development of all students. Such barriers have historically disproportionately disrupted the success of Black students. Systemic racism in schools is not new; however, school counseling that specifically addresses racism in schools is still not uniformly addressed in training programs and practice in K–12 schools. To be an effective antiracist school counselor, one must be well versed in approaches that actively name and disrupt white supremacist practices and the status quo that oppresses Black students educationally. Although no single approach serves as a panacea toward this end, elements such as critical consciousness, power, positive identity, and social action are particularly critical to antiracist work and the empowerment of Black students (Gutierrez, 1995; Harris, 2015; Hipolito-Delgado & Lee, 2007). Critical consciousness, a prerequisite for resistance and liberation, includes an awareness of anti-Black racism in America, the sociopolitical implications of it, and the actions necessary to appropriately prevent and resist racial trauma (Mosley et al., 2021). Critical consciousness must begin with the school counselor, though, for there to be any effective disruption and dismantling of racist school systems that wreak havoc on Black students. School counselors must first be trained over and above the well-intentioned foci of the Council for Accreditation of Counseling and Related Educational Programs (CACREP), which currently includes one 3-credit course on multicultural counseling within the 60-credit curriculum. Such critical consciousness on the part of the school counselor can then lead to a critically conscious comprehensive school counseling program that facilitates the same with Black students, leading to their positive identity amid structural racial bias designed to thwart it and resulting in further student-led and anti-Black social action.

The status quo, though, presents very real challenges to even the most prepared school counselor. This status quo includes, for example, unmanageably high student-to-counselor ratios in schools. Although ASCA recommends a ratio of 250:1, the average ratio nationwide is 464:1; it is even higher in high-poverty and high-BIPOC schools (Monaghan et al., 2020). The status quo also includes underresourced schools, which are most often attended by Black and Brown students (Monaghan et al., 2020). Still, school counselors can curate transformative experiences for all students using an antiracist lens and strategic consultative and collaborative efforts. Such efforts increase the number of students of color and the efficacy of significant others' influence on the CCR of students (Hines et al., 2019; Moore-Thomas & Day-Vines, 2010). ASCA (2019) recommends that 80% of school counselors' time be devoted to direct and indirect services, which includes consultation and collaboration. School counselors are uniquely situated in that by being in schools they have access to multiple stakeholders.

School Settings

When considering antiracist approaches, it is paramount to understand the various school and community contexts that contribute to strengths and challenges around CCR. Certainly, approaches may look similar across school settings, but a one-size-fits-all approach to antiracist CCR can miss the uniqueness of a given community and its associated challenges. Thus, here we talk briefly about challenges associated with different geographic settings that may help guide antiracist CCR practices.

Urban schools. Urban schools present a unique context, in particular for many Black and Brown students, who are likely to be enrolled in such schools. Our most vulnerable students (students of color, students from lower socioeconomic backgrounds, etc.) are most commonly enrolled in urban schools (Hussar et al., 2020). Although they may have great talent and potential among students and staff, urban schools are faced with limited structural and financial support and are often located in communities that are similarly resourced (Darling-Hammond, 2004, 2007). Moreover, although rigorous courses like honors and advanced placement courses may be available, Black and Brown students often have limited access to them despite making up the majority of the student population in these schools (Ford & Moore, 2013). Taken together, these challenges may lead to limited academic success and disengagement with school, including increased absences and dropout (Hannon, 2016). Given these challenges to academic success, it is no surprise that the CCR of students in urban schools can be impacted. Thus, graduation rates and college enrollment rates are lower for students from urban schools in comparison to students from more resourced schools (Hussar et al., 2020).

Rural schools. The challenges in rural schools can be similar to those seen in urban schools. Rural schools are often rife with limited resources, such as limited access to high-speed internet, few quality teachers, few teachers from diverse racial backgrounds, lack of college counseling, or lack of access to rigorous (e.g., advanced placement or honors) courses for college readiness (Byun, Irvin, & Meece, 2012; Byun, Meece, & Irvin, 2012; Kominak, 2018). Moreover, although students from rural areas are the fastest growing population in terms of college enrollment, they represent only a quarter of the U.S. population (Byun, Irvin, & Meece, 2012; Byun, Meece, & Irvin, 2012; Hines et al., 2015). Students from rural areas often encounter deficit narratives that may deter them from applying to and enrolling in college. Some of these narratives include a lack of motivation to be academically successful and a lack of interest in pursuing college. Rural students are less likely to be recruited by colleges because colleges typically target locations with an abundance of students who have less of a need for financial aid (Gettinger, 2019, as cited in Hines, Moore, et al., 2020, p. 60).

Suburban schools. Suburban schools are not without challenges or issues. Many suburban schools often employ teachers who lack experience working with students of color, vulnerable populations, and students of low socioeconomic status (Dell'Angela, 2016; McGhee, 2019). Furthermore, some suburban school districts mirror urban schools in that they are underresourced, have higher concentrations of students who live at or below the poverty line, have more students who qualify for free or reduced lunch, and have an increased number of English language learners (Gill et al., 2016). Moreover, resources that are usually allocated to address the aforementioned issues are usually located in urban areas, which makes it harder for suburban schools to access them (Gill et al., 2016). Finally, suburban schools are usually scored on metrics such as testing; however, these metrics cannot determine the quality of a school (Schneider, 2017).

State and National Impact on Community Settings

State Policies and Influences

State policies can have a significant impact on Black, Brown, and Indigenous students, especially around their postsecondary readiness and success. In particular, access and funding can vary by state, as states have more control over budget allocation and policy decisions than the federal government, which has a very limited role in education (U.S. Department of Education, n.d.). Different states have different definitions of what it means to be college and career ready (Southern Regional Education Board, 2019). Moreover, states allocate funding to colleges and universities differently; for example, some states appropriate more money for grants to lower the cost of tuition for students than other states (Urban Institute, n.d.). Also, research has shown that states can reduce tuition costs and improve accessibility by preparing students for postsecondary opportunities by bolstering and improving prekindergarten–Grade 12 academic preparation, which could lead to higher levels of college retention and reduced time to complete a degree (Urban Institute, n.d.). Furthermore, some states offer free tuition programs to improve accessibility, especially for students of low socioeconomic status or economically disadvantaged students (Urban Institute, n.d.).

National Policies and Influences

National policies have focused on CCR, but until recently most of these policies have lacked a clear equity focus for Black, Brown, and Indigenous students. In 1958, the National Defense Education Act was passed to increase the ability of the United States to compete with the Soviet Union in the Space Race and to ensure that students were prepared to enroll in science, mathematics, and foreign languages courses (National Defense Education Act, 1964). As a result of increased National Defense Education Act funding, a significant number of school counselors were hired to help students enroll in more rigorous courses. However, white and middle- and upper class students benefited while marginalized student groups were denied the guidance and access they needed to secure seats in these qualifying courses.

In 1965, the Elementary and Secondary Education Act, now know as ESSA, was passed by Congress to increase school funding with the aim of establishing equal access to education, decreasing the achievement gap, and providing additional support to low-income students. This law has been modified and reauthorized many times over its 55-year history, but it was not until 2015 that ESSA required CCR support for all students, including those with disabilities. The 2015 law advances equity by protecting disadvantaged and high-need students. For the first time since the law's inception, it requires that all students be taught to high academic standards that will prepare them to succeed in college and careers (English et al., 2016). ESSA also demands that educators, families, students, and communities be provided with information demonstrating each student's progress toward these high standards. It mandates accountability and action to effect change in the highest need schools, for groups of students not making significant progress, and where graduation rates are low over extended time frames. ESSA brings back local control and gives states and districts flexibility in implementing, measuring, and demonstrating accountability for long-standing equity issues. This shift may impact educational equity in both positive and negative ways (Malin et al., 2017).

In 2010, the College Board's National Office for School Counselor Advocacy (NOSCA) released the Eight Components of CCR Counseling to create a systemic approach to K–12 college and career counseling as well as to the development of state and national policies to ensure equitable CCR outcomes (NOSCA, 2010; see Figure 5.1). The eight components cover the elementary to high school spectrum of CCR counseling needs, and although they use a multicultural approach they fail to address the inherent racist ideas driving each of the components.

The Eight Components of College and Career Readiness Counseling provide a systemic approach for school counselors to implement, across grades K-12 — elementary through high school and beyond, to ensure equity both in process and results.

1. College Aspirations

Goal: Build a college-going culture based on early college awareness by nurturing in students the confidence to aspire to college and the resilience to overcome challenges along the way. Maintain high expectations by providing adequate support, building social capital and conveying the conviction that all students can succeed in college.

2. Academic Planning for College and Career Readiness

Goal: Advance students' planning, preparation, participation and performance in a rigorous academic program that connects to their college and career aspirations and goals.

3. Enrichment and Extracurricular Engagement

Goal: Ensure equitable exposure to a wide range of extracurricular and enrichment opportunities that build leadership, nurture talents and interests, and increase engagement with school.

4. College and Career Exploration and Selection Processes

Goal: Provide early and ongoing exposure to experiences and information necessary to make informed decisions when selecting a college or career that connects to academic preparation and future aspirations.

5. College and Career Assessments

Goal: Promote preparation, participation and performance in college and career assessments by all students.

6. College Affordability Planning

Goal: Provide students and families with comprehensive information about college costs, options for paying for college, and the financial aid and scholarship processes and eligibility requirements, so they are able to plan for and afford a college education.

7. College and Career Admission Processes

Goal: Ensure that students and families have an early and ongoing understanding of the college and career application and admission processes so they can find the postsecondary options that are the best fit with their aspirations and interests.

8. Transition from High School Graduation to College Enrollment

Goal: Connect students to school and community resources to help the students overcome barriers and ensure the successful transition from high school to college.

FIGURE 5.1 • Eight Components of College and Career Readiness Counseling

Note. From *Eight Components of College and Career Readiness Counseling*, by The College Board National Office for School Counselor Advocacy, 2010, College Board (https://secure-media.collegeboard.org/digitalServices/pdf/nosca/11b_4416_8_Components_WEB_111107.pdf).

Founded on colonial and Eurocentric approaches, multicultural theories have too often silenced minoritized voices and decreased outcomes for nondominant and diverse individuals and groups. Choosing to view these groups through a deficit lens allows the majority to sustain a system of oppression and marginalization (Sisko, 2021). The Eight Components of CCR Counseling call for a systemic approach but neglect to go far enough by calling out the very CCR system that reduced postsecondary opportunities and perpetuated the racist treatment of Black, Brown, and Indigenous students to begin with. For example, the College Aspirations goal assumes that students lack the confidence and resilience to overcome challenges. Problematizing students instead of addressing the flawed educational system that was designed and constructed to perpetuate inequitable opportunity creates a facade of fairness, allowing the dominant group to assume little if any responsibility by falsely displacing the blame on the individual who was targeted, pathologized, and denied support to begin with. All policies and CCR frameworks need to be reviewed through an antiracist lens.

The Reach Higher initiative was launched in 2014 to inspire every student in America to take charge of their future by completing some form of education past high school, whether through a professional training program, a community college, or a 4-year college or university. Although the intent was appropriate, the initiative neglected to powerfully and unapologetically call out the broken educational advising system, gatekeeping practices, and racist policies many educators endorse. Too many students are encouraged to attend college and university on campuses that provide painful encounters with white supremacy, white nationalism, and anti-Blackness. The Reach Higher initiative failed to challenge these long-standing practices and beliefs.

Brown et al. (2017) reviewed 6 years of research, national policies, and white papers on college and career advising specifically targeting school counselors' role in helping students navigate their postsecondary path. Their report included recommendations for the field in the areas of policy, credentialing, research, and practice. Yet they also neglected to call for a much-needed critical dialogue to discover an antiracist approach to CCR.

An Ecological Framework for Integrating and Dismantling Systems

To successfully prepare students for postsecondary opportunities using antiracist and culturally responsive lenses, we have created an ecosystem approach to integrating systems that work for students and dismantling systems that are racist, create barriers, and oppress students. This model merges Urie Bronfenbrenner's ecological systems theory (Bronfenbrenner, 1977) and the Eight Components of CCR Counseling (NOSCA, 2010). Below is the model with feature tenets:

A. *Individual Counseling (Microsystem).* Individual career counseling and coaching allows for the maximum amount of tailoring to the unique needs of the student with whom the school counselor is working (ASCA, 2017). At its core, individual counseling allows for strengths-based and empowerment-focused counseling that focuses on recognizing and honoring students' brilliance and resilience as a part of specific career planning and preparation activities. For example, school counselors may first seek to explore and understand more deeply who students are along with their hopes, desires, and anxieties about the future. In addition, more individualized activities such as a career assessment may be used to help link interests and characteristics with future careers (e.g., interest in building computers may be linked with a future career in science, technology, engineering, or mathematics; ASCA, 2017; NOSCA, 2010). This can allow for specific and collaborative planning related to coursework, extracurricular and community experiences, and skill development (ASCA, 2017; NOSCA, 2010). As a part of the collaborative planning process, it would be important to render explicit anti-Black and capitalist structures that the student may encounter to anticipate, navigate, resist, and dismantle them. Toward this end, school counselors should purposefully engage with race-conscious frameworks that illuminate social injustices while centering student voice and youth-driven advocacy as a part of counseling experiences (Coles & Powell, 2020; Harris et al., in press; Smith et al., 2010; Washington, 2018).

B. *Group Counseling (Mesosystem).* As school counselors are often pressed for time, meeting individually with students may not be a possibility. Thus, group counseling may offer a way to directly support and build connections among a smaller number of students (ASCA, 2020). These connections can offer an opportunity to not only take on CCR tasks but also allow for group efforts toward addressing related academic and social-emotional development (ASCA, 2020). For example, as a part of the group experience, students may share their frustrations with the ways in which they are constantly disciplined or why they rarely learn anything relevant to their lives or background. As in individual counseling, school counselors use the group experience to build on students' strengths and resilience while engaging with empowerment and youth-driven advocacy to develop CCR while also addressing barriers that may be impacting student success (ASCA, 2020; Coles & Powell, 2020; Smith et al., 2010; Washington, 2018). As a part of this process, it would be important for the school counselor to honor student voice and agency in the planning and implementation process while also committing to activities in which the school counselor can be a coconspirator in addressing students' concerns (Love, 2019).

C. *Classroom/Grade (Mesosystem).* Given the high numbers of students on school counselors' caseloads, especially in high-BIPOC and high-poverty districts, engaging students in large groups ensures everyone has access to school counseling services. There are many ways in which school counselors can partner with teachers at each grade level to provide counseling services that support existing learning objectives and standards and promote progress toward school improvement plan benchmarks.

For example, at the elementary level school counselors can partner with general education teachers to teach antiracist social-emotional skills, which not only supports teachers' efforts at preventive behavior management but also informs students about issues like racial microaggressions and biases that can create unhealthy interactions that lead to conflict. Art and music teachers would also make great partners for school counselors in that students can be encouraged to tell their stories through creative expression and be reinforced and validated for their unique contribution to the learning community. In an educational system in which curricula are historically biased, rooted in colonialist thought, and delivered through Eurocentric frameworks, such a strengths-based space could be empowering for an otherwise disempowered group of students.

The same would apply in middle schools, where school counselors could partner with social science teachers, for example, to speak to large groups of students about how mental health can be impacted by years of disenfranchisement. School counselors could create guidance lessons about why racial minorities are generally more hesitant to seek help because of historic large-scale exploitation by those in the helping profession (i.e., the Tuskegee experiment).

At the high school level, classroom guidance lessons on racialized trauma and depression would be incredibly relevant for any health and physical education curriculum. The obvious connection to mental health creates space for school counselors to design and execute large group lessons toward this end, highlighting unique dynamics that might contribute to disparate experiences and treatment. Furthermore, English teachers who are working on strengthening the writing skills of their students might use the college admissions essay as a way to do this. By having students write essays, high school counselors can ensure that all students, especially first-generation and otherwise marginalized groups, have a clear understanding of how to most effectively complete this part of their college application.

D. *School Level (Mesosystem).* First, school counselors can collect data on the racial and cultural climate of the school. They can use these data to plan and design interventions to implement at multiple levels in the school (ASCA, 2019; Erford, 2019). School counselors can interview students of color to uncover their experiences in classrooms and in particular courses. To that end, school counselors, administrators, and teachers can examine school data to determine where inequities exist in the areas of attendance; discipline; the representation of students of color in special education, gifted and talented programs, honors courses, and/or advanced placement courses; and representation among school personnel (Lee & Goodnough, 2019).

Second, school counselors can provide school-wide training to school personnel on antiracism, combating anti-Blackness, and culturally responsive practices (Holcomb-McCoy et al., 2020). In addition, school counselors can help educators infuse this pedagogy into their curriculum and assist administrators in integrating it into academic and discipline policies. A great example is to examine policies that hinder, prevent, or serve as a barrier to academic success or access to resources for postsecondary preparation for vulnerable populations and students of color. Making these changes allows school counselors to improve relationships with students through empathy and compassion, advocate for an equitable approach to ensuring students of color have access to and enroll in rigorous coursework to be college and career ready, and speak out against antiracist policies that deter or prevent students of color from pursuing postsecondary opportunities (Holcomb-McCoy et al., 2020; Kendi, 2019; NOSCA, 2010).

Finally, the school's mission statement and goals should reflect an antiracist perspective in addition to inclusive excellence that includes a commitment to equity and diversity. School leaders must ensure that the curriculum (and teachers) at all grade levels reflect the voices of Black, Brown, and Indigenous populations, avoid negative messaging about certain populations of people, and include inclusive language. Furthermore, school leaders (and personnel) must create a school climate in which all students feel that they are included and matter! This includes identifying inequitable practices when it comes to helping students identify their academic and career goals at each level as well as posting culturally responsive messages throughout the school about postsecondary readiness.

E. *District Level (Exosystem).* Students do not interact directly with stake-holders at the district level; nevertheless, policies and decisions at this level have an impact on students' academic and postsecondary trajectories. At the district level, there is usually a leader who is in charge of school counseling; often this person has the power to call district-wide meetings to bring school counselors together for goal setting, planning, and strategizing for student success. School counselors across the district should be collaborating and conversing around issues and initiatives specific to their district (Erford, 2019). District school counseling leaders can address the broader needs of students by having counselors collectively create goals to address issues while creating plans tailored to their respective schools to accomplish said goals. For example, a goal at this level could be to identify barriers at each school that contribute to the low graduation rate among Black males. School counselors across the district can look at the data at each of their schools and collectively identify themes or practices across the district that contribute to low graduation rates. Next school counseling leaders along with the school counselors can identify and implement training and best practices, such as providing anti-Blackness training, developing a uniform and culturally relevant group/classroom curriculum on postsecondary readiness at each school level, and creating a community and parent involvement component to ensure the academic and social needs of Black boys are met outside the school building. One intervention school counselors can use is a small-group curriculum created to assist Black males in 10th grade to prepare for college (Hines, Hines, et al., 2020).

F. *Community/Regional (Exosystem).* School-family-community partnerships are not only critical to the success of students but also important for supporting schools (Bryan & Henry, 2008). J. E. Epstein and associates (2019) suggested schools incorporate community resources and services that will support students' academic success, social-emotional development, and postsecondary readiness (ASCA, 2019; J. E. Epstein & Associates, 2019). Schools can partner with organizations that specialize in topics around racial justice and culturally responsive training. These organizations can assist school personnel with understanding the historical context of their students, especially students of color or those from vulnerable backgrounds. Moreover, school personnel can learn professional strategies for how to speak out against racism and oppressive practices that hinder postsecondary readiness for students of color.

School counselors and leaders can identify resources in the community to provide financial planning around college, train parents on completing the FAFSA, and discuss colleges and other postsecondary institutions that support students of color. Also, school counselors can invite community members who reflect the demographic of their student population to discuss racial and cultural experiences of getting to and getting through college as well as provide training for educators on how best to support students of color. Finally, school counselors need to identify financial resources for students of color who may not have the money to pay costs associated with postsecondary schooling. Such costs include fees for entrance exams (e.g., the SAT) or a deposit for room and board for college. Creating a scholarship fund or foundation account and soliciting donors can help improve postsecondary attendance rates and reinforce the high expectation that *all* students can pursue postsecondary opportunities.

G. *State Level (Macrosystem).* With the reauthorization of ESSA, states and school districts have been given more authority to set their college and career goals as well as identify the accountability metrics they will use to measure effectiveness and advance equity. States are required to hold all students to high academic standards, but what this looks like still varies significantly from state to state. Many states lack a director of school counseling, so school counselors are left to figure things out for themselves and often grapple with systemic barriers that prevent them from receiving guidance or giving input on state policies and practices. Most states have adopted the ASCA National Model (ASCA, 2019) to guide their college and career counseling work. However, Carey and Martin (2015) worried that most states lack the systemic structures needed to oversee the implementation of state models or evaluate the effectiveness of school counseling practices.

State school counselor associations frequently take on the responsibility of sharing standards and advocating for best practices at the state level. With so many community-based and college access organizations entering the college and career advising space, credentialing and licensure becomes an important issue. A new set of CCR competencies must be operationalized and applied equally across organizations and linked to training, credentialing, and licensing (Brown et al., 2017). Competencies need to be worded strongly enough to guide antiracist practice and outline the skills, knowledge, and aptitudes that all school counselors must possess. The competencies must be integrated into school counselor training, evaluation, and licensing practices. State policy is needed to build the capacity of state departments of education to promote these competencies and evaluate effective equity-centered college and career counseling practices in schools (Carey & Martin, 2015).

H. *Federal Level (Macrosystem).* Brown et al. (2017) called for national policy changes aimed at redefining and casting school counselors as leaders in college advising and postsecondary attainment. However, they warned that a lack of clarity around the school counselor's core role combined with high caseloads might make attempts to provide clear examples of effective leadership more difficult. Since the call for role clarification, a few studies have been published to help us better understand the school counselor's role in college and career advising. Many of these studies are directly linked to recommendations to increase college enrollment, persistence, and completion for low-income, first-generation, and Black, Brown, and Indigenous students.

Today's school counselors face daunting challenges as they serve as first responders in a rapidly changing postsecondary landscape, one that has been ravaged by the effects of the worldwide coronavirus pandemic. The pandemic has disproportionately impacted Black and Brown students and families, resulting in the removal, seemingly overnight, of many of the opportunity gains that were witnessed over the prior decade.

The unrelenting and ongoing murders of Black and Brown men, women, and children across the country combined with a long overdue racial reckoning prioritizes the need for school counselors who are ready to challenge implicit bias, advocate for antiracist practice, acknowledge spaces in which whiteness dominates, call out anti-Blackness, dismantle white privilege, and welcome more diverse advising professionals who are ready to lead and guide college and career counseling work. In response to the national Black Lives Matter movement, school counselors must address the unevenness of the lived experiences of Black, Brown, and Indigenous people in the United States. Mattering is a direct response to not mattering for hundreds of years. Counselors must be courageous and challenge old norms and racist ideas and beliefs about Black protests. Understanding and embracing this history (e.g., civil rights, Black Lives Matter) is critical for antiracist CCR work and requires more than just talking about race in a class. School counselors must collectively share the responsibility to address, eliminate, and prevent actions, decisions, and outcomes that result from and perpetuate racism, white privilege, white rage, and anti-Blackness.

School counselors are facing skyrocketing mental health needs among families, students, and staff. In light of this, as well as the impact of an economic downturn, the task ahead for school counselors and students becomes even more daunting. The postpandemic landscape will look quite different from where we were before, but each of these priority areas must be addressed if we are to adequately prepare students for their postsecondary opportunities.

Whether we are talking about ever-shifting test-optional policies or changing learning modalities (virtual vs. face to face), students and families are in dire need of school counselors and college advisers who are responsive to the quickly changing landscape and knowledgeable about the misinformation and barriers students face as well as the steps students need to take to stay on their postsecondary path. School counselors should consider partnering with local universities and researchers to identify counseling and advising strategies that best support equitable postsecondary attainment and allow for thriving postpandemic recovery.

I. *Training (Chronosystem).* Partnerships between universities and school counselors should be built on a solid foundation of antiracist practice cultivated in school counseling graduate programs. School counseling graduate programs across the country are continuously reflecting on how best to train school counselors to serve the increasingly diverse K–12 student population. Many are choosing to take their direction from CACREP. The standardization of graduate programs is well intentioned in that it can help ensure that school counselors across the country are gaining the same awareness, knowledge, and skills and that school administrators know exactly what to expect from their contribution to the school's mission. Those intentions, however, do not always translate into desired effective practice. This is particularly true for anti-Black, antiracist school counselor practice. For example, although every CACREP-accredited program has a multicultural counseling course included in its 60-credit curriculum, this does not ensure that students will graduate with cultural competence congruent with specific needs related to systemic anti-Black racism in schools. For school counselors to be prepared, such training needs to be infused throughout the curriculum and not relegated to one course. Every counseling and career theory, for example, must be interrogated through the lens of its applicability, or lack thereof, to Black and Brown students. Furthermore, there should be an intentional, curated space during a student's practicum and internship experience to analyze data, identify gaps, and design and evaluate interventions that target the closing of those gaps. The same critical consciousness that school counselors are expected to facilitate in their students must be similarly cultivated throughout their training experience.

Recommendations

Policy

School counselors are increasingly included in state and national policy, especially when equity and postsecondary attainment are the main focus. As new policies are developed, school counselors must advocate for dispositions that ensure that Black and Brown students matter and that racism, anti-Blackness, and white supremacy cannot exist in systems that claim to value all human life. School counselors must be aware of educational policies that impact their practice and understand how to leverage and advocate for equity-driven and antiracist practices that serve all students. The following are policy-related recommendations school counselors should consider:

1. Conduct an audit of documents, blueprints, and policy briefs to ensure anti-Blackness and white supremacy are in no way reflected in CCR policies.
2. Review the school's mission statement, goals, policies, and procedures to guarantee they incorporate principles and practices that promote diverse perspectives, cultural competence, and inclusive excellence.
3. Ensure that school policies represent the cultures, languages, and racial/ethnic backgrounds of your community.
4. Avoid imposing values that may conflict with those of racial, ethnic, or cultural groups in the community.
5. Ensure that all notices and policy communications to parents are written in their language of origin.
6. Make sure policies intentionally address practices that increase college enrollment, persistence, and completion for Black, Brown, and Indigenous students.
7. Recognize and challenge discrimination and discriminatory practices.
8. Identify federal funding opportunities that increase access and success for minoritized youth in higher education.
9. Establish college and career competencies that are centered in antiracism and equity-driven practice.

Practice

School counselors are in an important position to provide leadership in promoting antiracist practices and speaking out against anti-Blackness in postsecondary preparation. The following are recommendations for how school counselors can engage in antiracist CCR efforts:

1. School counselors should conduct systematic professional development workshops with faculty that illustrate how racism is perpetuated through certain policies and practices.
2. School counselors should facilitate an antiracist system audit in concert with the administration and adjust school handbooks and related policy guides accordingly.
3. School counselors should conduct listening sessions in and with Black, Brown, and Indigenous communities to develop a list of actionable steps to take to facilitate a sense of belonging for Black students. Then they should create partnerships with community members to execute a plan to achieve the identified goals.
4. School counselors should design and deliver large-group guidance lessons to students that promote their awareness, knowledge, and skills around racism, its deleterious effects in schools, and their power to change the narrative in their school and community.
5. School counselors should collaborate at district and school levels through horizontal and vertical teaming to implement and develop systematic antiracist practices that can be used by all schools but are customized to meet the needs of individual schools.
6. School counselors should work with high school graduates going off to college or any postsecondary institution to identify affinity groups, culturally relevant organizations, and offices that promote equity, diversity, and inclusion.
7. School counselors should be intentional about inviting historically Black colleges and universities, Hispanic-serving institutions, and minority-serving institutions to high school college fairs and student meetings rather than only inviting traditional flagship and Research 1 institutions that normally reflect white, middle-class, and suburban norms.
8. School counselors should work with school leaders to promote a school culture of respect and inclusivity for nontraditional families.
9. Messaging about postsecondary opportunities and high expectations must be promoted equitably and supported by school counselors as well as school leaders.
10. School counselors who engage in articulation from middle school to high school should ensure that every student is provided an equitable opportunity to take courses for postsecondary preparation as well as call out bias or racist practices that occur during this process, especially when it comes to students of color, English language learners, and students from economically disadvantaged backgrounds.

Conclusion

We acknowledge that the information presented in this chapter is not exhaustive, but it serves as a foundation for continually exterminating bias, racism, and oppression in the CCR process. Research is needed around using antiracism to promote CCR for students of color, specifically to understand how the implementation of antiracist policies can impact postsecondary aspirations. Finally, school counselors should not just speak up and speak out against these erroneous policies and practices; they must work with stakeholders in and outside the school building to create a sustainable and equitable school environment for students. The late Vivian E. Lee and Gary E. Goodenough so eloquently noted that courage and persistence are character traits of school counselors who want to change the structure of power to help traditionally underrepresented students (Lee & Goodnough, 2019, p. 69).

References

Alexander, M. (2010). *The new Jim Crow: Mass incarceration in the age of colorblindness*. The New Press.

American School Counselor Association. (2017). *The school counselor and individual student planning for postsecondary preparation*. https://www.schoolcounselor.org/Standards-Positions/Position-Statements/ASCA-Position-Statements/The-School-Counselor-and-Individual-Student-Planni

American School Counselor Association. (2019). *The ASCA national model: A framework for school counseling programs* (4th ed.).

American School Counselor Association. (2020). *The school counselor and group counseling*. https://www.schoolcounselor.org/Standards-Positions/Position-Statements/ASCA-Position-Statements/The-School-Counselor-and-Group-Counseling

Anderson, C. (2016). *White rage: The unspoken truth of our racial divide*. Bloomsbury.

Booth, J. (2019). Capitalism, anti-Blackness, and the law: A very short history. *Harvard BlackLetter Law Journal, 35*, 5–9.

Bronfenbrenner, U. (1977). Toward an experimental ecology of human development. *American Psychologist, 32*(7), 513–531. https://doi.org/10.1037/0003-066X.32.7.513

Brown, J., Hatch, T., Holcomb-McCoy, C., Martin, P., Mcleod, J., Owen, L., & Savitz-Romer, M. (2017, January). *The state of school counseling: Revisiting the path forward*. https://www.american.edu/centers/cprs/upload/revisiting-the-path-forward-report-full-report.pdf

Bryan, J., & Henry, L. (2008). Strength-based partnerships: A school-family-community partnership approach to empowering students. *Professional School Counseling, 2*(2), 149–156.

Byun, S., Irvin, M. J., & Meece, J. L. (2012). Predictors of bachelor's degree completion among rural students at four-year institutions. *The Review of Higher Education, 35*(3), 463–484.

Byun, S., Meece, J. L., & Irvin, M. J. (2012). Rural-nonrural disparities in postsecondary educational attainment revisited. *American Educational Research Journal, 49*(1), 412–437.

Carey, J. C., & Martin, I. (2015). *A review of the major school counseling policy studies in the United States: 2000-2014*. https://files.eric.ed.gov/fulltext/ED561867.pdf

Carnevale, A. P., Cheah, B., & Hanson, A. R. (2015). *The economic value of college majors*. https://cew.georgetown.edu/wp-content/uploads/Exec-Summary-web-B.pdf

Coles, J. A., & Powell, T. (2020). A BlackCrit analysis on Black urban youth and suspension disproportionality as anti-Black symbolic violence. *Race Ethnicity and Education, 23*(1), 113–133. https://doi.org/10.1080/13613324.2019.1631778

Conley, D. T. (2010). *College and career ready: Helping all students succeed beyond high school*. Jossey-Bass.

Crenshaw, K. (1989). Demarginalizing the intersection of race and sex: A black feminist critique of antidiscrimination doctrine, feminist theory and antiracist politics. *University of Chicago Legal Forum, 1989*(1), 139–167.

Crenshaw, K. (1991). Mapping the margins: Intersectionality, identity politics, and violence against women of color. *Stanford Law Review, 43*(6), 1241–1299.

Crenshaw, K. (2015, September 24). Why intersectionality can't wait. *The Washington Post.* https://www.washingtonpost.com/news/in-theory/wp/2015/09/24/why-intersectionality-cant-wait/

Darling-Hammond, L. (2004). The color line in American education: Race, resources, and student achievement. *Du Bois Review: Social Science Research on Race, 1*(2), 213–246. https://doi.org/10.1017/S1742058X0404202X

Darling-Hammond, L. (2007). Race, inequality and educational accountability: The irony of 'No Child Left Behind.' *Race Ethnicity and Education, 10*(3), 245–260. https://doi.org/10.1080/13613320701503207

Dell'Angela, T. (2016, May 17). *Suburban schools are not ready for big-city challenges.* Head in the Sand. https://headinthesandblog.org/2016/05/suburban-schools-are-not-ready-for-big-city-challenges/

English, D., Rasmussen, J., Cushing, E., & Therriault, S. (2016). *Leveraging the Every Student Succeeds Act to support state visions for college and career readiness.* www.ccrscenter.org/sites/default/files/AskCCRS_LeveragingESSA.pdf

Epstein, J. E., & Associates. (2019). *School, family, and community partnerships: Your handbook for action* (4th ed.). Corwin.

Epstein, R., Blake, J. J., & González, T. (2017). *Girlhood interrupted: The erasure of Black girls' childhood.* Georgetown Law Center on Poverty and Inequality. https://www.law.georgetown.edu/poverty-inequality-center/wp-content/uploads/sites/14/2017/08/girlhood-interrupted.pdf

Erford, B. T. (2019). *Transforming the school counseling profession* (5th ed.). Merrill Prentice Hall.

Every Student Succeeds Act, 20 U.S.C. § 6301 (2015). https://congress.gov/114/plaws/publ95/PLAW-114publ95.pdf

Ford, D. Y., & Moore, J. L., III. (2013). Understanding and reversing underachievement, low achievement, and achievement gaps among high-ability African American males in urban school contexts. *Urban Review, 45*(4), 399–415. https://doi.org/10.1007/s11256-013-0256-3

Gill, S., Posamentier, J., & Hill, P. T. (2016). *Suburban schools: The unrecognized frontier in public education.* https://www.crpe.org/sites/default/files/crpe.suburban_schools_5.2016.pdf

Goff, P. A., Jackson, M. C., Di Leone, B. A. L., Culotta, C. M., & DiTomasso, N. A. (2014). The essence of innocence: Consequences of dehumanizing Black children. *Journal of Personality and Social Psychology, 106*(4), 526–545.

Goldman, M., & Korn, M. (2020, November 9). College-admissions season was already stressful. Pandemic made it chaotic. *The Wall Street Journal.* https://www.wsj.com/articles/college-admissions-season-was-already-stressful-pandemic-made-it-chaotic-11604917801

Gould, E. (2020, February 27). *Black-white wage gaps are worse today than in 2000.* Economic Policy Institute. https://www.epi.org/blog/black-white-wage-gaps-are-worse-today-than-in-2000/

Gutierrez, L. M. (1995). Understanding the empowerment process: Does consciousness make a difference? *Social Work Research, 19*(4), 229–237.

Hannon, M. (2016). Professional development needs of urban school counselors: A review of the literature. *Journal of Counselor Preparation and Supervision, 8*(2), Article 8. https://doi.org/10.7729/82.1171

Harris, P. C. (2015). Urban Black male student athletes: School counseling interventions. In M. S. Henfield & A. R. Washington (Eds.), *Black male student success in the 21st century urban schools: School counseling for equity, access and achievement* (pp. 125–138). Information Age.

Harris, P. C., Seward, M., Mayes, R. D., Elopre, L. R., & Wengert, E. C. (in press). "We got to do better": Interactions between school counselors and Black male student athletes. *Professional School Counseling*.

Hines, E. M., Borders, L. D., & Gonzalez, L. M. (2015). "It takes fire to make steel": Stories of two African American males finding purpose through their college experiences. *Journal for Multicultural Education, 9*(4), 225–247.

Hines, E. M., Harris, P. C., Mayes, R. D., & Moore, J. L., III. (2020). I think of college as setting a good foundation for my future: Black males navigating the college decision making process. *Journal for Multicultural Education, 14*(2), 129–147.

Hines, E. M., Hines, M. R., Moore, J. L., III, Steen, S., Singleton, P., II, Cintron, D., Traverso, K., Golden, M. N., Wathen, B., & Henderson, J. A. (2020). Preparing African American males for college: A group counseling approach. *Journal for Specialists in Group Work, 45*(2), 129–145. https://doi.org/10.1080/01933922.2020.1740846

Hines, E. M., Moore, J. L., III, Mayes, R. D., Harris, P. C., Singleton, P., II, Hines, C. M., Harried, C. J., & Wathen, B. (2020). Black males in rural context: Challenges and opportunities. In C. R. Chambers & L. Crumb (Eds.), *African American rural education: College transitions* (pp. 53–66). Emerald Group.

Hines, E. M., Vega, D., Mayes, R. D., Harris, P. C., & Mack, K. (2019). College and career readiness: School psychologists and school counselors as collaborators. *Journal for Multicultural Education, 13*(3), 190–202.

Hipolito-Delgado, C. P., & Lee, C. C. (2007). Empowerment theory for the professional school counselor: A manifesto for what really matters. *Professional School Counseling, 10*(4), 327–332.

Holcomb-McCoy, C., Mayes, R. D., Savitz-Romer, M., Cheatham, C. B., & Sharp, S. (2020). *Antiracist school counseling: A call to action* [Webinar]. American University. https://youtu.be/JEjNaB2L3Vc

Horn, L., Cataldi, E. F., & Sikora, A. (2006). Waiting to attend college: Undergraduates who delay their postsecondary enrollment. *Education Statistics Quarterly, 7*(1&2). https://nces.ed.gov/programs/quarterly/vol_7/1_2/5_1.asp

Hussar, B., Zhang, J., Hein, S., Wang, K., Roberts, A., Cui, J., Smith, M., Bullock Mann, F., Barmer, A., & Dilig, R. (2020). *The condition of education 2020* (NCES 2020-144). National Center for Education Statistics. https://nces.ed.gov/pubs2020/2020144.pdf

Kendi, I. X. (2019). *How to be an antiracist*. One World.

Kominak, T. (2018, December 27). Top stories of 2018: Rural schools face common challenges, but need unique solutions. *TrustED.* https://www.k12insight.com/trusted/report-rural-schools/

LaPrade, K. (2011). Removing instructional barriers: One track at a time. *Education, 134*(4), 740–752.

Lee, V. L., & Goodnough, G. E. (2019). Systemic, data-driven school counseling practice and programming for equity. In B. T. Erford, *Transforming the school counseling profession* (5th ed. pp. 67–93). Pearson.

Love, B. L. (2019). *We want to do more than survive: Abolitionist teaching and the pursuit of educational freedom*. Beacon Press.

Malin, J. R., Bragg, D. D., & Hackmann, D. G. (2017). College and career readiness and the Every Student Succeeds Act. *Educational Administration Quarterly*, 53(5), 809–838.

Mayes, R. D., & Vega, D. (in press). Postsecondary readiness for Black girls with disabilities: The role of school counselors and school psychologists. In R. D. Mayes, M. Shavers, & J. L. Moore, III (Eds.), *African American female students in preK-12 schools and beyond: Informing research, policy, and practice*. Emerald Group.

McGhee, K. (2019, April 25). *What is a suburban school?* The Classroom. https://www.theclassroom.com/suburban-school-5108665.html

Monaghan, D. B., Hawkins, J., & Hernandez, A. (2020). Dream adjusters: High school counselors in a low-income school district. *Education and Urban Society*, 52(5), 704–733.

Moore-Thomas, C., & Day-Vines, N. L. (2010). Culturally competent collaboration: School counselor collaboration with African American families and communities. *Professional School Counseling*, 14(1), 53–63.

Mosley, D. V., Hargons, C. N., Meiller, C., Angyal, B., Wheeler, P., Davis, C., & Stevens-Watkins, D. (2021). Critical consciousness of anti-Black racism: A practical model to prevent and resist racial trauma. *Journal of Counseling Psychology*, 68(1), 1–16.

National Defense Education Act of 1958, Pub. L. No. 85-864, as amended by the 88th Congress. (1964).

National Office for School Counselor Advocacy. (2010). *Eight components of college and career readiness counseling*. College Board. https://secure-media.collegeboard.org/digitalServices/pdf/nosca/11b_4416_8_Components_WEB_111107.pdf

National Student Clearinghouse Research Center. (2020, December 10). *High school benchmarks 2020: National college progression rates*. https://nscresearchcenter.org/wp-content/uploads/2020_HSBenchmarksReport.pdf

Patrick, K., Rose Socol, A., & Morgan, I. (2020). *Inequities in advanced coursework*. The Education Trust. https://edtrust.org/resource/inequities-in-advanced-coursework/

Powell, T. (2014, July 24). My son has been suspended five times. He's 3. *The Washington Post*. https://www.washingtonpost.com/posteverything/wp/2014/07/24/my-son-has-been-suspended-five-times-hes-3/

Schneider, J. (2017, August 25). The urban-school stigma. *The Atlantic*. https://www.theatlantic.com/education/archive/2017/08/the-urban-school-stigma/537966/

Sisko, S. (2021). Cultural responsiveness in counselling and psychology: An introduction. In V. Hutton & S. Sisko (Eds.), *Multicultural responsiveness in counseling and psychology: Working with Australian populations* (pp. 1–21). Palgrave Macmillan.

Smith, L., Davis, K., & Bhowmik, M. (2010). Youth participatory action research groups as school counseling interventions. *Professional School Counseling*, 14(2), 174–182.

Southern Regional Education Board. (2019). *SREB regional overview*. https://www.sreb.org/regional-overview-and-trends

Teaching inequality: The problem of public school tracking. (1989). *Harvard Law Review*, 102(6), 1318–1341. https://doi.org/10.2307/1341297

Urban Institute. (n.d.). *Making college more affordable: State policies and programs*. http://collegeaffordability.urban.org/covering-expenses/state-policies/#/

U.S. Department of Education. (n.d.). *Laws and guidance.* https://www2.ed.gov/policy/landing.jhtml?src=ft

Washington, A. R. (2018). Integrating hip-hop culture and rap music into school counseling with Black males. *Journal of Counseling & Development*, *96*(1), 97–105. https://doi.org/10.1002/jcad.12181

Watson, A., & Pananjady, K. (2020, December 11). College financial aid applications down 16% this school year. *CT Mirror.* https://ctmirror.org/2020/12/11/college-financial-aid-applications-down-16-this-school-year/

Wright, B. L., Ford, D. Y., & Young, J. L. (2017). Ignorance or indifference? Seeking excellence and equity for under-represented students of color in gifted education. *Global Education Review*, *4*(1), 45–60. https://ger.mercy.edu/index.php/ger/article/view/290

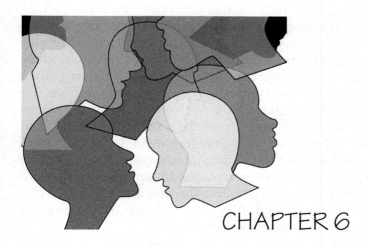

CHAPTER 6

An Antiracist Professional Development Curriculum for School Counselors

Traci Dennis, Joshua Schuschke, and Cheryl Holcomb-McCoy

Nationwide protests in response to racialized police brutality and an increase in white supremacist terrorist groups have led to a significant shift in conversations about racial inequities in schools. Although it may be premature to say that these conversations signal an awakening, there has been an uptick in educators' interest in professional development (PD) related to racial awareness and antiracist skills. PD is often the response to fixing the issue of racism in schools. However, access to high-quality training and PD is limited. This chapter focuses on a PD curriculum for providing school counselors with knowledge, awareness, and skill in antiracist counseling practice. The curriculum, the Antiracist Professional Development (APD) curriculum, was developed specifically for school counselors but can be adjusted for members of other counseling disciplines, helping professionals, and educators.

Background on the PD of Educators

PD is often understood as a broad system of learning experiences that aim for change (Fraser et al., 2007) and as an "uptake of formal and informal learning opportunities that deepen and extend one's professional competence, including knowledge, beliefs, motivation, and self-regulatory skills" (Richter et al., 2011, p. 116). For this reason, PD is often connected to many school improvement efforts to ensure that teachers, counselors, and other educators have the skills and/or knowledge to carry out a particular strategy or to ensure that outcomes of strategies are met. Guskey (2000) argued, "Never before in the history of education has greater importance been attached to the professional development of educators" (p. 3). Indeed, as Feiman-Nemser (2001) has claimed, if we want more antiracist, culturally competent school counselors, we must offer more effective learning opportunities for counselors.

Recent shifts in the need for more antiracist and culturally responsive counselors and educators have been documented by professional counseling associations (American Counseling Association, 2020; American School Counselor Association, 2020). These changes have been accompanied by parallel shifts in ideas about counselor learning and PD. Most experts in the field advocate moving away from an in-service training model, in which educators or counselors are expected to learn a clearly defined body of skills through a well-specified process, often in one-shot workshops or courses taught away from the school premises. These traditional approaches are generally viewed as overly fragmented, not connected closely enough to classroom practice, and out of alignment with current theories of learning and school reform. They are being replaced by approaches that are more closely aligned with constructivist and situative theories and reform efforts; specifically, these new approaches are grounded in actual practice and involve the formation of professional learning communities.

For many years, the literature and research on PD in education have suggested two features of effective PD. It should (a) situate the content in practice and (b) be focused (at least in part) on students' or clients' outcomes. More specifically, high-quality PD should be centered on practice as well as knowledge and skill-building. Another feature of high-quality PD is the use of modeling and/or activities that provide an opportunity for participants to engage in cycles of experimentation and reflection.

The remainder of this chapter includes a description of the APD curriculum, a PD curriculum for training school counselors to view their work through an antiracist lens.

A Description of the APD Curriculum and Its Modules

The APD curriculum provides school counselors with interdisciplinary content knowledge, skill development, and analytic tools to identify and disrupt structural and interpersonal forms of racism. Specifically, the APD curriculum is designed to achieve five goals: (a) promote critical reflections of counselors' experiences with racism, white supremacy, and anti-Blackness; (b) develop a structural and intersectional analysis of oppression within the U.S. educational system; (c) draw connections between counselor positionalities and educational institutions; (d) provide a set of skills in race consciousness that enable counselors to address issues of race and racism within school environments; and (e) cultivate an ongoing commitment to dismantling white supremacy through reflexive praxis and antiracist leadership within schools and communities. These goals are foregrounded in particular sessions while also reflected throughout the entire curriculum.

As counselors matriculate through the APD curriculum they receive specialized training to develop subject knowledge, self-evaluations, and practitioner skillsets through lessons and case studies, journal reflections, and workshop sessions. As shown in Figure 6.1, nine sessions in total are designed to build sequentially on previous lessons or workshops, culminating with counselors gaining self-sustaining practices and antiracist leadership skills that enable continuous development beyond their time as participants in APD. The important first session in the center of the figure is the foundational knowledge base that is used throughout the series. Sessions 2, 4, 6, and 8 are theory, history, and content sessions, whereas Sessions 3, 5, 7, and 9 are skill development and leadership training workshops.

Who can facilitate the APD curriculum? Facilitating discussions of racism is not easy. Derald Wing Sue (2020) recommended that "instructors need to understand not only the content of the communication but the process resulting from the interpersonal dynamics" (p. 2). We believe the facilitators of this curriculum must be highly knowledgeable on issues of racism in education and counseling. Also, they should have a keen awareness of their own racial identity and positioning in society.

In the remainder of this section, we describe each session by outlining its core content, objectives, and desired outcomes for knowledge and skill-building. See Figure 6.1 for the framework of the APD curriculum.

Session 1: Building an Antiracist Praxis

Session 1 begins the APD curriculum by outlining key definitions and providing a conceptual framework for understanding antiracist work. Specifically, this session introduces antiracism as an epistemology, advocacy practice, and educational policy tool. The purpose of Session 1 is to recognize various understandings of concepts related to race, racism, and antiracism and move participants toward more accurate and shared definitions that are used throughout the remainder of the APD curriculum. This process is achieved through co-constructing definitions of key terms in breakout groups to locate commonalities and differences in individuals' knowledge of the key terms. These definitions are then compared to scholarly definitions to help participants build their knowledge base with a correct(ed)

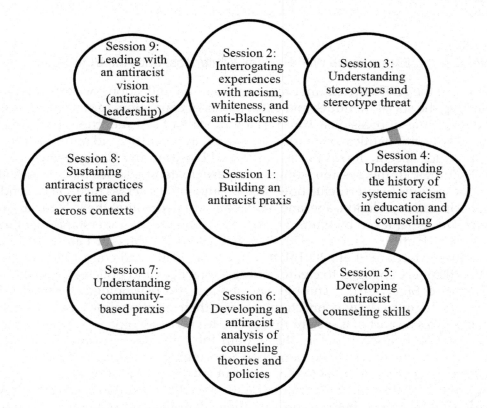

FIGURE 6.1 • Framework of the Antiracist Professional Development Curriculum

conceptualization of ideas. Specifically, participants are provided with definitions and theories of antiracism (Dei, 2013; Kendi, 2016) and antiracist education (Blakeney, 2005; Darling-Hammond, 2017; Denis & Schick, 2003). Counselors learn to differentiate among race, ethnicity, and nationality (Omi & Winant, 2015) while also understanding key terms and concepts such as intersectionality (P. H. Collins & Bilge, 2020; Crenshaw, 1989, 1991), decolonization (Arday et al., 2021; Zembylas, 2018), white supremacy (Bonilla-Silva, 2014), and anti-Blackness (Dumas, 2016; Dumas & ross, 2016). These definitions are foundational to the well-rounded antiracist knowledge base that counselors will use to evaluate their ideologies, practices, and school policies for the remainder of the PD series.

Session 1 also includes the perspectives of students of color through a round-table event in which they share their insights and perspectives on how to create more inclusive and antiracist school environments and experiences. The session concludes with breakout groups that challenge participants to critically evaluate and reflect on their own racialized belief systems and practices. These breakout sessions are bolstered by the firsthand accounts of the students of color and the definitions provided during the lesson, which give counselors the necessary language to reassess practices, ask questions relative to the series goals, and provide frameworks for structural analysis. By the end of Session 1, participants can define the key terms and are beginning to understand the nonlinear journey of building an antiracist praxis. A journal assignment that participants complete for the next session builds on the last breakout session by asking counselors to reflect on and write about their professional training and experiences and how these contributed to creating a racist or antiracist environment at their schools.

Session 2:
Interrogating Experiences With Racism, Whiteness, and Anti-Blackness

Session 2 of the APD curriculum builds on the initial reflections of participants by connecting the social identities and experiences of counselors to structural racism and intersecting oppressions. Through the process of self-reflection, participants locate their positionalities to identify how racist, Eurocentric, and anti-Black structures produce specific forms of inequities and biases in the United States and in school settings. In this session, counselors participate in a series of exercises and breakout sessions to interrogate how their positionalities across race, class, gender, sexual orientation, religion, age, and ability are situated within the U.S. racial caste system. This is achieved by guiding participants toward an understanding of how their social identities (Helms, 1990; Stets & Burke, 2000; Stets & Fares, 2019), positionalities (Merriam et al., 2001; Utt & Tochluk, 2020), and counseling methods can be reflexively engaged to create antiracist practices and policies (Feucht et al., 2017; Moss & Singh, 2015). Through sociological and psychological frameworks, counselors begin to draw connections among their positionalities, practices, and infrastructures as part of a system that promotes racist ideologies and outcomes.

This session helps counselors throughout the remainder of the APD curriculum as they critically evaluate how their upbringing, training, and internalized assumptions about students of color generate either antiracist or racist practices. For example, participants are provided with the APD self-interrogation tool (Appendix A), which asks them to consider their identities and professional training through a racialized lens, then reflect on experiences in schools when they may have performed racist and/or antiracist practices. Working in conjunction with their previous journal assignment, counselors see in detail how they perpetuate, and can ultimately subvert, racist practices and policies for an antiracist reimagining of the field of school counseling.

In addition to reflecting critically on their experiences and practices with students of color, participants also review their school counseling initiatives and protocols. The session concludes with counselors examining programming practices as a way of beginning to develop a critical analysis of school counseling practices, initiatives, opportunities, and mandates. These self-evaluations and critical analysis tools serve as building blocks for counselors as the series shifts toward direct impacts on the academic experiences of students and the history of racism in education. The journal assignment for this session asks counselors to reflect critically on a specific interaction with a student of color and how their actions may have been received by the student; what drove their actions; and how a better understanding of their identities, the student's identities, race, and positionality may have generated a different outcome.

Session 3: Understanding Stereotypes and Stereotype Threat

Session 3 of the APD curriculum transitions counselors from the process of self-reflecting to understanding the experiences of students of color. In this session, which functions as a workshop, participants learn about the history of, pervasive spread of, and academic outcomes associated with stereotypes about students of color and their intellectual and social-emotional abilities. The session begins with breakout sessions that require participants to reflect on stereotypes they have encountered, believe(d) in, or rejected, then consider where they heard these stereotypes and how they are used in educational contexts. After discussing the prevalence of stereotypes in society, participants are provided with a historical account of eugenics as an academic field that sought to reify race through scientific justification of the alleged intellectual inferiorities of people who were not white (Graves, 2008; Kendi, 2016). Next participants trace the deemphasizing of race science in favor of culturally deficit theories about Black and Brown communities' orientation toward education (Cokley, 2015; Harris, 2011). The historical content culminates with participants learning about the emergence of racist and anti-Black stereotypes relative to theories of "acting white" (Tyson, 2011), model minorities (Chou & Feagin, 2015), and Latinx resistance to schooling (Valenzuela, 1999).

The historical backdrops discussed in Session 3 pave the way for counselors to understand how they can design new counseling approaches in school contexts. Participants are introduced to stereotype threat as empirical evidence of the negative outcomes associated with racialized stereotypes, standardized testing, and their connected societal implications (Cokley, 2015; Nasir & Shah, 2011; Steele, 1997; Steele & Aronson, 1995). This lesson on stereotype threat is bolstered by encouraging counselors to problematize standardized testing as a Eurocentric and culturally biased form of assessment that problematizes Black students' behavior. During another breakout session, counselors are asked to discuss more culturally inclusive ways of assessing knowledge that they may advocate for in their schools. Participants leave their breakout sessions with innovative ideas that bolster students' identity, culture, and funds of knowledge that they can share with the broader collective.

Along with the results of the breakout sessions, participants are provided with identity-affirming practices, culturally responsive forms of assessment, and proof of their effectiveness as a way to combat stereotype threat and advocate for the implementation of antiracist practices and assessments in their schools (Livingston et al., 2008; McGee, 2013; McGee & Martin, 2011; Oliver et al., 2017; Scott & White, 2013). By the end of this session, counselors have acquired knowledge of the racist history of stereotypes, standardized tests, and theories of cultural deficits. Participants have also received training on various antiracist methods for combating stereotype threat and promoting student identity and culture. The journal assignment for this session asks counselors to operationalize one of the identity-affirming practices or culturally responsive assessments that they workshopped during the week at their school and write about their experience, successes, and difficulties using it.

Session 4:
Understanding the History of Systemic Racism in Education and Counseling

Session 4 provides counselors with additional core historical knowledge of the development of education as an institution in the United States. Specifically, participants learn about the denial of access to education to enslaved Africans, the indoctrination of First Nations people, and agentic ways in which these groups sought education and built their own schools (J. D. Anderson, 1988). In this session, counselors are expected to grapple with the history of schools and academic subjects as venues for resistance and oppression (Guthrie, 2004; Wilder, 2013). Essential to this session is tracing the rise of neoliberal politics in education and the role of private schools (Khan, 2010), charters (Frankenberg et al., 2011; Riel et al., 2018), and for-profit colleges (McMillan Cottom, 2017) as contemporary institutions that perpetuate racial inequality. During breakout sessions, participants are asked to locate the vestiges and reconfigurations of racist school policy and culture.

In addition to the broad impact and pervasiveness of racism within U.S. educational institutions, this session explores the role of counselors as important actors in mitigating the effects of racism in schools. Specifically, participants are provided with empirical evidence of the role of color-blind attitudes, white identity, and privilege as inhibitors to opportunity for students of color (Holcomb-McCoy, 2007; Pieterse, 2009; Sue & Sue, 1999). During breakout sessions, participants discuss how racist school counseling practices can lead to disproportionate numbers of Black students being tracked into remedial courses and suspended from school as well as the role of these practices as mediators of racist interactions between students and teachers. The session concludes with further empirical evidence of the effectiveness of school counselors as antiracist or social justice advocates and a preview of strategies deployed to achieve the five goals of the APD curriculum (Griffin & Stern, 2011; Holcomb-McCoy, 2007).

By the end of this session, counselors understand the racist genesis and transformation of public education as well as the rise of private education, and public education funding models, as neoliberal institutions that perpetuate inequality. Participants have also acquired foundational knowledge of the role of school counseling in relation to racism. These pieces of knowledge are essential for understanding how traditional or mainstream counseling practices perpetuate racism and advocating antiracism in schools. After this session, counselors write in their journal about a specific experience they had in their professional setting that dealt with issues of race and racism and their response to it.

Session 5: Developing Antiracist Counseling Skills

In Session 5 of the APD curriculum, school counselors workshop their practitioner skills to construct their antiracist praxis. Participants are introduced to an assortment of counseling paradigms, such as critical race, culturally responsive, multicultural, and social justice counseling, to have a wide pallet of options for engaging various issues in school counseling (Holcomb-McCoy, 2007). Through these various approaches, counselors gain the skills to address racism at multiple levels to ensure that the interpersonal needs of students are met through a structural framework. During this session, counselors work in groups to devise counseling plans to address topics such as the achievement gap, college preparation, and racial conflict in schools (Holcomb-McCoy, 2007; León et al., 2011; Moss & Singh, 2015; Savitz-Romer, 2012). The purpose of these group projects is for participants to begin to apply the knowledge and skillsets they acquired in the previous sessions to develop antiracist counseling practices.

This workshop provides participants with a set of content knowledge and empirical resources that help them evaluate white racial identities and attitudes toward counseling (Constantine, 2002; Moss & Singh, 2015), multicultural competencies (Holcomb-McCoy, 2004; Holcomb-McCoy et al., 2008), and racialized ecologies (Hines & Holcomb-McCoy, 2013). In addition, participants are trained on navigating issues of race and racism in online contexts. Specifically, participants receive training on the embedded nature of racism in technology and the internet while also locating sites and communities of resistance among communities of color (Brock, 2009; Daniels, 2009; Noble, 2018; Tynes et al., 2016). Counselors are then trained to leverage this understanding of racism and social activism on the internet to develop antiracist practices using social media platforms, websites, and blogs (Brock, 2020; Schuschke & Tynes, 2016; Tanksley, 2016). Through this knowledge, this session helps counselors leverage students' cultural funds of knowledge and identities; shows them how to mediate racial conflicts between students and teachers; and provides them with antiracist resources and materials to address structural and policies and issues, which they will build on in the next session. At the end of this session, participants write about how the confluence of existing counseling methods work in service of or can be adjusted to fit into antiracist counseling practice and how this has the potential to reshape their schools.

Session 6:
Developing an Antiracist Analysis of Counseling Theories and Policies

Session 6 provides counselors with analytic techniques and tools for identifying racist and antiracist school and district policy. Specifically, counselors are trained to analyze school syllabi, curricula, and educational policies to ensure they are culturally responsive, socially just, and antiracist. Participants begin to develop their analytical skills by assessing course syllabi and classroom curricula using culturally responsive frameworks that promote inclusive language and diverse course materials. During breakout sessions, they use the APD curriculum/syllabus evaluation tool (Appendix B) to analyze sample syllabi. This exercise in analyzing course documents builds up their skills so they can analyze more complex school policy.

During the policy portion of Session 6, participants are introduced to the concepts of technical problems and adaptive challenges (Heifetz & Laurie, 1997). The purpose of framing racist policy in this way is to provide counselors with an understanding of the complexities and discomforts of developing antiracist solutions. Counselors are trained to use critical race theory (Bell, 1995) and intersectionality (Crenshaw, 1989, 1991) to analyze educational policy. These theories help participants identify the ways in which policies operationalize color-blind language and multiple systems of oppression to disproportionally impact specific student groups (Bonilla-Silva, 2014; Pollock, 2004; Urrieta, 2006). Participants are given a mandate from their local school systems and are guided through the process of identifying potential racist or intersectional implications of the policy. Examples of policies counselors analyze are various zero-tolerance or school disciplinary policies (Golann & Torres, 2020; Love, 2016; Morris, 2016). Counselors analyze these policies alongside the empirical evidence of their racist impact.

This session concludes with participants acquiring a diverse set of analytic tools and materials to address systemic racism in school curricula and policy. Through the use of culturally responsive curriculum building, critical race theory, and intersectionality, counselors develop a multilayered analysis of how policy is designed and implemented in schools. This analysis and the ability to identify racism in policy serve as the building blocks for the construction of antiracist policy, which is workshopped in the following session. Before beginning the next session, however, participants write in their journals about their past PD training and any form of policy education they might have received in the past. Specifically, counselors are asked in what ways their understanding of racism in policy, either now or in the past, shapes their practices.

Session 7: Understanding Community-Based Praxis

In Session 7, school counselors are provided with resources and exercises to help conceptualize actions that engage their schools and local communities in ways that directly address white supremacy and center the strengths and needs of communities of color. Specifically, this workshop foregrounds social justice organizing, parents, and community involvement alongside counseling. The role of parents and community organizations as socializing agents and institutions for students of color is critical to their development when they are not in school (Hines & Holcomb-McCoy, 2013; Spencer, 1995). Thus, the APD curriculum facilitators foster collaborative opportunities by inviting parents, community leaders, and grassroots organizers to take part in this session. Counselors interact with a panel of parents and form breakout sessions with leaders and organizers to address specific issues relevant to school, home, and community contexts. Examples of topics that counselors and organizers collaborate on include bullying/cyberbullying, police interactions, and mentorship programs. These topics, among others, are considered critical issues that are properly addressed when schools and communities interface with each other (R. E. Anderson et al., 2015; Hines & Holcomb-McCoy, 2013; Ohrt et al., 2009; Tynes et al., 2015, 2019). APD prioritizes community engagement to center the needs of communities of color as a way to dislodge white supremacy and flatten social hierarchies and barriers in educational spaces.

This workshop also includes policy advocacy. During this session, participants and local organizers formulate a plan of action around a particular educational initiative, policy, or law. These plans of action include, but are not limited to, political campaigning, canvassing, online awareness-raising, and the development of new policies. After analyzing these mandates through the critical race and intersectional lenses provided in the previous session, counselors devise plans for how they can mitigate the effects of racist policies through the skillsets they have acquired through the APD. In addition to using their antiracist counseling skills, the participants also work in breakout groups to draft antiracist policies that address a racialized issue in K–12 settings.

By the conclusion of Session 7, counselors have forged relationships with local parents, community leaders, and organizations to develop an antiracist ecological approach to dealing with topics pertinent to students of color. Specifically, counselors have learned to leverage community strengths and funds of knowledge to dislodge white colonial practices in schools. This counseling practice is achieved through relationships with communities, antiracist skills, and critical/intersectional policy analysis. The journal assignment associated with this session asks counselors to identify a local community organization that offers innovative approaches to addressing racism and then draft a proposal to invite that organization into their school curriculum or programming.

Session 8: Sustaining Antiracist Practices Over Time and Across Contexts

Session 8 focuses on the long-term sustainability of antiracist practices. Participants gain an understanding of how reflexive praxis leads to a lifelong commitment to antiracism and how decolonizing white supremacist and anti-Black pedagogy is essential to providing quality counseling. This session also provides counselors with skills and resources to continue their antiracist journey along with training on handling resistance from various institutional actors and mandates. Specifically, participants take part in a series of activities and breakout sessions that prepare them for resistance to antiracist counseling from students, teachers, and administrators. Counselors are provided with Pieterse's (2009) strategies for handling resistance, which include constructivism, reliance on scholarship, reflective learning, systemic focus, and processing of emotion.

Sustaining an antiracist praxis beyond the APD includes not only handling resistance from individuals and institutions but continuing the self-reflection process. Session 8 provides counselors with a set of tools and practices that allow them to periodically reevaluate their belief systems, reassess their positionalities, and check their privileges as their contexts change and new developments related to race and racism emerge over time. The sustained practice of self-reflection returns participants to the foundational concepts of Session 1 so they understand antiracism as a nonlinear journey. Alongside training on encountering resistance, continuous self-reflection prepares participants for sustainable antiracist practices that they will carry into their school and counseling settings.

By the end of this session, participants have an expansive and foundational knowledge of racism and antiracism that will benefit their students, schools, and districts as a whole. At the conclusion of Session 8, the APD facilitators identify exemplary participants and request their participation in the final session. The requirements for participation in Session 9 include the following: (a) exhibited knowledge of the core competencies of antiracism, (b) exceptional self-reflections as demonstrated through course participation and journal entries, (c) unique leadership and counseling skills displayed during breakout sessions and workshops, and (d) an express desire to teach and train colleagues at their schools.

Session 9: Leading With an Antiracist Vision

The final session of the APD curriculum trains leaders in antiracist educational praxis. The purpose of this session is to identify exceptional participants who have demonstrated the capability to lead their school's antiracist efforts. In alignment with the existing research on PD, counselors participating in this session help expand and sustain antiracist training by becoming contextual experts who can build rapport with students, staff, and administrators (Darling-Hammond et al., 2017). The purpose of this leadership training is to provide schools with a well-rounded expert in antiracist education. School counselors serve as ideal candidates for this role, as they function as liaisons for interactions among students, their peers, teachers, and administrators.

The antiracist leaders who participate in this session leave with a set of skills tailored to training their peers and colleagues. Specifically, these leaders gain a thorough understanding of the essential content, exercises, and goals of the APD curriculum to conduct training at their schools that is designed to meet the needs of their schools. Leaders are provided with access to resources such as community forums, reports, and asynchronous training videos that will assist them in gaining expertise and workshop facilitation skills in several topics in antiracist education. In addition to these resources, participants exit the final APD session with the ability to provide training on antiracist teaching practices, curriculum building, and school policy analysis.

By the conclusion of the APD series, school counselors have accrued an array of content knowledge and skillsets that match the multidimensional nature of their jobs. This expertise and leadership training culminates in a certification in antiracist praxis, which we believe should be renewed annually. We recommend that school counselors gain recertification in antiracist praxis based on student data, school counseling program evaluation, and school racial climate data. This certification process ensures that counselors are adequately training their colleagues, promoting an antiracist educational environment, and actively revising school policy to ensure antiracist and intersectional equity.

The framework of the APD curriculum, which moves participants from individual and interpersonal understandings of racism toward a structural analysis that leads to an antiracist praxis, heightens the effectiveness of school counseling. This training provides schools with a professionally trained advocate who can locate racism at all levels and has the requisite tools and skillsets to undo or abolish racist policy and practices. When counselors receive this training and develop into antiracist leaders, they have a greater opportunity to improve the educational experience for students of color as their identities, cultures, and intellectual assets become the center of antiracist education.

APD Pitfalls and Possibilities

Citing McCarthy and Crichlow's (1993) work on race identity and representation in education, Denis and Schick (2003) addressed the concern that "antiracist teaching can unintentionally reinforce relations of domination in educational settings if the teaching fails to examine racist ideologies and the politics of racial identifications" (p. 57). To become actively antiracist, school counselor trainees[1] must clearly understand how race, racism, and white supremacy operate in our schools and society. Effective APD provides opportunities for participants to conduct an in-depth analysis of structural racism and the power relations behind it and to examine how their interactions with students of color are impacted by beliefs, ideologies, assumptions, and practices rooted in racism. According to Locke and Kiselica (1999), "Developing complex-thinking competencies about racism is different from transmitting a body of counseling knowledge" (p. 81). To this end, antiracist counselor training needs to involve a shift in focus. Instead of focusing on building the core competencies of an effective counselor, counselor educators[2] must first begin by taking trainees on a journey to an understanding of what racism is and what it does to human beings (Locke & Kiselica, 1999). We are all racial beings who internalize racist attitudes and exhibit racist behaviors; therefore, examining self and interrogating experiences with racism, white supremacy, and anti-Blackness is a critical first step. When implementing antiracist training, counselor educators must consider and address pitfalls and possibilities. Using the five goals and nine sessions of the APD curriculum as a springboard, here we use literature to explicate and illuminate three common pitfalls to avoid and possibilities to consider when delivering APD training to school counselor trainees.

Pitfall 1:
Failing to Promote Critical Reflections on School Counselor Trainees' Experiences With Racism, White Supremacy, and Anti-Blackness

A common pitfall of antiracist training is that participants are not required to focus on themselves before they begin to examine and interrogate the other (Matias, 2013). Self-interrogation reinforces the idea that everyone is a racialized being who harbors racist beliefs and ideas. In discussing how to build counselor trainees' racial/cultural awareness, N. M. Collins and Pieterse (2007) noted that the way in which counselor trainees are socialized impacts their ability to engage in racial awareness training. Because counseling work is carried out in a society in which racism and white supremacy are ubiquitous, it is critical that counselor trainees be given time, space, and opportunities to unpack positionalities, identities, and experiences relative to race, racism, power, and white supremacy. To avoid the pitfall of failing to first examine positionalities, identities, and experiences relative to race, racism, and white supremacy, counselor educators delivering antiracist training must engage counselor trainees in critical self-interrogation. *Self-interrogation* is defined as "considering how our own identities, socialization, affiliations, cultural practices and experiences impact our beliefs and shape how we see and understand children in ways that may be positive and negative, conscious and unconscious" (Teaching Works, 2019, p. 1). Session 2 of the APD curriculum is designed

---

[1]Counseling students are hereinafter referred to as school counselor trainees or counselor trainees.
[2]Counselor educators are those who are conducting the APD training.

to ensure that school counselor trainees work to examine, identify, and surface what they have been taught, experienced, and internalized that could negatively or positively impact their actions and interactions with students of color. In her racial literacy development model, Yolanda Sealey-Ruiz (2020) theorized five stages. The second stage, the archeology of self, is defined as a process of digging deep and peeling back layers of one's life experiences. This archeological dig brings to light some of the complex and underlying assumptions and beliefs that counselor trainees hold that are lurking beneath the surface but are not always recognized or acknowledged. The archeological dig reaffirms the idea that we must know our own story and be aware of who we are and what we bring to the school before we can begin to understand the story of others (Sealey-Ruiz, 2020).

Similar to Sealey-Ruiz's (2020) and Matias's (2013) beliefs and research on the importance of self-interrogation, R. T. Carter (2003) stated that "a psychologist or counselor needs to develop an understanding of his or her racial worldview as a prerequisite to understanding others" (p. 22). In 1995, Carter introduced the racial-cultural counseling competence model, which was developed on the premise that the counselor is a person with established histories, relationships, and beliefs (R. T. Carter, 2003). Carter indicated that whereas many trainings on race and culture focus on the minority person and attempt to uncover and understand the lived experiences of minority clients, his model acknowledges counselors as racial and cultural beings who bring their own social identities and reference group affiliations to their counseling work and relationships. This model centers on knowing self first before beginning to embark on the work of knowing other. Identities and affiliations impact how counselors approach their work. By centering and acknowledging identities and affiliations as critical factors in their relationships and interactions, counselor trainees can critically examine how prior learnings and group affiliations impact their practices and interactions with minoritized clients (R. T. Carter, 2003). Carter acknowledged that these identities and affiliations impact counselor trainees on three levels: cognitively, behaviorally, and emotionally. Counselor educators who engage in antiracist training must ensure that counselor trainees surface past and present beliefs and lived experiences. To understand other racialized beings, school counselor trainees must first understand themselves and their beliefs and attitudes about race and racism and how these beliefs and attitudes serve as resources or barriers to developing effective counseling relationships and interventions for students of color.

Building from R. T. Carter's (2003) racial-cultural counseling competence model, a critical component of antiracist training involves ensuring that school counselor trainees are given time and space to explore their own attitudes, beliefs, and values about diverse people and groups. From this deeper level of self-exploration, each counselor trainee will begin to develop and form a sense of self and others in the context of race. To ensure that they take the necessary steps to examine and critique their beliefs, values, and assumptions when it comes to students who do not share their same identities, counselor trainees should think back to their own schooling and specifically examine the following:

- Who was in your school, your community, your classes, and your neighborhood, and how did this impact what you believed about students who did not share your same identity?

- What was your curriculum like? Who was represented and who was invisible? What did you believe about the voices, views, and vantage points that were missing?
- Were students of color disproportionately disciplined? If so, why did you believe this was happening?
- Were there counselors, teachers, or school administrators who did not share your same identity? If so, what were your relationships and interactions with them like?
- Were race and racism openly discussed in your school and community?
- Were there school policies and practices that you felt were unfair or unequal? To whom? Why?

Self-interrogation enables counselor trainees to challenge and critique their beliefs, values, and assumptions based on their past and present lived experiences.

According to Choi (2008), as cited in Pabon and Basile (2019), "unlearning racism" (p. 635) involves recognizing and reckoning with one's beliefs and ideas about who is valuable, valued, and worthy. Studies have shown a connection among counselor attitudes on racism, white racial identity attitudes, and multicultural counseling competence (Constantine, 2002). Constantine (2002) conducted a study of 99 school counselor trainees in a master's-level school counseling course. The purpose of the study was to examine how the participants' racist attitudes and white racial identity attitudes contributed to their self-reported multicultural counseling competence. Constantine used a model of white racial identity development designed by Helms (1995). According to Helms (1995), through socialization white people in the United States learn that they are privileged relative to other racial groups, and they learn to protect their privilege through racist attitudes and behaviors (Helms & Cook, 1999). Helms (1995) identified five statuses that make up the white racial identity development process: (a) contact, in which whites are unaware of how they benefit from institutional and cultural racism and only superficially acknowledge their membership in the white racial group; (b) disintegration, in which whites become increasingly aware of their racial group status but are also ambivalent about being white because they receive more favorable treatment and benefits than other racial groups; (c) reintegration, in which whites behave in ways that maintain racism by embracing and advancing dominant, hegemonic narratives, histories, and ideologies that distort racism; (d) pseudo-independence, in which whites feel subtly superior to and lack acceptance of other racial groups; and (e) autonomy, in which whites internalize a positive racial identity, no longer impose racial definitions on others, and acknowledge and embrace racial differences and similarities (Helms, 1995).

The counselor trainees in Constantine's (2002) study received a survey packet that contained (a) the Multicultural Counseling Knowledge and Awareness Scale (MCKAS; Ponterotto et al., 2002), (b) the New Racism Scale (NRS; Jacobson, 1985), and (c) the White Racial Identity Attitude Scale (WRIAS; Helms, 1999; Helms & Carter, 1990). Instead of the WRIAS, counselor trainees who identified as persons of color completed the Visible Racial/Ethnic Identity Attitude Scale (Helms & Carter, 1986). Data from the Visible Racial/Ethnic Identity Attitude Scale were not included in this study. The NRS has seven items that measure white persons' attitudes toward Blacks. Scores on the NRS range from 7 to 25, with higher scores indicating more racist beliefs and attitudes. The MCKAS has 32 items and uses a 7-point Likert scale (1 = *not at all true*, 7 = *totally true*). Participants rank themselves according to their beliefs about their multicultural counseling efficacy. The two subscales of the survey are Knowledge and Awareness. Constantine (2002) included the full-scale score to determine participants' overall beliefs about their multicultural counseling abilities. The WRIAS contains 50 items and uses a 5-point Likert scale (1 = *strongly disagree*, 5 = *strongly agree*). It requires participants to rank themselves on the five white racial identity statuses outlined earlier: contact, disintegration, reintegration, pseudo-independence, and autonomy.

To disaggregate the data Constantine (2002) followed two steps. First, she identified the number of formal multicultural counseling courses taken. Second, she factored in the race-related attitudinal variables (NRS, WRIAS). Constantine (2003) found that after she accounted for the number of multicultural counseling courses taken, the NRS and WRIAS scores together illuminated significant variance in the MCKAS scores. She noted a specific relationship between NRS scores and disintegration racial identity attitudes. Constantine (2002) found that higher NRS scores were associated with lower self-reported multicultural counseling competence. She also found that higher disintegration racial identity attitudes were also associated with lower self-reported multicultural counseling competence (Constantine, 2002). From these study results it is clear that counselor trainees, especially white counselor trainees, must be afforded opportunities to explore and critique their racist attitudes and white racial identity attitudes.

Constantine's (2002) study demonstrates that race-related attitudinal variables matter and are important to consider when delivering antiracist school counselor training. If they do not understand their own experiences with race and racism, counselor trainees' ability to become competent counselors of culturally diverse students is compromised (Constantine, 2002). Constantine outlined two important insights from this study that have important implications for antiracist school counselor training. First, counselor trainees who have strong racist attitudes and beliefs about students of color are less equipped to deliver high-quality counseling to students who are experiencing challenges with bias, stereotypes, microaggressions, imposter syndrome, and a myriad of other race-based challenges and circumstances that arise in oppressive and marginalized school environments. Second, holding racist beliefs and ideologies makes counselor trainees less attuned to blind spots and barriers that impair and hinder their ability to support students of color. Conversely, counselor trainees who have advanced racial identity attitudes are more likely to be effective at supporting and nurturing culturally diverse students; addressing racially and culturally sensitive issues; and building their awareness to challenge and confront racist policies, practices, and beliefs that harm and hinder minoritized students academically, socially, and emotionally. Moreover, Constantine et al. (1998) noted that school counselors' racist attitudes can impact the way in which they provide career counseling services to students of color. The researchers noted that harboring racist attitudes and beliefs can lead to school counselors not recognizing the full potential of students of color, failing to provide them with appropriate career and college advice or opportunities, and perpetuating further inequalities by denying them access to opportunities and experiences that will enhance their college and career aspirations and outcomes (Constantine et al., 1998).

Supporting the social-emotional health and well-being of students of color is as important as supporting their academic achievement and success. If counselors are not aware of the biases, harmful beliefs, and negative assumptions they are holding, then antiracist training is less likely to move counselor trainees forward in their journey to becoming antiracist counselors. Building counselor trainees' awareness of their attitudes toward white racial identity and racism will enable them to become attuned to blind spots, biases, and barriers that will prevent them from supporting and nurturing culturally diverse students and addressing racially and culturally sensitive issues that these students encounter. As a final note, when conducting self-interrogation, intersectionality must also be presented as a framework and an analysis tool. Coined by Crenshaw (1989, 1991), the term "intersectionality" is used to define how race, class, gender, and other systems intersect with one another and overlap to uniquely oppress women of color. When counselor trainees are pushed to reflect on how their multiple intersecting identities (race, gender, sexuality, ability, class) provide unearned advantages or disadvantages, it serves to deepen their social and political analysis of inequality and why it exists (Denis & Schick, 2003). Self-interrogation also surfaces ideologies and assumptions that counselor trainees hold that may prevent them from beginning the journey to becoming actively antiracist.

Pitfall 2:
Failing to Include Structural and Intersectional Analyses of Racism and Oppression Within the U.S. Educational System

To understand and challenge the racism, discrimination, oppression, and prejudice that students of color face daily in schools, counselor trainees must first believe that racism truly exists. In his *New York Times* best selling book *How to Be an Antiracist*, Ibram Kendi (2019) asserted that "the only way to undo racism is to consistently identify and describe it—and then dismantle it" (p. 9). Antiracist training and workshops often shy away from explicitly acknowledging racist policies and practices in our schools and classrooms. This leads to a reproduction of the status quo, in which established systems and structures of racism, white supremacy, and anti-Blackness reign supreme. When conducting effective antiracist training for school counselor trainees, counselor educators must acknowledge and problematize race as central to disparities in discipline, achievement outcomes, educational and economic advancement, housing, employment, and health care. Failure to surface and challenge these disparities through a racialized lens reinforces color-blind epistemologies (Pabon & Basile, 2019); the myth of meritocracy (Denis & Schick, 2003); and deficit thinking that blames students of color, their families, and their communities for their disparate outcomes (Ford & Grantham, 2003; Lewis et al., 2008).

Denis and Schick (2003) identified three ideological assumptions about inequality that counter antiracist work and can undermine effective antiracist training. These ideologies further enable and sustain personal and systemic racism. The three ideologies are (a) race does not matter; (b) everyone has equal opportunity (meritocracy); and (c) by individual acts and good intentions, one can secure innocence as well as superiority (goodness and innocence; Denis & Schick, 2003). These pervasive ideologies mask the structural and systemic nature of racism and instead reinforce color-blind ideologies; bootstrap mentalities; and the erroneous belief that our schools are fair and equal places where everyone is provided the same experiences, opportunities, supports, and considerations. These beliefs are introduced and reinforced not only in our schools but also in our society and our nation's history (Denis & Schick, 2003).

According to Denis and Schick (2003), antiracist education requires us to examine the practices of individuals and institutions, ideological assumptions, dominant identifications, and power relations. Making counselor trainees aware that they have a racial identity and that it is socially constructed enables them to critically examine how racism operates and how racial classifications have been created and designed to benefit some and oppress others. Counselor trainees must also begin to understand that those dominant representations are constructed and remain active as a result of the silencing of other histories (Denis & Schick, 2003). It is the other histories that must be surfaced and centered so the counterhistories of racialized groups are understood and destigmatized.

P. L. Carter et al. (2016) addressed the harmful impact of unstated and unexamined biases when examining discipline disparities. Studies reveal that when it comes to teacher reactions to misbehavior and school pushout, the differential treatment of white and Black students can be based on beliefs and assumptions rooted in negative stereotypes (Blake et al., 2011; P. L. Carter et al., 2016; Lewis et al., 2010; Lindsay & Hart, 2017; Skiba et al., 2011). Often Black and Brown students receive harsher punishments than white students for the same infractions and behaviors (P. L. Carter et al., 2016). In antiracist training, counselor trainees need to be made aware that disproportionate suspensions and expulsions, arrests, and zero-tolerance consequences are patterns that need to be critiqued and challenged with a racialized lens.

According to P. L. Carter et al. (2016), to counter racial inequality we must examine not only policies but also our own practices and interactions. They also asserted that we cannot address racial disparities without addressing race. Pollock (2004) referred to resistance to race talk as color muteness. The problem with color muteness is that it prevents training participants from engaging in a race-based analysis of the decisions, policies, actions, and interactions that continue to marginalize and oppress students of color. To develop mind-sets, beliefs, and behaviors that challenge racism, counselor trainees must understand and acknowledge that we are all racial beings who internalize racist attitudes and exhibit racist behaviors. In addition, returning to the self-interrogation mentioned earlier, counselor educators must explicitly push counselor trainees to examine what they think about different types of students and how these thoughts consciously or unconsciously guide actions and interactions that counselors have with students of color. P. L. Carter et al. also mentioned the importance of engaging in conversations about race. Not only is this important when discussing discipline disparities, but it is key when discussing all disparities. One important item to note is that these conversations surface "false or harmful notions about 'races' we carry around with us as we interact" (P. L. Carter et al., 2016, p. 220). Having this dialogue during antiracist training is critical because, as these researchers stated in the title of their article, "you can't fix what you don't look at." Engaging in what the researchers called *race consciousness discussions* will enable counselor trainees to unpack and critically analyze how racial dynamics factor into their relationships and interactions with students of color (P. L. Carter et al., 2016).

Becoming actively antiracist requires an ongoing awareness of harmful policies and practices and a steadfast commitment to eradicating them at the individual and institutional levels. Harmful race-based beliefs, stereotypes, and biases that counselor trainees may hold will reinforce and perpetuate institutionalized racism that harms and hinders the achievement of students of color and prevents them from self-actualizing and thriving. One of the ways to counter these harmful policies and practices, which are reinforced by racist ideas and deficit ideologies, is to build the racial literacy of counselor trainees. *Racial literacy* is defined as the knowledges, skills, awareness, and dispositions to talk about race and racism (Howard, 2020). According to Pabon and Basile (2019), to eradicate school-based racial oppression teachers must be able to see it and understand how they are contributing to its reproduction. In understanding how to effectively train school counselors to be antiracist, this same message rings true. Antiracist counselors must be able to understand and interrogate how their beliefs, assumptions, actions, and interactions either advance racist ideas and practices or disrupt them. To disrupt racially oppressive and marginalizing school environments, counselor trainees must engage in critical race reflection. Developing counselor trainees' racial literacy will assist them in translating antiracist theories and research into practice in their daily work and their lives. Three theories that are beneficial for counselor educators to unpack and explore during antiracist counselor training are (a) critical race theory (Bell, 1995), (b) intersectionality (Crenshaw, 1989), and (c) the typology of ethnic identity (Banks, 2004). Being familiar with these theories enables school counselor trainees to more fully explore and understand how race, gender, identity, and multiple intersecting identities, both achieved and ascribed, impact how students of color interact with adults and how adults interact with students of color. Understanding students' racialized identities and experiences and building racial literacy through discussion of how race and racism operate at the individual and institutional levels both historically and currently provide counselor trainees with knowledge and literacies to cultivate an ongoing commitment to dismantling white supremacy and racism through reflexive praxis.

Pitfall 3:
Positioning Counselor Trainees of Color as Cultural Experts, Aides, and Witnesses During Antiracist Training

A common practice in some antiracist training and courses that focus on race and culture is for students of color to take on the role of having to teach white students about racism (Jackson, 1999). In these instances, students of color take on the role of enlightening white students to the pain and realities of racism by sharing personal encounters and experiences with stereotypes, bias, microaggressions, and other verbal and nonverbal assaults. As stated by Pieterse (2009), there are several negative consequences to adopting this methodology or using this practice as a pedagogical tool. For one thing, this approach does not allow for a critical examination of whiteness, as the minoritized student and their experiences are the source and topic of conversation and evaluation. This also allows for the notion and belief of other to exist and whiteness to remain the dominant, uncritiqued norm; thus, white as a racial group and whiteness as a construct remain invisible and uninterrogated. Another problem with centering students of color to teach white students about race and racism is that it robs the students of color from learning about themselves and their beliefs and assumptions relative to race (Pieterse, 2009). Students of color have understandings and experiences of race and racism that they need to unpack and examine. They also need space to process and interrogate how internalized racism and the effects of daily racial encounters have impacted them socially, emotionally, and academically. White students and students of color may understand and experience race and racism differently, yet they should all be afforded opportunities to grapple with, examine, critique, and interrogate their own lived experiences, actions, and interactions.

In problematizing the principles and practices of antiracist educators, Blackwell (2010) spoke to the pitfall of white professors using students of color to advance the learning of white students. In her article, she recounted personal experiences with being relegated to the sidelines in antiracist courses (Blackwell, 2010). She also mentioned the tendency of white educators to use the personal stories of students of color to benefit white students and white educators (Blackwell, 2010). Blackwell urged antiracist educators to place the same level of importance on the educational needs of students of color in antiracist classrooms alongside their white classmates.

One of the main concerns Blackwell (2010) outlined is positioning students of color to be experts on racial identity and racial oppression, which only serves the interests of white students. Hearing stories from marginalized students for the purpose of building white students' racial consciousness not only is unfair and unethical but sidelines and discounts students of color in the classroom and their learning and growth in antiracist education (Blackwell, 2010). Blackwell also asserted that this type of teaching serves to dehumanize students of color and can be damaging to them. She suggested that a more productive approach would be to allow students of color to decide how they want to critique their experiences and to assist them in defining how they would like to build their racial awareness (Blackwell, 2010).

Blackwell (2010) acknowledged that what some white educators and white students may consider antiracist may reinforce racism for racialized students. For example, she listed three roles in which students of color in antiracist classrooms often find themselves: cultural expert, aide, and witness. The cultural expert is expected to provide insight into racism. They provide anecdotes and narratives outlining firsthand experiences with race and racism. The cultural expert is often called on to affirm, authenticate, or absolve (Blackwell, 2010). The aide assists the antiracist educator in dealing with white fragility (DiAngelo, 2018). When white students experience discomfort or become defensive regarding race and racism, the student of color aids the teacher in proving that the allegations or assertions about racism are true and valid (Blackwell, 2010). The student of color provides evidence that the antiracist educator's assertions are valid and accurate. This role can be retraumatizing for a student who has experienced prejudice, racism, and discrimination and also absolves the trainer or instructor from having to argue that racism truly exists and deal with uncomfortable situations and hostility from students. The final role that serves to marginalize and oppress students in antiracist training and classrooms is the witness. Students of color act as witnesses when antiracist educators focus exclusively and solely on "the race-conscious raising and crises of White students" (Blackwell, 2010, p. 486). In this scenario, the needs and desires of white students are paramount, and students of color are once again relegated to the sidelines.

Part of the concern with asking students of color to take on these roles in antiracist courses and training is that their educational goals for the training are now sidelined as they are busy filling a role they did not sign up for and are not being paid to take on. Antiracist trainers would best serve the needs of participants of color by ensuring that (a) they are not positioned as experts, aides, or witnesses; (b) they are not sidelined for white students to gain an understanding of race and racism; and (c) they have critical learning moments and are guided and supported in developing transformative antiracist knowledge, literacies, and capacities.

Implications for Research

Researchers who use antiracism as a theoretical framework or epistemology or study the role of school counselors who adopt an antiracist framework need to have a fundamental understanding of the structural nature of racism within schools and counseling as an academic field. Methodologies used in antiracist research should be rooted within an ethic of dismantling white supremacy and intersectional forms of oppression. Specifically, antiracist research should seek to flatten social hierarchies in practice, which means researchers should consider their positionalities and relationships to their topic of inquiry and ensure that their methodologies are in service of communities of color. The APD series offers those in the field of school counseling the opportunity to conduct research that ties structural racism in educational spaces to the interpersonal interactions that occur among various groups of students, staff, and administrators.

Conclusion

This chapter has outlined the APD curriculum, a nine-session APD curriculum for school counselors. Because school counselors are in a position to positively impact the racial climate of schools as well as the academic and social-emotional outcomes of students, it is fitting that school counselors be the focus of intensive PD to increase their skills to eradicate racism and racist practices in schools.

References

American Counseling Association (2020, June 22). *ACA anti-racism statement.* https://www.counseling.org/news/updates/news-detail/2020/06/22/aca-anti-racism-statement

American School Counselor Association. (2020). *Standards in practice: Eliminating racism and bias in schools: The school counselor's role.*

Anderson, J. D. (1988). *The education of Blacks in the South, 1860-1935.* University of North Carolina Press.

Anderson, R. E., Hussain, S. B., Wilson, M. N., Shaw, D. S., Dishion, T. J., & Williams, J. L. (2015). Pathways to pain: Racial discrimination and relations between parental functioning and child psychosocial well-being. *Journal of Black Psychology, 41*(6), 491–512.

Arday, J., Zoe Belluigi, D., & Thomas, D. (2021). Attempting to break the chain: Reimaging inclusive pedagogy and decolonising the curriculum within the academy. *Educational Philosophy and Theory, 53*(3), 298–313.

Banks, J. A. (2004). Teaching for social justice, diversity, and citizenship in a global world. *The Educational Forum, 68*(4), 296–305.

Bell, D. A. (1995). Who's afraid of critical race theory? *University of Illinois Law Review, 1995,* 893–910.

Blackwell, D. M. (2010). Sidelines and separate spaces: Making education antiracist for students of color. *Race Ethnicity and Education, 13*(4), 473–494.

Blake, J. J., Butler, B. R., Lewis, C. W., & Darensbourg, A. (2011). Unmasking the inequitable discipline experiences of urban Black girls: Implications for urban educational stakeholders. *The Urban Review, 43*(1), 90–106.

Blakeney, A. M. (2005). Antiracist pedagogy: Definition, theory, and professional development. *Journal of Curriculum and Pedagogy, 2*(1), 119–132.

Bonilla-Silva, E. (2014). *Racism without racists: Color-blind racism and the persistence of racial inequality in the United States* (4th ed.). Rowman & Littlefield.

Brock, A. (2009). "Who do you think you are?" Race, representation, and cultural rhetorics in online spaces. *Poroi, 6*(1), 15–35.

Brock, A. (2020). *Distributed Blackness: African American cybercultures.* New York University Press.

Carter, P. L., Skiba, R., Arredondo, M. I., & Pollock, M. (2016). You can't fix what you don't look at: Acknowledging race in addressing racial discipline disparities. *Urban Education, 52*(2), 207–235.

Carter, R. T. (2003). Becoming racially and culturally competent: The racial-cultural counseling laboratory. *Journal of Multicultural Counseling and Development, 31*(1), 20–30.

Chou, R. S., & Feagin, J. R. (2015). *Myth of the model minority: Asian Americans facing racism.* Routledge.

Cokley, K. (2015). *The myth of Black anti-intellectualism: A true psychology of African American students.* ABC-CLIO/Praeger.

Collins, N. M., & Pieterse, A. L. (2007). Critical incident analysis based training: An approach for developing active racial/cultural awareness. *Journal of Counseling & Development, 85*(1), 14–23.

Collins, P. H., & Bilge, S. (2020). *Intersectionality.* Wiley.

Constantine, M. G. (2002). Racism attitudes, white racial identity attitudes, and multicultural counseling competence in school counselor trainees. *Counselor Education and Supervision, 41*(3), 162–174.

Constantine, M. G. (2003). Multicultural competence in supervision: Issues, processes, and outcomes. In D. B. Pope-Davis, H. L. K. Coleman, W. M. Liu, & R. L. Toporek (Eds.), *Handbook of multicultural competencies in counseling and psychology* (pp. 383–391). Sage.

Constantine, M. G., Erickson, C. D., Banks, R. W., & Timberlake, T. L. (1998). Challenges to the career development of urban racial and ethnic minority youth: Implications for vocational intervention. *Journal of Multicultural Counseling and Development, 26,* 83–95.

Crenshaw, K. (1989). Demarginalizing the intersection of race and sex: A Black feminist critique of antidiscrimination doctrine, feminist theory and antiracist politics. *University of Chicago Legal Forum, 1989*(1), 139–167.

Crenshaw, K. (1991). Mapping the margins: Intersectionality, identity politics, and violence against women of color. *Stanford Law Review, 43*(6), 1241–1299.

Daniels, J. (2009). *Cyber racism: White supremacy online and the new attack on civil rights.* Rowman & Littlefield.

Darling-Hammond, L. (2017). Teaching for social justice: Resources, relationships, and anti- racist practice. *Multicultural Perspectives, 19*(3), 133–138.

Darling-Hammond, L., Hyler, M. E., & Gardner, M. (2017). *Effective teacher professional development.* Learning Policy Institute.

Dei, G. J. S. (2013). Reframing critical antiracist theory (CART) for contemporary times. In G. J. S. Dei & M. Lordon (Eds.), *Contemporary issues in the sociology of race and ethnicity: A critical reader* (pp. 1–14). Peter Lang.

Denis, V. S., & Schick, C. (2003). What makes anti-racist pedagogy in teacher education difficult? Three popular ideological assumptions. *Alberta Journal of Educational Research, 49*(1), 55–69.

DiAngelo, R. (2018). *White fragility: Why it's so hard for white people to talk about racism.* Beacon Press.

Dumas, M. J. (2016). Against the dark: Antiblackness in education policy and discourse. *Theory Into Practice, 55*(1), 11–19.

Dumas, M. J., & ross, k. m. (2016). "Be real Black for me": Imagining BlackCrit in education. *Urban Education, 51*(4), 415–442.

Feiman-Nemser, S. (2001). From preparation to practice: Designing a continuum to strengthen and sustain teaching. *Teachers College Record, 103*(6), 1013–1055.

Feucht, F. C., Lunn Brownlee, J., & Schraw, G. (2017). Moving beyond reflection: Reflexivity and epistemic cognition in teaching and teacher education. *Educational Psychologist, 52*(4), 234–241.

Ford, D. Y., & Grantham, T. C. (2003). Providing access for culturally diverse gifted students: From deficit to dynamic thinking. *Theory Into Practice, 42*(3), 217–225.

Frankenberg, E., Siegel-Hawley, G., & Wang, J. (2011). Choice without equity: Charter school segregation. *Education Policy Analysis Archives, 19*(1), 1–96.

Fraser, C., Kennedy, A., Reid, R., & Mckinney, S. (2007). Teachers' continuing professional development: Contested concepts, understandings and models. *Journal of In-Service Education, 33*(2), 153–169.

Golann, J. W., & Torres, A. C. (2020). Do no-excuses disciplinary practices promote success? *Journal of Urban Affairs, 42*(4), 617–633.

Graves, J. L. (2008). *The emperor's new clothes: Biological theories of race at the millennium.* Rutgers University Press.

Griffin, D., & Stern, S. (2011). A social justice approach to school counseling. *Journal for Social Action in Counseling & Psychology, 3*(1), 74–85.

Guskey, T. R. (2000). *Evaluating professional development.* Corwin.

Guthrie, R. V. (2004). *Even the rat was white: A historical view of psychology.* Pearson Education.

Harris, A. L. (2011). *Kids don't want to fail.* Harvard University Press.

Heifetz, R. A., & Laurie, D. L. (1997). The work of leadership. *Harvard Business Review, 75*(1), 124–134.

Helms, J. E. (Ed.). (1990). *Black and white racial identity: Theory, research, and practice.* Greenwood Press.

Helms, J. E. (1995). An update of Helms's white and people of color racial identity models. In J. G. Ponterotto, J. M. Casas, L. A. Suzuki, & C. M. Alexander (Eds.), *Handbook of multicultural counseling* (pp. 181–198). Sage.

Helms, J. E. (1999). Another meta-analysis of the White Racial Identity Attitude Scale's Cronbach alphas: Implications for validity. *Measurement and Evaluation in Counseling and Development, 32*(3), 122–137.

Helms, J. E., & Carter, R. T. (1986). *Manual for the Visible Racial/Ethnic Identity Attitude Scale* [Unpublished manuscript]. Psychology Department. University of Maryland, College Park.

Helms, J. E., & Carter, R. T. (1990). Development of the White Racial Identity Inventory. In J. E. Helms (Ed.), *Black and white racial identity: Theory, research, and practice* (pp. 67–80). Greenwood Press.

Helms, J. E., & Cook, D. A. (1999). *Using race and culture in counseling and psychotherapy: Theory and process*. Allyn & Bacon.

Hines, E. M., & Holcomb-McCoy, C. (2013). Parental characteristics, ecological factors, and the academic achievement of African American males. *Journal of Counseling & Development, 91*(1), 68–77.

Holcomb-McCoy, C. (2004). Assessing the multicultural competence of school counselors: A checklist. *Professional School Counseling, 7*(3), 178–186.

Holcomb-McCoy, C. (2007). *School counseling to close the achievement gap: A social justice framework for success*. Corwin Press.

Holcomb-McCoy, C., Harris, P., Hines, E. M., & Johnston, G. (2008). School counselors' multicultural self-efficacy: A preliminary investigation. *Professional School Counseling, 11*(3), 166–178. https://doi.org/10.1177/2156759X0801100303

Howard, T. C. (2020, June 19). *Racial literacy: A call to action for teachers*. Houghton Mifflin Harcourt. https://www.hmhco.com/blog/racial-literacy-a-call-to-action-for-teachers

Jackson, L. C. (1999). Ethnocultural resistance to multicultural training: Students and faculty. *Cultural Diversity and Ethnic Minority Psychology, 5*(1), 27–36.

Jacobson, C. K. (1985). Resistance to Affirmative Action: Self-Interest or Racism? *Journal of Conflict Resolution, 29*(2), 306–329.

Kendi, I. X. (2016). *Stamped from the beginning: The definitive history of racist ideas in America*. Nation Books.

Kendi, I. X. (2019). *How to be an antiracist*. One World.

Khan, S. R. (2010). *Privilege: The making of an adolescent elite at St. Paul's School*. Princeton University Press.

León, A., Villares, E., Brigman, G., Webb, L., & Peluso, P. (2011). Closing the achievement gap of Latina/Latino students: A school counseling response. *Counseling Outcome Research and Evaluation, 2*(1), 73–86.

Lewis, C. W., Butler, B. R., Bonner, F. A., III, & Joubert, M. (2010). African American male discipline patterns and school district responses resulting impact on academic achievement: Implications for urban educators and policy makers. *Journal of African American Males in Education, 1*(1), 7–25.

Lewis, C. W., James, M., Hancock, S., & Hill-Jackson, V. (2008). Framing African American students' success and failure in urban settings: A typology for change. *Urban Education, 43*(2), 127–153.

Lindsay, C. A., & Hart, C. M. D. (2017). Teacher race and school discipline. *Education Next, 17*(1), 72–79.

Livingston, J., Pipes-McAdoo, H., & Mills, C. J. (2008). Black studies and political ideology as predictors of self-esteem: A call for a new direction. *Journal of Black Studies, 40*(4), 726–744.

Locke, D. C., & Kiselica, M. S. (1999). Pedagogy of possibilities: Teaching about racism in multicultural counseling courses. *Journal of Counseling & Development, 77*(1), 80–86.

Love, B. L. (2016). Anti-Black state violence, classroom edition: The spirit murdering of Black children. *Journal of Curriculum and Pedagogy*, *13*(1), 22–25.

Matias, C. E. (2013). Check yo'self before you wreck yo'self and our kids: Counterstories from culturally responsive white teachers? … to culturally responsive white teachers! *Interdisciplinary Journal of Teaching and Learning*, *3*(2), 68–81.

McGee, E. (2013). Young, Black, mathematically gifted, and stereotyped. *The High School Journal*, *96*(3), 253–263.

McGee, E. O., & Martin, D. B. (2011). "You would not believe what I have to go through to prove my intellectual value!" Stereotype management among academically successful Black mathematics and engineering students. *American Education Research Journal*, *48*(6), 1347–1389.

McMillan Cottom, T. (2017). *Lower ed: The troubling rise of for-profit colleges in the new economy*. The New Press.

Merriam, S. B., Johnson-Bailey, J., Lee, M. Y., Kee, Y., Ntseane, G., & Muhamad, M. (2001). Power and positionality: Negotiating insider/outsider status within and across cultures. *International Journal of Lifelong Education*, *20*(5), 405–416.

Morris, M. (2016). *Pushout: The criminalization of Black girls in schools*. The New Press.

Moss, L. J., & Singh, A. A. (2015). White school counselors becoming racial justice allies to students of color: A call to the field of school counseling. *Journal of School Counseling*, *13*(5), 1–35.

Nasir, N. I. S., & Shah, N. (2011). On defense: African American males making sense of racialized narratives in mathematics education. *Journal of African American Males in Education*, *2*(1), 24–45.

Noble, S. U. (2018). *Algorithms of oppression: How search engines reinforce racism*. New York University Press.

Ohrt, J. H., Lambie, G. W., & Ieva, K. P. (2009). Supporting Latino and African-American students in advanced placement courses: A school counseling program's approach. *Professional School Counseling*, *13*(1), 59–63. https://doi.org/10.1177/2156759X0901300104

Oliver, A., Andemeskel, G., King, C. R., Wallace, L., Monteiro, K. P., & Ben-Zeev, A. (2017). "I'm Black and I'm proud": A majority ecological context protects affective aspects of Black identity under stereotype threat. *Race and Social Problems*, *9*(4), 313–320.

Omi, M., & Winant, H. (2015). *Racial formation in the United States* (3rd ed.). Routledge.

Pabon, A. J. M., & Basile, V. (2019). Can we say the "r" word? Identifying and disrupting colorblind epistemologies in a teacher education methods course. *Educational Studies*, *55*(6), 633–650.

Pieterse, A. L. (2009). Teaching antiracism in counselor training: Reflections on a course. *Journal of Multicultural Counseling and Development*, *37*(3), 141–152.

Pollock, M. (2004). *Colormute: Race talk dilemmas in an American school*. Princeton University Press.

Ponterotto, J. G., Gretchen, D., Utsey, S. O., Rieger, B. P., & Austin, R. (2002). A revision of the Multicultural Counseling Awareness Scale. *Journal of Multicultural Counseling and Development*, *30*(3), 153–180. https://doi.org/10.1002/j.2161-1912.2002.tb00489.x

Richter, D., Kunter, M., Klusmann, U., & Ludte, O. (2011). Professional development across the teaching career: Teachers' uptake of formal and informal learning opportunities. *Teaching and Teacher Education*, *27*(1), 116–126.

Riel, V., Parcel, T. L., Mickelson, R. A., & Smith, S. S. (2018). Do magnet and charter schools exacerbate or ameliorate inequality? *Sociology Compass*, *12*(9), 1–15.

Savitz-Romer, M. (2012). The gap between influence and efficacy: College readiness training, urban school counselors, and the promotion of equity. *Counselor Education and Supervision, 51*(2), 98–111.

Schuschke, J., & Tynes, B. M. (2016). Online community empowerment, emotional connection and love in the #Blacklivesmatter movement. In S. Y. Tettegah (Ed.), *Emotions, technology, and social media* (pp. 25–48). Academic Press.

Scott, K. A., & White, M. A. (2013). COMPUGIRLS' standpoint: Culturally responsive computing and its effect on girls of color. *Urban Education, 48*(5), 657–681.

Sealey-Ruiz, Y. (2020). *Arch of Self, LLC.* https://www.yolandasealeyruiz.com/archaeology-of-self

Skiba, R. J., Horner, R. H., Chung, C. G., Rausch, M. K., May, S. L., & Tobin, T. (2011). Race is not neutral: A national investigation of African American and Latino disproportionality in school discipline. *School Psychology Review, 40*(1), 85–107.

Spencer, M. B. (1995). Old issues and new theorizing about African American youth: A phenomenological variant of ecological systems theory. In R. L. Taylor (Ed.), *Black youth: Perspectives on their status in the United States* (pp. 37-69). Praeger.

Steele, C. M. (1997). A threat in the air: How stereotypes shape the intellectual identities and performance of women and African-Americans. *American Psychologist, 52*(6), 613–629.

Steele, C. M., & Aronson, J. (1995). Stereotype threat and the intellectual test performance of African-Americans. *Journal of Personality and Social Psychology, 69*(5), 797–811.

Stets, J. E., & Burke, P. J. (2000). Identity theory and social identity theory. *Social Psychology Quarterly, 63*(3), 224–237.

Stets, J. E., & Fares, P. (2019, May). The effects of race/ethnicity and racial/ethnic identification on general trust. *Social Science Research, 80*, 1–14.

Sue, D. W. (2020). *Facilitating difficult race discussions: Five ineffective strategies and five successful strategies.* Wiley.

Sue, D. W., & Sue, D. (1999). *Counseling the culturally different: Theory and practice.* Wiley.

Tanksley, T. C. (2016). Education, representation, and resistance: Black girls in popular Instagram memes. In S. Noble & B. Tynes (Eds.), *The intersectional internet* (pp. 243–259). Peter Lang.

Teaching Works. (2019). *General curriculum materials: Building respectful relationships. Activity 2: Interrogating the self.* https://library.teachingworks.org/curriculum-resources/materials/general-building-respectful-relationships/downloads/#docModal

Tynes, B. M., Del Toro, J., & Lozada, F. T. (2015). An unwelcomed digital visitor in the classroom: The longitudinal impact of online racial discrimination on academic motivation. *School Psychology Review, 44*(4), 407–424.

Tynes, B. M., Schuschke, J., & Noble, S. U. (2016). Digital intersectionality theory and the #Blacklivesmatter movement. In S. Noble & B. Tynes (Eds.), *The intersectional internet* (pp. 21–40). Peter Lang.

Tynes, B. M., Willis, H. A., Stewart, A. M., & Hamilton, M. W. (2019). Race-related traumatic events online and mental health among adolescents of color. *Journal of Adolescent Health, 65*(3), 371–377.

Tyson, K. (2011). *Integration interrupted: Tracking, Black students, and acting white after* Brown. Oxford University Press.

Urrieta, L., Jr. (2006). Community identity discourse and the heritage academy: Colorblind educational policy and white supremacy. *International Journal of Qualitative Studies in Education, 19*(4), 455–476.

Utt, J., & Tochluk, S. (2020). White teacher, know thyself: Improving anti-racist praxis through racial identity development. *Urban Education, 55*(1), 125–152.

Valenzuela, A. (1999). *Subtractive schooling: Issues of caring in education of US-Mexican youth.* State University of New York Press.

Wilder, C. S. (2013). *Ebony and ivy: Race, slavery, and the troubled history of America's universities.* Bloomsbury Press.

Zembylas, M. (2018). Affect, race, and white discomfort in schooling: Decolonial strategies for "pedagogies of discomfort." *Ethics and Education, 13*(1), 86–104.

CHAPTER 7

Infusing an Antiracist Framework Into School-Family-Community Partnerships

Julia Bryan, Lynette M. Henry, Aubrey D. Daniels, Mary Edwin,
and Dominiqua M. Griffin

Antiracism is the active identification, description, and dismantling of racism, racist ideas, and racist policies (Kendi, 2019). Counselors and educators can partner with family and community stakeholders to center the needs of and empower students and families of color. Children's outcomes improve when their families are engaged in partnership programs and interventions in schools and communities. Indeed, school-family-community partnerships can augment programs for children as well as provide education, support, and advocacy for parents and family members that can further support their children's success. Recently, a body of literature has emphasized the importance and characteristics of equity-focused partnerships (Bryan, Griffin, Kim, et al., 2019; Bryan et al., 2020; Griffin et al., in press). Scholars recognize the crucial leadership role school counselors and other educators can play in creating partnerships that engage families and community members in mutually beneficial ways and create equity-focused programs and policies that increase resources and opportunities and improve educational environments and outcomes for students of color. However, this literature on equity-focused partnerships has not focused directly on racism or antiracism in schools and educational settings, where whiteness and white middle-class norms are centered.

Racism in schools takes a variety of forms that present barriers for students and families of color and allow educators and counselors to perpetuate racism in their partnerships with families and communities of color. Kohli et al. (2017) identified three types of racism perpetuated in schools under the guise of equity and social justice: evaded racism, antiracist racism, and everyday racism. Evaded racism occurs when educators and counselors discuss and address inequities without examining institutional barriers, simultaneously silencing views about racism.

For example, evaded racism occurs when educators and counselors discuss the achievement gap with a focus on short-term rather than systemic solutions while blaming Black and Brown parents and depicting them as the problem. Antiracist racism occurs when racist policies and practices are promoted as the answer to racism. Antiracist racism is perpetuated in numerous ways, for example, through social-emotional learning, growth mind-sets, grit, and other programs that are color-blind, integrate deficit narratives and white norms, and promote individual rather than systemic change; through color-blind classroom management and disciplinary practices, including dress and hair codes based on white norms, that exclude children of color, push them out of the classroom, and create racially hostile and unsafe climates for students of color; and through school choice policies and charter school programs that use young white teachers while displacing teachers of color. Everyday racism shows up in seemingly small events, microaggressions that take place in white teachers' and administrators' daily interactions with children and families of color that make them feel excluded, like outsiders. For example, everyday racism is seen in the mispronunciation of the names of students of color, the small insults and hostilities to which students and families of color are treated, and the negative stereotypes and narratives that paint Black parents as incapable and irresponsible.

Counselors and educators, who are primarily white, may promote equity for students of color in schools, family engagement, and school-family-community partnerships while simultaneously centering and normalizing whiteness, promoting racism and deficit narratives about students and families of color (Kohli et al., 2017; Yull et al., 2014). When counselors do not directly acknowledge and address racism and racist structures in schools, equity initiatives often reproduce the structural racism in the school (Kohli et al., 2017; Wilson, 2019). Racism and implicit bias also influence school-family-community partnerships but typically go unrecognized. When partnerships between school, family, and community partners do not confront the reality of racism and the way it works in schools, then the structures, policies, and practices that maintain racism and racial disparities continue to create racially unsafe spaces for children and families of color in school and community settings.

In this chapter, we discuss how school counselors, educators, and family and community stakeholders can use an antiracist lens to address and eliminate all types of racism in partnerships. Although this chapter focuses on children of color, we pay particular attention to Black children, who are daily targets of pervasive anti-Black racism in the United States. We use the terms "Black students," "Black and Brown students," and "students of color" interchangeably in the chapter. To build antiracist partnerships, school, family, and community stakeholders must examine their beliefs and narratives about students and their families, their relationships and interactions with students and families of color, the goals and outcomes they have for students, and the policies and practices that need to be disrupted or implemented to interrupt the racism that children of color experience in schools.

In this chapter, we describe four antiracist foci counselors need to address as they build antiracist partnerships, discuss four essential equity-focused partnership principles (democratic collaboration, empowerment, social justice, and a strengths focus), and present a seven-step partnership process model (Bryan, Griffin, Kim, et al., 2019; Bryan & Henry, 2012; Bryan et al., 2020; see Figure 7.1). These antiracist foci and equity-focused principles enable counselors and educators to build school-

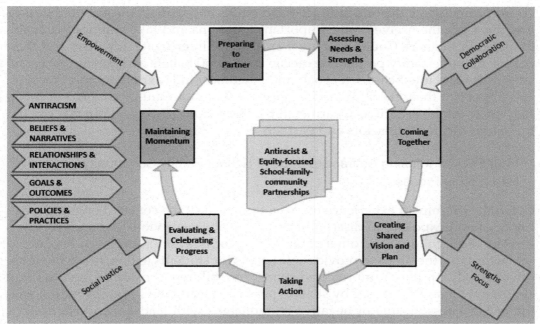

FIGURE 7.1 • Infusing Antiracism Foci Into an Equity-Focused Model
of School-Family-Community Partnerships

family-community partnerships suitable for supporting children of color and other marginalized students without perpetuating racism and inequity. Using this seven-step partnership process model, counselors can intentionally build school-family-community partnerships that provide antiracist interventions to tackle trauma, promote college and career readiness and access, and foster protective factors and racially safe school environments for children and families of color.

An Antiracist School-Family-Community Partnership Process Approach

School-family-community partnerships are consistently used in schools to address inequities and challenges students face, such as trauma (including racial trauma), lack of access to college and career readiness opportunities, and disproportionate discipline referrals and suspension from school. Yet these well-intentioned partnerships may perpetuate racism, ethnocentrism, and inequity if counselors, educators, and other stakeholders are not intentionally antiracist. Counselors must be courageous leaders of antiracist work in schools. They are in a unique position to promote and lead these equity-focused and antiracist school-family-community partnerships, as the American Counseling Association and the American School Counselor Association delineate equity, social justice, and antiracism as expressed roles of counselors. Counselors and educators must approach their partnership efforts with an intentional antiracist lens or approach, regardless of the type of partnership interventions they implement to support students of color, including trauma-informed care, college and career readiness, academic enrichment, or mentoring programs. To be intentional in antiracist partnership work and to create partnerships that are antiracist and equity focused, counselors and educators must ask themselves some important questions and take courageous action in four critical areas. Counselors must examine or interrogate how they and their partners inadvertently perpetuate racism in their (a) beliefs and narratives, (b) relationships and interactions, (c) goals and outcomes, and (d) policies and practices. It is important that school counselors address these four antiracist areas or foci if they are to establish antiracist partnership programs and interventions. We discuss these four foci for counselors and partners below.

Four Foci for Infusing Antiracism Into the School-Family-Community Partnership Process

Given the prominent experience of racial trauma (i.e., the constant ongoing experience of and exposure to discrimination, bias, abuse, or violence based on one's race) by Black children and other students of color, it is important that school counselors form partnerships to provide safe spaces for students to flourish. Schools are often racially unsafe or unprotected spaces for children of color, especially Black children, who are burdened by stereotypes and deficit views and the pathologizing of Blackness, hostile or negative relationships with teachers and counselors, low expectations, and harsh discipline and exclusionary policies (Jenkins, 2021; Wilson, 2019; Yull et al., 2014). Jenkins (2021) described how students experience schools as places of racialized terror where they are seen as problems and illegitimate, where their identities and cultures are rejected, and where they constantly experience other Black students being removed, often forcefully from classrooms and the school building. Despite these ongoing traumatic experiences, Black students are typically told to get over these racially traumatic experiences (Nadal et al., 2019), which leads to them bottling up painful emotions and feeling unsafe at school or in community settings. Through antiracist partnerships, school counselors can collaborate to implement programs and activities that enhance and validate the experiences that Black students and their families have in schools and communities and tackle race-based barriers to students' academic success, college and career readiness and access, and social-emotional development. School counselors can lead the way in enacting antiracism in schools by intentionally identifying and naming racism and developing partnerships to foster antiracist school and community environments, racially safe spaces in which students of color and family members feel validated and empowered rather than traumatized.

In a recent statement, the Association for Multicultural Counseling and Development acknowledged the negative impact of racial trauma, specifically the ways in which it manifests in people of color through symptoms such as depression, a range of emotions such as anger, avoidant behavior, agitation, and hypervigilance (Association for Multicultural Counseling and Development, 2020; Comas-Díaz, 2016; McIntosh, 2019). Other responses to racial trauma include hypersensitivity to possible threats, unhelpful stress responses such as hostility, and substance abuse (Comas-Díaz, 2016; McIntosh, 2019). Multiple exposures to racial trauma are correlated with even more intense symptoms over time (McIntosh, 2019; Wade et al., 2014). Thus, it is imperative that counselors and educators partner with family and community members to address antiracism in schools. To infuse antiracist practices into their partnerships, school counselors must address the following four antiracist foci: (a) beliefs and narratives, (b) relationships and inter-actions, (c) goals and outcomes, and (d) policies and practices.

Beliefs and Narratives

White values, norms, standards, beliefs, and stories/narratives and manifestations of white supremacy and power are front and center in education and many institu-tions (Earick, 2018). The first area of antiracism focus for counselors is their own beliefs, values, norms, and narratives about students and families of color. It is im-portant that counselors, especially white counselors, do the critical work of reflect-ing on and challenging their own beliefs, expectations, and narratives about chil-dren of color, in particular Black children, and the ways in which they perpetuate stereotypes about them. Students and families of color are aware of the negative and racist beliefs and stereotypes that adults in schools and the wider community have about them and unconsciously experience the toxic stress of stereotype threat and racial trauma as a result. As counselors initiate and coordinate partnership interventions to meet the needs of students of color, they must help school, family, and community partners examine their own beliefs and narratives about students of color and their families. Indeed, counselors, educators and community partners must recognize the value of diverse parents and family members and make them feel valued in the school and at the partnership table.

Despite the need for parent/family engagement in their children's education, parents of color often experience marginalization and disempowerment in schools (Baquedano-López et al., 2013; Kim & Bryan, 2017; Kim et al., 2017). In particular, Black parents and family members often feel unwelcome in schools where teachers and administrators often promulgate the deficit narrative that parents and family members do not care about their children and are not involved in their children's education (Baquedano-López et al., 2013; Bryan, Griffin, Kim, et al., 2019; Kohli et al., 2017; Wilson, 2019; Yull et al., 2014). Indeed, school administrators, teach-ers, and counselors often see Black families and their children as angry, threaten-ing, delinquent, and not caring or invested in education. Black mothers are often depicted as child abusers and Black fathers as absent and irresponsible. These pervasive beliefs make schools unwelcoming, dangerous, and violent places for Black children and their families, where educators exclude or punish them. Fur-thermore, the pathologizing and criminalization of students and families of color in schools make it more likely that these family members will avoid interactions and engagement with school personnel.

Frequently school staff make assumptions that promote negative views and narratives about families of color, especially Black families' aspirations and edu-cational values for their children. Yet research has shown that families of color often have high academic and college and career expectations for their children even when they lack the resources and information necessary to support their chil-dren's endeavors. School counselors and other educators and stakeholders can inadvertently invalidate family members' contributions to their children's college and career development by not acknowledging those expectations. Moore-Thomas and Day-Vines (2010) posited that deficit-based narratives, low expectations, and misperceptions of Black students in schools act as barriers to children's educa-tional success and emotional well-being. Indeed, presenting educational dispari-ties between Black children and white children as an achievement gap ignores the structural barriers that restrict opportunities and support for children of color. Indeed, the concept of the achievement gap perpetuates the racist idea that there is a hierarchy between Black and white student subgroups (Reynolds & Kendi, 2020). A need exists for counselors to shift the narrative to a focus on changing policies, programs, and structures rather than implying there is something inherently wrong with Black students and their families.

School counselors support an antiracist approach to developing partnerships by addressing and correcting faulty beliefs and narratives of partners and intentionally acknowledging the strengths of families of color, including the high expectations they have for their children's academic, college, and career outcomes and the multiple ways in which they are engaged in their children's education. Counselors can work to help school stakeholders and partners reframe deficit narratives to emphasize the strengths and high expectations of Black students and students of color. Counselors, school personnel, youth, and community partners must take a strengths-based approach to partnership programming. For example, rather than presenting students of color in deficit terms such as "at risk," "needy," or "aggressive" and their parents as "disinterested" or "incompetent" or other deficit narratives, school counselors can shift partnership conversations to focus on students' strengths and academic outcomes and address ways to build on student successes. For example, partnership programs to increase college and career opportunities should involve successful college students of color as mentors for Black and Brown students aspiring to college (Bryan, Griffin, Henry, & Gilfillan, 2019; Bryan, Williams, & Griffin, 2016; Bryan, Young, et al., 2016; Edwin et al., in press).

Relationships and Interactions
The beliefs and narratives of adults in schools directly impact the relationships and interactions they have with Black students. Furthermore, counselors must help educators, family, and community partners understand how the interactions and partnerships between school personnel and parents and family members of color often reflect racism in the wider society. Indeed, counselors and other educators who embrace color blindness and deficit thinking in approaching students of color and their families foster cultural mistrust and negative interactions with students and families of color. It is imperative that counselors help educators and partners understand that color blindness is racism, not antiracism. Indeed, equity work in schools is often masked as color-blind approaches, which blinds educators and other partners to the realities, oppression, and trauma that students of color face (Kohli et al., 2017; Wilson, 2019). The belief that all students have a level playing field and the same experiences in schools normalizes and centers whiteness at the expense of students of color, in particular Black students (Benson & Fiarman, 2020; Pollock, 2009). It is also essential that counselors understand and acknowledge—and help their partners understand and acknowledge—the racial trauma that Black students and other students of color often experience in toxic or hostile relationships with administrators, teachers, psychologists, mentors, tutors, and other stakeholders. In schools, adults' negative attitudes toward Black children are often displayed in punitive or harsh relationships with students of color. Children of color are typically aware of the ways in which they are treated differently by counselors, teachers, and administrators and experience schools as unsafe and negative places—as places of punishment and racial threat—where they are not given the same protections or considerations as white children (Wilson, 2019).

As a result, students of color feel hypervisible, hypervigilant, unsafe, and unprotected in relationships with polite teachers and adults in schools (Wilson, 2019).

Counselors who intend to be antiracist must lead in helping educators, families, and community members understand how to create caring and antiracist partnerships with the protective factors that children of color need. Indeed, counselors recognize that antiracist trauma-informed partnerships must make it a goal to provide safe spaces for Black and Brown students and their families where they are not retraumatized. For example, schools with police roaming the halls and metal detectors do not provide safety for Black students. Rather, they can retraumatize Black students, who are rightfully afraid of the police because of the police profiling and brutality they consistently witness in their communities and in the media. Meanwhile, white students may feel safe with metal detectors and police present, as they do not perceive them as a threat to their safety. Therefore, it is imperative that school counselors encourage and collaborate with partners to structure partnership programs to focus on providing safe, antiracist spaces for students of color that do not involve retraumatizing Black and Brown students. School counselors can do this through antiracist social-emotional learning programming, restorative justice practices, trauma-informed care interventions, and mentoring programs. In addition, counselors must help partners design programs and build relationships that create a safe space for students to process trauma, especially race-based trauma. Counselors can help develop partnerships that promote relationships with caring adults that result in increased developmental assets for students to foster their resilience and well-being (Henry & Bryan, 2021; Henry et al., 2017). When counselors, educators, and other stakeholders acknowledge racism and racial trauma and recognize how they may harm children as a result of deficit thinking and pathologizing, they are able to develop healthier and more trusting relationships with children and families of color. They are able to better support students with feelings of validation and safety and open the door for students to share when they feel demeaned or discriminated against in partnership programs and activities in the school building or community setting.

Goals and Outcomes

Often counselors, teachers, administrators, and other school stakeholders fail to focus on important goals and indicators that enhance the opportunities, skills, and success of students of color, in particular Black students. Schools center white norms and values and focus on students (and parents) following white mainstream norms. For example, curriculum and partnership programs and interventions in schools that focus on social-emotional learning, grit, and resilience de-emphasize race and center whiteness and white norms and values, excluding the perspectives, values, and culture of students, parents, and communities of color. However, afro-affirmative programs and partnerships decenter whiteness, intentionally including the experiences, strengths, aspirations, and needs of students and families of color (Wilson, 2019). Counselors and partnership teams that seek to develop antiracist partnership programs and interventions must be afro-affirmative, focusing their goals and outcomes on the experiences, strengths, aspirations, and needs of Black students and on creating the developmental assets and protective factors that help Black students succeed and thrive in schools and in postsecondary settings. Given the academic, economic, and structural barriers Black youth face, antiracist and equity-focused partnerships can provide academic and enrichment programs that produce the college knowledge, information, and counseling supports these youth need to succeed (Bryan, Williams, & Griffin, 2016; Bryan, Young, et al., 2016). For example, college and career readiness partnership programs can include college students of color or volunteers of color who graduated from college as mentors to aid students in seeing representations of themselves making successful postsecondary transitions (Bryan, Griffin, Henry, & Gilfillan, 2019; Bryan, Williams, & Griffin, 2016; Bryan, Young, et al., 2016; Edwin et al., in press). Furthermore, in addition to academic success and college and career readiness, partnership teams should focus interventions and programs for students of color on noncognitive outcomes such as racial identity development, racial literacy, leadership and self-advocacy skills, critical consciousness and empowerment, college and career aspirations, and self-efficacy. It is important that counselors and partners target partnership interventions toward creating both cognitive and noncognitive factors that help students succeed. Above all, counselors should encourage adults in schools and partners to consider the effects of racism on student performance and how to build antiracist interventions to support the academic success of students of color. Partnership programs should incorporate critical pedagogy and other culturally appropriate experiences to increase students' critical consciousness, enhance their racial identity development, and teach them about how racism affects them in and out of college and how to navigate that racism and resulting trauma (Majors, 2019). School counselors can also create partnerships to implement staff trainings that support teachers and other stakeholders in examining the goals and outcomes they establish for students and ensure that they are intentionally decentering whiteness as they create student outcomes.

Policies and Practices

Policies in schools are the most effective tools of racism that adults in schools use to exclude, alienate, punish, and disadvantage students of color, depriving them of opportunities, support, encouragement, and educational equity. Too often schools and school systems have used color-blind approaches school-wide in their discipline policies, curricular content, and student tracking and in programs such as trauma-informed care, social-emotional learning, and multitiered systems of support, thereby restricting and limiting opportunities of students (Joseph et al., 2020; Kohli et al., 2017; Wilson, 2019). For example, college and career readiness frameworks and partnership programs are often color-blind, excluding consideration of the structural inequities and racism that limit the opportunities of Black students and other students of color; instead, they focus solely on the skills and knowledge students of color need for college entry and success. However, enhancing students' skills and knowledge without dismantling inequitable policies and structural inequities puts all of the onus on Black students and families to navigate a system that provides them with fewer opportunities and less information and support than white and more affluent students.

This incorrect and ineffective approach of color blindness to serving students of color has led to the continuation of unjust school policies, with teachers and administrators meting out harsh punishments, blaming students without considering the relationship of trauma to their behavior, and failing to implement a trauma-informed approach to educating students of color (Joseph et al., 2020). Similarly, a color-blind approach in partnerships leads counselors and other partners to focus on individual-level rationales and solutions rather than the vehicles of racism, that is, racist policies and practices in schools that continue to disadvantage and traumatize students of color (Kohli et al., 2017). For example, they may focus on the achievement gap as opposed to attending to and challenging educational and societal policies that limit learning opportunities and support for children of color from birth to 12th grade, such as resource-poor or no libraries in the schools and communities of children of color (Kendi, 2019).

Thus, in addition to the implementation of partnership programs such as mentoring and tutoring programs, parent education, academic and college access programs, and many others, advocacy for dismantling policies that restrict the educational success of children of color must be at the forefront of partnership building. School counselors must disaggregate data and assess the ways in which programs and policies disadvantage children of color, as disaggregating data reveals racial inequities masked by aggregate data. It is imperative that counselors use the data to call educators', family members', and partners' attention to the ways in which policies, such as zero-tolerance policies, act to harm Black children and other children of color and to advocate for new antiracist policies.

Regarding partnerships, school counselors must not carry out or support colorblind practices. Rather, they should address and help partners address the fact that students of color and their families are experiencing or have experienced racial trauma and stress. One cannot overstate the importance of counselors, educators, and youth workers acknowledging a student's race and other sociocultural factors as opposed to focusing solely on individual-based outcomes such as coping skills, academic performance, and social-emotional competencies. Furthermore, colorblind approaches to partnership programs keep school, family, and community partners from addressing racism and inequity and advocating for antiracist interventions and policies that help children of color thrive.

The four antiracist foci bring critical attention to the ways in which antiracism operates in schools and must be integrated into partnerships designed to support children and families of color. Below we describe four principles of equity-focused partnerships detailed in previous work (Bryan, Griffin, Kim, et al., 2019; Bryan et al., 2020; Griffin et al., in press). Here we examine these partnership principles through an added lens of antiracism with the recognition that when counselors and educators engage in equity work without a consideration of racism, equity discourse and approaches merely mask racism and the mechanisms of systemic racism and result in individual-level solutions and practices. Such individual-level solutions neither result in racially safe school climates nor promote the academic and social-emotional well-being of students of color.

Key Principles for Building School-Family-Community Partnerships

Four principles guide school-family-community partnerships that are focused on equity and antiracism to best support students of color: democratic collaboration, empowerment, social justice, and a strengths focus (Bryan, Griffin, Kim, et al., 2019; Bryan & Henry, 2012; Bryan et al., 2020; Griffin et al., in press). These principles help counselors take the lead in building partnerships that include diverse stakeholders as partners, empower and embrace the strengths of students and their families, challenge racist and deficit views and practices in schools and communities, and promote equity and antiracism.

Democratic Collaboration

Although schools often create partnerships to support students of color, the partnership leadership team (PLT) often excludes from the team the parents of the students they plan to support. Counselors must emphasize the importance of the involvement of families of color in key decisions about their children's education. Counselors should ensure not only that the PLT includes parents and families of color at the table but that they come to the table as mutual, equal partners sharing power in problem-solving; decision-making; and planning, implementing, and evaluating partnership programs and events. Counselors can play a critical role in helping families feel welcome and valued by encouraging the partnership team and partners to challenge their deficit and antiracist beliefs and narratives about students and families of color and what families need to do to help their children succeed.

Empowerment

As schools, family, and community members seek to build partnerships to design programs and strategies to support students of color, they often ignore or exclude the voices and perspectives of families of color. Counselors can help the partnership team and partners design programs and build relationships with students and families of color that validate and center the voices of students and families of color rather than center white norms and voices. To facilitate empowering relationships with families of color, counselors, educators, and other partners must recognize the power dynamics in schools. Often white and affluent families are listened to and welcomed while families of color are not welcomed, are marginalized, and are seen as aggressive as they advocate for their children. Building partnerships that are empowering for families of color involves counselors and partners recognizing families of color as the experts in their children's lives and consulting with and believing them concerning the challenges and experiences their children face in schools, especially around race and racist ideas. Antiracist counselors, educators, and other partners listen to families' and students' voices, stories, concerns, and ideas as they examine student data, develop goals, and plan programs and outcomes.

Social Justice

Students of color, especially Black students, often lack or are excluded from pertinent information, opportunities, resources, and networks that increase safety and support for academic success and trauma recovery and increase access to postsecondary education and careers. Not only should partnerships redistribute power so families are at the table and center students' and families' voices, concerns, and perspectives but they should also increase students' and their families' access to information, resources, opportunities, and networks and address and eliminate academic, college and career, and social-emotional disparities. As counselors partner with educators, family members, and community and youth workers to implement programs and provide support services for students, they must keep social justice and antiracism at the forefront. This involves partnership teams examining student and school data to examine educational disparities and reveal policies and practices that limit the chances of success of children of color. Furthermore, partnership teams and stakeholders must understand the importance of not taking a color-blind approach to social justice and equity as they develop partnership programs, as color-blind partnerships merely mask racism.

A Strengths Focus

Students and families of color, especially Black students and their family members, are often seen and discussed in deficit ways in schools. Despite their strengths, resilience, and diverse experiences, they are often seen as deficient. Counselors, partnership teams, and other school and community stakeholders who are antiracist recognize and highlight the strengths of students of color and their families. They do not evaluate students' and families' strengths based on white norms but decenter whiteness so their behaviors and ways of being are not measured against white norms and behaviors. For example, counselors emphasize that families of color are not uninvolved in their children's education but involved in culturally relevant or distinct ways. Counselors encourage educators and the partners they work with to examine their views and narratives about students and families of color and to reframe them. Furthermore, counselors encourage partners to create partnership goals focused on increasing developmental assets and protective factors that foster the educational success, safety, and strengths of children of color (Bryan, 2005; Bryan et al., 2020; Henry & Bryan, 2021). Furthermore, partners consider the strengths of students of color and their families and communities, which they may build on, for example, by connecting them to mentors and tutors of color and enrichment programs that incorporate their cultures and by creating programs that focus on celebrating children and families of color.

Below we describe the seven steps of the partnership process model (see Table 7.1), which is built on the four equity-focused principles and infuses the four antiracist foci. To exemplify each step of the partnership model, we share the stories of a school counselor (the second author, Lynette M. Henry) and how she used the partnership model to support children of color and other marginalized students in her schools. We set each step of the model in bold and italicize important tasks at each step.

The Seven-Step Partnership Process Model: A Counselor's Story of Building Antiracist and Equity-Focused Partnerships

To adopt antiracist partnerships in a practical manner, school counselors can use the seven steps of the partnership process model to help them navigate the process. Building effective antiracist, equity-focused partnerships with school, family, and community members comprises seven steps: (a) preparing to partner, (b) assessing needs and strengths, (c) coming together, (d) creating shared vision and plan, (e) taking action, (f) evaluating and celebrating progress, and (g) maintaining momentum (Bryan, Griffin, Kim, et al., 2019; Bryan & Henry, 2012; Bryan et al., 2020; Griffin et al., in press). The essential tasks counselors and educators should implement at each step of the partnership process can be found in Table 7.1. As school counselors work through the model, they should ask questions at each step that direct their focus to antiracism and really interrogate whether they are really being antiracist. See Griffin et al. (in press) for specific questions about antiracism to ask at each step. Here we

Step	Partnership Tasks
1. Preparing to partner How and where do I begin in building an antiracist partnership?	• Recognize and challenge one's own biases, racist beliefs, and stereotypes • Become familiar with the school's racial groups and history of oppression, marginalization, and disenfranchisement • Challenge racist ideas, beliefs, and stereotypes about Black and Brown students and families • Align the partnership's vision of antiracism and equity with the school's vision • Examine racial inequities in student outcome data • Get principal and teacher buy-in using a rationale based on research on the benefits of partnership for students of color
2. Assessing needs and strengths How do I identify antiracist goals for the partnership?	• Conduct a needs and strengths assessment (interviews, surveys, focus groups), especially with students and families of color • Center the perspectives and voices of students and families of color • Meet cultural brokers and persons of influence from communities of color • Identify potential partners in the school and community, including racially diverse partners • Create a community assets map (including cultural services, resources, organizations, spaces)
3. Coming together How do I bring antiracist partners together?	• Create an antiracist partnership leadership team • Reach out and send invitations to racially diverse potential partners, cultural brokers, and persons of influence • Share data and identified needs and strengths to get partners' buy-in • Discuss principles of antiracism • Discuss partner commitments and contributions that relate to empowering racially diverse students and families
4. Creating shared vision and plan How do I get everyone on board and on the same page with building antiracist programs?	• Brainstorm nontraditional and culturally relevant ways to partner with diverse families • Create goals and outcomes related to antiracist practices and programs and empowering students of color • Determine how each partnership will be evaluated in formal and informal ways • Identify instruments and surveys for measuring outcomes that were normed on this population • Share the plan with stakeholders (school staff, families, community members) and include their feedback on antiracist procedures
5. Taking action What will we do and how will we build antiracist partnership programs?	• Recruit leaders and volunteers, including racially diverse ones • Delegate leadership and responsibilities for each event • Delegate based on each team member's strengths (skills, resources) • Start small • Plan for barriers and challenges, implement anyway, and advocate • Implement activities according to a timeline
6. Evaluating and celebrating progress How will I measure the success of the antiracist partnership programs?	• Conduct collaborative evaluation (before and after events, at identified points in the school year), including evaluation by racially diverse team members • Analyze student outcome data and create a user-friendly presentation of the data that explains technical information for a variety of audiences • Evaluate and analyze measures of partnership effectiveness concerning antiracism and equity • Share outcomes and accomplishments with all stakeholders (administrators, teachers, other staff, students, families, community) • Celebrate and empower all partners and partnership accomplishments
7. Maintaining momentum How will I sustain this antiracist partnership?	• Discuss evaluation results as they relate to empowering racially diverse students • Contact partners before and early in the school year (retreat) • Consider extensions of existing partnerships • Identify possible new members and partners for the partnership leadership team • Build alliances with other organizations with antiracist programs and practices • Repeat steps in the partnership building process

TABLE 7.1 • Essential Tasks for Implementing an Antiracist School-Family-Community Partnership Process Model for Empowering Racially Diverse Youth

Note. Adapted from "A Model for Building School–Family–Community Partnerships: Principles and Process," by J. Bryan and L. Henry, 2012, *Journal of Counseling & Development, 90*(4), pp. 408–420. Adapted with permission.

present a concrete case study of the experiences of Lynette M. Henry while she was a school counselor. Writing in the first person, we describe how she infused antiracism and equity into building school-family-community partnerships across a range of school settings at the elementary, middle, and high school levels using the seven-step model of school-family-community partnerships.

Case Study:
A School Counselor's Story of Implementing the
Antiracist Seven-Step Partnership Process Model

To **prepare to partner,** you first must take time to get familiar with the cultural groups within your schools. One elementary school I worked in, Charisma Elementary School (a pseudonym), was in a high-poverty area. Many students came from single-parent homes, had parents who were incarcerated, and experienced drug and violence in the community and other forms of trauma; 99% of students were on free and reduced lunch, and 85% were Black students (Bryan & Henry, 2008; Henry, 2014; Henry & Bryan, 2021; Henry et al., 2017). Some school personnel held stereotypes and deficit views about the students and their parents, for example, that Black parents have low expectations for their children and Black children do not care about their education. The need for school personnel to *examine and challenge their beliefs and stereotypes* and *recognize their conscious and unconscious biases* about racially diverse students and families was demonstrated in an experience I had. A Black Haitian American girl in fifth grade was often absent from school. What school personnel often assumed and said (without proof) was that she was skipping school because she was out on the streets participating in risky sexual and other behaviors. This racist belief and narrative had to do with the color of her skin and where she lived; it demonstrated white supremacy. When I visited this family at their home, I realized the mother needed additional resources and support. We were able to help get the mother connected to a Head Start program for her younger child (whom her fifth-grade daughter often stayed home to help babysit while her mother went to work to provide for her family). The fifth-grade girl joined our Ladies Club, a partnership program, which provided an empowerment and support group for girls to enhance current and future opportunities available to them, especially college and career readiness. It was important to *challenge the stereotypes, biases, and deficit narratives* of the school staff, pointing out the wrong and deficit assumptions and biases about this young fifth-grade student. Furthermore, *preparing to partner* involves helping school personnel and partners *understand the strengths and resilience of Black students and families*.

Assessing needs and strengths is essential to determining the goals of the partnership. It is important that counselors not only look at school data but take time *to listen to the voices of diverse stakeholders* and ensure that they *include Black student and family voices*. Data are not just numbers; data are people. *Listening to the perspectives and narratives of Black students* is important to truly understand what they need. Numerical data can miss or leave out systemic barriers that hinder students from accessing services and the supports they need. As a counselor at a high school with an International Baccalaureate (IB) program and a General Education (GE) program, I examined school data, which showed a high percentage of seniors overall applying to college. However, on further disaggregating the data, we found that most of the students applying to college were in the IB program.

Many of these students' families had college degrees. Typically, IB and magnet schools have *policies and systems* in place to identify students for their programs that marginalize Black and Brown students. To interrupt and dismantle the system in the high school that tracked students into the GE program, I had to *be intentional in building partnerships that could truly expand the opportunities and college access of the GE students.* One partnership involved collaborating with some of the parents of IB students to support the GE students in the college application process. Many of these students were the first in their family to go to college. I partnered with the IB parents to meet one-on-one with GE students to help them with their college applications and to network with their parents to build social capital, that is, to *increase their college knowledge and access to the same information and resources* as more affluent families. Forming partnerships with universities also allowed students to be mentored and provided families of color access to one-on-one advising when it came to financial planning.

In one middle school where I was a counselor, we aggregated data to determine who was participating in Algebra I by eighth grade. We found a proportionate representation of students across all student racial groups participating in Algebra I. However, when we *disaggregated the data* further, *within each racial subgroup,* we found disproportionately larger numbers of Black and Hispanic students who had earned As and Bs in seventh-grade math yet were not participating in eighth-grade Algebra I. Participation in eighth-grade algebra is a gateway to students accessing more advanced math courses, a requirement of many 4-year colleges. Many of the *conversations I challenged* in this school were conversations concerning Black and Hispanic students not being ready, about their standardized scores not being high enough, or questioning whether these students would earn a good grade if they took Algebra I. The racist belief that white and Asian students are capable of doing better academically than Black and Hispanic students is an example of what Ibram Kendi (2019) called a *racist idea,* or the tendency to see one racial group as inferior or superior to another racial group. Kendi said that educators' faith in standardized tests causes us to believe that the racial gap in test scores means something is wrong with Black test takers—and not the tests themselves. As a result of disaggregating the data by racial subgroup, we built equity-focused partnerships that *disrupted these policies* and *intentionally put supports, resources, and practices in place to increase the number of Black and Brown students in Algebra I.*

Coming together or *bringing diverse stakeholders together* is important to building partnerships. *Assessing needs and strengths* and *coming together* often overlap as the PLT brings together partners to engage in discussions and brainstorming about needs and strengths. As we were examining inequities related to eighth-grade Algebra I participation for Black and Hispanic students, we needed to examine the reasons these students were not accessing Algebra I by eighth grade. In seeking to understand the problems and issues around this inequity, the PLT brought together a group of diverse stakeholders, including administrators, teachers, school counselors, district personnel and community members, and especially Black and Brown parents. The group of stakeholders shared their insights into why Black and Brown students were not accessing Algebra I in eighth grade and brainstormed strategies for change. Members of a brainstorming team may also be potential members of the PLT who coordinate the partnership programs and interventions. Contrary to common belief, families of color want to be involved with and in the school making key decisions about their children's education. Because we included diverse stakeholders, especially people of color (in this case Black and Hispanic families), our understanding of the problem was more comprehensive and accurate, as we *included those who were directly impacted by the racist policy*. However, it is imperative that counselors *value families' knowledge and input as equal and mutual partners in the partnership process* and not make families feel further marginalized.

As the PLT **creates a shared vision and plan** for building antiracist, equity-focused partnerships, *the vision and plans should be shared with the school and all stakeholders*. It is important that counselors and educators invite families of color and community leaders of color (e.g., Black churches) to the school to become involved in planning and implementing partnership programs and activities. After reviewing the needs and strengths assessment we conducted, the PLT at Charisma Elementary School decided to develop the Just Love partnership (described in Henry, 2014; Henry & Bryan, 2021; Henry et al., 2017). This faith-based partnership provided mentoring (Just Mentor), classroom adoption (Just Connect), and various other school-wide and community initiatives (Just Rewards). Many of the children had experienced trauma, including race-based trauma, and lacked trust, especially for white people. Like most children, they knew what genuineness looked like and tested people to see whether they were truly sincere before allowing them to be a part of their lives. Therefore, volunteers and mentors needed to be patient and understand that the children's (and their parents') experiences of racism had resulted in mistrust. Trust takes time to build. "Trust isn't built by hearing people's good intentions. Trust grows from witnessing people's actions" (Benson & Fiarman, 2020, p. 78).

As the PLT creates its plans, it should brainstorm nontraditional and culturally appropriate ways to partner with diverse families. For example, Black community and faith-based leaders and Black-based or culturally linked organizations, such as Black churches, are critical and valuable partners and cultural brokers in partnership programs. One of our cultural brokers from the community, a grandmother, was part of our PLT in the elementary school. Her insights and perspectives were invaluable in building the partnership. She always knew what was going on in the community and where the greatest needs were, and this information helped us better target our partnership programs to students' and families' needs. She was the one who told me that our students at Charisma Elementary School never had birthday parties, so we started celebrating students' birthdays as part of our partnership (on the stage in the cafeteria every birthday with cupcakes; the neighborhood McDonald's donated the toys). Students of color want to feel valued and supported. Eventually this grandmother became the head custodian of the school. One of our mothers became president of the parent-teacher association, and one father went back to school and eventually earned a higher income. Partnerships enhance students' success, and they can *empower families of color* and help transform communities.

Taking action means the counselor and the PLT implement planned partnership programs and events despite the inevitable barriers and challenges. Here are two examples of partnership programs and interventions the PLT and I implemented at different schools and some of the challenges and barriers we faced. First, at Charisma Elementary School almost every student was a student of color and economically disadvantaged. To meet the needs of so many students, we used a multitiered systems approach. We developed a variety of partnership programs as part of Just Love, including mentoring (individual level), classroom support and resources (group level), and school-wide incentives as well as parent support services and resources. Using a community asset map, we identified a range of partners from the community and partnered with nearby businesses, community agencies, universities, mental health agencies, wrap-around services, grocery stores, restaurants, judges, parents, churches, a children's board, the housing authority, and other organizations to implement programs to foster protective factors and developmental assets (Henry, 2014; Henry & Bryan, 2021; Henry et al., 2017).

Second, while I was a school counselor in the high school I discussed earlier, a major challenge I faced was helping first-generation, immigrant, and undocumented students go to college. They did not have the information, finances, or resources for college. Once again, I built multilevel partnerships that involved partnering with parents who had information and knowledge about college; college admission recruiters; and district experts on scholarships and financial aid for these students, the Deferred Action for Childhood Arrivals program, and immigration policy. These partnerships provided parents and students with culturally specific information, resources, and activities that enhanced their academic preparation and helped increase opportunities for their students to go to college (Bryan, Griffin, Henry, & Gilfillan, 2019).

Evaluating partnership programs and celebrating progress are essential steps that are often ignored. Even when programs sound good and seem beneficial, they are not always effective at enhancing academic achievement, social-emotional or mental health, or college and career outcomes. If a partnership program is not effective, then it needs to be revised or a new partnership needs to be developed. *Evaluation of partnerships should be done collaboratively with diverse stakeholders, including Black families.* All stakeholders who contribute to the partnership should feel involved, valued, and empowered, especially students of color and their families. Their efforts are integral to the evaluative process and should be celebrated. Evaluating outcomes can help identify what is working, what barriers may be impacting outcomes, what needs to be done to continue to make a positive impact, and how programs can be improved. Just Love, the partnership at Charisma Elementary School, comprised three programs (as described earlier in this case study). We evaluated these programs to understand how they affected the outcomes (academic outcomes, behavior, and attendance) of students who participated in the programs (Henry, 2014; Henry & Bryan, 2021; Henry et al., 2017). We found that third-grade students' reading scores increased from 85% to 97%, discipline referrals decreased from 718 to 133, and attendance increased from 91% to 93%. When asked what they liked most about the Just Love programs, 60% of students said having a mentor. Over the years as Just Love was evaluated, teachers, parents, volunteers, and students spoke of "extravagant love," caring, and reciprocal relationships. Parents shared that they liked that their children had another adult who cared about them to talk to and give them advice. The evaluations showed that stakeholders in this partnership had high expectations for Black students and other students of color and inspired and empowered students to be successful. At the end of each school year, the Just Love partnership team at Charisma Elementary School shared the evaluation results with all stakeholders and the entire school. We held a breakfast for parents, family and community members, teachers, and students to share the results of the programs. We also held a large festive celebration to honor school and community partners and parent volunteers.

Maintaining momentum is a significant step and a continuous stage that involves *maintaining contact with partners during the year and in the summer, continually* *looking for ways to build the partnership team,* and helping partners grow in their understanding of what it means to be antiracist and equity focused in the context of school-family-community partnerships. While working in a middle school, I developed an equity-focused school-family-community partnership, a mentoring program called CAREing Mentors. The goal of the program was to provide Black and Brown students with a caring and supportive adult mentor. Research indicates that many students benefit from having a mentor, yet students often lack mentors, especially mentors of color. Antiracist partnerships intentionally focus on providing resources and support to students who need them most. Many times programs and interventions focus on equality and creating programs that are for *all* students. When we do this, we are decreasing access to programs for students who need it most. CAREing Mentors provided students with mentors, many of them mentors of color. We also focused on providing mentors who had high expectations and positive views of students of color. In CAREing Mentors, we sought to diversify the type of adult mentor, intentionally seeking community and school staff volunteers of color. As the program grew, we partnered with churches, military officers, community organizations, and college students. Maintaining this partnership required a consistent and strategic effort. I continually reached out to mentors and volunteers from these groups, inviting them to come alongside me on the PLT. For example, I reached out to volunteers and partners during the summer to maintain connections and involve them in planning for the next year. I also reached out to organizations and people who were not current partners, inviting them to celebrations and events throughout the year so they could learn about the partnership and its accomplishments. This ongoing outreach to engage potential volunteers and partners helped us to continuously recruit partners each year.

Finally, to do antiracist partnership work as an individual is to do tough, critically reflective work related to antiracism, including reading books on racism; doing research; and participating in professional development on partnerships, equity, and Black students and families. Antiracism is uncomfortable, but you cannot just talk about it. You need to be a courageous leader, to be actively involved in dismantling systemic and institutional racism. As Bettina Love (2019) said, we want to become coconspirators. Take risks, use your privilege, use your power to change policies for Black youth, create opportunities, and open doors (Love, 2019). Show up personally and remember that racism, not Black people, is the problem in need of changing (Reynolds & Kendi, 2020). As you continue to work collaboratively to build antiracist and equity-focused partnerships, continue to assess how bias and racism arise within your data, programs, services, systems, structures, and policies and create partnership plans and processes to address them. Examine implicit and explicit biases and beliefs about students and families of color and your interactions with them. Consider how you are building partnerships to ensure that they are antiracist and equitable and increase access and opportunities for youth of color.

Implications

Antiracist school counselors recognize that communities of color have historically faced systematic disenfranchisement and exclusion within the American school system and American culture that have had significant negative effects on students of color, especially Black and Brown students. Efforts to provide inclusive and equity-focused services are imperative, and school counselors can play a vital leadership role in promoting family and community engagement that is actively antiracist. This means moving beyond merely communicating respect for families, recognizing their strengths, and building trust with families—all of which are important—to highlighting and eliminating racist systemic barriers in schools.

Engaging in antiracist partnerships requires school counselors to be courageous to self-reflect and consider their own biases and the racist ways in which they experience and see Blackness and Black culture. They will need to challenge their stereotypical views and opt for a more antiracist, strengths-based perspective on Black people and Black community. They must acknowledge the historical trauma and pain experienced by Black people and see the possibility in partnering to create antiracist schools and partnership programs so Black students do not experience schools as places of racial violence and terror. When school counselors make conscious decisions to be intentionally antiracist, they can build more impactful partnerships with and for Black students and families. Equally important is that counselors help partners acknowledge that racism exists and persists in this country and that schools systemically exclude Black and Brown students and families from opportunities, equitable outcomes, and success. Partners must be willing to transform schools. They must be willing to advocate for Black and Brown students; to use data to show that these communities have been disenfranchised; and to help dismantle rules and policies that perpetuate racial disparities in discipline, academic opportunities, and college and career readiness and access. One important aspect of being antiracist is intentionally inserting antiracist actions into partnership work and programs, including lifting up Black voices and representing Black and Brown students, families, and communities as positive, desirable, and strong as opposed to deficient and problematic.

Additional research is needed to explore antiracist partnerships, including their process and outcomes. Although research on partnerships has begun, antiracist framing should be at the center of partnership research, examining how partnerships promote antiracist beliefs and narratives, relationships and interactions, goals and outcomes, and policies and practices among partners and educators and in schools. Antiracism objectives must include intentionality in attacking racism and inequity in schools; validating students' and families' experiences and contributions; and making sure whiteness and white voices are not centered in school curricula, policies, narratives, and goals. Research on antiracist partnerships should comprise both quantitative and qualitative methods so the voices of Black students and families and their experiences in partnership activities and programs and in schools are centered.

Antiracist partnerships have important implications for policies; partners must ensure that their policies and practices are not discriminatory in practice and do not hinder students and families. Partnership policies may help contribute to Black and Brown students' overrepresentation in special education and placement in the school-to-prison pipeline rather than interrupt these policies. Punitive policies should undergo reform so Black students are not criminalized. Counselors should be proactive (and encourage partners to be proactive) in reviewing policies that negatively and disproportionately impact Black and Brown students, bringing them to partners' attention, and working together to transform these policies. Any policies or procedures in which Black students are disproportionately represented and disadvantaged should be further investigated and changed. School counselors who are intentionally antiracist also consistently aim to understand policies that discriminate against students of color. This awareness will lead to greater change in the school system, providing students with safer spaces in schools and more support and energy to focus on their education, future careers, and wellness.

Conclusion

School counselors have a vital part to play in fostering antiracism in schools, especially through leadership in building and promoting partnerships with families and communities of color. Antiracist and equity-focused partnerships make possible the delivery of equitable programs that do not retraumatize students of color. These programs support the resilience of students who have experienced trauma, increase their access to college and career readiness opportunities, and create safer spaces for students and parents of color in schools, empowering spaces as they engage in education. Antiracist partnerships are essential to the success of youth of color, including immigrant youth, as they can provide a strong network of support, resources, and increased educational opportunities, all of which contribute to positive academic outcomes for youth of color.

Antiracist partnerships are essential to fostering positive student outcomes. School counselors are equipped with the leadership, advocacy, and collaboration skills needed to engage in such antiracist work. Therefore, they should be courageous leaders, intentional in including race-based discussions in forming partnerships and deliberately creating antiracist partnership programs, goals, policies, practices, and research to foster Black and Brown students' success and well-being. Although antiracist work requires much self-reflection, it is necessary work that will move the counseling field forward and make resources, opportunities, and success more tangible for students and families who have traditionally been marginalized.

References

Association for Multicultural Counseling and Development. (2020, June 3). *AMCD statement on racialized violence and discrimination.* https://www.counseling.org/news/updates/2020/06/03/amcd-statement-on-racialized-violence-and-discrimination

Baquedano-López, P., Alexander, R. A., & Hernandez, S. J. (2013). Equity issues in parental and community involvement in schools: What teacher educators need to know. *Review of Research in Education, 37*(1), 149–182.

Benson, T. A., & Fiarman, S. E. (2020). *Unconscious bias in schools: A developmental approach to exploring race and racism.* Harvard Education Press.

Bryan, J. (2005). Fostering educational resilience and achievement in urban schools through school-family-community partnerships. *Professional School Counseling, 8*(3), 219–227.

Bryan, J., Griffin, D., Henry, L., & Gilfillan, E. (2019). Building culturally relevant school-family-community partnerships that promote college readiness and access. In National Association for College Admission Counseling (Ed.), *Fundamentals of college admission counseling* (5th ed., pp. 467–488). National Association for College Admission Counseling.

Bryan, J., Griffin, D., Kim, J., Griffin, D. M., & Young, A. (2019). School counselor leadership in school-family-community partnerships: An equity-focused partnership process model for moving the field forward. In S. Sheldon & T. Turner-Vorbeck (Eds.), *The Wiley handbook on family, school, and community relationships in education* (pp. 265–287). Wiley. https://doi.org/10.1002/9781119083054.ch13

Bryan, J., & Henry, L. (2008). Strengths-based partnerships: A school-family-community partnership approach to empowering students. *Professional School Counseling*, 12(2), 149–156.

Bryan, J., & Henry, L. (2012). A model for building school–family–community partnerships: Principles and process. *Journal of Counseling & Development*, 90(4), 408–420. https://doi.org/10.1002/j.1556-6676.2012.00052.x

Bryan, J., Williams, J. M., & Griffin, D. (2016). Closing opportunity gaps for Black male students through school-family-community partnerships. In M. S. Henfield & A. R. Washington (Eds.), *School counseling for Black male student success in 21st century urban schools* (pp. 75–98). Information Age.

Bryan, J., Williams, J. M., & Griffin, D. (2020). Fostering educational resilience and opportunities in urban schools through equity-focused school–family–community partnerships. *Professional School Counseling*, 23(1), 1–14. https://doi.org/10.1177/2156759X19899179

Bryan, J., Young, A., Griffin, D., & Henry, L. (2016). Preparing students for higher education: How school counselors can foster college readiness and access. In J. L. DeVitis & P. Sasso (Eds.), *Higher education and society* (pp. 149–172). Peter Lang.

Comas-Díaz, L. (2016). Racial trauma recovery: A race-informed therapeutic approach to racial wounds. In A. N. Alvarez, C. T. H. Liang, & H. A. Neville (Eds.), *The cost of racism for people of color: Contextualizing experiences of discrimination* (pp. 249–272). American Psychological Association. https://doi.org/10.1037/14852-012

Earick, M. E. (2018). We are not social justice equals: The need for white scholars to understand their whiteness. *International Journal of Qualitative Studies in Education*, 31(8), 800–820.

Edwin, M., Haynes-Thoby, L., & Bryan, J. (in press). Using school-family-community partnerships to enhance career development and postsecondary transitions for students of color. In E. M. Hines & L. Owens (Eds.), *Equity-based career development and postsecondary transitions*. Information Age.

Griffin, D., Williams, J. M., & Bryan, J. (in press). School-family-community partnerships for educational access and equity for Black male students. *Professional School Counseling*.

Henry, L. M. (2014). *Just love: A collaborative evaluation of a faith-based school-family-community partnership through the voices of the children* [Doctoral dissertation, University of South Florida]. University of South Florida Scholar Commons. http://scholarcommons.usf.edu/cgi/viewcontent.cgi?article=6433&context=etd

Henry, L. M., & Bryan, J. (2021). How the educator–counselor–leader–collaborator creates asset-rich schools: A qualitative study of a school–family–community partnership. *Professional School Counseling*, 24(1) 1–13. https://doi.org/10.1177/2156759X211011907

Henry, L. M., Bryan, J., & Zalaquett, C. (2017). The effects of a counselor-led, faith-based, school–family–community partnership on student achievement in a high-poverty urban elementary school. *Journal of Multicultural Counseling and Development*, 45(3), 162–182. https://doi.org/10.1002/jmcd.12072

Jenkins, D. A. (2021). Unspoken grammar of place: Anti-Blackness as a spatial imaginary in education. *Journal of School Leadership*. Advance online publication. https://doi.org/10.1177/1052684621992768

Joseph, A. A., Wilcox, S. M., Hnilica, R. J., & Hansen, M. C. (2020). Keeping race at the center of school discipline practices and trauma-informed care: An interprofessional framework. *Children & Schools*, 42(3), 161–170.

Kendi, I. X. (2019). *How to be an antiracist*. One World.

Kim, J., & Bryan, J. (2017). A first step to a conceptual framework of parent empowerment: Exploring relationships between parent empowerment and academic performance in a national sample. *Journal of Counseling & Development*, 95(2), 168–179. https://doi.org/10.1002/jcad.12129

Kim, J., Fletcher, K., & Bryan, J. (2017). Empowering marginalized parents: An emerging parent empowerment model for school counselors. *Professional School Counseling*, 21(1). https://doi.org/10.1177/2156759X18773585

Kohli, R., Pizarro, M., & Nevárez, A. (2017). The "new racism" of K–12 schools: Centering critical research on racism. *Review of Research in Education*, 41(1), 182–202. https://doi.org/10.3102/0091732X16686949

Love, B. L. (2019). *We want to do more than survive: Abolitionist teaching and the pursuit of educational freedom*. Beacon Press.

Majors, A. T. (2019). From the editorial board: College readiness: A critical race theory perspective. *The High School Journal*, 102(3), 183–188.

McIntosh, M. L. (2019). Compound fractures: Healing the intersectionality of racism, classism and trauma in schools with a trauma-informed approach as part of a social justice framework. *Journal of Educational Leadership and Policy Studies*, 3(1). https://files.eric.ed.gov/fulltext/EJ1226938.pdf

Moore-Thomas, C., & Day-Vines, N. L. (2010). Culturally competent collaboration: School counselor collaboration with African American families and communities. *Professional School Counseling*, 14(1), 53–63.

Nadal, K. L., Erazo, T., & King, R. (2019). Challenging definitions of psychological trauma: Connecting racial microaggressions and traumatic stress. *Journal for Social Action in Counseling & Psychology*, 11(2), 2–16.

Pollock, M. (2009). *Colormute: Race talk dilemmas in an American school*. Princeton University Press.

Reynolds, J., & Kendi, I. X. (2020). *Stamped: Racism, antiracism, and you*. Little, Brown Books for Young Readers.

Wade, R., Jr., Shea, J. A., Rubin, D., & Wood, J. (2014). Adverse childhood experiences of low-income urban youth. *Pediatrics*, 134(1), e13–e20. https://doi.org/10.1542/peds.2013-2475

Wilson, C. M. (2019). Critical approaches to educational partnerships with African American families: The relevancy of race in ideology and practice. In S. Sheldon & T. Turner-Vorbeck (Eds.), *The Wiley handbook on family, school, and community relationships in education* (pp. 51–69). Wiley.

Yull, D., Blitz, L. V., Thompson, T., & Murray, C. (2014). Can we talk? Using community-based participatory action research to build family and school partnerships with color. *School Community Journal*, 24(2), 9–32.

CHAPTER 8

Dismantling White Supremacy in School Counselor Training Programs: Preparing Counselors to Enact Antiracist Practices

Whitney Polk, Mandy Savitz-Romer, and Gretchen Brion-Meisels

Across the globe, persistent violence against Black and Indigenous people has led to increasingly frequent calls for antiracist schools and communities. The murders of Ahmaud Arbery, Breonna Taylor, George Floyd, and too many others by police, and the ensuing protests demanding justice, compelled tens of thousands of people across the globe to exit their homes during a global health pandemic, march together, and righteously declare once again that "Black Lives Matter." Knowing that schools play a critical role in the interrogation of pervasive racism, discrimination, and oppression within society, educators across the United States committed to incorporating antiracist approaches into their teaching and practice. This movement included school counselors and counselor educators, many of whom set out to unlearn socialized anti-Blackness in schools and revisit their social justice advocacy. They joined webinars, book clubs, and other professional learning opportunities focused on overt and covert racism in schools and began to interrogate themselves and their profession. However, noticeably absent from the surge of interest in antiracist education was attention to the preservice training that indoctrinates counselors into the field.

School counselors and counselor educators have traditionally pioneered social justice and multicultural advocacy in educational research and practice (Grzanka et al., 2019; E. M. Vera & Speight, 2003). For many years, counselor educators have taught multicultural counseling competencies that require counselor trainees to consider their own biases and skills to better understand the contexts and belief systems of BIPOC (Goodman et al., 2015). Graduate programs in counseling have also incorporated data-driven counseling approaches that position school counselors to identify and interrupt practices that actively discriminate against BIPOC in curricula and educational settings (Holcomb-McCoy, 2007). However, these programs rarely acknowledge Whiteness[1] in a field that is overwhelmingly White in terms of research, practice, and training. When Whiteness is deracialized and removed from the conversation, it tacitly becomes the norm, asserting its power and inhibiting antiracist efforts. The absence of Whiteness in discussions of discrimination, inequality, and oppression both reifies and obscures the power dynamics of racism, in which Whiteness and White people are positioned atop the hierarchy.

The presence of White supremacy culture (WSC) in counselor education programs—spaces that indoctrinate school counselors into the field—reinforces the racism present in schools and school counseling practices. WSC, which includes both overt expressions of White power and authority and subtle manifestations of White dominance, is present in our cultural, political, economic, educational, and social institutions. The pervasiveness of WSC manifests not just in counselor education classrooms but across the entirety of the field. Dismantling this culture is paramount to engendering subsequent antiracist school counseling practices.

In this chapter, we describe how the centrality of WSC in many higher education institutions leads school counselor education programs to center Whiteness in their curricula, fieldwork, and pedagogy. This reality works to maintain the status quo and undermines any intentions of teaching multicultural competencies. Worse, it harms the students and communities our graduate students aim to support. In this chapter, we first describe the importance of calling for antiracist, antioppressive school counseling and the consequences of failing to subvert WSC in our work. We then describe WSC, as defined by K. Jones and Okun (2001), and illustrate how WSC specifically manifests in counselor education programs. We describe selected elements of this cultural framework using examples across curricular, pedagogical, and applied elements of graduate programs in school counseling. We then illustrate an alternative approach to counselor education using a case vignette to illustrate recommendations for change. By providing you with the language to talk about harmful practices, and concrete examples of where they emerge, we hope to begin a dialogue that will end with the collective reimagining of why, how, and with whom school counselors prepare for the profession. We end this chapter with a set of antidotes that we hope might inspire counselor educators to enact new ways of designing and delivering school counseling programs and courses.

Our Positionality

In writing this chapter, we began by thinking and talking about our positionalities. As is always the case, who we are and how we come to our work as counselors has a significant impact on how we make meaning of our experiences within it.

---

[1]In this chapter, we have chosen to capitalize "White" in line with style advice offered by the American Psychological Association and the Center for the Study of Social Policy, among others. We have elected to capitalize "Black," "Brown," and "BIPOC" alongside "White," "Whiteness," and "White power/privilege" not to confer some sort of misguided notion of language equality or deference. A primary purpose of this chapter is to name and identify White supremacy culture (WSC), which insulates Whiteness and White people, to root it out and in turn reduce the dominance it has imbued by virtue of its invisibility and normalization. Truly, the capitalization of "White" and its other iterations throughout the chapter may be jarring, especially for BIPOC and so many other people experiencing the weight of WSC. Still, we reason that it is important to interrogate that discomfort, especially for those new to feeling uncomfortable, and challenge WSC where we see it enacted. We reason that a chapter calling for decentering Whiteness in counselor education programs should avoid deracializing Whiteness, illustrating its central point through such an editorial choice. However, we recognize both the benefit and potential harm of capitalizing "White" and thus encourage you to review insightful perspectives on this topic (e.g., Nell Irvin Painter, Eve Ewing, Kwame Anthony Appiah, the Associated Press).

As I grapple with the realities of White supremacy in our world and chosen field, I (Whitney) am cognizant of my identity as a Black, straight, cisgender woman. As an early career researcher, it is also important for me to consider the power dynamics of coconstructing a chapter on White supremacy with two more senior faculty White women, who are also two of my closest mentors. Despite an early history of economic hardship, I have been privileged to learn and train in overresourced yet underscrutinized predominantly White institutions. Learning and growing as a Black counselor and now academic on elite campuses with violent, racist, and colonial pasts and presents demands constant negotiations and counternarratives to preserve my humanity and the humanity of others. And yet, given that same education, I too am required to unlearn aspects of WSC that interfere with those demands. Seeing the privileges afforded to my White peers juxtaposed against my own intersectional experiences of oppression and those of my BIPOC students and colleagues fuels my commitment to disrupting racism and White supremacy.

As a White, Jewish, straight, cisgender woman, my (Mandy) understanding of counselor education and WSC in particular is shaped by the racial and educational privilege I have experienced as a student, as a school counselor, and now as a counselor educator. My training in counseling affirmed the White cultural norms and expectations that I was socialized to uphold; now, as the director of a school counseling program, I am deeply committed to unlearning this part of my training and interrogating perceptions I had about the appropriate way to train preservice counselors. This is a journey that I expect will be lifelong.

As a White, queer, cisgender woman who grew up in a racially and socioeconomically diverse context, I (Gretchen) was raised to think critically about my own racial and socioeconomic privilege. Nevertheless, every day I become newly aware of how racism, misogyny, racial capitalism, and class privilege have shaped my perceptions of the world and my ways of being within it. Although I was trained as a teacher, I have always been drawn to school counseling because of its commitment to supporting whole children. And like Mandy, I consider the unlearning of WSC to be a lifelong journey that I know will bring both deep pain and important moments of liberation.

Collectively, the three of us have spent much of our educational and pedagogical journeys in elite institutions. We recognize that our firsthand experiences in counselor education programs reflect elements of those institutions and in particular their predominantly White faculty and student bodies. Two of us work at Harvard University, which sits on the ancestral land of the Massachusett people, and one of us works at the University of Pennsylvania, which is in Lenapehoking territory. Thus, we are mindful of the privileges and autonomy we have in constructing our pedagogies and programs.

Interrogating Whiteness in Counselor Education

Although there is limited research on the explicit role of WSC (or White dominant culture) in U.S.-based school counselor education programs, there is a deep history of critically oriented scholars and practitioners calling for a more antiracist, antioppressive approach to this work. Given the racist origins of the field of psychology (e.g., eugenics, intelligence testing, criminalization; Fernando, 2017; Winston, 2020; Yakushko, 2019) and the assimilationist origins of the field of school counseling (e.g., Halpern, 1999), this sustained, powerful resistance to hegemonic notions of health, well-being, success, and happiness is not surprising. In our reviews of this literature, we have observed that writing about antiracist, antioppressive counseling is much more common in the fields of social work and psychology than in the smaller field of school counseling itself. Even so, there is certainly a history of multicultural and antiracist school counseling, much of which has inspired us and helped us think more carefully about these issues. Although we cannot do justice to this vast body of work, we think it critical for you to engage with it, either by exploring more recent texts published by Atkins and Oglesby (2018) or Holcomb-McCoy (2007) and/or by digging into its emancipatory roots across education (Freire, 2018; Ivey & Collins, 2003), critical studies of race and education (Delgado & Stefancic, 2017; Ladson-Billings & Tate, 1995, 2016), psychology, and theology (Fanon, 1963, 2008; Martín-Baró, 1994). We also encourage you to engage with scholars who are working to decolonize school counseling (see, e.g., the authors published in Goodman & Gorski, 2015). We appreciate, honor, and seek to build on this work in our writing. In particular, this chapter builds on the work of Smith and Geroski (2015), who called for a social justice model of alterity for the field of professional school counseling, and the work of Grzanka et al. (2019), who argued for (a) rejecting racial progress narratives, (b) engaging in social justice–oriented practice with White clients, and (c) dismantling White supremacy as critical steps for the field of counseling psychology.

Seeking to contribute to this ongoing call for antiracist, antioppressive school counseling, we argue that identifying and dismantling WSC within the context of school counseling and school counselor education is a critical step to decolonizing our field. Just as Smith (2017, p. 2) suggested that critical consciousness is the lens through which school counselors might better identify the "damaging forces in our culture that negatively affect the health, wellness, and psycho-social development of students and families"—the pathogen that threatens "human wellness and development"—we argue that WSC is a large part of that pathogen. By learning to see how and when the pathogen shows up (and spreads) within ourselves, our relationships, our offices, and the schools where we work, we can begin to reimagine our work in antioppressive ways. Later in this chapter, we provide concrete examples of how different elements of WSC show up in school counseling and school counselor education. To do this, we briefly connect our work to three existing movements within our field that highlight the dangers of addressing the symptoms of racism without ameliorating the pathogen itself.

Fundamentally, our argument builds on arguments about the importance of centering sociocultural factors in ecological systems theory. In 1996, when Cynthia García Coll et al. were finally able to publish their seminal piece "An Integrative Model for the Study of Developmental Competencies in Minority Children," their writing catalyzed 3 decades of explicit calls for bringing the outer (more systemic) systems of Bronfenbrenner's (1977) ecological systems theory into the center of that model. Specifically, the authors argued that for many marginalized children and youth, sociopolitical, cultural, and historical factors shape elements of the interactions that drive development. Although García Coll et al. were writing specifically about the impact of factors of social positioning on marginalized children, subsequent work has also highlighted the role that these macrolevel systems can play in the everyday interactions of children with privilege. All children and adults are directly impacted by their relationships to systems of oppression.

Decades of research in developmental psychology suggest that meeting the American School Counselor Association (ASCA) goal of providing school counseling programs that "are delivered to all students systematically, include a developmentally appropriate curriculum focused on the mindsets and behaviors all students need for postsecondary readiness and success, close achievement and opportunity gaps, [and] result in improved student achievement, attendance and discipline" (ASCA, 2017, "The Rationale," para. 1) requires identifying and dismantling the systems, policies, and practices that continue to reinforce inequities within schools. Including an analysis of power in our data-based decision-making is critical to authentically using an ecological systems model for our work. Failing to consider sociopolitical, cultural, and historical factors that reinforce WSC is akin to ignoring the pathogen and instead treating only the symptoms.

Multicultural, Social Justice, and Antiracist Movements in Counselor Education

For several decades, counselor education and training focused on the development of multicultural competence (Gorski & Goodman, 2015) and presumed to push the field toward a more pluralistic understanding of culture, race, and identity in the client-counselor relationship (Smith & Geroski, 2015). Multicultural counseling competencies encouraged counselors to become culturally skilled by developing an awareness of their own biases and assumptions, attempting nonjudgmental cross-cultural understanding, and implementing culturally sensitive interventions with those culturally different from themselves (Sue et al., 1992). As the fourth force of counseling, multiculturalism offered a more inclusive approach to supporting BIPOC clients with an emphasis on assisting White counselors either unaccustomed to, ignorant of, or apathetic toward race, racism, and White supremacy in the lives of their clients (Sue et al., 1992). Critiques of multiculturalism highlight this exclusive focus on White counselor development for their work with BIPOC clients (Miller et al., 2018). Despite initial calls for context and oppression analyses with clients, multiculturalism quickly became equated with non-White or racial/ethnic minority issues, devoid of any substantive interrogations of Whiteness or oppression (Bartoli et al., 2015; Singh et al., 2020). Impacted by the dearth of BIPOC counselors, researchers, and advocates and opposition to early movements around multicultural counseling competencies (see Weinrach & Thomas, 2004), multiculturalism became centered less on cultural pluralism and more on the othering of folks from White, nondominant cultural backgrounds (Drake & Oglesby, 2020), in particular through the emphasis on the one-to-one relationship in cross-cultural counseling approaches (Bartoli et al., 2015). As a result, the original arguments put forth by Sue et al. (1992) were diluted and Whiteness was again centered in conversations about counseling. Multicultural approaches to counseling that failed to confront Whiteness ultimately reinforced the very cultural power dynamics they intended to counter and diminished their intended utility.

Noting the increasing diversity of public school student populations, ASCA developed several multicultural competency frameworks and position statements (ASCA, 2012; Holcomb-McCoy, 2004). Still, in an explicit exploration of the role of othering or alterity in school counselor education, Smith and Geroski (2015) argued that the language of the multicultural competencies still did not adequately address issues of power and cultural hegemony. Multiculturalism that lacks explicit discussions of power and privilege may inadvertently replicate oppressive systems by denying their existence. Furthermore, Gorski and Goodman (2015) argued that promoting multiculturalism sans collective and corrective action does little to advance calls for social justice and equity. Without a plan for addressing power (e.g., without explicit discussions of how power and privilege oppress those outside the White dominant culture) multiculturalism is easily whitewashed (Drake & Oglesby, 2020). Moreover, focusing on culture as opposed to cultural power and privilege likens the effects of racism and oppression to cultural happenstance rather than intentional and "purposeful societal arrangements" (Gorski & Goodman, 2015, p. 3). This devolution of the framing of multicultural competence compelled counselor educators and researchers to generate competencies that centered antiracism.

The Multicultural and Social Justice Counseling Competencies (Ratts & Greenleaf, 2017; Ratts et al., 2016) were developed in response to calls for multicultural competencies that specifically addressed the impact of both privileged and marginalized counselor identities on work with clients. These more recent movements specifically demand social justice and aim to disrupt racism in our training and practice. The Multicultural and Social Justice Counseling Competencies explicitly call for the interrogation of power and the problematization of privilege, both of which are intended to address oppression and help counselors advocate for equity (Singh et al., 2020). For school counselor educators and trainees, the Multicultural and Social Justice Counseling Competencies require exploration of how power and oppression impact students' academic, social-emotional, and career development (Ratts & Greenleaf, 2017).

Despite the limited reach of multicultural counseling competencies, their focus on narratives of diversity and inclusivity, emphasis on counselor self-awareness and bias, and appreciation for holistic views of clients have become integral to counselor education and training programs (Nassar & Singh, 2020). Social justice and antiracist counseling movements have extended these ideas, ensuring that the merits and underlying principles of multiculturalism are upheld within counseling relationships, especially cross-cultural relationships (E. M. Vera & Speight, 2003). Social justice counseling strives to "promote human development and the common good" by directly addressing both individual and systemic injustice (Crethar & Ratts, 2008, p. 24). Social justice counseling advocacy requires counselors to be trained to center issues of resource equity; access to services, power, and information; participation in society and societal decision-making; and harmony that prioritizes the collective good (Crethar & Ratts, 2008). As the fifth force of counseling, social justice counseling builds on and is entwined with multicultural approaches that view "clients as cultural beings who exist within systems and contexts" (K. A. Tate et al., 2015, p. 41). Still, in practice social justice movements in counseling have experienced a knowledge-skill gap. Like multiculturalism movements, social justice counselor training has produced counselors who can articulate (or know of) inequities and structural barriers but lack the requisite skills (or know-how) to implement effective interventions or support meaningful systemic change in clients' lived experiences (Arthur et al., 2013; J. M. Jones et al., 2013). Counseling that advocates social justice falls short without naming or counteracting the powerful patriarchal, colonial, and racist oppressive systems it intends to undo or correct.

Movements to decolonize counseling counter injustice and cultural monism by speaking directly to the coloniality of U.S. history and the client-counselor relationship. Decolonization of counseling requires an understanding of the constancy of power and racism embedded within the U.S. context, specifically violent colonial pursuits, beginning with the genocide of Native Americans and the enslavement of Africans (Fernández, 2018) and continuing through the existing marginalization and disenfranchisement of BIPOC (Hunter et al., 2010). Moreover, the focus on coloniality offers a more direct course of action by naming the oppressive force to be dismantled. In contrast, efforts to disrupt an unknown or unnamed oppressive entity are easily neglected when that which must be undone is elusive or intangible. Colonialism denotes the intentional subordination and dehumanization in both body and ideology of BIPOC through violence and dominance in the name of Eurocentrism or European racial supremacy (Moe et al., 2020; Young, 2016). Proponents of decolonized multicultural counseling suggest that disrupting powerful colonial hierarchies requires problematizing entrenched power structures positioned at the top. Moreover, decolonizing counselor education and practice require attending to who is affected and why; what can be done to support those impacted by colonialism; and how we might restructure counseling theory, practice, and training toward more socially just ends (Gorski & Goodman, 2015).

Because racism is a primary feature of the maintenance of colonialism, explicit calls for antiracist counselor education (Atkins & Oglesby, 2018; Holcomb-McCoy, 2007)—and more recently for abolitionist teaching and learning (Love, 2019)—have demanded that counselor educators explicitly advocate for antiracist policies and practices within their schools and communities. Racism functions as both a system of disadvantage and a pattern of interpersonal denigration through the enforcement of a racial hierarchy (Ladson-Billings & Tate, 1995; Tatum, 2017). Our commitment to social justice demands a both/and understanding of the interpersonal and systemic manifestations of racism to shape how we conceptualize and work to dismantle racism in our clinical practice, educational praxis, and pedagogy. Integrating García Coll et al.'s (1996) arguments about the central importance of sociopolitical, cultural, and historical systems in the everyday lives of individuals with Tervalon and Murray-García's (1998) notion of cultural humility,[2] this writing has demanded that school counselors see themselves as antiracist advocates at both the individual and systems levels. Rightfully, much of our advocacy work and dedication to disrupting and eradicating racism is reactionary, focusing on the disadvantages and dehumanization experienced by BIPOC in anticipation of it occurring or after it occurs, when the harm and impact are most visible and apparent. However, too little attention is paid to what underpins the harm and disadvantage: the enforcement of a racial hierarchy.

In the U.S. context, Whiteness and White supremacy are seated atop the racial hierarchy (Chrobot-Mason et al., 2020), sustaining vertical stratification of BIPOC and White folks across various social sectors (Grzanka et al., 2019). In a field that is overwhelmingly White in terms of research, practice, and training, to relegate multicultural, racial, and social justice practice and pedagogy to the realm of *not* White, and to avoid direct discussions of Whiteness, power, and White supremacy, is to uphold the racial hierarchy. Antiracist counseling, then, must be committed to actively dismantling the racial hierarchies that reify Whiteness as the dominant cultural frame and uphold White supremacy ideology and culture. This chapter

---

[2]Cultural humility calls on clinicians to "continually engage in self-reflection and self-critique as lifelong learners and reflective practitioners," "check the power imbalances that exist" in both their own interpersonal relationships and the larger systems in which they work, and "maintain mutually respectful and dynamic partnerships with communities in service of their patients and communities in the context of community-based clinical and advocacy training models" (Tervalon & Murray-García, 1998, pp. 118–119).

focuses on the ideology and subsequent culture of White supremacy that is produced, maintained, and replicated in counseling and school counselor education.

WSC

White supremacy is both an ideology and a system through which White people and their ideas, beliefs, and humanity are individually valued and advantaged over people of color (Ansley, 1997; Grzanka et al., 2019). Although the term "White supremacist" conjures specific imagery of the Ku Klux Klan, Nazis, and violent White nationalist separatists, White supremacy includes both overt expressions of White power and authority and subtle manifestations of White dominance present in our cultural, political, economic, educational, and social institutions. Like racism, White supremacy materializes and is reproduced in all our interactions and institutions through "implicit and explicit ideas about White people's superiority" (Grzanka et al., 2019, p. 479; see also Ansley, 1997). Grzanka et al. (2019) articulated three primary aims of White supremacy: (a) the subjugation of BIPOC, (b) the promotion of White interests, and (c) hostility toward any perceived or real threats to White power and privilege. White supremacy is entwined with Eurocentrism, patriarchal notions of gender, heteronormativity, and Christianity and is preoccupied with the normalization of these concepts through violence and marginalization, such that any deviation is regarded as deficient. Challenges to Whiteness and the superiority of White folks directly threaten White notions of normativity and universality (Chrobot-Mason et al., 2020; Parker et al., 2017). A primary goal of White supremacy is to retain authority and control of the social order through explicit ownership and possession of normality as well as property, resources, and knowledge (Frediani, 2020). This is partly accomplished by exclusively exalting the interests, needs, and wants of White peoples at the expense of groups that are not White. Adopting a colonial lens, Frediani (2020) understood White supremacy "as a matrix of patterns of coloniality of knowledge, coloniality of being, and coloniality of power" that seeks to control, among other things, the formation of knowledge (p. 544).

Exclusive rights to normative ways of being, knowing, and doing imbue Whiteness with the authority to define reality (Sue, 2013, 2016). In defining reality, White supremacy can simultaneously assert itself and render itself invisible, as long as its existence and permeance are ignored or rejected by complicit beneficiaries. This kind of White epistemological ignorance represents a willful rejection of histories of colonialism, enslavement, disenfranchisement, and violence; the persistence and permanence of racism; and their continued impact on current racial inequality and stratification (Mills, 2014; Steinberg, 2018). It is simultaneously a rejection of reality and a self-assured retelling of reality to which others must also subscribe.

White supremacy thrives in part because of epistemological ignorance. Beneficiaries of White supremacy can at once deny its existence and impact and, through this denial, legitimize its efficacy and sustain its power. Racial color blindness serves as an unambiguous manifestation of epistemological ignorance. Color blindness, or the denial or ignorance of racial differences, confers innocence and relinquishes responsibility regarding the realities of racial inequality (Bonilla-Silva, 2006). Color blindness enables racism and White supremacy through the erasure of BIPOC experiences (Kohli et al., 2017). Color-blind approaches to race and racism are dehumanizing, as they strip BIPOC of their agency and self-narratives and silence their experiences of injustice (e.g., If you do not see color, you do not see my full experience as a person of color). Fernández (2018) suggested that historical amnesia coupled with racial color blindness inhibits pursuits of equity and justice. If the world is color-blind, then any racial differences in opportunities or outcomes rest within the individual or their community (Kohli et al., 2017). While at once denying knowledge or the existence of racial differences and inequality, White supremacy ideology affirms the privileged position of Whiteness, pathologizes legitimate anger and challenges to oppression (Nelson & Prilleltensky, 2010; Shin, 2015), and places accountability for change among marginalized individuals and communities.

For example, Black Lives Matter (BLM) began as a direct call for justice and recognition of Black humanity following the murder of Trayvon Martin and subsequent acquittal of his killer, George Zimmerman. In its fight against police brutality and White supremacy, BLM has been vilified by both liberal and conservative political and media circles as too aggressive, aimless, and disrespectful of the legacies of nonviolence of the civil rights movement. BLM has been consistently told that to be taken seriously it should tone down or centralize its message and appeal to a broader (read Whiter) audience. Despite developing a detailed platform of demands, securing front-door meetings with top political candidates, and peaceably protesting as one of the largest multiracial coalitions in recent history, BLM is continually met with backlash, police violence, and public derision for challenging racism and White supremacy. Saying "Black Lives Matter" forces folks to bear witness to discrimination, racism, and anti-Blackness, whereas the glib response "All lives matter" attempts to delegitimize the necessity of BLM despite ample evidence of racial disparities in policing and systemic oppression. The invisibility of Whiteness and White supremacy renders them imperceptible, obscuring their oppressive power. It is the insidiousness of Whiteness and White supremacy that makes them difficult to combat. This process not only obscures White supremacy and Whiteness but also succeeds in divorcing explorations of Whiteness and power from multicultural, social justice, and antiracist approaches to counseling.

Both the normative and invisible nature of White supremacy espouse a culture of supremacy endemic to our norms, attitudes, and behaviors as well as our educational organizations and institutions. K. Jones & Okun (2001) defined WSC as "the explicit to subtle ways that the norms, preferences, and fears of White European descended people overwhelmingly shape how we organize our work and institutions, see ourselves and others, interact with one another and with time, and make decisions" (p. 1). K. Jones and Okun (2001) developed a WSC framework that offers insight into the ways in which White supremacy can operate, in particular in professional settings. Through our exploration of multicultural, social justice, and antiracist approaches to counseling and counselor education, we articulate a common through-line: Direct and explicit naming of the sources of injustice is necessary to actively disrupt and dismantle racism, eradicate inequality, and end the marginalization and dehumanization of oppressed groups. Furthermore, counselors occupy a unique space in the action and advocacy needed to pursue these goals. Actions to directly dismantle racism and oppressive systems are prioritized within social justice counselor education (DeBlaere et al., 2019). To continue the tradition of social justice advocacy and to adequately socialize and support the next generation of counselors, antiracist counselor education necessitates explicit targeting of WSC to understand how, why, and where WSC materializes in counseling and preservice training.

Though seemingly counterintuitive, centering White supremacy differs from centering Whiteness or White people (Grzanka et al., 2019). First, White supremacy is an ideology and system that is not exclusively upheld by White-identified folks. The culture of White supremacy is so pervasive and normalized that our social, political, and educational systems promote White, dominant culture as the ethos to which all people should aspire. BIPOC individuals are not immune and can also enact aspects of WSC in their personal and professional lives. The research on *internalized racism,* or "the acceptance, by marginalized racial populations, of the negative societal beliefs and stereotypes about themselves" (Williams & Williams-Morris, 2000, p. 255), highlights the individual psychological injury wrought by internalized inferiority as well as potential harm directed toward other marginalized groups (David et al., 2019; Speight, 2007; Williams & Williams-Morris, 2000). Second, centering Whiteness as the norm while evading analyses of White privilege, domination, and power is the core of White supremacy—its power lies within its invisibility. In contrast, centering and interrogating White supremacy shatters the illusion of invisibility, revealing WSC as an ever-present malevolent ideology and system of oppression. Centering WSC serves to disrupt the racial hierarchy; demands accountability from the oppressive class; and situates the work within individuals, communities, and institutions, especially those in power. To center and thus excavate WSC, we identify characteristics of WSC (K. Jones & Okun, 2001) across multiple sectors of school counselor education and training: curriculum, pedagogy, recruitment and retention, clinical experiences and fieldwork, licensure and credentialing, and scholarship.

WSC in School Counselor Education

K. Jones and Okun's (2001) WSC framework describes 14 tenets of WSC that can be harmful when enacted without question. School counselor education, like any other educational system, is susceptible to WSC and the replication of harmful oppressive structures. As school counselor educators, we must ensure that training supports the development of strong counseling skills. The competencies gained through our curricula, pedagogy, recruitment and retention efforts, and field placements must reflect the social justice and antiracist aims of our programmatic missions and standards of our field. Thus, we examine the WSC framework concerning what, how, who, and where we teach and prepare school counselor trainees. Furthermore, we explore the presence of WSC tenets among our avenues of credentialing and scholarship. Licensure and credentialing and the production of academic research in counseling serve as markers of knowledge and expertise. Unexamined White supremacy within accreditation and licensing bodies may confer unlearned or unearned skill and capability on poorly trained or vetted institutions, educators, trainees, and supervisors. Likewise, unchecked counseling scholarship may promote harmful, hegemonic narratives about marginalized groups and exclude research topics, methods, and analyses that prioritize community and non-Eurocentric knowledge (Fernández, 2018). Thus, we applied the 14 tenets of WSC across six sectors of counselor preparation: curriculum, pedagogy, recruitment and retention, clinical experiences and fieldwork, licensure and credentialing, and scholarship.

The characteristics that typify WSC include paternalism; power hoarding; individualism; objectivity; perfectionism; worship of the written word; either/or thinking; only one right way; sense of urgency; progress is bigger, more; quantity over quality; fear of conflict; right to comfort; and defensiveness (K. Jones & Okun,

2001). Although these characteristics are not exhaustive of the manifestations of WSC in counseling and other institutions, they do illuminate observable processes and practices inherent to White, dominant cultural ways of being, doing, and knowing. Though each tenet depicts a unique feature of WSC, there is crossover in how they function and attempt to preserve the hierarchy of White dominance. To explore the continuity among WSC characteristics, we developed four thematic categories of WSC inclusive of these tenets: Power, Rightness, Perpetual Progress, and Civility (see Figure 8.1).

The primary aim of WSC is the maintenance of Power; it is through the imposition of power that Whiteness and White-identified folks retain their position atop the racial hierarchy. Power is expected, felt to be deserved, and taken for granted through a sense of moral and nominal Rightness. Challenges to White power and presumptions of Rightness are suppressed by promises of eventual Perpetual Progress, such that if inequality exists it will be attended to in due time. Finally, calls for Civility allow Power, Rightness, and Perpetual Progress myths to persist, such that antiracist voices are silenced or accused of wrongdoing for challenging White supremacy, oppression, and injustice. An exploration of these WSC categories, associated tenets, and illustrative examples of their presence across school counseling curriculum, pedagogy, recruitment and retention, clinical experiences and fieldwork, licensure and credentialing, and scholarship follow.

Power

In the context of White supremacy, power maintains control, authority, and influence over groups that are not White through "practices and institutional structures that keep White people in power and privilege a White perspective" (Baima & Sude, 2020, p. 62; DiAngelo, 2018; Helms, 2017). Power perpetuates oppression and is preserved through unrelenting accumulations of interpersonal, intergenerational, and systemic power that secures White advantage. Denying power to marginalized groups sustains WSC and is accomplished through characteristics like paternalism, power hoarding, and individualism. Refusal to share in power is justified through paternalism and similar attitudes of White superiority.

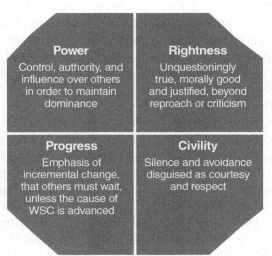

FIGURE 8.1 • Thematic Categories of White Supremacy Culture (WSC)

Institutional paternalism relies on and exalts the knowledge and know-how of those in positions of authority, ignoring the viewpoints and perspectives of those without power (K. Jones & Okun, 2001). Paternalist attitudes are propelled by the notion that one group not only knows more but knows better and therefore can and should dictate the course and direction of the lives of those without power. This lack of transparency leaves those without power perennially in the dark about how decisions are made; allows decision-making to be rooted in White, cultural assumptions; and indicates whose input is and is not valued. A paternalistic approach rejects collaboration, collective responsibility, and accountability. Instead, this atmosphere promotes individualism and separateness, or the expectation of independence and autonomy as paramount, and the idea that individuals are the sole arbiters of their environment (K. Jones & Okun, 2001; Potapchuk, 2012). Threats to paternalism and individualism are met with power hoarding. Ideas, knowledge, and suggestions from those without power threaten the status quo. Calls for transparency, accountability, and power sharing are met with resistance and explained away via myths about the scarcity of resources and reverence for what has always been done. In Table 8.1, we describe manifestations of paternalism, individualism, and power hoarding across multiple sectors of counseling and preservice training.

School counseling is grounded in vocational guidance, counseling psychology, and psychotherapy (Drake & Oglesby, 2020). Thus, school counseling finds its roots in Western philosophies of illness and wellness and in White, dominant cultural expectations of care and healing (Moe et al., 2020; Sue & Sue, 2008). Despite a commitment to multicultural and social justice education, our curricula largely rest on theories and foundational content that pathologizes or altogether excludes non-White cultural modes of success and wellness (Moe et al., 2020). Liberation and community psychology perspectives are generally absent from standard curricula and texts and are treated as fringe or experimental when introduced. The White experience is centered in our coursework and course offerings, and the inclusion of BIPOC perspectives is consciously or unconsciously sidelined (Watkins et al., 2018). Though most graduate training programs and licensure bodies require coursework on multiculturalism, these courses are viewed as auxiliary to normative models of school counselor education instead of integrated across curricula and programming (Motulsky et al., 2014). Multiculturalism itself is othered when relegated to 1 week on a syllabus or a single required course instead of being integrated across lessons and among courses (Goodman et al., 2015). Although questions of power, privilege, and oppression may be highlighted in these courses, their integrity and value are dependent on the knowledge, skill, and willingness of the school counselor educator and the social justice commitment of the program and institution (Motulsky et al., 2014).

Power dynamics shape content delivery and deficit-based ideologies inform deficit-based pedagogy. Training that promotes theories, ideas, or skills that undervalue client and community input centers the school counselor in relationships with students and families. Though demographics are shifting, the majority of the school counseling field is made up of White women (Packer-Williams et al., 2010), which places undue burden on educators and trainees of color to incorporate antioppressive theories and therapies into the curriculum. BIPOC counselor educators and trainees are tasked with the extra responsibility of educating their colleagues and peers. In the case of BIPOC trainees, the added pressure to serve as cultural experts or brokers further marginalizes BIPOC preservice counselors

TABLE 8.1 • Illustrations of White Supremacy Culture in Counselor Education Programs

Power	Rightness	Progress	Civility
Curriculum			
Paternalism: Content that pathologizes, excludes, or devalues nondominant cultural modes of expression (verbal, emotional, physical) equating multicultural counseling with Blacks, Indigenous people, and people of color **Power hoarding:** Reliance on experts and exclusion of community members to learn skills **Individualism:** Counselor-student dynamic positioned as a hierarchy exalting individual change over social or systemic change	**Perfectionism:** Expectation of the ideal **Worship of the written word:** Highly text-based, limited observational learning **Either/or thinking:** Pass/fail approach to content knowledge **Only one right way:** Emphasis on foundational content that marginalizes critical texts **Objectivity:** Approaching counselors as blank slates	**Sense of urgency:** Instructive coursework more than collaborative coursework **Progress is bigger, more:** Multicultural coursework without multicultural lenses **Quantity over quality:** Breadth over depth	**Fear of conflict:** Focus on individual reflection over group reflection **Right to comfort:** Promotion of de-escalation tactics that devalue nondominant modes of expression **Defensiveness:** Critical approaches to texts unwelcome
Pedagogy			
Paternalism: Promotion of theories, ideas, and skills that pathologize students and lack student input **Power hoarding:** Knowledge derived from instructor and texts only **Individualism:** Focus on counselor-student one-to-one dynamic neglecting student in relation to school, family, community	**Perfectionism:** Emphasis on mistakes rather than growth areas **Worship of the written word:** Reliance on written assignments to assess skill development **Either/or thinking:** Simplification of complex topics **Only one right way:** Promotion of ideal outcomes that are culturally exclusive **Objectivity:** Ignoring or glossing over emotional responses (indifference, fear, anxiety) to content and learning skills	**Sense of urgency:** Results focused **Progress is bigger, more:** Addressing diversity, equity, and inclusion (DEI) without the notion of why we need DEI initiatives in the first place **Quantity over quality:** Task oriented versus process oriented, emotion focused	**Fear of conflict:** Discouraging conflict in classroom discussions Preoccupation with appropriateness, civility, and decorum at the expense of some over others **Right to comfort:** Difficult dialogues that exclusively protect those with limited knowledge at the expense of others Instructor or trainee preserves their own comfort in response to criticism, conflict, or racism **Defensiveness:** Challenges to instructor or content viewed as threatening
Recruitment and Retention			
Paternalism: Savior complex toward trainees, students, and communities	**Perfectionism:** Anticipated performance over mastery potential **Worship of the written word:** Reliance on essay application over interview or practical assessment **Either/or thinking:** Excellent or poor trainee candidates	**Quantity over quality:** Admitting more trainee candidates rather than quality trainee candidates	**Fear of conflict:** Lacks systems for addressing struggling trainees

(Continued)

in the classroom (Coleman, 2006; Paone et al., 2019). Furthermore, assuming that BIPOC trainees are already multiculturally competent provides them little space to deepen their advocacy work (Coleman, 2006). Positioning the counselor as an expert or guide as opposed to a parallel support reinforces a hierarchy within

TABLE 8.1 • Illustrations of White Supremacy Culture in Counselor Education Programs (*Continued*)

Power	Rightness	Progress	Civility
		Clinical Experiences and Fieldwork	
Paternalism: Branding students or communities as resistant when our services do not meet their needs Assigning inexperienced trainees to high-needs schools to learn **Individualism:** Focus on one-to-one counseling placement, not structured around advocacy or addressing systemic bias or racism	**Worship of the written word:** Bracketing **Either/or thinking:** Students viewed as well or unwell **Only one right way:** Emphasis on trainees or students adapting to institution only	**Sense of urgency:** Assigning field sites without proper vetting **Progress is bigger, more:** Emphasis on how many students are served regardless of the quality of service **Quantity over quality:** Emphasis on hour attainment rather than the quality of training	**Fear of conflict:** Training avoids addressing student/trainee/supervis ruptures **Defensiveness:** Retainin inadequate supervisors without addressing urge growth areas
		Licensure and Credentialing	
Individualism: No specific advocacy requirements No service hours required beyond practicum or internship **Power hoarding:** Credentialism	**Perfectionism:** Viewed as end point, implies that the work is not ongoing **Worship of the written word:** Emphasis on written exam **Only one right way:** Universalizing competency criteria	**Progress is bigger, more:** More training hours or higher exam scores indicative of success **Quantity over quality:** Emphasis on hour completion rather than the quality of training	**Fear of conflict:** Credentialing or graduating underqualifie and inadequately trained preservice counselors
		Scholarship	
Paternalism: Little emphasis on qualitative and participatory research **Individualism:** Writing in isolation Peer accountability excludes nonacademic/ nonpractitioner community	**Perfectionism:** Focus on traditional research methods **Worship of the written word:** Scholarship as pinnacle of expert knowledge **Objectivity:** Impersonal, detached methodologies	**Sense of urgency:** The push to publish **Quantity over quality:** Emphasis on measurement, quantifiable goals versus process	**Fear of conflict:** Deferenc to seminal frameworks **Right to comfort:** Use of passive voice to discuss race and oppression

the educator-trainee relational dyad—a relationship that is mirrored in school counselor-student relationships.

Current ASCA national standards to eliminate racism and bias in schools encourage counselors to help students cultivate mind-sets of belonging and inclusion to cope with experiences of oppression (Drake & Oglesby, 2020). Individualism occupies a dual role here: individuals as controlling their environments and, by extension, individuals as solely responsible for teaching or saving others. Shin et al. (2010) found that providing training that supports reciprocity and equalizing school counselor-student relationships empowers students and promotes positive development. Furthermore, DiAngelo (2010) argued that downplaying the influence of structures and systems in individuals' lives diminishes their experiences and confines those experiences to the interpersonal. Any struggles or triumphs experienced are devoid of context, which makes it easier to assign individual blame for social inequities. Programming and interventions that advocate individual behavioral change among students and families fail to interrogate the dysfunctional and inequitable systems in which they are educated, live, and work. Promoting individualism in this way serves to "obscure and maintain racism" (DiAngelo, 2010, p. 3). Still, school coun-selors are often isolated in their role at schools. This reality not only concretizes a sense of being the only one to save their students but also complicates their role as collaborators and advocates. White saviorism serves as a symptom of both pater-nalism and individualism in WSC (Gorski & Goodman, 2015; Grzanka et al., 2019). Savior complexes infantilize students, communities, and new or struggling trainees as individuals or groups to be rescued. Students and trainees become passive recep-tors, which results in lowered expectations and restricted access to information and opportunities (Gorski & Goodman, 2015; Li, 2010; Perera-Diltz & Greenidge, 2018). The superiority of the savior is preserved, and dependence and reliance on the sav-ior as a source of power is reaffirmed. Power is hoarded and reserved for those in positions of ascribed or appropriated authority.

Rightness

Exclusive maintenance of power is explained by presumptions of the rightness and goodness of the beliefs and motivations central to Whiteness. WSC assump-tions of rightness are manifested via objectivity, perfectionism, either/or thinking, worship of the written word, and only one right way. Rightness occupies a White master narrative of "sincere fictions" (H. Vera et al., 1995) in which White power and privilege are rationalized given beliefs in White fairness, morality, good inten-tions, and color blindness (Feagin, 2014; Sue, 2013). This narrative asserts that rac-ism is something that happened a long time ago; racism that still exists is enacted interpersonally by a few bad actors. Similarly, it suggests that inequality is a thing of the past that, if it does still exist, is the fault of unmotivated individuals. These sincere fictions are upheld by notions of White innocence and goodness in which Whiteness is divorced from power and oppression and any evidence of White supremacy, in belief or action, is simply a consequence of merit or effort. The un-derlying message is that White supremacy does not exist, but if it does then it is driven by a few evil White supremacists, and any advantages or power acquired by White people are a function of aptitude. This nonchalant attitude toward rac-ism and inequality helps to absolve complicity in WSC and racial inequality. Smith and Geroski (2015) argued that the disruption of racism and White supremacy requires direct, empathy-driven action. However, in an effort to diminish the reali-ties of racism, WSC rejects empathy in favor of intellectualization to rationalize the exclusive authority of one group over others.

Objectivity in WSC prioritizes rationality and logic and positions emotionality as detrimental to decision-making (K. Jones & Okun, 2001). K. Jones and Okun (2001) questioned the validity of objectivity as a concept, given that its utility lies in the dismissal of experiential knowledge and reality. Counseling is as much an emotion-centered art of healing and support as it is centered on cognition and behavior. The ASCA National Model mandates that school counselors encourage the social-emotional well-being of their students (ASCA, 2012), yet we struggle to encourage emotionality in our preservice training classrooms. Truly, the emotional work of counseling is challenging. Trainees often lack adequate preparation in their coursework and field experiences to support the emotional needs of their students or their own emotional regulation needs when working with schools, students, and families (Prikhidko et al., 2020). Training that values reason over feelings de-prives trainees of opportunities to observe modeling and facilitation of supporting students' emotional growth. Promoting the concept of objective knowledge can easily trap educators and trainees into patterns of either/or thinking and expectations that there is only one right way to gain and assess counseling skills.

Our recruitment strategies zero in on excellent trainee candidates as measured by merit-based systems of achievement like grades, Graduate Record Examination test scores, writing samples, and one-on-one interviews. This is especially true of school counselor training programs within elite and predominantly White institutions. In an attempt to screen quality candidates versus poor candidates we reify White dominant cultural expectations about what makes a good student as opposed to a good school counselor. Our admission criteria knowingly prioritize past academic achievement and test-taking ability without questioning whether those criteria are indicative of relative success in a helping profession that requires leadership and communication as well as advocacy and collaboration. When assessing changes in school counselor program admission processes between 2000 and 2015, researchers found that grade point average and statements of purpose were the most preferred sources of information used for screening trainee candidates (Perusse et al., 2015). This emphasis on grades, exams, and writing potentially discourages applicants and may serve as a barrier to entry for folks from historically underserved backgrounds. Although reliance on Graduate Record Examination scores has decreased, so has reliance on evidence of work or volunteer experiences, and the use of written documents has increased by more than 14% (Perusse et al., 2015). Our admissions processes emphasize only one right way of recruiting potential school counselors that discounts other forms of knowledge, skill demonstration, and communication and are bound by worship of the written word. In lionizing empirical knowledge over experiential knowledge, didactic pedagogies take precedent over more collaborative, process-oriented, or service-learning pedagogical models (Killian & Floren, 2020). This process encourages perfectionism in prioritizing grades, academic performance, and content knowledge over the development of practical or clinical skills. In an antioppressive and critical context, mastery frames of learning can be problematic given their focus on individual successes (Drake & Oglesby, 2020). However, here, in reaction to perfectionism, we might understand mastery as the expectation of skill practice in community with fellow trainees, where success is less dependent on initial performance than a commitment to process and skill development. This is particularly relevant for multicultural and social justice coursework in schools.

Although multicultural and social justice coursework is more widely available than in previous decades, the content is often siloed. When multicultural competencies are integrated across school counselor coursework, trainees report higher levels of competence and multicultural self-efficacy but report feeling less prepared to integrate these skills into practice (DeCino et al., 2018; Packer-Williams et al., 2010). For many BIPOC trainees, the courses seem geared toward addressing White students with rudimentary understandings of race, racism, and inequality (Paone et al., 2019; Seward, 2014). Trainees generally leave these courses feeling inadequately trained and apprehensive about employing antiracist practices in the field (Prikhidko et al., 2020). Either/or thinking relates closely to perfectionism, which makes learning from mistakes, confronting hard truths, and struggling through conflict difficult (K. Jones & Okun, 2001). Like objectivity, the danger of either/or thinking lies in the simplification of our complex, layered social realities. K. Jones and Okun (2001) suggested that either/or thinking reduces things to good or bad, right or wrong, for or against. More than that, the either/or thinking that follows a reductionist "either racist or not racist" view of how racism and White supremacy persist makes challenging those systems seem insurmountable. Guided and scaffolded coursework and fieldwork enhances trainees' self-awareness, bias, and confidence to engage in advocacy work (Cook et al., 2015; Hayden et al., 2015). However, school counselor training that promotes "rightness" makes it difficult for counselor educators and trainees to lean into the mistakes and messiness that accompany disruption.

Progress

Social progress myths protect White dominance by placating subjugated groups, promising that their time will come. More specifically, narratives of racial progress indicate that although change is slow and incremental, it does occur and does so linearly. Perpetual progress suggests that things are better now than they were in some distant past. Vague references to acts of exclusion, genocide and relocation of Indigenous people, chattel slavery, and Jim Crow are offset with evidence of the civil rights movement and the election of Barack Obama as President of the United States (Bonilla-Silva, 2006; Onyeador et al., 2020). Yet this evidence fails to interrogate the power structures that made the civil rights movements and affirmative action necessary or why President Obama's election was revelatory to many. Racism and subjugation are easier to avoid or evade when they are decontextualized. Moreover, the assumption that progress occurs automatically and without intentional action may defeat its presumed purpose (Onyeador et al., 2020). Progress myths of WSC inadvertently expose the fact that although the road to progress is eventual, it is also perpetual, acquiescing to some degree to the ongoing realities and persistence of inequality. Progress narratives fail to specify how and when progress can be achieved. Sense of urgency narratives offer a reactive rather than proactive strategy toward progress. Here the rush of urgency provides little time to include all voices in decision-making or consider long-term effects (K. Jones & Okun, 2001). As a tenet of WSC, a sense of urgency frequently results in "sacrificing interests of communities of color for quick or highly visible results ... [and] sacrificing communities of color in order to win victories for White people" (K. Jones & Okun, 2001, p. 1). There are continued calls for more participatory action research (PAR) in the counseling field (Baranowski et al., 2016; DeBlaere et al., 2019; Kidd & Kral, 2005; K. A. Tate et al., 2015). However, PAR, youth participatory action research (YPAR), and other liberatory methods are time consuming and likely interfere with academic pressures to publish. YPAR and PAR have been successfully implemented by schools and educators to support student development; however, few studies have highlighted their use and efficacy among school counselors (Smith et al., 2014). Smith et al. (2014) proposed that YPAR specifically offers a framework for implementing approaches to multicultural and social justice counseling that provide youth with opportunities for empowerment and action that positively impacts their community. Baranowski et al. (2016) found that in addition to including student and community input into scholarship, PAR was particularly useful in training and supporting counseling trainees and in building their own self-efficacy for social justice and advocacy.

Uninterrogated progress narratives allow for the existence of multicultural course requirements; diversity, equity, and inclusion initiatives; and social justice frameworks that never wrestle with why the work is necessary. Preservice counselors are readily dispatched to underserved and underresourced schools to learn about diversity and challenge their biases. This unidirectional relationship prioritizes the urgent needs of the trainee and perhaps the immediate needs of the school given high counselor-student ratios. However, using students and families as a testing ground for challenging trainee biases is a colonial exercise. Progress is bigger, more seeks to use the training space to kill two birds with one stone: Trainees become more aware of their biases, and underresourced schools receive more help. However, when issues of power and privilege are not mandatory aspects of the field supervisor-trainee relationship or the practicum curriculum, more progress may be indicative of more harm. Progress is bigger, more poses risks to communities and schools when the number of people served is prioritized over the quality of services. When the students and families whom trainees serve in their field placements are viewed solely as a or the source for trainees' personal diversity-building/cultural competence development, trainees are at risk of providing inadequate care and developing passive empathy (Goodman et al., 2015). Passive empathy, like White guilt, may arouse feelings of sadness or even shame related to awareness of oppression but does not necessarily motivate collective social action or shift trainee worldviews away from White supremacy paradigms (DiAngelo, 2018; Goodman et al., 2015; Grzanka et al., 2019). Given the didactic nature of most school counselor education programs, the field placement serves as the primary source of practical, hands-on learning. However, Perusse et al. (2015) found that in the past 2 decades, the significance of clinical and nonclinical school counseling supervision has declined among school counselor educators. Furthermore, despite requirements emphasizing the quantity of hours that satisfies licensure and certification standards, the quality of those hours is rarely addressed. Supervisor training and thus the support of trainees varies widely (Tang, 2019). Training that simultaneously relies on the field placement to provide a concrete evaluation of skill progress and development but undervalues the professional development of supervisors and the supervisor-trainee relationship undermines the quality of service offered to students and families.

Civility

Developing and sustaining antioppressive cultures and climates demands that we name and talk directly about racism and White supremacy and how they function in our daily lives (Bonds & Inwood, 2016). Still, so much of the power of WSC lies in its subterfuge. That WSC is indistinguishable from Western understandings of culture is intentional and serves to reify its primacy in maintaining the social order. WSC is the materialization of an ideology that has adopted strong self-serving and self-aggrandizing narratives about justice, equity, and meritocracy. Sue (2013) contended that counternarratives that "talk back" to White supremacy narratives of rightness and progress threaten WSC because they expose White power and privilege and the realities of inequality (p. 665). Thus, race talk is generally discouraged in organizational and educational settings under the guise of maintaining civility or politeness. Calls for civility allow difficult dialogues about Whiteness, White supremacy, and racism to be shut down, avoided, or evaded (Kohli et al., 2017; Sue, 2005, 2016). Those who offer counternarratives by questioning White dominance or dismissing Whiteness as the norm are maligned as inappropriate or disrespectful, in particular when those counternarratives are broached by BIPOC (Smith et al., 2014). Expectations of this so-called civility, especially in the classroom, not only promote racial avoidance but affirm WSC by prioritizing the safety and care of White people over BIPOC. The mere suggestion that White power, privilege, and beliefs of supremacy contribute to oppression violates a kind of pact of silence around WSC. Those who interrupt this carefully crafted silence are branded instigators. The emotional and cognitive safety of these disruptors, especially BIPOC, is largely discounted. Despite the costs of daring to broach discussions of oppression and racism, the perspectives of BIPOC are readily downplayed, their feelings ignored, and their experiences marginalized again. WSC suppresses discussions of race, racism, and other forms of inequality by prioritizing the right to comfort, acquiescing to a fear of conflict, and responding with defensiveness when counternarratives are presented.

Race dialogues are considered difficult or challenging (Chung et al., 2018). Classes that address racism and oppression may cause emotional stress and cognitive dissonance for trainees and faculty unaccustomed or apathetic to these discussions. In contrast to expectations of objectivity and reason, racial and antioppressive dialogues disrupt a presumed right to comfort. BIPOC trainees and faculty experience their own racial stress and discomfort in these spaces. BIPOC trainees wage an internal struggle of whether to educate their peers and faculty, face external pressures to represent their racial or ethnic identity group, and feel compelled to correct racist statements made by peers and faculty (Paone et al., 2019; Seward, 2014; Seward & Guiffrida, 2012). Thus, these dialogues are often discouraged, diverted, or shut down by peers, colleagues, and faculty who either are ill equipped to facilitate these conversations or disagree with the content (Sue, 2013). White faculty are less likely than their colleagues of color to draw attention to race in the classroom (Haynes, 2017), and supervisors are not likely to address White trainees who struggle with cross-racial interactions (Helms & Cook, 1999; Utsey et al., 2005). This racial avoidance may be driven by a fear of conflict. Beyond a fear of appearing ill informed, racial dialogues might expose an individual's own racism, making silence preferable (Grzanka et al., 2019). In WSC, the fear of being called a racist often outweighs the racism exposed and the impact of that racism on someone else, triggering resistance and defensiveness (Chung et al., 2018). This fear is driven in part by White fragility, in which White-identified folks find even minimal racial stress unbearable and respond defensively (DiAngelo, 2018). Without adequate and responsive facilitation, White fragility not only impedes necessary interrogations of Whiteness but also trivializes the utility of diversity training altogether (Chrobot-Mason et al., 2020; S. A. Tate & Page, 2018). Furthermore, White faculty are less likely than their colleagues of color to name racism and oppression in classrooms (Haynes, 2017) and may become defensive when their authority is challenged by BIPOC colleagues or trainees.

According to BIPOC trainees, difficult racial dialogues in their classrooms are almost always triggered by microaggressions (Sue, 2013). When White faculty and trainees downplay racism and oppression or ignore the perspectives and feelings of their BIPOC colleagues and trainees, White comfort is prioritized. This process compounds the microaggressive experience, as BIPOC are first subjected to some form of racism in their learning and training space and then asked to suffer a second indignity of being either diminished or admonished for pointing out the offense. When faculty fail to support or protect all students, BIPOC students must publicly renegotiate their humanity in the presence of their peers. Similarly, when BIPOC faculty challenge power structures and narratives in school counselor education, they may similarly be met with resistance and challenges to their authority by White students (Chung et al., 2018; Grzanka et al., 2019). Overreliance on faculty and trainees of color to initiate challenges to oppressive structures diminishes the cost of their emotional labor and offers it up for public consumption.

Emphasizing BIPOC voices and perspectives in the classroom is critical to challenging WSC; however, BIPOC students are often expected to act as experts on racism and oppression (Chung et al., 2018). In this way, BIPOC are deprived of their right to exist as trainees and take on the role of educator. Here school counselor training programs prioritize the consciousness-raising of White trainees, situating antiracist work as the work of White counselors and disempowering both BIPOC and White trainees. Civility demands that BIPOC ignore race in the classroom yet simultaneously act as the sole keepers of racial knowledge. Furthermore, BIPOC trainees and faculty are expected to tread lightly to avoid interracial discomfort, minimize racial stress, and prevent interracial conflict. Ultimately, civility allows WSC to flourish as White trainees and faculty stay silent or less informed of past and present realities of racial oppression and inequality and BIPOC trainees and faculty are subjugated into silence.

What Would It Look Like to Operate a Program That Does Not Embody WSC?

As counselor educators ourselves, each of us is on a lifelong journey to resist and dismantle WSC in our classrooms. We are by no means done. A critical part of our continued commitment to growth has been the desire to collectively imagine different ways of being (and doing) in our work. To this end, we close with a vignette that showcases some possible ways for counselor educators to resist traditional academic practices and norms that reflect WSC. Note both structural choices as well as pedagogical moves made by a White counselor educator aiming to shift the culture in her program.

> As Professor Sonia Levy prepared to teach the required Issues in School Counseling class, she was excited about the opportunity to redesign the course. She knew there was room for improvement to the course, which had until now lacked attention to critical perspectives or discussions of power and oppression. The multicultural counseling class was historically the only place in the curriculum expected to incorporate content and skills regarding race, racial identity, justice, or specific antiracist counseling practices. Professor Levy spent the better part of her summer updating content, identifying new scholars of color for readings, reframing assignments, and considering multiple ways to assess students' learning and deliver feedback. By summer's end, Professor Levy developed a syllabus she felt incorporated antiracist, antioppressive counseling texts; diverse learning goals and assessments; and a set of principles to guide her teaching and students' learning. To enhance her growth and institute a check for her own bias, Professor Levy sought support from the Faculty Consultancy Group, a group of faculty who volunteered to consult with faculty to improve pedagogy and instructional practices. Through that process, Professor Levy

received support from two of her colleagues, a Latinx man and a White woman. Her male Latinx colleague suggested she find ways to incorporate decision-making with students into the curriculum or assignments. Her White colleague suggested she bring in youth from the community to share their experiences in schools to provide additional perspectives and model for the preservice counselors how to incorporate the voices of youth and adults from the community into their future work.

On the first day of class, Professor Levy coconstructed norms with students and even role-played how they might handle conflict should it come up. Her rationale was that the sooner they began to talk about how to use conflict to enhance discussion, the more likely they could distance themselves from the fear of conflict. She also discussed how the class would collectively monitor their norms to share the responsibility for upholding them.

Four weeks into the course, students were given their first major assignment. The students were asked to use an ecological framework to create a case study of a high school student who was struggling in school. Students were invited to submit work in a variety of formats (written work, visual representations, oral reflections) as a way to practice moving away from worshipping the written word. The assignment was meant to decolonize counselees' orientation to problems or concerns about students. As Professor Levy began to read through the papers, she noticed that most students of color in the class used the ecological framework to highlight racist systemic forces and structures that influenced the student's struggles. And almost without exception, the majority of White students wrote about the student's experience from a deficit lens, rarely pointing to the systemic racism that was responsible for the student's experience. Professor Levy felt a familiar pain realizing that despite her attempts, she was still seeing the reproduction of White supremacy among her White students. Rather than grade the assignments right away, she revisited relevant course principles she had set for the class, including the following:

- The class will take the form of a learning organization, one that recognizes the value of making mistakes and learning from them.
- This class will prioritize quality over quantity, which means there may be times when we pause our agenda to address underlying concerns or allow extra time to process.
- All members of our learning organization will contribute to the learning and course format, which means all knowledge and perspectives will be valued and input will be solicited regularly.
- This class will challenge deficit-based ideologies regarding students and education.

Professor Levy decided she wanted to enact these principles of the learning organization and invite feedback to shape how she would respond to the trend in the assignments. Moreover, she recognized this as an opportunity to act on her commitment to pushing and holding accountable students with White privileges. She knew that failing to do so would lead to (or perpetuate) a savior orientation among some of the trainees. She decided to share her observation with her students, recognizing and validating students' different approaches as is consistent with rejecting the only one way tenet of WSC. Professor Levy cancelled the next class and told students she would be holding two separate working sessions to expand on the projects and students' knowledge and understanding. This approach allowed her to differentiate students' learning and enabled students to join affinity spaces with others who were at similar developmental points or levels of understanding. Once the students chose their groups, Professor Levy used a feedback form to coconstruct how they would use the time together. She then gave all students the choice to complete another, new assignment or reproduce the first assignment with new learning.

In this fictitious vignette, a White faculty member disrupts some of the traditional practices in the academy that maintain WSC. By allowing the students who need additional support to work on their racial and ethnic identity and relationship to power more time and space for that learning, Professor Levy challenges the norm that assumes that all students will meet the exact same standard. As noted elsewhere, efforts to respect everyone's antiracism journey almost always default to prioritizing folks without knowledge instead of folks with knowledge. By holding a separate session for those students who accurately identified the systemic forces at play in the assigned case study, Professor Levy avoids prioritizing those who lack this critical knowledge. Furthermore, she holds the White students in the class accountable for understanding that systemic racism exists, reinforcing the notion that counseling practice goes beyond individual work to include systemic change. In addition, the ecological approach embedded in the assignment challenges the individuation that permeates the counseling canon. Even before the assignment, we see examples of how counseling faculty can structure a course with reading selections, course principles, and assignments to achieve a different standard of teaching. Likewise, the vignette illustrates Professor Levy's explicit intention to center and incorporate voices that are traditionally marginalized in higher education through the youth and adult voice panel. Finally, Professor Levy challenges patterns of civility with early norming for how the learning organization will manage difficult conversations.

For the three of us, teaching in a school counseling program and committing to dismantling practices and policies that uphold WSC has required a shift toward an explicit analysis of systems of power in schools and communities and a commitment to considering how these systems both shape and are shaped by our work. This commitment helps us to center sociopolitical, cultural, and historical factors in our ecological systems work. Moreover, it forces us to turn our focus inward and engage in deeper, more meaningful work on our own biases and blind spots. For the White faculty and students at our institution, this means investigating not only the explicit upholding of racism but also the more subtle, insidious ways in which our failure to challenge racist assumptions or values constitutes tactic approval of them. Although this work is particularly important for White school counselors, the dominance of Whiteness in educational institutions makes it important for many of our trainees of color to examine their relationship to these cycles of socialization as well.

As the field of school counseling commits to training school counselors who will work with students of different racial, ethnic, and cultural backgrounds, we believe that looking inward and centering an analysis of our own cycles of socialization (Harro, 2000) as well as our participation in the socialization of our students is critical. We recognize, however, that some counselor educators may question their authority and efficacy in challenging WSC, especially tenure-track faculty for whom the pressure to publish is strong. In Table 8.2, we offer alternative approaches to traditional practices that will aid counselor educators in their efforts to disrupt academic cultures that prioritize Whiteness and the associated norms that privilege WSC.

TABLE 8.2 • Antidotes to White Supremacy Culture in Counselor Education

...wer	Rightness	Progress	Civility
Curriculum			
...reful attention to voice, ...uthorship, and worldview ...n content, such that ...iverse perspectives are ...nvited to the table ...rriculum coconstructed ...vith students to be ...ulturally and contextually ...elevant ...commitment to ...nly voluntary and ...ompensated labor on the ...art of students ...pportunities for parents, ...tudents, and other ...takeholders to contribute ...o decisions about ...urriculum and learning	Flattening of expertise such that multiple ways of knowing are invited into the space Opportunities for students to engage in self-reflection and hold multiple truths around their own positionalities and experiences Rubrics that center personalized learning and growth and include a requirement for self-reflection Multiple ways of demonstrating learning, including but not limited to the written word	Focus on process over progress or metrics Creation of space to acknowledge and work on self-identified growth edges Opportunities to gather feedback from many different stakeholders (including students), not just those with power Scaffolding to develop a lifelong professional development and healing plan Focus on equitable and distributed learning, not just increasing outcomes	Scaffolding and explicit discussions of group dynamics, including how power and positionality enter into these Normalization of discomfort and support for how to move through it with a learning stance Opportunities to witness and practice speaking truth to power Engagement with a restorative justice, healing-centered approach to learning
Pedagogy			
...omotion of critical ...pedagogies ...plicit thinking about ...classroom processes and ...dynamics ...pportunities to learn from ...nultiple voices, including ...ther students and ...community members ...cus on ecological ...systems theory with ...a commitment to ...pringing issues from the ...nacrosystem into the ...everyday and addressing ...power imbalances	Celebration of mistakes and growth rather than "correct" answers Multiple ways of demonstrating learning, including visual, oral, and embodied practices Queering of the curriculum and work, with a focus on dismantling binaries and either/or thinking Welcoming of emotions and embodied knowledge into our practices	Careful attunement to process and its effects on members of a community Diversity, equity, and inclusion work that starts with reflexivity and self-work Recognition that there are multiple end points and therefore multiple definitions of progress, some of which are culturally bound	Encouragement of conflict and disagreement in the class, with scaffolding to help students move through it Focus on caring for those most marginalized during difficult conversations Support for students to develop a self-awareness around their reactions and coping mechanisms and the effects these have on others Respectful challenges to the instructor and content welcomed
Recruitment and Retention			
...n application that takes ...cultural humility and cross-...cultural skills into account ...as much as test scores ...and grades ...n explicit commitment ...o weeding out students ...vho demonstrate a savior ...complex or committed ...responsibility to working ...vith student to improve	Focus on mastery potential and a growth mind-set over past performance Possible inclusion of performance tasks on applications	A focus on the quality of candidates rather than the need to meet a quota with admissions or the desired school ranking	Feedback provided to students about their applications regardless of their acceptance

(Continued)

Conclusion

As school counselors and mental health clinicians are increasingly seen as plausible alternatives to security and policing, the importance of developing antiracist school counselors becomes even more salient. Antiracist counseling and counselor

TABLE 8.2 • Antidotes to White Supremacy Culture in Counselor Education (*Continued*)

Power	Rightness	Progress	Civility
Clinical Experiences and Fieldwork			
Focus on long-term relationships in authentic partnerships between higher education and districts or schools Coconstruction of goals and outcomes with both students and site partners Explicit antiracist training for students and supervisors Accountability for supervisors	Focus on training for what is possible or best for children, not training for what is practical or likely Clear training around how to acknowledge and work with one's own triggers and reactions, such that we do not project them onto students Emphasis on one definition of healthy for students and families	Careful vetting of site placements to ensure an antioppressive lens is present Emphasis on the quality of relationships between interns and students or supervisors rather than the number of relationships Emphasis on active engagement with students, families, or educators, not administrative tasks	Supervisors who invite feedback and conflict with their interns Scaffolded processes for moving through conflict in healthy and healing ways Explicit feedback for supervisors who are not addressing their own growth areas Explicit feedback for supervisors and sites around issues of power
Licensure and Credentialing			
Pathways to licensure that are affordable and accessible to community members and parents Review of licensure done by communities, children, and parents Hiring of faculty from the educational communities that hire school counselors	Ongoing approach to professional development that requires ongoing antioppressive work Multiple ways to demonstrate knowledge other than a written exam Locally generated competency criteria	Emphasis on the quality of training and its connection to antioppressive work rather than simply the number of hours of training	Requirements for antioppressive self-work, interactive work, and systems work as part of licensure
Scholarship			
Requirement for recognition of author positionality Required engagement with systems of power and macrosystems as relevant More cowriting Accountability and review that includes the nonacademic/practitioner community	Wider representation of epistemological and cultural perspectives Wider definition of methods that can be used for inquiry More opportunities for practitioners, students, and families to generate knowledge, either alone or in partnership with university researchers	A recentering of action as it relates to improving schools and communities rather than publication and presentation Emphasis on scholarship that reflects community experiences and resonates with community members Less emphasis on generalizability and scaling projects	

education requires a steadfast commitment to dismantling systems, structures, and ideologies that maintain and reinforce the marginalization and subjugation of BIPOC. Current discussions of antiracist efforts too often focus on the "after," when the harm and the impact of racism and discrimination are most readily visible and apparent. However, too little attention is paid to the "before," or how we train educators to enact antiracist practices, especially within a profession that currently is overwhelmingly White.

Centering Whiteness in any discussion of our practice always runs the risk of redirecting our attention yet again to dominant ways of being and doing. However, if we do not articulate the ways in which culture, power, and race are playing out in our graduate programs and practices, then we often subconsciously default to these dominant practices, harming ourselves and one another in the process. In other words, to dismantle WSC within the field of school counseling, we must first learn to see it. We hope this chapter serves as a first step in this journey.

References

American School Counselor Association. (2012). *ASCA national model: A framework for school counseling programs.*

American School Counselor Association. (2017). *The school counselor and school counseling programs.* https://schoolcounselor.org/Standards-Positions/Position-Statements/ASCA-Position-Statements/The-School-Counselor-and-School-Counseling-Program

Ansley, F. L. (1997). White supremacy (and what we should do about it). In R. Delgado & J. Stefancic (Eds.), *Critical white studies: Looking behind the mirror* (pp. 592–595). Temple University Press.

Arthur, N., Collins, S., Marshall, C., & McMahon, M. (2013). Social justice competencies and career development practices. *Canadian Journal of Counselling and Psychotherapy, 47*(2), Article 2. http://136.159.200.199/index.php/rcc/article/view/60929

Atkins, R., & Oglesby, A. (2018). *Interrupting racism: Equity and social justice in school counseling.* Routledge.

Baima, T., & Sude, M. E. (2020). What white mental health professionals need to understand about whiteness: A Delphi study. *Journal of Marital and Family Therapy, 46*(1), 62–80. https://doi.org/10.1111/jmft.12385

Baranowski, K. A., Bhattacharyya, S., Ameen, E. J., Herbst, R. B., Corrales, C., Gonzalez, L. M. C., González, D. M., Jones, S., Reynolds, J. D., & Goodman, L. A. (2016). Community and public arena advocacy training challenges, supports, and recommendations in counseling psychology: A participatory qualitative inquiry. *Journal for Social Action in Counseling & Psychology, 8*(2), 70–97. https://doi.org/10.33043/JSACP.8.2.70-97

Bartoli, E., Bentley-Edwards, K. L., García, A. M., Michael, A., & Ervin, A. (2015). What do white counselors and psychotherapists need to know about race? White racial socialization in counseling and psychotherapy training programs. *Women & Therapy, 38*(3–4), 246–262. https://doi.org/10.1080/02703149.2015.1059206

Bonds, A., & Inwood, J. (2016). Beyond white privilege: Geographies of white supremacy and settler colonialism. *Progress in Human Geography, 40*(6), 715–733. https://doi.org/10.1177/0309132515613166

Bonilla-Silva, E. (2006). *Racism without racists: Color-blind racism and the persistence of racial inequality in the United States.* Rowman & Littlefield.

Bronfenbrenner, U. (1977). Toward an experimental ecology of human development. *American Psychologist, 32*(7), 513–531.

Chrobot-Mason, D., Campbell, K., & Vason, T. (2020, March 31). *Whiteness in organizations: From white supremacy to allyship.* Oxford Research Encyclopedias: Business and Management. https://doi.org/10.1093/acrefore/9780190224851.013.195

Chung, R. C.-Y., Bemak, F., Talleyrand, R. M., & Williams, J. M. (2018). Challenges in promoting race dialogues in psychology training: Race and gender perspectives. *The Counseling Psychologist, 46*(2), 213–240. https://doi.org/10.1177/0011000018758262

Coleman, M. N. (2006). Critical incidents in multicultural training: An examination of student experiences. *Journal of Multicultural Counseling and Development, 34*(3), 168–182. https://doi.org/10.1002/j.2161-1912.2006.tb00036.x

Cook, A. L., Hayden, L. A., Gracia, R., & Tyrrell, R. (2015). Exploring outcomes of a targeted supervisory training curriculum on developing multicultural competency and social justice advocacy. *Counseling Outcome Research and Evaluation*, 6(2), 126–140. https://doi.org/10.1177/2150137815594201

Crethar, H. C., & Ratts, M. J. (2008). Why social justice is a counseling concern. *Counseling Today*, 50(12), 24–25.

David, E. J. R., Schroeder, T. M., & Fernandez, J. (2019). Internalized racism: A systematic review of the psychological literature on racism's most insidious consequence. *Journal of Social Issues*, 75(4), 1057–1086. https://doi.org/10.1111/josi.12350

DeBlaere, C., Singh, A. A., Wilcox, M. M., Cokley, K. O., Delgado-Romero, E. A., Scalise, D. A., & Shawahin, L. (2019). Social justice in counseling psychology: Then, now, and looking forward. *The Counseling Psychologist*, 47(6), 938–962. https://doi.org/10.1177/0011000019893283

DeCino, D. A., Strear, M. M., & Olson, S. (2018). Exploring school counselors' social desirability, multicultural counseling competence, and demographics in the Midwest. *Journal of School Counseling*, 16(2). http://jsc.montana.edu/articles/v16n2.pdf

Delgado, R., & Stefancic, J. (2017). *Critical race theory: An introduction* (3rd ed.). New York University Press. https://doi.org/10.2307/j.ctt1ggjjn3

DiAngelo, R. J. (2010). Why can't we all just be individuals? Countering the discourse of individualism in anti-racist education. *InterActions: UCLA Journal of Education and Information Studies*, 6(1). https://doi.org/10.5070/D461000670

DiAngelo, R. (2018). *White fragility: Why it's so hard for white people to talk about racism.* Beacon Press.

Drake, R., & Oglesby, A. (2020). Humanity is not a thing: Disrupting white supremacy in K-12 social emotional learning. *Journal of Critical Thought and Praxis*, 10(1), Article 1. https://doi.org/10.31274/jctp.11549

Fanon, F. (1963). *The wretched of the earth.* Grove Press.

Fanon, F. (2008). *Black skin, white masks.* Grove Press.

Feagin, J. R. (2014). *Racist America: Roots, current realities, and future reparations.* Routledge.

Fernández, J. S. (2018). Decolonial pedagogy in community psychology: White students disrupting white innocence via a family portrait assignment. *American Journal of Community Psychology*, 62(3–4), 294–305. https://doi.org/10.1002/ajcp.12282

Fernando, S. (2017). *Institutional racism in psychiatry and clinical psychology.* Springer. https://doi.org/10.1007/978-3-319-62728-1

Frediani, S. (2020). Utilizing pedagogy for disrupting white supremacy. *Religions*, 11(11), 544–554. https://doi.org/10.3390/rel11110544

Freire, P. (2018). *Pedagogy of the oppressed: 50th anniversary edition.* Bloomsbury.

García Coll, C., Lamberty, G., Jenkins, R., McAdoo, H. P., Crnic, K., Wasik, B. H., & Vázquez-García, H. (1996). An integrative model for the study of developmental competencies in minority children. *Child Development*, 67(5), 1891–1914. https://doi.org/10.2307/1131600

Goodman, R. D., & Gorski, P. C. (Eds.). (2015). *Decolonizing "multicultural" counseling through social justice.* Springer. https://doi.org/10.1007/978-1-4939-1283-4

Goodman, R. D., Williams, J. M., Chung, R. C.-Y., Talleyrand, R. M., Douglass, A. M., McMahon, H. G., & Bemak, F. (2015). Decolonizing traditional pedagogies and practices in counseling and psychology education: A move towards social justice and action. In R. D. Goodman & P. C. Gorski (Eds.), *Decolonizing "multicultural" counseling through social justice* (pp. 147–164). Springer. https://doi.org/10.1007/978-1-4939-1283-4_11

Gorski, P. C., & Goodman, R. D. (2015). Introduction: Toward a decolonized multicultural counseling and psychology. In R. D. Goodman & P. C. Gorski (Eds.), *Decolonizing "multicultural" counseling through social justice* (pp. 1–10). Springer. https://doi.org/10.1007/978-1-4939-1283-4_1

Grzanka, P. R., Gonzalez, K. A., & Spanierman, L. B. (2019). White supremacy and counseling psychology: A critical–conceptual framework. *The Counseling Psychologist, 47*(4), 478–529. https://doi.org/10.1177/0011000019880843

Halpern, R. (1999). *Fragile families, fragile solutions: A history of supportive services for families in poverty.* Columbia University Press. https://doi.org/10.1177/088610990001500114

Harro, B. (2000). The cycle of socialization. In M. Adams, W. J. Blumenfeld, R. Castañeda, H. W. Hackman, M. L. Peters, & X. Zúñiga (Eds.), *Readings for diversity and social justice: An anthology on racism, anti-Semitism, sexism, heterosexism, ableism, and classism* (pp. 15–21). Routledge.

Hayden, L., Cook, A., Gracia, R., Silva, M. R., & Cadet, M. (2015). Evaluating fieldwork and a targeted curriculum on urban counselor trainees' self-efficacy. *Counseling Outcome Research and Evaluation, 6*(1), 33–46. https://doi.org/10.1177/2150137815573789

Haynes, C. (2017). Dismantling the white supremacy embedded in our classrooms: White faculty in pursuit of more equitable educational outcomes for racially minoritized students. *International Journal of Teaching and Learning in Higher Education, 29*(1), 87–107. https://eric.ed.gov/?id=EJ1135971

Helms, J. E. (2017). The challenge of making whiteness visible: Reactions to four whiteness articles. *The Counseling Psychologist, 45*(5), 717–726. https://doi.org/10.1177/0011000017718943

Helms, J. E., & Cook, D. A. (1999). *Using race and culture in counseling and psychotherapy: Theory and process.* Allyn & Bacon.

Holcomb-McCoy, C. (2004). Assessing the multicultural competence of school counselors: A checklist. *Professional School Counseling, 7*(3), 178–186.

Holcomb-McCoy, C. (2007). *School counseling to close the achievement gap: A social justice framework for success.* Corwin Press.

Hunter, S., Swan, E., & Grimes, D. (2010). Introduction: Reproducing and resisting whiteness in organizations, policies, and places. *Social Politics, 17*(4), 407–422. https://doi.org/10.1093/sp/jxq020

Ivey, A. E., & Collins, N. M. (2003). Social justice: A long-term challenge for counseling psychology. *The Counseling Psychologist, 31*(3), 290–298. https://doi.org/10.1177/0011000003031003004

Jones, J. M., Sander, J. B., & Booker, K. W. (2013). Multicultural competency building: Practical solutions for training and evaluating student progress. *Training and Education in Professional Psychology, 7*(1), 12–22. https://doi.org/10.1037/a0030880

Jones, K., & Okun, T. (2001, May). White supremacy culture [Online workbook]. In *Dismantling racism: A workbook for social change groups.* Change Work. https://www.dismantlingracism.org/

Kidd, S. A., & Kral, M. J. (2005). Practicing participatory action research. *Journal of Counseling Psychology, 52*(2), 187–195. https://doi.org/10.1037/0022-0167.52.2.187

Killian, T., & Floren, M. (2020). Exploring the relationship between pedagogy and counselor trainees' multicultural and social justice competence. *Journal of Counseling & Development, 98*(3), 295–307. https://doi.org/10.1002/jcad.12324

Kohli, R., Pizarro, M., & Nevárez, A. (2017). The "new racism" of K–12 schools: Centering critical research on racism. *Review of Research in Education, 41*(1), 182–202. https://doi.org/10.3102/0091732X16686949

Ladson-Billings, G., & Tate, W. F. (1995). Toward a critical race theory of education. *Teachers College Record, 97*(1), 47–68.

Ladson-Billings, G., & Tate, W. (2016). Toward a critical race theory of education. In A. D. Dixson, C. K. R. Anderson, & J. K. Donnor (Eds.), *Critical race theory in education* (pp. 10–31). Routledge.

Li, H.-L. (2010). From decolonisation of alterity to democratic listening. *Social Alternatives, 29*(1), 29–33.

Love, B. L. (2019). *We want to do more than survive: Abolitionist teaching and the pursuit of educational freedom.* Beacon Press.

Martín-Baró, I. (1994). *Writings for a liberation psychology.* Harvard University Press.

Miller, M. J., Keum, B. T., Thai, C. J., Lu, Y., Truong, N. N., Huh, G. A., Li, X., Yeung, J. G., & Ahn, L. H. (2018). Practice recommendations for addressing racism: A content analysis of the counseling psychology literature. *Journal of Counseling Psychology, 65*(6), 669–680. https://doi.org/10.1037/cou0000306

Mills, C. W. (2014). *The racial contract.* Cornell University Press. https://doi.org/10.7591/9780801471353

Moe, J., Carlisle, K., Augustine, B., & Pearce, J. (2020). De-colonizing international counseling for LGBTQ youth. *Journal of LGBT Issues in Counseling, 14*(2), 153–169. https://doi.org/10.1080/15538605.2020.1753625

Motulsky, S. L., Gere, S. H., Saleem, R., & Trantham, S. M. (2014). Teaching social justice in counseling psychology. *The Counseling Psychologist, 42*(8), 1058–1083. https://doi.org/10.1177/0011000014553855

Nassar, S. C., & Singh, A. A. (2020). Embodying the multicultural and social justice counseling competency movement: Voices from the field. *Journal of Counseling & Development, 98*(3), 253–260. https://doi.org/10.1002/jcad.12320

Nelson, G. B., & Prilleltensky, I. (2010). *Community psychology: In pursuit of liberation and well-being* (2nd ed.). Palgrave Macmillan.

Onyeador, I. N., Daumeyer, N. M., Rucker, J. M., Duker, A., Kraus, M. W., & Richeson, J. A. (2020). Disrupting beliefs in racial progress: Reminders of persistent racism alter perceptions of past, but not current, racial economic equality. *Personality and Social Psychology Bulletin, 47*(5), 753–765. https://doi.org/10.1177/0146167220942625

Packer-Williams, C. L., Jay, M. L., & Evans, K. M. (2010). Understanding the contextual factors that influence school counselors' multicultural diversity integration practices. *Journal of School Counseling, 8*(6), 1–34. http://jsc.montana.edu/articles/v8n6.pdf

Paone, T. R., Malott, K. M., Pulliam, N., & Shannon, J. (2019). Experiences of counselor students of color in the classroom: A qualitative study. *Race Ethnicity and Education,* 1–17. https://doi.org/10.1080/13613324.2019.1579186

Parker, P. S., Jiang, J., McCluney, C. L., & Rabelo, V. C. (2017, January 25). *Race, gender, class, and sexuality.* Oxford Research Encyclopedias: Communication. https://doi.org/10.1093/acrefore/9780190228613.013.204

Perera-Diltz, D. M., & Greenidge, W. L. (2018). Mindfulness techniques to promote culturally appropriate engagement. *Journal of Creativity in Mental Health, 13*(4), 490–504. https://doi.org/10.1080/15401383.2018.1459215

Perusse, R., Poynton, T. A., Parzych, J. L., & Goodnough, G. E. (2015). Changes over time in masters level school counselor education programs. *The Journal of Counselor Preparation and Supervision, 7*(3), Article 8. https://doi.org/10.7729/73.1072

Potapchuk, M. (2012). *White culture* [Worksheet]. https://www.seattle.gov/documents/Departments/RSJI/GRE/whiteculturehandout.pdf

Prikhidko, A., Su, Y.-W., Houseknecht, A., & Swank, J. M. (2020). Emotion regulation for counselors-in-training: A grounded theory. *Counselor Education and Supervision, 59*(2), 96–111. https://doi.org/10.1002/ceas.12169

Ratts, M. J., & Greenleaf, A. T. (2017). Multicultural and social justice counseling competencies: A leadership framework for professional school counselors. *Professional School Counseling, 21*(1b), 1–9. https://doi.org/10.1177/2156759X18773582

Ratts, M. J., Singh, A. A., Nassar-McMillan, S., Butler, S. K., & McCullough, J. R. (2016). Multicultural and social justice counseling competencies: Guidelines for the counseling profession. *Journal of Multicultural Counseling and Development, 44*(1), 28–48. https://doi.org/10.1002/jmcd.12035

Seward, D. X. (2014). Multicultural course pedagogy: Experiences of master's-level students of color. *Counselor Education and Supervision, 53*(1), 62–79. https://doi.org/10.1002/j.1556-6978.2014.00049.x

Seward, D. X., & Guiffrida, D. A. (2012). Deciding how much to share in class: A study of the experiences of students of color enrolled in multicultural counseling courses. *International Journal for the Advancement of Counselling, 34*(4), 286–296. https://doi.org/10.1007/s10447-012-9157-5

Shin, R. Q. (2015). The application of critical consciousness and intersectionality as tools for decolonizing racial/ethnic identity development models in the fields of counseling and psychology. In R. D. Goodman & P. C. Gorski (Eds.), *Decolonizing "multicultural" counseling through social justice* (pp. 11–22). Springer. https://doi.org/10.1007/978-1-4939-1283-4_2

Shin, R. Q., Rogers, J., Stanciu, A., Silas, M. Brown-Smythe, C., & Austin, B. (2010). Advancing social justice in urban schools through the implementation of transformative groups for youth of color. *Journal for Specialists in Group Work, 35*(3), 230–235.

Singh, A. A., Appling, B., & Trepal, H. (2020). Using the multicultural and social justice counseling competencies to decolonize counseling practice: The important roles of theory, power, and action. *Journal of Counseling & Development, 98*(3), 261–271. https://doi.org/10.1002/jcad.12321

Smith, L. C. (2017). Critical consciousness and school-based family counseling: "Seeing" the pathogen in order to dismantle the pump of oppression. *International Journal for School-Based Family Counseling, 8.* https://www.instituteschoolbasedfamilycounseling.com/docs/IJSBFC%20-%20critical%20consciousness%20-%20final_LS.pdf

Smith, L., Beck, K., Bernstein, E., & Dashtguard, P. (2014). Youth participatory action research and school counseling practice: A school-wide framework for student well-being. *Journal of School Counseling, 12*(21). http://jsc.montana.edu/articles/v12n21.pdf

Smith, L. C., & Geroski, A. M. (2015). Decolonizing alterity models within school counseling practice. In R. D. Goodman & P. C. Gorski (Eds.), *Decolonizing "multicultural" counseling through social justice* (pp. 99–116). Springer. https://doi.org/10.1007/978-1-4939-1283-4_8

Speight, S. L. (2007). Internalized racism: One more piece of the puzzle. *The Counseling Psychologist, 35*(1), 126–134. https://doi.org/10.1177/0011000006295119

Steinberg, S. (2018). The whiteness of race knowledge: Charles Mills throws down the gauntlet. *Ethnic and Racial Studies, 41*(3), 541–550. https://doi.org/10.1080/01419870.2018.1389970

Sue, D. W. (2005). Racism and the conspiracy of silence: Presidential address. *The Counseling Psychologist, 33*(1), 100–114.

Sue, D. W. (2013). Race talk: The psychology of racial dialogues. *American Psychologist, 68*(8), 663–672. https://doi.org/10.1037/a0033681

Sue, D. W. (2016). *Race talk and the conspiracy of silence: Understanding and facilitating difficult dialogues on race.* Wiley.

Sue, D. W., Arredondo, P., & McDavis, R. J. (1992). Multicultural counseling competencies and standards: A call to the profession. *Journal of Counseling & Development, 70*(4), 477–486. https://doi.org/10.1002/j.1556-6676.1992.tb01642.x

Sue, D. W., & Sue, D. (2008). *Counseling the culturally diverse: Theory and practice.* Wiley.

Tang, A. (2019). The impact of school counseling supervision on practicing school counselors' self-efficacy in building a comprehensive school counseling program. *Professional School Counseling, 23*(1). https://doi.org/10.1177/2156759X20947723

Tate, K. A., Rivera, E. T., & Edwards, L. M. (2015). Colonialism and multicultural counseling competence research: A liberatory analysis. In R. D. Goodman & P. C. Gorski (Eds.), *Decolonizing "multicultural" counseling through social justice* (pp. 41–54). Springer.

Tate, S. A., & Page, D. (2018). Whiteliness and institutional racism: Hiding behind (un)conscious bias. *Ethics and Education, 13*(1), 141–155.

Tatum, B. D. (2017). *Why are all the Black kids sitting together in the cafeteria? And other conversations about race.* Basic Books.

Tervalon, M., & Murray-García, J. (1998). Cultural humility versus cultural competence: A critical distinction in defining physician training outcomes in multicultural education. *Journal of Health Care for the Poor and Underserved, 9*(2), 117–125. https://doi.org/10.1353/hpu.2010.0233

Utsey, S. O., Gernat, C. A., & Hammar, L. (2005). Examining white counselor trainees' reactions to racial issues in counseling and supervision dyads. *The Counseling Psychologist, 33*(4), 449–478. https://doi.org/10.1177/0011000004269058

Vera, E. M., & Speight, S. L. (2003). Multicultural competence, social justice, and counseling psychology: Expanding our roles. *The Counseling Psychologist, 31*(3), 253–272.

Vera, H., Feagin, J. R., & Gordon, A. (1995, Summer). Sincere fictions of the white self. *Journal of Negro Education, 64*(3), 295–306.

Watkins, M., Ciofalo, N., & James, S. (2018). Engaging the struggle for decolonial approaches to teaching community psychology. *American Journal of Community Psychology, 62*(3–4), 319–329. https://doi.org/10.1002/ajcp.12295

Weinrach, S. G., & Thomas, K. R. (2004). The AMCD multicultural counseling competencies: A critically flawed initiative. *Journal of Mental Health Counseling, 26*(1), 81–93. https://doi.org/10.17744/mehc.26.1.p20t16tdhpgcxm3q

Williams, D. R., & Williams-Morris, R. (2000). Racism and mental health: The African American experience. *Ethnicity & Health, 5*(3–4), 243–268. https://doi.org/10.1080/713667453

Winston, A. S. (2020, May 29). *Scientific racism and North American psychology.* Oxford Research Encyclopedias: Psychology. https://doi.org/10.1093/acrefore/9780190236557.013.516

Yakushko, O. (2019). Eugenics and its evolution in the history of Western psychology: A critical archival review. *Psychotherapy and Politics International, 17*(2), e1495. https://doi.org/10.1002/ppi.1495

Young, R. J. C. (2016). *Postcolonialism: An historical introduction.* Wiley. https://doi.org/10.1002/9781119316817

CHAPTER 9

The Antiracist Inclusive Model
of Systems Supervision

Kara Ieva, Kaprea Johnson, M. Ann Shillingford, and Sam Steen

Counselors in prekindergarten–Grade 12 and higher education settings work and are prepared in these same educational systems, which are often centered in whiteness and perpetuate systemic racism. *Systemic racism* is a form of oppression that subjugates people and groups who embody characteristics associated with any racial group other than the dominant race (Roysicar et al., in press). Antiracist professional school counselors believe that (a) racism can be dismantled because it is learned and (b) it is their duty to actively confront and challenge systemic racism within the school and the broader community. Navigating the complexities of systemic racism on the individual and collective levels demands an interconnected supervisory experience guided by an antiracist framework that supports the development of school counselors (Ieva et al., 2021). However, research on antiracist and antioppressive supervision is present in the social work literature (Bhatti-Sinclair, 2011; Hair, 2015; Hair & O'Donoghue, 2009) but currently absent from the literature on counselor education. An antiracist supervisory framework provides an ideal space in which to address gaps in the current understanding of antiracist practices, increase accountability for taking action within oppressive and racist systems, and allow for personal and professional growth on the antiracist continuum for school counselors. This chapter presents the antiracist inclusive model of systems supervision (AIMSS), a conceptual framework that fosters critical reflection on systemic racism and extends traditional models of supervision and peer consultation through its roots in antiracist tenets. Following is a brief overview of the realities of current supervision practices in schools. The general tenets of supervision and peer consultation practice are juxtaposed with the AIMSS in Table 9.1.

TABLE 9.1 • A Comparative Analysis of Supervision and Peer Consultation Models and the Antiracist Inclusive Model of Systems Supervision

Aspect of Process	Consultation and Supervision	Antiracist School Counseling Consultation and Supervision
Goals	• Interpersonal relationship designed to foster personal and professional development as a counselor • Growth model in which participants learn from each other and grow • Focus on developing one's style of counseling • Leads to autonomy • Seeks consultation when needed	• Reciprocal, critically reflective and accountable relationship that supports and challenges school counselors to develop critical consciousness and a coconspirator identity to further their equity lens, agency and voice in dismantling racist practices, dismantling systemic inequities, and addressing collective racial trauma in schools • Strengths-based growth model • Focus on developing an equity lens and coconspirator identity • Leads to critical consciousness rather than autonomy • Commitment to learning together
Tenets	• Hierarchy (supervisor/supervisee or consultation/consultee) • Developmental • Manage counselors' anxiety to confidence • Move through counselor, teacher, and supervisor • Interventions are for the counselor • Shadow/observe • Build relationships and network with others • Apply skills and build confidence • Learn and practice new skills • Continue defining a theoretical orientation • Apply theoretical approaches	• Absence of hierarchy, peer collaboration • Transparent and straightforward/less developmental (no politics, no agenda); no evaluation • Intentional, moving toward self-awareness or critical consciousness • Uses basic counseling skills to affirm and challenge • Move through educator, counselor, active listener, and challenger • Interventions are for the system first • Promote awareness of systemic racism • Promote understanding of policies and practices connected to the system • Explore counselors' contribution to complacency versus challenging racist practices • Bring blind spots to the forefront • Awareness of parallel process • Applicable across the school/university level (e.g., intern, professional school counselor, supervisor, university supervisor)
Skills and dispositions	• Self-confidence • Self-direction • Independence • Flexibility • Openness • Peer and self-assessment • Skills from theoretical orientations (potentially antiquated)	• Humility • Appropriate self-disclosure • Ability to challenge self and others • Critically conscious • Critical thinking • Cognitively flexible • Self-appraising and reflexive • Courageous • Confront conflict • Interrogate and challenge theoretical orientations of self and others • Selflessness • Openness • Ability to discuss race and explain how racism impacts inequities • Ability to address systemic racism • Risk-taker • Leadership

(Continued)

TABLE 9.1 • A Comparative Analysis of Supervision and Peer Consultation Models and the Antiracist Inclusive Model of Systems Supervision (*Continued*)

pect of Process	Consultation and Supervision	Antiracist School Counseling Consultation and Supervision
neficiaries	• Primary: counselor • Secondary: students (clients) • Tertiary: school (setting)	• Primary: system • Secondary: students and stakeholders • Tertiary: counselor
actical features Duration/frequency	• Weekly for approximately 1 hour • Approximately 10–14 sessions per semester • Occurs until licensure hours are met • Predetermined schedule	• Provided during the workday • Uninterrupted time and space (can be virtual) • Recommended weekly (at a minimum monthly) for 1–2 hours depending on the frequency
ession materials	• Answers to predetermined structured questions • Prerecorded counseling session	• Varies • Can be reflective thoughts, programming insights, reactions to reading (or listening to) materials, reactions to policies, answers to predetermined structure questions, artifacts from incidents since the last session, etc.

School Counselor Practice

School counselors practice in complex school systems, often in isolation, without clinical supervision, and with limited peer consultation (Lambie & Sias, 2009). They face a plethora of challenges as part of the profession, including supporting (a) students who are suicidal and combating mental health issues, (b) families who are homeless, (c) students who experience consistent racial microaggressions from their teachers, (d) students with academic concerns, and (e) exceptionally gifted individuals who need more than can be offered by traditional structure of school academically and emotionally. School counselors do not just treat individual students; they also provide school, family, community, and systems triage for the benefit of all students. Through comprehensive school counseling programs, school counselors provide prevention, intervention, and postvention at the individual, collective, and systems levels, which may result in policy change. Therefore, school counselors require foundational knowledge based on best practice at each level as well as a formalized supervisory process to continue to develop their identity as individuals and systems counselors. The varying school counselor roles and responsibilities necessitate continual support to meet consistent and evolving societal needs, and an opportune way of receiving that support is through supervision.

School Counseling Supervision and Consultation

Supervision is an integral part of counseling practice in general (American Counseling Association, 2014; National Board for Certified Counselors, 2020). It is important to acknowledge that supervision started as an apprentice model, as it was believed that because the master was quite good at doing the work, they would be equally good at teaching or supervising other counselors (Smith, 2009). Scholars have attempted to use clinical supervision models with school counselors (Luke & Bernard, 2006; Rutter, 2006; Wood & Rayle, 2006); however, formalized practices for school counselor supervision have yet to be implemented (Bryant-Young et al., 2014; Tang, 2020). In the absence of clinical supervision, school counselors typically receive supervision from school administrators (e.g., principals) or counseling supervisors who may not have any school counseling experience or the necessary knowledge and dispositions to foster school counselor development through continuous support and challenge. The purpose of administrative supervision is to ensure compliance with laws and policies, cultivate a working relationship with other stakeholders, utilize appropriate data sources (e.g., work schedules, record keeping, school information, and documentation systems), and work effectively within the school system (Henderson, 1994). Although administrative supervision is warranted, it lacks a process to further the development of professional identities and provide insight into the clinical and systems knowledge required of school counselors.

In the absence of clinical supervision, one suggestion is to provide programmatic counseling (clinical) supervision in addition to administrative supervision (Quitanna & Gooden-Alexis, 2020). Programmatic counseling supervision advances school counselors' clinical skills to do triage, provide individual and group counseling, and refer students. Programmatic counseling supervision is vital to monitoring skills and interventions and to ensuring that students and stakeholders are protected from harm. Programmatic counseling supervision aims to enhance school counselors' professional development in terms of implementing a comprehensive school counseling program (Quitanna & Gooden-Alexis, 2020). This type of supervision is commonly provided by a school counselor district or school supervisor. In theory, programmatic counseling supervision provides insight into program management, accountability, in-service training, school- or district-wide concerns, and evaluation of programming efforts.

Without clinical supervision, with limited programmatic counseling supervision, and with mostly only administrative supervision, school counselors have relied on peer supervision/consultation individually and within group settings to foster their development. Peers are individuals who are considered to be on equal footing based on social location characteristics such as qualifications, years of experience, or other values deemed important. Peer consultation, sometimes called *peer supervision*, describes a mutually agreed-on collaborative support system among peers. Both peer consultation and supervision can be structured voluntary or involuntary processes conducted in dyads or groups. Numerous social media sites have provided space for these consultations locally and nationally through private groups and served as a starting point for connection (e.g., Facebook: Elementary Exchange and Caught in the Middle, Twitter: #scchat and #antiracistsc, Instagram: Brown Girls Who Counsel, #SchoolCounselorsofInstagram; Ieva, 2020). However, there is no accountability except to gather numerous consultative points of view and share resources. Although there is diversity among these social media groups, school counselors more broadly still lack racial representation, as nearly 62% of all school counselors identify as white (U.S. Census Bureau, 2018). Therefore, collectively these online groups might lack the knowledge and skills needed to push others further along an antiracist continuum to dismantle systemic racist policies in schools founded on white, middle-class norms that are continually perpetuated throughout generations.

Based on the complexities in schools—including the growing number of racially and ethnically diverse students and families, the political unrest that affects minoritized children and families, long-standing health and economic disparities that affect low-income communities and schools, standardized testing, the ongoing coronavirus pandemic and its aftermath, as well as the use of Eurocentric supervision and peer supervision/consultation models—an innovative supervision model for counselors in educational systems is needed. The AIMSS assists school counselors in developing an antiracist lens and further develops counselor and coconspirator identities in tandem. Furthermore, the AIMSS framework can assist in providing development to analyze programmatic, school, and district data to interrogate school climates and policies that perpetuate racist practices and to advocate for change. Finally, it also enhances consultative skills to challenge school counseling peers, complacent teachers, administrators, and communities who interact with and create classroom and school policies that affect all students. Table 9.1 highlights the goals, tenets, beneficiaries, associated skills, and practical features of traditional consultation and supervision juxtaposed with the AIMSS framework.

School counselors are tasked with acknowledging inequities and systemic barriers that exist in schools and that impact students' social-emotional, academic, and career development (American School Counselor Association [ASCA], 2014, 2020). Antiracist school counselors "are charged to ensure the success of all students by playing a role as leaders, systemic change agents, and advocates who dismantle and remove barriers while providing antiracist, systemic prevention and intervention practices that bring about equity in schools" (R. Mayes, personal communication, August 11, 2020). To make this more common, social justice, antiracism, and advocacy must be at the core of training, supervision, and practice (American Counseling Association, 2014; ASCA, 2014, 2020; Ieva et al., 2021; Mayes, personal communication, August 11, 2020).

A Comparative Analysis of Traditional Models and the AIMSS

Table 9.1 outlines goals, tenets, skills and dispositions, beneficiaries, and practical features of traditional consultation and supervision and antiracist school counseling consultation and supervision. Furthermore, it highlights how the AIMSS either expands on, modifies, or is completely innovative as it relates to traditional consultation and supervision.

By definition, goals are developed to achieve a particular outcome or result. In traditional models of consultation and supervision, goals are focused on supervisees, skills, strengths, and areas for growth (Crunk & Barden, 2017). However, goals may vary based on the supervisor, the supervisee, and anticipated therapeutic outcomes. One major difference between traditional models and the AIMSS is that the AIMSS is concerned more with approaches to engaging in the system than with the development of one's individual counseling style. Another notable difference is that supervision traditionally leads toward autonomy as a clinician. In contrast, the AIMSS recognizes that school counselors operate independently from their first day on the job, and therefore it does not promote autonomy but rather promotes a continuous journey toward critical consciousness. In addition, the AIMSS lacks the hierarchy and power in traditional supervisor/supervisee and consultant/consultee frameworks. The AIMSS is a co-led process that is not dependent on any particular hierarchy, strengths, or experiences; it necessitates a committed school counselor who accepts the responsibility of engaging in antiracist practice and is willing to use various roles within the AIMSS framework (e.g., counselor, educator consultant, challenger, active listener) to eradicate systemic racism.

The tenets or principles of traditional models of consultation and supervision focus on the professional development of the supervisee by examining the working alliance, instilling hope in the supervisee, enhancing supervisee self-awareness, promoting knowledge and skill acquisition, and so on (Milne et al., 2008). Although these tenets may seem advantageous, they severely lack guidance and direction on how and where to challenge and address systemic racism in educational settings and communities. Without a structured antiracist framework, blind spots related to opportunities to challenge systemic racism may not be illuminated. One deficit of traditional consultation and supervision is that they do not center on the eradication of systemic racism. Unfortunately, this deficiency may lead to well-intentioned professional school counselor perpetuating or following racist practices and policies without challenge and engaging in consultation and supervision that only benefits them on an individual level. In fact, traditional consultation and supervision practices often exclude impacts at the systems level, which disproportionately hinders, hurts, and harms marginalized students and their families.

Skills are beneficial in assessing the transition from knowledge to practice. As depicted in Table 9.1, skills consistent with traditional models of consultation and supervision, such as flexibility, independence, and self-confidence, are just as important and relevant for the AIMSS approach. The skills and dispositions defined for the AIMSS approach extend the traditional skills by addressing racism in all forms (e.g., challenge inequities; ability to discuss racism; ability to address systemic racism; ability to identify, map, and utilize resources; leadership; self-disclosure; risk-taking; selflessness). Therefore, although traditional models of supervision highlight useful skills to support supervisee growth and development, a more intentionally, systemically focused approach that challenges antiquated counseling theories and interventions and promotes antiracist behaviors and practices is warranted.

There is a clear distinction between the traditional approach and the AIMSS in terms of who is the beneficiary of supervision. For instance, in traditional models, the development of counselor identity and self-efficacy is the main priority, and therefore the school counselor benefits most, followed by students in educational settings. Within the AIMSS framework, the main beneficiary is the system, followed by students and stakeholders, and finally the counselor. In other words, the growth of the counselor is further developed by attending to the system and those encompassed within that system.

Finally, the practical features of the two approaches in Table 9.1 are similar but are distinct in two areas: duration/frequency and session materials. Per accreditation standards (Council for Accreditation of Counseling and Related Educational Programs [CACREP], 2016), traditional supervision is assigned in graduate school in conjunction with a clinical course that typically meets weekly for group supervision and individual and/or triadic supervision and is mandated until the completion of state hours for licensure (not education related). Therefore, sessions are dependent on the orientation and theory of the supervisor and are structured accordingly with materials. The AIMSS is flexible enough to accommodate an array of scheduling factors with strong recommendations and a dedicated space for work that is dependent on where school counselors are, what challenges they faced in practice since their last session, and how they are moving toward the goals of their programs. Therefore, the structure, other than time, is intentional but flexible.

Table 9.1 highlights some of the similarities and differences between traditional supervision and consultation and the AIMSS framework. The following section provides a brief overview of antiracist school counseling and offers further justification, description, explanation, and practical steps for implementing the AIMSS.

Moving Forward Toward Antiracist School Counseling and Supervision

Antiracist School Counseling

To situate school counseling peer consultation or supervision from an antiracist framework, one must conceptualize antiracist school counseling practice. Antiracist school counselors actively fight racism in everyday practice (Ieva et al., 2021). In her keynote address at the University of Virginia's School Counseling Summit, Cheryl Holcomb-McCoy foundationally defined antiracist school counseling as

> recogniz[ing] and affirm[ing] the wholeness and humanness of students, families, and their communities. This requires an *action-oriented pursuit* to not only understand, but to address and dismantle racist ideologies, policies, and practices in [prekindergarten–Grade 12] schools. School counselors commit to developing antiracist practices, engage in a continuous process of self-reflection and inquiry that enable them to identify and correct racist, "White-centered" cultures in schools. (University of Virginia School of Education and Human Development, 2020, 28:20)

Hence, antiracist school counselors continuously work toward critical consciousness by holistically interrogating the profession, the educational system, and personal views and biases; practice critical reflection; and become coconspirators in dismantling historical unjust practices (Ieva et al., 2021). Antiracist school counseling is a conscious choice to center equity, humanity, and justice consistently, every day, in all that counselors do. To do this work, school counselors need a structured process, time, and environment in which to continually engage in critical self-reflection. Antiracist peer consultation or supervision offers a process that supports the development of antiracist school counselors with the flexibility to create the time that works with the collective schedule and environment (the room or space with the school or district). Therefore, we present a framework for antiracist peer consultation or supervision and a systems perspective below.

The AIMSS

Given the dynamic needs of school counselors and the urgency to address systemic racism in schools with limited training and supervision, we offer a conceptual framework for all supervisors and counselors currently functioning under the influence of a Eurocentric mind-set. The model is based on our collective research, collaborations, professional development, experiences as school counselors and counselor educators, and encounters facilitating individual and group supervision of master's- and doctoral-level and practicing school counselors. The AIMSS is a peer supervision framework that utilizes a reciprocal, critically reflective, and accountable cosupervisory relationship. Within these interactions, peers support and challenge one another to develop coconspirator school counselor identities that further their equity lens, agency, and voice in dismantling racist practices, addressing systemic inequities, and addressing individual and collective racial trauma in schools and connected communities. Although the model is focused on race, it is inclusive of all intersecting identities (see Figure 9.1 for an overview).

The AIMSS, which is rooted in antiracist tenets, expands on best practices in clinical supervision and peer consultation while remaining flexible enough to be implemented in educational settings that might not have the resources for additional positions and professional training. Unlike other models, the AIMSS is nuanced enough to create a comprehensive school counseling program within a system known for perpetuating racism and contributing to disparities in education, such as disproportionality in discipline practices (e.g., the school-to-prison pipeline), special education, achievement, course-taking patterns, and so forth (Roysicar et al., in press).

Goals

The AIMSS focuses on providing continuous professional development and peer supervision through a process of self-reflection and collective reflection (i.e., reflecting on your school and colleagues) and critical inquiry with four main goals:

1. Promote the ongoing development (e.g., knowledge, skills, and dispositions) of school counselors' antiracist lens and critical consciousness.
2. Foster the continuous development of school counselors' counselor, educator, and coconspirator identities and the connection to program delivery, the

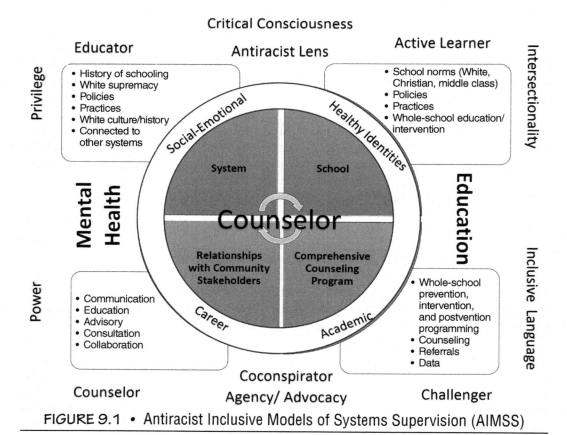

FIGURE 9.1 • Antiracist Inclusive Models of Systems Supervision (AIMSS)

school, and the system.

3. Empower school counselors' agency and voice to advocate on behalf of others and the system.
4. Advance systems knowledge and comprehensive program evaluation skills to address systemic inequities.

Delivery and Environment

As stated previously, delivery and environment can be utilized in counselor education training and for ongoing development with collaboratives of practicing school counselors. We advocate that sessions should become a dedicated part of the professional workday, and thus school counselors might want to advocate for this dedicated time and seek administrative approval. The duration and frequency can be flexible to accommodate counselors' schedules within districts (regardless of level), although we recommend a weekly session (at a minimum monthly sessions) ranging from 1 to 2 hours (depending on frequency) to reach a level of depth. Because the number of counselors in a district can range from 1 to 100, it is recommended that if counselors are unable to meet with other school counselors in their districts county and/or state associations or universities offer varying time slots to increase options for counselors who work in school districts without other counselors. Moreover, school counselors work with other wellness professionals, like social workers, child study team individuals, and school psychologists. The AIMSS encourages interprofessional collaboration to provide cosupervision, as other wellness professionals may be more knowledgeable about systems and could serve as an integral part of the process. Specifically, in rural settings, in which the number of mental health professionals may be limited, interprofessional collaboration may be beneficial (Steen et al., 2021). Furthermore, school counselor educators may also use this model with one another to continue their professional growth.

Cosupervisory Relationship and Roles

In all models of supervision and consultation, trust is foundational to the supervisory alliance and relationship. Many factors contribute to building trust (similar to building group cohesion), in particular in a cosupervisory relationship, in which counselors may not have the flexibility to choose with whom they are in the relationship. Authentic trust is a process that unfolds over time in which counselors are genuine in presenting thoughts, responses, actions, fear judgments, and evaluations and appreciate the same from their collaborators. It involves the vulnerability of understanding that there will always be more to learn to grow professionally (and personally). When thinking about the trust you have developed with a colleague, it is helpful to reflect on the following questions and share those responses: (a) How did you come to trust them? (b) Are there caveats to the trust? and (c) How do you know they trust you? The answers will help establish a cosupervisory relationship that requires vulnerability and self-disclosure.

One way to begin this process in the first established session is to coconstruct norms and rules that encompass trust-building environments: confidentiality; an attempt to suspend judgment; the ability to accept critical feedback as a part of growth; the acceptance of challenge and support from peer counselor(s) regarding values, beliefs, biases, and professional interaction; and the awareness that there will be moments of uncomfortableness that will lead to growth. After counselors establish norms and rules, a first activity should include reviewing all identities that the counselors hold, the spaces in which they hold power and privilege, and the spaces in which they might be marginalized. This sets an immediate tone of self-reflection, self-disclosure, and recognition of where they are on the antiracist continuum. Furthermore, this discussion allows for the inclusiveness of individual and collective identities that build trust and provide a lens that can provide a framework for professional practice.

Similar to other supervision and consultation models, the roles of the cosupervisees can fluctuate depending on topic and circumstance. Operating from a critical stance, the fluctuating roles include educator consultant, active learner, challenger, and counselor. There may be times when a counselor might alternate between all roles within a session or be in more than one role simultaneously. For example, it is plausible that one might be able to challenge someone while also operating as a counselor or educator. Furthermore, one might be challenged and also be an active learner in the process. The roles are described as follows:

- *Educator consultant.* At times within the supervisory relationship, one counselor might have more insight into a particular topic, intervention, critical reflection, or various other topics and responses. Thus, the counselor will impart information based on various learnings (e.g., readings, experiences, policies).
- *Active learner.* As the work is centered on critical inquiry, being an active learner is a requirement for growth. School counselors are often consulting, educating, and counseling others. In the active learner role, the counselor gets to take a timeout to process and become a learner as opposed to the go-to person and expert, which enhances wellness.
- *Challenger.* Although challenging others can create a level of discomfort, it is part of critical inquiry to confront previously conditioned thoughts, ideologies, beliefs, and values. Therefore, the model calls for counselors to challenge one another to increase their coconspirator identity and push beyond the surface level to see connections between programming and the system and racist policies.
- *Counselor.* As mentioned previously, these sessions may leave counselors feeling vulnerable and insecure or facing burnout and exhaustion from continuously trying to address a system riddled with racist ideologies and standards. Thus, at times it will be appropriate to use counseling skills and techniques to explore, support, listen, and validate one another.

Critical Consciousness

The AIMSS attempts to further school counselors' critical consciousness. Critical consciousness refers to the ability to recognize and analyze systems of inequality and the commitment to taking action against those systems (Freire, 1978). The development of critical consciousness comes from reading; studying; engaging in deep scholarship; practicing humility; listening to and interacting with others; and consistently examining and reexamining one's ideas, beliefs, and truths (Pitts, 2020). Inherent in school counselors participation in the AIMSS is a commitment to lifelong learning toward critical consciousness. Moving toward critical consciousness will provide school counselors with knowledge and insight to contribute to dismantling racism in schools. Therefore, the following key concepts are at the forefront of each supervision session as well as programmatic decisions: (a) intersectionality, (b) power, (c) privilege, and (d) inclusive language as they contribute to creating a more inclusive school climate. Although standards for counselor education (CACREP, 2016) discuss aspects of power and privilege through a multicultural lens, intersectionality is a rather newer concept not necessarily discussed across the counseling curriculum. To ensure consistent understanding, we describe the definitions and how they apply in this context and questions to keep in mind when reflecting on experiences and decision-making, as follows:

Power. In the context of working in schools, power refers to having influence, authority, or control over people and/or resources. Society is affected by many different power systems: Patriarchy, white supremacy, heterosexism, cissexism, and classism are only a few of them. Together they interact in a larger oppressive system that disenfranchises those with limited access to power. In your work setting, reflect on the following:

A. What are the power structures in your setting (i.e., who are the feared and who are the fearless)? Typically the feared represent the people who have the most power.
B. Who has the power in certain spaces (e.g., a teacher in a classroom vs. the school counselor in the teacher's classroom, the principal in the school vs. the principal in a meeting with the superintendent)?
C. How do people use their power in these spaces to eradicate or uphold systemic racism?
D. How is power weaponized in your setting?
E. Who rarely has power, and is this lack of power situational? Are there high stakes (i.e., expulsion, advanced placement/International Baccalaureate placement, etc.)?
F. How does one obtain power? What is or can be your role in assisting in increasing the power of historically disenfranchised and other-ized groups in your setting?
G. How is power used in decision-making?
H. How is power used in creating policies?
I. How do you use your power? Give an example of how you used your power to eradicate a racist policy or practice in your setting.
J. In what ways have you convinced others to use their power or advocated that they do so?
K. How has someone used their power recently toward the shared goal of eradicating systemic racism, oppressive policies, and/or practices in your setting? How did you acknowledge or celebrate this person's antiracist actions?

Privilege. Recognizing privilege is a critical element in the process of achieving racial equity. Society grants privilege to people based on certain aspects of their identity, which can include but are not limited to race, class, gender, ethnicity, sexual orientation, language, geographic location, ability, religion, and diagnosis (Ferguson, 2014). Privilege can operate on a personal, interpersonal, cultural, or institutional level and confers advantages, favors, and benefits to members of dominant groups at the expense of members of target groups (Leaven Center, 2003). It is often easier to see oppression than to see privilege, as seeing privilege requires critical reflection and self-awareness. For perspective, consider that all counselors earn a master's degree and therefore hold privilege in spaces over 86.9% of the population (U.S. Census Bureau, 2018). In your work setting, reflect on the following:

A. Name your privilege and how it has benefited you. Where have you publicly and privately acknowledged your privilege, including how it serves to disenfranchise others? It is an intentional responsibility and our job to reverse the impact of our privilege on others.

B. When was the last time you led a discussion of the impact of unjust power and privilege on the students and families you serve in your setting? How did you do it?

C. How does privilege show up in your work, school, or district? Who has advantages because of privilege?

D. Who is oppressed as a result of privilege? To whom does your comprehensive program confer privilege?

E. How does your privilege shape your thoughts and opinions on how you operate as a school counselor and make decisions?

F. Which school policies advantage those with the most power, privilege, and resources in your school setting? How can these policies be reshaped, rethought, or eradicated to be more just to all in your setting?

Intersectionality. The term "intersectionality" was coined by Kimberlé Crenshaw (1989, 1991) to describe a framework for conceptualizing how systems of oppression overlap to create distinct experiences for people with multiple identity classifications (e.g., race, class, gender identity, sexual orientation, religion, and other identity markers). It takes into account people's overlapping identities and experiences to understand the complexity of the multiple prejudices and oppression they face. Crenshaw originally used it to describe the experiences of Black women, who experience both sexism and racism. Although all women experience sexism, the sexism that Black women experience is unique in that it is informed by racism (Ferguson, 2014). School counselors need to understand how identities, oppression, systems, and policies are all connected. Reflect on the following and how it relates to your work setting:

A. What are the identities you hold? Which one of them is privileged, and which might be oppressed?

B. How do your privileged and oppressed identities influence your role as a school counselor? How do they influence your ability or inability to act on equity and justice issues in the school setting?

C. What district or school policies oppress other identities?

D. What aspects of your programming might oppress identities?

Inclusive language. Inclusive language is communication that includes people regardless of identity (e.g., gender, language, culture, religion, race, ability, family structure, marital status, sexuality, origin). People who use inclusive language avoid using words, expressions, or assumptions that unnecessarily exclude people, specifically stakeholders. An example of inclusive language in schools is the use of "parent," "guardian," or "caregiver" as opposed to "mom" or "dad" to be more inclusive of genders and family structures. Person-first language for people with disabilities is also a type of inclusive language. That is, when referring to a person with a disability, one should put the person first rather than the disability (e.g., "a person who is blind or visually impaired" rather than "a blind person"). Reflect on the following and how it relates to your work setting:

A. How is the language you use informed by your implicit bias?

B. How do you use inclusive language in your daily interactions?

C. What documents, websites, and other artifacts can you change to include more inclusive language?

D. What can your school change to include more inclusive language?

Interconnected Reflective Practice

School counselors build on their knowledge and skills in mental health and education to deliver comprehensive counseling programs (focused on academic development, social-emotional development, career development, and the development of healthy identities), cultivate relationships with stakeholders, and address the whole-school climate. Yet they are also part of a broader system (e.g., district) as part of their practice. The main focus of AIMSS sessions is for counselors to critically reflect on and understand the interconnectedness of their practice and connected systems. This means school counselors must fully acknowledge and understand the historical nature of the educational system broadly and their school context specifically, school culture, comprehensive school counseling programs, and roles of community stakeholders. Once they understand the interconnectedness and interdependence of their practice, school counselors can then begin to challenge previously conceived and conditioned thoughts, ideologies, beliefs, and values at different points across and within the school system.

> **System.** The educational system comprises all things related to schooling students, including policies, laws, funding, regulations, and strict adherence to conformity. Working in isolation and without acknowledging the racialized system in which you work can lead to missed opportunities to support students, families, and communities. Opportunity for engagement with the system can take on many forms, but it is important to remember that the system is steeped in white supremacy and was structured historically to marginalize, oppress, and exclude students of color. Addressing the system in AIMSS sessions will take intentionality and an interrogation of policies, procedures, and practices that are widely adopted and accepted by the majority. Challenging the system will take bold, selfless action; the development of coconspirators; leadership; a questioning of how you have contributed to the system; and a commitment to achieving long-term goals through small gains. The system cannot be overlooked in AIMSS sessions because it is the originator of the oppressive chaos students and families of color experience while navigating school. For example, if in an AIMSS session the focus is on increasing graduation rates among students of color in your school, and the discussion stops at innovative programming, then the session is not engaging the system. Engaging with the system would involve discussing innovative programming and interrogating the low graduation trends through data and inquiries. Such an interrogation might include asking questions such as the following:
>
> A. What policies coincide with changes in graduation rates?
> B. What policies can impact or have inadvertently impacted graduation rates (e.g., zero-tolerance policies, attendance policies, dress codes, bussing, school start and end times)?
> C. What funding is available to support students and families, and what is the history or trend in funding at the state level (e.g., has it increased, has funding shifted to new programs)?
> D. Which elected official is focused on graduation rates, what is their plan, and how has their plan impacted policies and procedures at your school?
>
> This level of engagement with the system is an important part of the AIMSS approach. It is OK to not have answers, but it is important to ask the questions because you are shifting your thinking from impacting an individual to impacting

an individual and the collective (i.e., the system). As you start to reflect on your engagement with the system, think through the following questions:

A. What policies appear neutral but unjustly impact students of color? What has historically been the impact of these policies on students of color (e.g., increased disciplinary action, harsher discipline)?

B. Who is the elected official presiding over the community in which your school is located?

C. How is your school system related to other systems in your community (e.g., health care, justice, business)? How does it influence or impact these other systems?

D. What do you view as the most pressing needs of your school community, and are these needs aligned with the stated goals, missions, and values of elected official(s)?

E. In what ways do you interrogate your adherence to racialized policies and practices?

F. What are three ways in which you can develop an intentional practice of interrogating policies and procedures within your system?

G. What are your internal and external fears related to interrogating and engaging the system in supervision and practice? How do you plan on overcoming those fears (e.g., developing coconspirators, getting involved with the community, engaging more stakeholders)?

School, community, and comprehensive school counseling program. The school is the physical, intangible, and contextual environment in which you work, which includes but is not limited to context (e.g., ecological systems, historical knowledge, the physical environment, resources, white culture/ Eurocentrism), culture (e.g., beliefs, perceptions, relationships, attitudes, written/ unwritten rules that shape and influence how your school functions equitably or inequitably), climate (the National School Climate Center defines this as the quality and character of school life based on patterns of students', parents', and school personnel's experience with school life), norms (e.g., written and unwritten expectations and rules of the school codeveloped over time by leaders, often with limited input from students and families), and place (e.g., your place, status, and influence within the school as it relates to interactions with other school personnel, administrators, leaders, students, families, and the community).

Areas related to school-community partnerships offer starting points for understanding, engagement, and whole-school education and intervention. Within the AIMSS, increasing understanding and engagement with and about the school may include learning more about the context, culture, climate, norms, and physical environment of your school site. Gathering the information that will help you understand your school more holistically can include engaging public databases (i.e., examining school statistics, connecting to the community surrounding your school, being informed about the feeder schools for your school, etc.), reading archived materials on school policies, talking with long-term employees about the history of the school's leadership or administration (including decision-making), collecting data on how others view important processes and decision-making (e.g., whether people feel it is equitable), and so on.

In the case study presented below, understanding, engagement, and whole-school intervention and programming may include the school counselor seeking to understand dress code policies at nearby schools and feeder schools, gathering information on when the dress code policy went into place and whether it had minimized the occurrence of violations or inappropriate dress, seeking to understand whether other personnel deemed the policy valuable (or necessary, or problematic, etc.), and presenting her findings to the leadership or administration. Whole-school education and programming can include engaging teachers in educating on how dress code policies can be anti-Black or oppressive to Blacks, Indigenous people, and people of color; brainstorming solutions to eradicating inequitable policies; or debunking any myths or misinformation school personnel might have as it relates to the policy (i.e., does it reduce infractions, how many instances have been found of head scarves being related to gang activity, etc.). As you start to reflect on your understanding, engagement, and whole-school intervention efforts within your school, think through the following questions:

A. What areas related to the school context, school counseling program, culture, climate, norms, and physical environment do you know the most and least about? Develop a plan to learn more about the areas in which you are lacking knowledge.
B. Who might benefit from the materials you gather in your endeavor to learn more about the school and the community and its stakeholders? How can you share the materials with these communities and groups?
C. With which area of the school have you avoided engagement and why? How might this avoidance impact students of color, special education students, and other marginalized students within your school counseling program?
D. What areas can you impact the most at your school? Who should be your collaborators within the school and community to have a positive impact in the school counseling program and other areas?
E. What are your fears related to understanding, engaging, and fostering school-wide comprehensive programming efforts that include specific intervention and education in your school? What is your plan to overcome these fears and barriers to antiracist practices?
F. What do you think a target school area(s) should be during your time in AIMSS supervision with your peer(s)? Why do you choose this area(s)?
G. Where can antiracist practice and tenets be incorporated into your school? Who is the leader or administrator of that particular area, and what is your plan to engage them in this discussion? Who will be your co-conspirators in this discussion?

Case Illustration Using the AIMSS

Setting

The Charter High School was located in a large metropolitan area that had seen an uncontrolled expansion of housing and commercial development. The school demographics had recently shifted from 25% Black-identifying families to 40% Black-identifying families, 40% white-identifying families, 15% Latinx-identifying families, and 5% of families identifying as multiracial. The school staff and administrators identified predominantly as white. The mismatch between school staff and students/families had recently been discussed in parent-teacher association meetings, leading to a few heated discussions.

Case

Cassie was settled into her role as a school counseling intern at The Charter High School and was currently well into her second month. Ms. M, her site supervisor, had done a great job getting Cassie acclimated and assisting her in developing a reasonable caseload. Cassie even had regular students who came in to say hello and students with whom she met in group counseling. One group that was going well was her Girls in STEAM group, which focused on demystifying science, technology, engineering, art, and mathematics (STEAM) futures and connecting girls to opportunities to engage in more STEAM activities. The group was small, so when one person was missing it was obvious; this week Imani was missing from the group. Cassie asked the group whether anyone knew where Imani was, and they noted she was in in-school suspension because she had refused to take off her scarf during breakfast. Someone else noted that Imani had started braiding her hair the previous day but had not finished, hence the scarf.

Cassie noted the information and continued with the group activity. After the group was dismissed, Cassie asked Ms. M what they could do about Imani being in in-school suspension because of her headscarf. Ms. M noted, "We could take her scarf off" and chuckled. Cassie asked again, noting that she did not feel that punishing someone for wearing a headscarf was just or logical. Ms. M noted that although she appreciated Cassie's opinion the rules were there for a reason and they were rules and not opinions. Ms. M concluded the conversation by noting, "We follow the rules in this office; we are not here to be a student's friend."

Feeling dismissed by Ms. M, Cassie brought this concern up to the career and college access counselor, Mx. Willard. After the discussion, Mx. Willard asked Cassie whether they had permission to relay this concern to Ms. M. Cassie agreed that it would be helpful for another person to broach the topic. Mx. Willard had worked with Ms. M for more than a decade and had a very stable and collegial relationship with her. Mx. Willard discussed the concern Cassie noted and also asked whether they could engage in peer supervision because they also had not recognized this policy as problematic until the discussion with Cassie.

Getting Started With the AIMSS

In the case above, Mx. Willard and Ms. M jointly decided to use the AIMSS to guide their peer supervision relationship and experience. Although in this case a single incident precipitated the initiation of this relationship, this is not a necessary precursor in the aforementioned case. To get started using the AIMSS, both parties must agree that it is a good fit for their supervision experience, align and agree on their goals, and acknowledge a willingness to interrogate systems and structures that perpetuate oppressive racialized experiences for students and families. Note that the sessions below are not linear and do not correspond to a set number of meetings but rather are indications of progress and can be read as guidance on how to enact the AIMSS.

Session A

Discuss basic expectations for the peer supervision relationship, including confidentiality, trust, and a culture of openness. Set norms for the relationship, goals, and timelines (i.e., when you will meet and for how long). Also, discuss any pressing challenges you want to engage (e.g., dress code policies, graduation rates) and longer term goals as they relate to these challenges and other opportunities for eradicating racism in your setting.

Session B

Refocus attention on the pressing challenge. To start the supervision experience, both parties should be open about their knowledge of the challenge, their awareness of its impact, and their skills for navigating the challenge. Develop a document that notes the shared understanding of the challenge, how it impacts the school and specific students (i.e., review data, anecdotal information, etc.), and systems-level influences (i.e., policy, practices, etc.). After the challenge is documented note what ongoing development might be needed (e.g., readings about anti-Blackness, racialized discipline policies), engage with stakeholders (i.e., community members, students, and families at the school), and jointly develop a reading list that you will engage with throughout the relationship to further develop your antiracist lens and critical consciousness.

Session C

Review your progress on your goals and your commitment to challenging the system and addressing the pressing challenge. Using your shared document, discuss and note how your understanding of the challenge has matured, assess any actions and inaction thus far, note whether there have been other instances of the same challenge, and reflect (and write) on the experience of engaging with antiracist readings. Assess and interrogate your practices thus far using the reflection questions in the chapter, as this will assist you as you start to track the development of your coconspirator identity.

Session D

You have collected data on the pressing challenge and now are more informed about how the challenge has disproportionately impacted marginalized students and understand how the system contributes to racialized policies that cocreate pressing challenges. It is thus time to use your agency and voice to educate others about the challenge. Using your agency and voice starts the process of developing coconspirators. Your coconspirators are developed and engaged through your activism (i.e., your sharing of information about the pressing challenge—who it impacts, why it is wrong, its potential negative impact on groups of students and the school, etc.). The information you share may vary by stakeholder; for example, teachers may be moved by the inequitable application of specific school policies (i.e., some teachers apply them and some do not), whereas community members and families may be moved by understanding how policies unjustly oppress Black students. Developing your coconspirators leads to action planning for change. For example, your effort should be focused on both engaging people to inform them of the challenge and recruiting them to be part of developing the action plan.

Session E

Discuss the next steps for the action plan. Record who your coconspirators are and who you will engage at the systems level (this can include the principal or those higher up). Document your timeline, potential challenges to implementing your plan, and ways to overcome these challenges. Include a plan to evaluate the effectiveness of the collective effort to dismantle systemic equities.

Session F

Review your goals and the implementation plan. In what ways did the plan change the experience for students of color at the school? Who was the most receptive to the plan, and who required the most support in understanding the goal? (It is important to document this because you will want to continue developing the difficult relationships in case other issues arise.) What methods did you use to evaluate the plan and its effectiveness? How did you share the results with your coconspirators? How will you celebrate and acknowledge the change publicly? There must be a public acknowledgment of the eradication of a racialized and unjustly oppressive policy. This acknowledgment signals to the students who have been unjustly impacted that those in power do care, it signals to those in power that people are watching and are willing to sacrifice for the greater good, and it invigorates others to learn more and get involved.

Session G

Assess the supervisory relationship and next steps. Were the shared goals accomplished? If not, what is the plan to move forward? Do any goals need to be revised? Develop your ongoing antiracist identity development plan and your self-accountability plan (i.e., what specific readings you will engage, what conferences you will attend, what community events you will attend, what community service you will engage in, how you will get involved). Use the reflection questions in the chapter to develop other areas of growth and to assess your development thus far.

Reflective Questions

Drawing on the case illustrations, we offer sample reflective questions for discussion in clinical peer supervision as follows:

- How does the group get prepared? How do you get prepared?
- What are critical reflection questions, and what should you start with?
- Protecting thyself is a convenient way to keep silent and be content with inaction. Sometimes it involves asking yourself to reflect on the sayings "silence is violence" and "inaction is an action." Think about how you protected thyself this week. What groups were or could be most impacted?
- What personal values and biases collude with protecting thyself?
- An important part of interrogating yourself and your practices is acknowledging your fear and fearlessness. What fear (e.g., a fear of being wrong, a fear of disappointing a supervisor, a fear of your voice not being heard) colluded with protecting thyself this week and caused inaction?
- How will you overcome this fear? What is your plan? How will you recognize when you are making progress on overcoming this fear?
- What fearless act did you engage in this week? Remember that fearlessness can reveal itself in different ways. It can be a gentle challenge, emailing a teacher advocating for a child, coordinating services for a child, sending resources to a family, or writing to your elected official.

- How are you developing coconspirators? What action or inaction was taken this week toward this goal?
- Who have you identified as potential or possible coconspirators and why?
- How will you develop, maintain, and activate this relationship to accomplish antiracist goals in your school?
- Who have you left off the list and why? What is your plan to engage your colleague, educator, or school leader?
- Are you able to identify a systemic challenge at your school?
- What data (quantitative, qualitative, and anecdotal) substantiate this challenge?

Implementing the AIMSS in Counselor Education

Above we depicted the use of the AIMSS with practicing school counselors. However, the intent of the model is to change the system while building counselor, educator, and coconspirator identities. Consequently, the use of a systemic implementation plan is in direct alignment with the tenets of the model. In addition, school counselor educators can engage with one another using the AIMSS and/ or implement them within their own counselor education departments, as higher education is also a system that perpetuates systemic racism.

Counselor Educators

As mentioned previously, there are a few ways the AIMSS can be implemented in counselor education. One is to have counselor education departments and program faculty engage in this model of supervision with one another. Counselor educators work and educate others in an educational system that may oppress both students and faculty and share a similar goal of promoting student success. Engaging in the model may lead to deeper understandings of the systems in which they are operating and how the delivery of their training programs might need to be altered based on outcomes (e.g., curriculum, policies, evaluation). Counselor educators (and adjuncts) are the first to model awareness, dispositions, knowledge, and skills for dismantling racist practices both in higher education and in counselor education. This may lead to a deeper understanding of school counseling, potential research endeavors, and continuous programmatic improvement.

Preservice School Counselors

In addition to a lack of clinical supervision, another impetus for the model is the fact that practicing school counselors may not be trained in antiracist work. One way to reach them is through the placement of interns and the creation of university partnerships. When the model is introduced in coursework prior to clinical practice, it creates a framework for students to understand schools and systems, defines an expectation of ongoing development, and defines key concepts that further awareness of systemic racism (e.g., power, privilege, intersectionality, critical consciousness). Once students reach clinical practice, the AIMSS may be used with interns in university group supervision, which mirrors a group of practicing school counselors at different schools within a district. The use of the model provides continuous development and training in cosupervision simultaneously.

Therefore, students are prepared to implement the AIMSS on graduation in their school counseling roles.

According to CACREP (2016), universities must provide site supervisor training. Another way to reach school counseling site supervisors is to train them to use this model with interns as an expectation and hence assist in their development and implementation of an equitable comprehensive school counseling program. Programs might also invite site supervisors to group supervision a set number of times as part of the program supervisor expectations to engage simultaneously with counselor educators, interns, and other practicing school counselors serving as site supervisors. This will create a cadre of practicing and future school counselors who will be able to implement the AIMSS in the field and therefore reach other practicing school counselors.

Practicing School Counselors

Reaching practicing school counselors is challenging for a variety of reasons, including the fact that these counselors might not all belong to the same professional organizations, states have different methods of overseeing school counseling, and counselors may have different professional identities based on when they received their training and what type of master's degree they hold. It would be advantageous for universities to provide spaces for practicing school counselors to not only train but also model implementation monthly. In addition, professional organizations can provide spaces and opportunities to engage school counselors in this work nationally, regionally, and at the state and local levels. The model is developed in such a way that regardless of when school counselors begin the cosupervisory experience the system remains the focus, and counselor developmental readiness is not a factor in beginning the work.

Future Practice Considerations

As this is a conceptual framework, there is room for improvement. For example, although four potential roles are listed, as counselors engage in this process there might be a need to add more roles. Likewise, counselors might coconstruct structured supervisory sessions that work for them and deviate from what is presented here. We welcome any feedback one may find useful to further improve this model and thus the professional growth of school counselors. Our hope is that counselor education programs move toward more of an antiracist approach to clinical supervision so interns and site supervisors gain the knowledge, awareness, and skills to promote the success of all students.

Future Research Considerations

The AIMSS is in the nascent phase of conceptualization, and much of the understanding is based on our collective experiences as practitioners and counselor educators. The need to explore strengths and areas to improve is duly noted. Specifically, it would be imperative to determine the best practical features, including the duration, frequency, and session structure most feasible for implementation. For example, currently it is suggested that those using the AIMSS framework meet regularly (e.g., weekly or monthly) during the workday for 1 to 2 hours at a time.

Even though we know from clinical experience that it is necessary for regular and ongoing discussions and interactions to occur because systemic racism is persistent, to what extent is this feasible and sustainable? Furthermore, given a typical 8-hour workday and the added stressors of the current coronavirus pandemic, what is the minimum amount of time that would lead to the most optimal outcome?

Another important line of inquiry related to the AIMSS would be to gain a deeper understanding of the perceived cost and benefits of using such a framework among counselors and counselor educators who are engaged in antiracist work. The current version of the AIMSS was created by and derived from school counselor educators and practitioners immersed in combating systemic racism within schools. Finally, as the AIMSS continues to develop, there is a need to create appropriate strategies to evaluate the model and its various components. Along those lines, school counselors using this model will benefit if evaluation considerations are more clearly provided in a multimodal fashion to account for the complexities of the intersections of identities counselors hold and those identities represented within the schools and communities served.

Conclusion

This chapter has highlighted the shift from traditional clinical supervision and peer consultation to a more antiracist approach specific to school counseling. The AIMSS conceptual framework is a starting point for developing coconspirator school counselor identities among both preservice and practicing school counselors with a strong commitment to eradicating racism and promoting equity in schools.

References

American Counseling Association. (2014). *ACA code of ethics*. https://www.counseling.org/resources/aca-code-of-ethics.pdf

American School Counselor Association. (2014). *ASCA ethical standards for school counselors*.

American School Counselor Association. (2020). *Standards in practice: Eliminating racism and bias in schools: The school counselor's role*.

Bhatti-Sinclair, M. K. (2011). *Anti-racist practice in social work*. Macmillan International Higher Education.

Bryant-Young, N., Bell, C. A., & Davis, K. M. (2014). *A supervisory issue when utilizing the ASCA National Model framework in school counseling* (EJ1084445). ERIC. https://eric.ed.gov/?id=EJ1084445

Council for Accreditation of Counseling and Related Educational Programs. (2016). *2016 CACREP standards*. www.cacrep.org/for-programs/2016-cacrep-standards/

Crenshaw, K. (1989). Demarginalizing the intersection of race and sex: A Black feminist critique of antidiscrimination doctrine, feminist theory and antiracist politics. *University of Chicago Legal Forum, 1989*(1), 139–167.

Crenshaw, K. (1991). Mapping the margins: Intersectionality, identity politics, and violence against women of color. *Stanford Law Review, 43*(6), 1241–1299.

Crunk, A. E., & Barden, S. M. (2017). The common factors discrimination model: An integrated approach to counselor supervision. *The Professional Counselor, 7*(1), 62–75.

Ferguson, S. (2014, September 29). *Privilege 101: A quick and dirty guide*. Everyday Feminism. https://everydayfeminism.com/2014/09/what-is-privilege/

Freire, P. (1978). *Pedagogy of the oppressed*. Continuum.

Hair, H. J. (2015). Supervision conversations about social justice and social work practice. *Journal of Social Work, 15*(4), 349–370.

Hair, H. J., & O'Donoghue, K. (2009). Culturally relevant, socially just social work supervision: Becoming visible through a social constructionist lens. *Journal of Ethnic & Cultural Diversity in Social Work, 18*(1–2), 70–88. https://doi.org/10.1080/15313200902874979

Henderson, P. (1994). *Supervision of school counselors* (Report No. EDO-CG-94-21). Office of Educational Research and Improvement.

Ieva, K. P. (2020, September). Filling the emotional cup: Growing your own support network. *Counselor News*. https://asca-prod.azurewebsites.net/newsletters/september-2020/filling-the-emotional-cup-growing-your-own-suppor?st=NJ

Ieva, K. P., Beasley, J., & Steen, S. (2021). Equipping school counselors for antiracist healing centered groups: A critical examination of preparation, connected curricula, professional practice and oversight. *Teaching and Supervision in Counseling, 3*(2), Article 7. https://trace.tennessee.edu/tsc/vol3/iss2/7

Lambie, G. W., & Sias, S. M. (2009). An integrative psychological developmental model of supervision for professional school counselors-in-training. *Journal of Counseling & Development, 87*(3), 349–356. https://doi.org/10.1002/j.1556-6678.2009.tb00116.x

Leaven Center. (2003). *Doing our own work: A seminar for anti-racist white women*. Indiana University Bloomington.

Luke, M., & Bernard, J. M. (2006). The school counseling supervision model: An extension of the discrimination model. *Counselor Education and Supervision, 45*(4), 282–295. https://doi.org/10.1002/j.1556-6978.2006.tb00004.x

Milne, D. L., Aylott, H., Fitzpatrick, H., & Ellis, M. V. (2008). How does clinical supervision work? Using a "best evidence synthesis" approach to construct a basic model of supervision. *The Clinical Supervisor, 27*(2), 170–190. https://doi.org/10.1080/07325220802487915

National Board for Certified Counselors. (2020). *Approved Clinical Supervisor (ACS) program*.

Pitts, J. (2020, September 11). *What anti-racism really means for educators*. Learning for Justice. https://www.tolerance.org/magazine/what-antiracism-really-means-for-educators

Quitanna, T., & Gooden-Alexis, S. (2020). *Making supervision work*. American School Counselor Association.

Roysicar, G., Steen, S., & Cole, K. (in press). *Anti-Black racism in contemporary America*. Cognella.

Rutter, M. E. (2006). Group supervision with practicing school counsellors. *Guidance & Counseling, 21*, 160–167.

Smith, K. L. (2009, September). *A brief summary of supervision models*. https://www.marquette.edu/education/graduate/documents/brief-summary-of-supervision-models.pdf

Steen, S., Schimmel, C. J., Melfie, J. M., & Carro, A. M. (2021). *Applying the achieving Success Everyday (ASE) group counseling model in rural schools: Implications for school counselor training* [Manuscript submitted for publication]. George Mason University.

Tang, A. (2020). The impact of school counseling supervision on practicing school counselors' self-efficacy in building a comprehensive school counseling program. *Professional School Counseling, 23*(1). https://doi.org/10.1177/2156759X20947723

University of Virginia School of Education and Human Development. (2020, November 2). *2020 UVA school counseling summit* [Video]. YouTube. https://www.youtube.com/watch?v=pPoD5lIXXZI

U.S. Census Bureau. (2018). *Public Use Microdata Sample (PUMS)*. https://www.census.gov/programs-surveys/acs/data/pums.html

Wood, C., & Rayle, A. D. (2006). A model of school counseling supervision: The goals, functions, roles, and systems model. *Counselor Education and Supervision, 45*(5), 253–266. https://doi.org/10.1002/j.1556-6978.2006.tb00002.x

CHAPTER 10

A Personal Essay:
The Costs of Being an Antiracist School Counselor

Dana Griffin

It feels hypocritical for me to write this personal essay about being an antiracist school counselor because when I was a professional middle school counselor, I was not an antiracist school counselor. When I reflect on my time spent as a middle school counselor in Virginia, the first thought that comes to mind is sorrow—sorrow for all the Black students who needed me to advocate for them. Instead I chose to uphold the policies that continued to marginalize them through suspensions, lowered expectations, and higher grade-level retentions. If I could see them again, I would apologize to every one of them, but all I can do now is hope and pray they were able to overcome the racist treatment they received by the very people who were supposed to educate, guide, and support them. I start this essay by sharing my own story because I want you to know that I have not always been antiracist, but it is never too late to change. Although this chapter is about the personal costs of being an antiracist school counselor, I begin with a personal account of my work as a school counselor to hopefully show the professional school counselors reading this that the cost of *not* having an antiracist school counseling program is much higher than the personal costs of being an antiracist school counselor.

I remember one Black male student, retained in the eighth grade, whom the teachers loathed. One of his teachers approached me at the beginning of the school year, demanding that I remove him from her class because she had him the year before and did not want him on her team. This student was angry; he pushed buttons; he was often suspended. When I worked with him, I engaged in anger management techniques, teaching him how to control the anger he had toward his teachers. I was not successful, for what I failed to realize at that time was that his anger was justified and my efforts should have been on reducing the racist treatment he received from his teachers instead of only teaching him to deal with his anger over the racist interactions. One day this student said he was going to blow up the school, effectively ending his middle school career. My advocacy was telling the principal that he did not mean it, that he had only said it in anger. His white teachers said they were afraid of him and thought he would bring a gun into the school, although we knew at that time that all perpetrators of school shooting violence had been white. The white principal considered the student's comment a direct threat and had him expelled. We failed this student. I failed this student.

I remember the Black female student, diagnosed with bipolar disorder at the age of 11, who was expelled for running out of the school when the white male principal and Black male school resource officer took her into the principal's office and closed the door. As I had worked with the student for more than a year, I knew how to calm her down when she was enraged. I told them that taking her into a closed room and shutting the door would scare the student and that, at a minimum, I should be a part of this meeting. They did not listen. I should have argued. This student ended up expelled, but because of her special education status she was reinstated after a 10-day suspension. We failed this student. I failed this student.

I remember my Black female seventh grader who identified as a lesbian. She was suspended for hitting on another student. I remember the Black student wrongly accused of cheating, the Black student who was disruptive in the classroom, the Black student who yelled in the classroom. They were all suspended, and not one of these students deserved the treatment they received. I could share numerous stories of failure during my years as a school counselor, for I did not engage in any advocacy on behalf of my students. In essence, I maintained the status quo, allowed the white supremacy that ran rampant in our school to continue to harm student after student. I was not an antiracist school counselor, and thus we failed these students. I failed these students.

Although I do not have exact data from my time working at this school, I can vividly recall that we had higher numbers of Black students than white students being suspended, expelled, and sent to in-school suspension. Black students also accounted for the highest number of grade retentions. Furthermore, the Black students at this school were least likely to be enrolled in gifted math and English classes. I am sure this information is not surprising, as much has been written about the suspension rates, retention rates, and gifted and advanced placement course rates of Black students. I am also sure it is not surprising that the school did nothing to address this, placing the blame on the students and the families themselves. Daily I would hear comments about how the students and their parents did not care about their futures. When parents would advocate on behalf of their students, they were labeled "problem parents" and vilified.

During a webinar on antiracism, Angela Davis said, "Engaging in antiracism means you are making a commitment to recognizing and ending systemic structures that uphold racism" (personal communication, September 17, 2020). Education has been and continues to be a systemic structure that upholds racism. An antiracist school counselor develops and implements an antiracist school counseling program dedicated to ending the practices and policies that schools use to uphold racism. Being an antiracist school counselor demands perseverance, fortitude, commitment, and caring. It involves engaging in abolitionist work. Bettina

Love (2019) defined *abolitionist teaching* as "tearing down old structures and ways of thinking" and

> forming new ideas, new forms of social interactions, new ways to be inclusive, new ways to discuss inequality and distribute wealth and resources, new ways to resist, new ways to agitate ... and new ways to establish an educational system that works for everyone, especially those who are put at the edges of the classroom and society. (pp. 88–89)

In essence, professional school counselors need to not only become antiracist but also embody an abolitionist mind-set.

The chapters in this book detail various ways in which school counselors can engage in antiracist and abolitionist work. However, this particular chapter focuses on the personal costs of engaging in antiracist practices. Far too often, counselor educators research and document what needs to be done on behalf of our Black students but fail to engage in conversations about the personal costs of this work—both professionally and personally. Therefore, in this chapter I remedy this by first providing an overview of antiracism as it is used in different fields and then discussing the need for antiracism pedagogy in school counseling. I end with a discussion of the personal and professional costs of taking on an antiracist agenda as shared by three professional school counselors.

A Historical Look at Antiracism

Antiracism education has been the topic of much discourse across many academic fields, such as teacher education, sociology, medicine, and school leadership, but the concept of antiracism is not a new one. Even the Bible discusses acting out against oppression: "And oppress not the widow, nor the fatherless, the stranger, nor the poor" (Syswerda, 1984, Zechariah 7:8) or "Do not mistreat an alien or oppress him" (Syswerda, 1984, Exodus 22:21). Indeed, in 1999, Geoffrey Short wrote an article on the need for antiracism education using the Holocaust as the motive for including antiracist education in schools. He stated that although 11,000 people risked their lives to protect the Jews from persecution, so many more functioned as bystanders, passively allowing the horror to occur. As he wrote in his article, most Germans were against the brutality toward Jews but did not take action to speak out against it, fight against it, or help their Jewish countrymen. Short (1999) continued by stressing that what we must learn from what happened during the Holocaust is that action must be taken, that "we must nurture in students to act out against racism" (p. 50).

In teacher education, scholars discuss the need to enact culturally responsive and culturally relevant pedagogy (Gay, 2000; Howard, 2010; Ladson-Billings, 2009). Ladson-Billings's (2009) culturally relevant pedagogy calls on educators to have knowledge and awareness of social inequities, to critique these social inequities, and to draw on students' cultural funds of knowledge and engage them in social justice advocacy. Culturally responsive teaching calls for educators to use cultural knowledge and prior experience to make learning more relevant and responsive to students of color (Gay, 2000; Howard, 2010). However, in this field, much of the work on antiracism education has focused on preparing preservice teachers who are not white for work with students identified as Black, Indigenous, or people of color (Ohito, 2019), not necessarily teaching them how to engage in antiracist work such as dismantling the systems that continue to oppress these students.

In school administration, Jean-Marie and Mansfield (2013) discussed the importance of courageous conversations for school leaders in creating an antiracist school environment. In their chapter, they cited the work of Solomon (2002), who stated that school leaders need to reflect on the development of their consciousness of race and racial differences, which may help them become more effective antiracism educators. However, Short (1999) asserted that one cannot take for granted the fact that simply knowing racism exists guarantees antiracist behavior. The field of nursing also addresses the need for both cross-cultural understanding and antiracism training for nursing students, citing that cross-cultural understanding is insufficient to promote antiracist health systems for culturally diverse populations and that antiracism training is needed to change racist beliefs and attitudes as well as to focus on the social and political structures underpinning racism in health care systems (Allen, 2010). In her literature review on antiracism in nursing education, Allen (2010) cited Johnstone and Kanitsaki (2008) and Narayanasamy and White (2005) in stating that health care inequities exist for culturally diverse populations not only because of the lack of access to health care services due to language and cultural barriers but also because of institutional racism embedded in health care organizations that fail to provide appropriate services to people of color.

Social workers also address the need for antiracism education in their work, also concluding that simply teaching cultural competence does not necessarily lead to someone being antiracist (Hamilton-Mason & Schneider, 2018). In 2002, a small group of social workers developed the Anti-Racist Alliance, the purpose of which is to undo structural racism in their profession, organization, community, and university (Blitz et al., 2014). This organization has since grown and now has thousands of members dedicated to an antiracist agenda. However, social work scholars have also found that although one may commit to an antiracist agenda, controversies exist around antiracism education, including what and how to teach (Hamilton-Mason & Schneider, 2018), a conclusion also found in nursing education (Allen, 2010). In summary, antiracism is not a new phenomenon, and many scholars across different fields of study have expressed the need to engage in antiracist education. Yet significant barriers exist to engaging in antiracism, mainly in the training and practice of antiracism, and nowhere do we see this play out more than in the field of professional school counseling.

The Need for Antiracist School Counseling

The events of January 6, 2021, vividly and explicitly demonstrated the need for antiracism in educational settings. A white terrorist group stormed the U.S. Capitol, a government building, angry at how our democratic process had failed to keep their preferred candidate in office, even as white elected officials were in the process of voting to overturn the election results because they too were angry about how the democratic process had failed to keep their preferred candidate in office. We need to realize that at some point all these people, more likely than not, were students in K–12 schools. All these terrorists and elected officials, who openly espoused racist rhetoric to their constituents—the same racist rhetoric used by racist groups such as neo-Nazis, the Ku Klux Klan, and the Proud Boys—had some type of K–12 education. We need to realize that this mob that attacked the Capitol justified their actions by calling themselves patriots fighting to save their country and live up to President Donald Trump's motto, a motto that won him the 2016 presidential election, "to make America great again." At some point, these "patriots" had teachers, counselors, administrators, school social workers, and school nurses, all members of professions with scholars asserting that antiracism needs to be incorporated into their fields. However, in school counseling antiracism is still far from being widely accepted and implemented.

In fact, not only is it a struggle to implement antiracism in schools, but many actively fight against having antiracism education in schools. One of the most well-known attempts to ban antiracism education occurred in Tucson, Arizona, in 2007, when the state superintendent of public instruction, Tom Horne, fought to ban ethnic studies programs in schools, writing an open letter to the citizens of Tucson. His argument in this letter was that an ethnics studies program is a resentment-based program that creates fear (Horne, 2007). More recent attacks against antiracism education have occurred, most notably an Executive Order issued by President Trump on September 22, 2020, that prohibited discussions of critical race theory and antiracism as they are "offensive and anti-American" (Exec. Order No. 13,950, 2020, p. 60683). These events speak to the need for school counselors themselves to be antiracist and to develop and implement an antiracist school counseling agenda.

Antiracism in school counseling is not new; it has just been couched in different language. In a webinar on antiracist school counseling, Cheryl Holcomb-McCoy discussed the evolution of counseling in terms of issues of race, detailing how scholarship on racial issues began in Black psychology with such scholars as Asa Hilliard, Wade Nobles, and Faye Belgrave; evolved to cross-cultural counseling and psychology with scholars such as Derald Wing Sue and Clemmont Vontress; evolved again to multicultural counseling with scholars such as Courtland Lee and Michael D'Andrea; and is manifested in the latest iteration of social justice counseling helmed by scholars such as Holcomb-McCoy herself, Fred Bemak, Rita Chung, and Rebecca Toporek (personal communication, November 2, 2020). However, social justice counseling focuses on human rights and oppression broadly. To truly engage in social justice school counseling, we need to move the profession toward understanding antiracism. We need to not only be aware of how racist ideas, policies, and procedures continue to harm Black youth and families but also know how to dismantle policies and procedures that impact the academic, social, and emotional development of Black youth.

One positive is that research on antiracism in counseling has been conducted. For example, Malott et al. (2015) conducted a qualitative study framed by Janet Helms's model of white racial identity development to ascertain the characteristics of white counselors engaged in antiracist activities. Helms's model is composed of six statuses, from those who uphold the status quo and continue to oppress people of color to those who abandon racist ideologies and commit to a nonracist identity (Malott et al., 2015). Just as in teacher education, this work focuses on white counselors and individuals and their experiences with antiracism (see Malott et al., 2015, 2019; Todd & Abrams, 2011). The work of Malott et al. (2015, 2019) and Todd and Abrams (2011) details how participants who identify as antiracist struggle with relationships and making lifestyle decisions that align with and honor their antiracist beliefs as well the backlash and alienation they receive from their white peers, colleagues, and family members. However, in this chapter, and in alignment with who I am as a Black woman who strives to be antiracist, I want to focus on the personal and professional costs of antiracism among Black school counselors, giving voice to those who are often overlooked and omitted from conversations.

Personal and Professional Costs of Being Antiracist

"I'm tired. I'm sad. I'm frustrated. I'm angry. I'm overwhelmed. But most of all, I'm sad." These are the sentiments of a professional school counselor on how she feels having to fight the system just so her Black students can receive the same access to education as her white students. Mary-Frances Winters (2020) called racism that erodes the mind, body, and spirit *Black fatigue*, meaning "fatigue that comes from the pain and anguish of living with racism every single day of your life" (p. 4). Although this phenomenon is what Black people experience, those who engage in antiracist work also experience fatigue—fatigue at having to fight racist policies and practices that continue to harm and oppress Black students on a daily basis, often at the expense of their own emotional and professional well-being. Following are the actual words of current Black professional school counselors—those on the front line, in the schools—who are tired and experiencing fatigue from the difficulties they face fighting to dismantle systemic oppression and racism.

Reflections From the Field (In Their Own Words)

Elementary School Counselor, North Carolina, Second Year, Female

I took this job because I wanted to help all students, to be a resource for them, to support them and help them develop the social-emotional learning skills they need to thrive. Personality wise, I feel I'm more suited for the young ages, and as I am young I feel I have more to offer this age group than the older kids. From my counseling program and my own experience as a Black person, I know that inequities in the school system exist and that Black students are often hurt and harmed in schools. I see it in my school. Our Black male students are suspended more than other students and are referred to me for discipline issues more than any other students. I try to advocate on their behalf, but no one listens to me. I mean, they *hear* me, but they do not *listen* to me. And I have no support in this fight. I am alone. This doesn't deter me from wanting to continue to fight, but I often wonder what good I am truly doing. I don't care that I may rub my coworkers the wrong way and that they may be tired of me always bringing up race in our meetings. I don't even care if they don't like me. I don't need their friendship to do my job, although it would make my job much easier. But when it comes to antiracism—fighting the polices in our school—yeah, I'm fighting a losing battle. I know that I am helping students, but I am not really *helping* students. If I leave this school, the same system will be in place. And there will be no one left to fight the good fight. Unless they hire another Black counselor. But then that person will face what I'm facing. I strive to be an antiracist, but I do not know if I am truly running an antiracist school counseling program because the systems that cause harm to my Black students are still here.

Personally, outside of school, I surround myself with people who feel the same way I feel about the plight of African Americans in our society, how we are brutally killed for the enjoyment of white supremacists, how those who kill us rarely face any consequences. We are angry. I am angry. I have to work hard not to hate white people for their role in the state of affairs and their passivity to it. It angers me that they [white people] feel they can tweet or make a hashtag and that makes them activists. White people tweeting pics of themselves with the hashtag #IrunwithAmaud almost made me leave Twitter. Yes, I am angry. I feel this is their mess, and they want us [Black people] to clean it up, but they don't want to change, because deep down, they [white people] know they benefit from it all.

Middle School Counselor, North Carolina, Fifth Year, Female

I work in a majority-minority middle school. A lot of my colleagues are Black. But we do not all have the same mind-set when it comes to antiracism. I am sad to say that a lot of my colleagues view these students in the same way the white people do. They talk about them negatively, hold low expectations, and will even say, "This student is a lost cause" or "We need to get this student out of this school." Our principal is a Black man and does not advocate for our students. He wants our students to follow the rules—rules created for white students, rules that do not take into account the poverty and violent neighborhoods from which my students come. I do try to fight for my students, and others do too, but when you have a leader who sees things differently, there is only so much you can do. I knew this wouldn't be easy, but I did choose to work in this type of school because I thought it would be easier to advocate for Black students in a majority-Black school than to advocate for Black students in a majority-white school. I understand that we need to have an antiracist agenda, but please tell me how to do that when leadership doesn't have an antiracist agenda.

Personally, I am angry. No ifs, ands, or buts. Just angry. I'm angry at the injustice of it all. I'm angry that I still have to live in a world that does not want me in it. I never want my students to feel this way, but they know the truth. And it makes me angry that we are raising yet another generation of Black kids who know that the world hates them and have to experience the hatred.

High School Counselor, North Carolina, Eighth Year, Female

I do not engage in antiracism in any shape, form, or fashion. It's not that I do not want to do so, but I am tired. I'm ready to leave the profession. It's not what I thought it would be. I rarely get to counsel students. Students only come to us for information or help related to their course schedule and college. We have a career counselor too, so students wanting to go to work mainly go to him. I don't even know if he has a degree in school counseling or counseling in general. I think I started out thinking I could change the system, but the system changed me. I am ashamed to admit it, but it has. I felt I was doing this alone and I felt that no one else cared, not even the students themselves. And definitely not the parents. I could never get the parents to come out for anything, at least the Black parents. I gave up on doing parent workshops. I guess I gave up on a lot. I come to work, do my job, and go home. That's it. So no, I do not engage in any antiracist work as a school counselor. But I did vote for Joe Biden. Does that count for anything?

Personally, I feel a lot of anger on so many levels, but I think I am most angry with white people who are passive; those who do nothing to change the system; those who claim to be outraged at events, but their outrage quickly dies down and they go on with their lives, and I can't go on with my life. It stays with me. I'm ready to settle down, and I would love to have children, but I do not want to bring a Black child into this world, and that makes me angry because I have to give up on a dream that I have always had. You know, I never told anyone that. I always say that I just don't want to be a mother, but the truth is, I want to be a mother; I want to have kids, but I know I can't save them from the hate they will experience, and I just do not want to do that to a child, to my child.

The Personal Costs of Being an Antiracist School Counselor

Based on my experiences, and the voices of these three school counselors, I would say the first cost of choosing to follow an antiracist path is loneliness. Anyone committed to this work must know that not everyone will be committed to and engaged in antiracism. You may be the only one in your school committed to this work. There are ways to work around this. One strategy is to connect with others engaged in antiracism work. Joining professional organizations such as the American Counseling Association, the Association for Multicultural Counseling and Development, and the National Association for Multicultural Education is a great way to meet others committed to doing antiracist work. Attend their annual conferences and go to sessions that focus on issues related to race and antiracism in schools. Meet other attendees and make connections with those who are committed and willing to remain in contact with you.

When I first began my job as an assistant professor, it was an isolating experience until I found my people. My people were not even in the state of North Carolina, but they were my support group whom I could call on to help with anything I needed relating to my work. Connecting with others will be the key to combatting loneliness and staying committed in this work. They can be teachers and counselors in your school or in different schools. They can be former professors, or they can be friends who also do this work but in different fields. They are out there, but you may have to take time to cultivate this support network. Do not give up. Find your people.

The second cost is anger. Seeing the injustices happening, the anti-Black sentiment overtly or covertly expressed, and not having the power to address it is enraging. Having your ideas dismissed, having your suggestions ignored is enraging. Hearing teachers, principals, school counselors, social workers, school psychologists, school nurses, and other school stakeholders express their love for all students and then seeing them enact racial harm against Black students is enraging. Having people go about their lives, the outrage they once felt when hearing the news of another murder of a Black person long gone and relegated to the furthest recesses of their mind, when you must face this knowledge daily is enraging. Just as experiencing racism has a psychological effect on individuals, so does seeing these racial injustices happening and seeing inaction and a moving on after they occur. Utsey and Ponterotto (1996) stated that the racism and discrimination Black individuals experience daily are inescapable and a painful reality of daily life, and they do impact their psychological well-being, which includes being angry. These psychological responses are what Utsey et al. (2000) called *coping strategies* that we as Black people use to deal with the stress of racism. But as we tell our students, it is OK to be angry. What we need to focus on is what we do with our anger.

So what should you do with your anger? Use your anger to propel yourself to continue to fight for your students. We often think of anger as a negative emotion, but there are positives to feeling anger. One main positive is that anger energizes and is motivating. Use that energy and motivation to continue fighting racial injustice. Winters (2020) stated that Black people need to continue to use their voice, remain vigilant, and speak out against and reframe the deficit narrative that schools currently use to explain Black academic performance. For example, when we hear that Black children are not succeeding at the same rate as white children, we need to reframe the situation. To state this more accurately, schools are structured to disadvantage Black children (Winters, 2020). Use your anger.

The third cost of being an antiracist school counselor is hopelessness and resignation. As expressed by the high school counselor above, burnout, the physical and emotional exhaustion one feels doing one's job, runs rampant in the school counseling profession. No extant research exists exploring school counselor burnout and antiracist work, but given the difficulty and isolation in this work, I am sure many antiracist school counselors experience burnout. Three key dimensions of burnout are emotional exhaustion, depersonalization, and diminished personal accomplishment (Maslach et al., 1996), which the three counselors interviewed for this chapter and I have all expressed.

What does this mean for the training and education of future professional school counselors? Simply put, it means we cannot give up. It means I cannot give up. Yes, those of us committed to antiracism know that this work is isolating; it is enraging; it is frustrating; it is difficult. But those of us committed to antiracism also know that the burden falls on us to engage in this work. It is our responsibility to stay committed, doing whatever we need to do for self-care in the process. It is our responsibility to fight the racist ideas, policies, and procedures that continue to create racial trauma for Black people in this country; it is our responsibility to continue to fight the racists who enact the racist ideas, policies, and procedures that continue to create racial trauma for Black people in this country. So to the high school counselor who asks whether voting for a candidate who stands up for antiracist policies counts as an antiracist act, I say yes. Casting a vote to eliminate a president who upholds racist beliefs is an antiracist act. To the elementary school counselor who wonders whether she is truly running an antiracist school counseling program, I say you are if you are acting against injustice (Love, 2019). To the middle school counselor who has to operate in a school whose leadership is not committed to antiracism, I say there is no one way to do this work (Love, 2019). Find what works for you. To everyone out in the field doing this work, whether as a professional school counselor or in academia training the next cohort of school counselors, Love (2019) wrote about teachers doing abolitionist work:

> Some teachers will create a homeplace for their students while teaching them with the highest expectations; some will protest in the streets; some will fight standardized testing; some will restore justice in their classrooms; some will create justice-centered curriculums and teaching approaches. . . . Some will leave the profession mentally, physically, and spiritually depleted looking for a way to make an impact on education outside the classroom, but all are working to restore humanity with their eyes on abolishing the educational system as we know it. (pp. 89–90)

The point is that we do not have the luxury of giving up, but you can find ways to continue to fight that work for you. Our ancestors before us—our great-great-grandparents, our great-grandparents, our grandparents, and for some of us our parents—did not give up even after atrocities were committed against them: the 1963 Alabama church bombing that killed Addie Mae Collins, Cynthia Wesley,

Carole Robertson, and Carol Denise McNair; the 1921 Tulsa, Oklahoma, race massacre that killed hundreds of Black men, women, and children and destroyed a thriving town; the 1898 Wilmington, North Carolina, massacre that again saw white Americans killing Black men, women, and children and destroying a thriving town all over a fear of Negro domination; the 1923 Rosewood Massacre in which Black Americans were lynched and an entire town burned; the 2015 Charleston, South Carolina, church murders (Zinn Education Project, n.d.). There are so many more. The common denominator is what Carol Anderson (2016) called *white rage*, the hatred and anti-Black sentiment overtly expressed by white Americans. This white rage is embedded in the very fabric of our nation; it ebbs and flows, but it is always present, whether overtly or covertly.

#SayTheir Names. We do not have the luxury of giving up. When anger, sadness, frustration, and resignation creep upon us, we need to remember the faces of Andre Hill, Casey Goodson, Jr., Angelo Crooms, Sincere Pierce, Marcellis Stinnette, Jonathan Price, Dijon Kizzee, Rayshard Brooks, Carlos Carson, David McAtee, Tony McDade, George Floyd, Sean Reed, Breonna Taylor, Botham Jean, Korryn Gaines, Philando Castile, Alton Sterling, Sandra Bland, Freddie Gray, Michael Brown, John Crawford III, Eric Garner, Rekia Boyd, Tamir Rice, Trayvon Martin. So many more can be added to this list—all murdered based on racist ideas and all whose murderers walk free based on racist policies.

Discussion

Malcolm X, the civil rights advocate, said, "The most disrespected person in America is the Black woman. The most unprotected person in America is the Black woman. The most neglected person in America is the Black woman" (Bihibindi News, 2016, 2:26). I add this quote because the three school counselors whose perspectives I shared are all Black, cisgender women, and their voices cry out: "We are tired. We are overwhelmed. We are unsupported. We are alone. We are angry. And we give up." And I understand and recognize all of it, for today, as I write this, I too feel the same way, alone and unsupported, fighting a losing battle against people with more power than I have, who do not have the same mind-set when it comes to antiracism. As Winters (2020) discussed in her work on Black women, I have also been called angry, opinionated, and aggressive by those who are white and criticized for my looks and actions by those who are Black. In fact, almost every day I receive a phone call from a Black colleague who proceeds to provide constructive feedback on why I fail in my job as a diversity, equity, and inclusion fellow and what I need to be doing differently. Personally, my friends and families agree with me about the inequities that Black people face, but I know they do not want to discuss it or talk about it; instead, they choose to focus on the regular everyday life experiences that all people share, in my opinion, striving to be normal. So for me, the choices in my life are to discuss this at work with people who tell me I am bad at my job, to not discuss this at all, or to keep going, keeping in mind the high stakes of not engaging in this work. I choose the last option, and I hope that everyone stepping into the role of school counselor also decides to be committed to and engaged in antiracist work despite the personal costs of being an antiracist school counselor.

Conclusion

One strategy I strongly suggest for all people engaging in antiracist work is to constantly engage in self-reflection. When confronted with the negative, overwhelming magnitude of the work in which we engage, taking time to think about how you are helping your students, families, and communities can be the panacea you need to keep going. I constantly reflect on the work, what I am doing well, and what I need to do better. I also take time (although I know I need to take more time) to engage in self-care, to get the rejuvenation I need to keep going, for I know that I do not have the luxury of giving up. I see the young faces of my own two beautiful Black children (Madison and Joe), my beautiful Black nieces (Nicole, Ashlii, Sydney, and Jordan), and my beautiful Black nephews (Andre, AJ, and Michael) who deserve, just as all Black men, women, and children deserve, to be free from white supremacy and systemic racism. Say their names too. As I wrote at the beginning of this chapter, the costs of not being an antiracist school counselor are much higher than the personal costs of being one.

References

Allen, J. (2010). Improving cross-cultural care and antiracism in nursing education: A literature review. *Nurse Education Today, 30*(4), 314–320. https://doi.org/10.1016/j.nedt.2009.08.007

Anderson, C. (2016). *White rage*. Bloomsbury.

Bihibindi News. (2016, June 28). *Who taught you to hate yourself—Malcolm X* [Speech audio recording]. YouTube. https://www.youtube.com/watch?v=sCSOiN_38nE

Blitz, L. V., Greene, M. P., Bernabei, S., & Shah, V. P. (2014). Think creatively and act decisively: Creating an antiracist alliance of social workers. *Social Work, 59*(4), 347–350. https://doi.org/10.1093/sw/swu031

Exec. Order No. 13,950, 3 C.F.R. 60683 (2020). https://www.govinfo.gov/content/pkg/FR-2020-09-28/pdf/2020-21534.pdf

Gay, G. (2000). *Culturally responsive teaching: Theory, research, and practice*. Teachers College Press.

Hamilton-Mason, J., & Schneider, S. (2018). Antiracism expanding social work education: A qualitative analysis of the Undoing Racism workshop experience. *Journal of Social Work Education, 54*(2), 337–348. https://doi.org/10.1080/10437797.2017.1404518

Horne, T. (2007, June 11). *An open letter to the citizens of Tucson*. https://www.faculty.umb.edu/lawrence_blum/courses/CCT627_10/readings/horne_open_letter_tucson.pdf

Howard, T. C. (2010). *Why race and culture matter in schools: Closing the achievement gap in America's classrooms*. Teachers College Press.

Jean-Marie, G., & Mansfield, K. C. (2013). School leaders' courageous conversation about race: Race and racial discrimination in schools. In J. S. Brooks & N. W. Arnold (Eds.), *Anti-racist school leadership: Toward equity in education for America's students* (pp. 19–36). Information Age.

Ladson-Billings, G. (2009). *The dreamkeepers: Successful teachers of African American children*. Jossey-Bass.

Love, B. L. (2019). *We want to do more than survive: Abolitionist teaching and the pursuit of educational freedom*. Beacon Press.

Malott, K. M., Paone, T. R., Schaefle, S., Cates, J., & Haizlip, B. (2015). Expanding white racial identity theory: A qualitative investigation of whites engaged in antiracist action. *Journal of Counseling & Development, 93*(3), 333–343. https://doi.org/10.1002/jcad.12031

Malott, K. M., Schaefle, S., Paone, T. R., Cates, J., & Haizlip, B. (2019). Challenges and coping mechanisms of whites committed to antiracism. *Journal of Counseling & Development, 97*(1), 86–97. https://doi.org/10.1002/jcad.12238

Maslach, C., Jackson, S. E., & Leiter, M. (1996). *The Maslach Burnout Inventory manual* (3rd ed.). Consulting Psychologists Press.

Ohito, E. (2019). Mapping women's knowledges of antiracist teaching in the United States: A feminist phenomenological study of three antiracist women teacher educators. *Teaching and Teacher Education, 86,* Article 102892. https://doi.org/10.1016/j.tate.2019.102892

Short, G. (1999). Antiracist education and moral behaviour: Lessons from the Holocaust. *Journal of Moral Education, 28*(1), 49–62.

Syswerda, J. (1984). *Women of faith study Bible.* Zondervan.

Todd, N. R., & Abrams, E. M. (2011). White dialectics: A new framework for theory, research, and practice with white students. *The Counseling Psychologist, 39*(3), 353–395. https://doi.org/10.1177/0011000010377665

Utsey, S. O., & Ponterotto, J. G. (1996). Development and validation of the Index of Race-Related Stress (IRRS). *Journal of Counseling Psychology, 43*(4), 490–501.

Utsey, S. O., Ponterotto, J. G., Reynolds, A. L., & Cancelli, A. A. (2000). Racial discrimination, coping, life satisfaction, and self-esteem among African Americans. *Journal of Counseling & Development, 78*(1), 72–80. https://doi.org/10.1002/j.1556-6676.2000.tb02562.x

Winters, M.-F. (2020). *Black fatigue: How racism erodes the mind, body, and spirit.* Berrett-Koehler.

Zinn Education Project. (n.d.). *Nov. 10, 1898: Wilmington massacre.* https://www.zinnedproject.org/news/tdih/wilmington-massacre-2/

CHAPTER 11

Sustaining Antiracism in the Counseling Profession

Cheryl Holcomb-McCoy, Joshua Schuschke, and Malik S. Henfield

Talking about the need for change is easy, but bringing about sustained change requires action and planning. In this chapter, we introduce five steps for creating immediate change in one's antiracist efforts and then describe more structural, long-term efforts to change counselor training and research to reflect a commitment to racial justice and antiracism.

Immediate Steps to Becoming an Antiracist Counselor

In his classic book *How to Be an Antiracist*, Ibram Kendi draws on his own experiences and family narratives to illustrate his journey to becoming antiracist. He begins his book by telling a story about his own internalized racist ideas about Blackness as a 17-year-old high school student. The book, in essence, is a description of Kendi's antiracism journey, including faulty interpretations and aha moments. As professional counselors ponder how to create justice for their Black and Brown students, we believe that committing to the lifetime journey is the first step. There is never a sense of completion. Every day we learn more about ourselves and our practice. The journey requires us to share our personal stories of challenge, resistance, and joy. As a matter of fact, it is our openness and love of humanity that drive this work. Below are five immediate steps that can jumpstart the journey.

Step 1: Know the Definition of Racism and Racist

To fully understand one's role in being antiracist, one must first understand the concept of racism. *Merriam-Webster's Collegiate Dictionary* defines *racism* as "a belief that race is the primary determinant of human traits and capacities and that racial differences produce an inherent superiority of a particular race" ("Racism," 2009). Understanding racism must be coupled with fully understanding the concepts of white supremacy and structural racism. All in all, antiracist counselors spend considerable time and effort building a keen understanding of the history of racism in the United States and beyond. Reading the work of Black and Brown scholars who study racism and its effects on disparities in economics, housing, health, and education is a necessary component of this step.

Step 2:
Accept That Racism Exists and Place Antiracism in
One's Organization or School's Vision, Mission, and Core Values

The words "diversity," "inclusion," and "equity" are in the mission and vision statements of many schools and organizations. However, the antiracism framework is often missing. Another step in the journey is to be sure racism is not avoided as a core value in one's mission or vision.

Step 3: Identify Racist Practices in One's Counseling Program and/or Training

Once one understands racism, it is essential to accept it and then identify where racist practices exist in one's counseling program or practice. For instance, it is well known that gifted and talented programs reinforce racial hierarchies and ultimately result in uneven and inequitable pathways to postsecondary opportunities. In New York City, where 65% of kindergartners are Black and Latinx, the school district offered only 18% of gifted and talented kindergarten seats to Black and Latinx students in 2019 (Kirkland, 2019). It is important to note that gifted and talented programs are linked to the eugenics movement (Stoskepf, 1999). For many years, gifted and talented programs have relied on teacher and parent recommendations as a significant part of the identification process. Black and Brown students are historically underidentified for these programs because there is bias among teachers and Black and Brown parents often lack the information needed to recommend their children. This is a racial inequity in many schools. Antiracist school counselors would identify this inequity through the use of data (which is evidence!) and advocate for changing the policy and/or identification process. An antiracist analysis of gifted programs would clarify that the problem is not the students but the policies that put Black and Brown students at a distinct disadvantage.

Step 4: Understand That Antiracism Is Intersectional

Racist policies impact many of our students and clients, but we must not forget that race intersects with multiple aspects of people's identities, including gender, sexuality, religion, and ethnicity. Antiracist school counselors must use an intersectional approach. When examining the outcomes of racist school discipline policies, it is essential to pay particular attention to the impact of those policies on intersectional groups: Black Queer students, Native American women, Latinx males, and so on.

Step 5: Support Antiracist Groups and Organizations

An essential aspect of being an antiracist counselor is supporting organizations that fight policies that create racial disparities. One might volunteer with or fund these organizations. Recently, the Black Lives Matter movement and the Indigenous communities organized at Standing Rock repeatedly made visible the vast need for legislative and economic change. These groups are just some of the groups antiracist counselors might support. More important, antiracist school counselors support students who are fighting against injustice as well. For instance, counselors and educators must not shun students who are vocal about their involvement in the Black Lives Matter movement. Empowering students to be active advocates for justice and humanity is a step toward becoming an antiracist counselor.

Sustaining Antiracism Through Counseling Research

To sustain antiracism in the counseling profession, counseling research and scholarship must also become more antiracist through its implementation and understanding. Antiracist researchers acknowledge racism and center the experiences, strengths, and knowledge produced by Black and Brown people. Specifically, antiracist researchers recognize participants' full humanity and multiple existing systems of oppression to analyze data properly. This means that counselor education scholars must adopt antiracist paradigms and account for the ways in which white supremacy, anti-Blackness, and settler colonialism have shaped traditional ways of knowing. Researchers studying race and racism need to reject notions of detached objectivity and invest in epistemologies of liberation (DeCuir-Gunby, 2020; Dixson et al., 2018; Harper & Kuh, 2007). In this way, over time, antiracist research can sustain the field's antiracist stance and approach by ensuring that the research and knowledge base is based on justice and antioppressive themes.

To achieve an antiracist research base, counseling researchers must first grapple with the racism embedded in their training and practice. Antiracist researchers must account for how institutions and disciplines have attempted to erase, displace, and enact violence on particular groups (Graves, 2008; Guthrie, 2004; Wilder, 2013). For counselor educators specifically, understanding how policies and practices such as tracking (Legette, 2018; Tyson, 2011), zero tolerance (Crenshaw et al., 2015), and standardized testing (Harris, 2011) contribute to ongoing systematic racism is critical to correctly choosing methodologies and interpreting data. Having antiracist codes of ethics requires that scholars fundamentally question racist policy and push for abolishing it through their work (Kendi, 2016, 2019; Love, 2019). Recognizing how scholarship shapes and is shaped by racist institutions enables researchers to begin the process of generating antiracist academic discourse and advocacy.

At the core of this antiracist ethic are the Black people, Brown people, and people of color whom this research is designed to center and elevate. Moving beyond standard ethics that seek to ensure participants' safety, which historically have not applied to people of color (Graves, 2008), antiracist researchers must account for the specific experiences and culture of the groups they study. First, they must value the ideas, principles, and practices of historically marginalized groups. Second, researchers must understand and respect the hesitancy, mistrust, and resistance to participating in data collection among particular groups, given the violent history of academic exploration (Graves, 2008; Wilder, 2013). Third, to conduct antiracist research alongside communities of color researchers must become advocates in service of the studied groups' needs and desires. Valuing, respecting, and advocating for people of color when conducting research are the most direct ways in which scholars embody antiracist ethics.

To properly advocate for groups in ways that are antiracist, researchers must understand their own positionalities and relationships to the individuals, groups, and topics being studied. Individuals' social identities and positionalities may generate potential biases, interactions, and outcomes when engaging in race and racism issues. It is critical to understand researcher positionality, as social hierarchies and power dynamics can shape research throughout all phases of a study, in particular during data collection and analysis (Merriam et al., 2001; Milner, 2007). Researchers must know how their multiple identities and group memberships may place them inside and/or outside a particular community. Understanding when positionalities may be leveraged to gain credibility and build rapport is just as important as knowing when to accept and learn from an outsider's perspective.

Upon understanding the role of positionalities, whether as the member of an in-group or an out-group, it is vital to remember that the role of researcher comes with inherent social power and privilege, in particular when the researcher is engaging communities of color (Merriam et al., 2001; Milner, 2007; Utt & Tochluk, 2020). Antiracist researchers can check these privileges and power dynamics by ensuring that their participants' perspectives, responses, and lifestyles are appropriately recorded, conveyed, and analyzed. Although it is essential to use antiracist methodological approaches that ensure validity and reliability (discussed below), researching in a way that creates trust between the researcher and participant by accurately accounting for their data is vital for building individual and communal trust in antiracist scholarship.

In addition to using positionality to build trust, providing space for people and communities of color to lead and showcase their intellectual, cultural, and political strengths throughout data collection and analysis is vital to conducting antiracist research. Highlighting participants' practices and responses, and their general voice, to dislodge white supremacy while (re)moving white logics and interpretations to the margins is central to the antiracist goal of disrupting oppressive institutions. Centering and supporting participants of color within a system that historically erased and misrepresented them or profited from their experiences provides the opportunity to reimagine academic spaces as sites of resistance, decolonization, and liberation.

Sustaining Antiracism Through Counselor Training Policies

Accrediting and licensing boards can play a significant role in sustaining antiracist practice in the counseling profession. The body that accredits counselor education programs, the Council for Accreditation of Counseling and Related Educational Programs (CACREP), is positioned to ensure the explicit inclusion of antiracism and antidiscrimination in its standards, which include the number of credit hours for programs (tuition implications), and training areas of focus: The Learning Environment, Professional Counseling Identity, Professional Practice, Evaluation in the Program. Here are three distinct ways in which antiracism can be included in accreditation and training standards (our proposed additions are in bold):

1. Currently the CACREP Board of Directors has a set of five core values: (a) advancing the counseling profession through quality and excellence

in counselor education; (b) ensuring a fair, consistent, and ethical decision-making process; (c) serving as a responsible leader in protecting the public; (d) promoting practices that reflect openness to growth, change and collaboration; and (e) creating and strengthening standards that reflect the needs of society, respect the diversity of instructional approaches and strategies, and encourage program improvement and best practices (CACREP, n.d., "Core Values"). We propose revising (e) to include "creating and strengthening standards that **reflect the distinct needs of racially and culturally diverse populations in society**."

2. The program objectives for CACREP-accredited programs are the core of the training protocol. It is here that we propose a revision to include antiracism as a foundational element of training. Currently, guidelines for program objectives state the following:

> The program objectives (1) reflect current knowledge and projected needs concerning counseling practice in a multicultural and pluralistic society; (2) reflect input from all persons involved in the conduct of the program, including counselor education program faculty, current and former students, and personnel in cooperating agencies; (3) address student learning; and (4) are written so they can be evaluated. (CACREP, 2016, Section 2, Standard B)

Following is our recommended revision of the CACREP guidelines for program objectives:

> The program objectives (1) reflect current knowledge and projected needs **for promoting antiracism** and counseling in a multicultural and pluralistic society …

3. In the section describing aspects of social and cultural diversity in the training curriculum (CACREP, 2016, Section 2, Standard F.2.), there is no mention of racism or antiracism. We propose the following revisions:

> 2. SOCIAL AND CULTURAL DIVERSITY
> a. multicultural and pluralistic characteristics within and among diverse groups nationally and internationally
> b. theories and models of multicultural counseling, cultural identity development, **antiracist practice,** and social justice and advocacy
> c. multicultural counseling competencies
> d. **the impact of historical policies and practices (e.g., enslavement of persons of African descent, internment of Japanese American, colonialization of Native Americans); attitudes, beliefs, understandings, and acculturative experiences on an individual's views of others**
> e. **the effects of power, privilege, intersectionality, and white supremacy on the counseling process**
> f. help-seeking behaviors of diverse clients
> g. the impact of spiritual beliefs on clients' and counselors' worldviews
> h. **strategies for identifying and eliminating barriers and processes of intentional and unintentional racism, oppression and discrimination**

Changing the language in accreditation standards is the least that can be done to ensure an antiracist counseling profession. Counselor education programs must also revise admissions and program policies to ensure that racially diverse students have equitable access to all program opportunities. The following questions can be used to determine whether a program is antiracist: Are admissions interviews accessible to all students? Are admissions materials in the native languages of racially diverse prospective students? Do admissions costs and tuition create disproportionate barriers for certain racial groups? Does the time of day when program courses are offered disproportionately affect working students and students of color?

Conclusion

In this book, we have attempted to weave a path forward for developing a sustainable, antiracist counseling profession. The book began with a statement of urgency given the countless number of Black and Brown people who have been hurt, discriminated against, killed, and/or murdered based on faulty racist ideas and practices. It is our belief that racial disparities in education, health care, and other systems will continue to plague our society if a critical mass of counselors do not stand up to do their part to correct past and current injustices. This book started with the words of poet Amanda Gorman, and it ends with her words of wisdom and inspiration:

> We've learned that quiet isn't always peace,
> and the norms and notions of what "just" is isn't always justice.
> … even as we grieved, we grew.
> … even as we hurt, we hoped.

> —**Amanda Gorman,** "The Hill We Climb"

References

Council for Accreditation of Counseling and Related Educational Programs. (n.d.). *About CACREP: A brief history.* https://www.cacrep.org/about-cacrep/#the-cacrep-board-of-directors

Council for Accreditation of Counseling and Related Educational Programs. (2016). *2016 CACREP standards.* www.cacrep.org/for-programs/2016-cacrep-standards/

Crenshaw, K., Ocen, P., & Nanda, J. (2015). *Black girls matter: Pushed out, overpoliced, and underprotected.* Columbia University, Center for Intersectionality and Social Policy Studies.

DeCuir-Gunby, J. T. (2020). Using critical race mixed methodology to explore the experiences of African Americans in education. *Educational Psychologist, 55*(4), 244–255.

Dixson, A. D., James, A., & Frieson, B. (2018). Taking it to the streets: Critical race theory, participatory research and social justice. In J. T. DeCuir-Gunby, T. K. Chapman, & P. A. Schutz (Eds.), *Understanding critical race research methods and methodologies: Lessons from the field* (pp. 64–75). Routledge.

Graves, J. L. (2008). *The emperor's new clothes: Biological theories of race at the millennium* (6th ed.). Rutgers University Press.

Guthrie, R. V. (2004). *Even the rat was white: A historical view of psychology.* Pearson Education.

Harper, S. R., & Kuh, G. D. (2007). Myths and misconceptions about using qualitative methods in assessment. *New Directions for Institutional Research, 2007*(136), 5–14.

Harris, A. L. (2011). *Kids don't want to fail*. Harvard University Press.

Kendi, I. X. (2016). *Stamped from the beginning: The definitive history of racist ideas in America*. Nation Books.

Kendi, I. X. (2019). *How to be an antiracist*. One World.

Kirkland, D. (2019, September 20). What the gifted education fight is really about. *New York Daily News*. https://www.nydailynews.com/opinion/ny-oped-what-the-gifted-education-fight-is-really-about-20190920-vry2cqgpyvhw7or-4jft3qa2eqm-story.html

Legette, K. (2018). School tracking and youth self-perceptions: Implications for academic and racial identity. *Child Development, 89*(4), 1311–1327.

Love, B. L. (2019). *We want to do more than survive: Abolitionist teaching and the pursuit of educational freedom*. Beacon Press.

Merriam, S. B., Johnson-Bailey, J., Lee, M. Y., Kee, Y., Ntseane, G., & Muhamad, M. (2001). Power and positionality: Negotiating insider/outsider status within and across cultures. *International Journal of Lifelong Education, 20*(5), 405–416.

Milner, H. R. (2007). Race, culture, and researcher positionality: Working through dangers seen, unseen, and unforeseen. *Educational Researcher, 36*(7), 388–400.

Racism. (2009). In *Merriam-Webster's collegiate dictionary* (11th ed.). Merriam-Webster.

Stoskepf, A. (1999). The forgotten history of eugenics. *Rethinking Schools, 13*(3). https://rethinkingschools.org/articles/the-forgotten-history-of-eugenics

Tyson, K. (2011). *Integration interrupted: Tracking, Black students, and acting white after Brown*. Oxford University Press.

Utt, J., & Tochluk, S. (2020). White teacher, know thyself: Improving antiracist praxis through racial identity development. *Urban Education, 55*(1), 125–152. https://doi.org/10.1177/0042085916648741

Wilder, C. S. (2013). *Ebony and ivy: Race, slavery, and the troubled history of America's universities*. Bloomsbury Press.

APPENDIX A

Self-Interrogation of Identities and Locating of Positionalities

Traci Dennis and Joshua Schuschke

Critically reflecting on your identity and contexts from childhood to adulthood is vital to the sustained development of an antiracist praxis. This tool is designed to help counselors reflect on the ways in which they have been socialized. In addition, some items require counselors to reflect on their interactions with students of color.

Evaluating your personal and professional journey is key to locating racialized biases and blind spots at multiple levels and in various educational contexts.

Individual

1. What was your first awareness of your own race? What did that moment reveal to you?

   _____

   _____

2. In what ways do you see your privileges shaping your day-to-day interactions? Your privileges might be based on race, gender, class, etc.

   _____

   _____

3. Think about your circle of friends, your work colleagues, and your family. How racially diverse are they, and how does that shape how you think and interact with others?

   _____

   _____

4. How many different languages do you speak? When did you learn them? How important are these languages to what you do now?

   _____

   _____

5. Think of a time when your perspective on race was challenged. What was your gut reaction? How did that moment change you?

   _____

   _____

Home, Family, and Neighborhood

6. In what ways did your family discuss race or racism while you were growing up, and how do they do so currently?

7. What did your neighborhood look like when you were growing up in terms of race and class? How close were you to your neighbors?

8. What type of learning materials or media were in your home? Did you have ways of learning about Black and Brown people or people of different cultures other than your own?

9. What type of restaurants, stores, or community centers were in your neighborhood? What was it like going to those places?

10. When you visited other neighborhoods, cities, states, or countries, did you notice any differences? If so, what were they and how did they impact you?

School and Community

11. Describe the racial diversity of the school and/or community where you work. How do you think your school and/or community shapes your interactions with racially diverse students?

12. How might your beliefs, identities, and experiences shape what you value and/or expect from students or clients?

13. What might be your blind spots? What do you still need to learn about and practice to build respectful relationships with children?

14. If your school district or community agency were to mandate an initiative with BIPOC (Black, Indigenous, and people of color) communities, how comfortable would you feel and why?

15. When you are planning counseling sessions, how do you decide what types of materials or media you are going to use? Are these resources developed by Black and Brown people or counselors?

APPENDIX B

Antiracist Syllabus Review Protocol

Traci Dennis, Joshua Schuschke, and Cheryl Holcomb-McCoy

PART 1 • Description

Reviewers: _____

Date: _____ / _____ / _____
            (month/day/year)

Teacher Name: _____

Subject: _____

No. of class sessions: _____

No. of assignments: _____ / _____
                    (in class/homework)

No. of semesters taught: _____

Syllabus File Name: _____

Course Title: _____

School Name: _____

City: _____

No. of breaks: _____

No. of assigned readings: _____ / _____

Grade Level(s): _____

PART 2 • Antiracist Content

Purpose
What is the purpose of this course? _____
_____

Is the purpose of the course conveyed accurately? Does the purpose of the course convey an antiracist disposition?	❑ Clear purpose ❑ Antiracist ❑ Other Notes: _____

Description
How is the course described? _____
_____

Does the course description address race and/ or racism?	❑ Clear description ❑ Addresses race ❑ Addresses racism ❑ Other Notes: _____

(Continued)

PART 2 • Antiracist Content (*Continued*)

Goals
What are the goals of this course? _____

Are the goals oriented to social justice, equity, and antiracism? Are the goals presented as tangible and attainable for all students?	❏ Clear goals ❏ Antiracist goals ❏ Attainable goals ❏ Other Notes: _____

Required Resources
What resources, technologies, and materials are needed for students to complete the course? _____

Are these resources accessible to all students?	❏ Textbooks ❏ Laptop ❏ Desktop ❏ Cellphone ❏ Internet ❏ Calculator ❏ Other Notes: _____

Course Materials
What type of content will students engage with? _____

Does the content include people of color as experts or topics? Are there antiracist materials? Is the course material accessible physically and conceptually?	❏ Inclusive materials ❏ Inclusive topics ❏ Developmentally appropriate ❏ Antiracist ❏ Other Notes: _____

Assignments
What type of in-class assignments are there? _____

What type of homework assignments are there? _____

Do assignments directly engage with issues of race and racism? Are assignments geared toward social justice? Are students asked to collaborate with peers? Are students asked to engage with communities?	❏ Centers on race and racism ❏ Oriented to social justice ❏ Community based activities ❏ Supports collaborative learning ❏ Other Notes: _____

Grading Are the grading rubrics clear and equitable? Is grading in alignment with the course goals?	❏ Equitable grading practices ❏ Clear grading system ❏ Aligned with course goals ❏ Other Notes: _____

PART 3 • Antiracist Language

Effectiveness of Communication Does the syllabus accurately convey the course goals, expectations, assignments, and grading?	❏ Purpose ❏ Goals ❏ Expectations ❏ Assignments ❏ Grading ❏ Other Notes: _____
Supportive Resources and Language Does the syllabus include supportive resources and welcoming language?	❏ Antiracist/discrimination policy ❏ Offers social-emotional support resources ❏ Offers support resources for special needs ❏ Provides generally supportive language throughout ❏ Other Notes: _____
Inclusive Language Does the syllabus operationalize language and a tone that is responsive to people of different racial/ethnic groups, gender identities, abilities, etc.?	❏ Uses gender-inclusive terms/pronouns ❏ Uses easy-to-read font ❏ Provides resources for language translation ❏ Provides culturally responsive resources ❏ Other Notes: _____

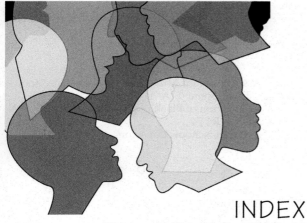

INDEX

Figures and tables are indicated by f and t following the page number.

(Continued)

(Continued)